S. Hrg. 113–845

WHY NET NEUTRALITY MATTERS: PROTECTING CONSUMERS AND COMPETITION THROUGH MEANINGFUL OPEN INTERNET RULES

HEARING

BEFORE THE

COMMITTEE ON THE JUDICIARY
UNITED STATES SENATE

ONE HUNDRED THIRTEENTH CONGRESS

SECOND SESSION

SEPTEMBER 17, 2014

Serial No. J–113–73

Printed for the use of the Committee on the Judiciary

U.S. GOVERNMENT PUBLISHING OFFICE

21–221 PDF   WASHINGTON : 2017

For sale by the Superintendent of Documents, U.S. Government Publishing Office
Internet: bookstore.gpo.gov   Phone: toll free (866) 512–1800; DC area (202) 512–1800
Fax: (202) 512–2104   Mail: Stop IDCC, Washington, DC 20402–0001

COMMITTEE ON THE JUDICIARY

PATRICK J. LEAHY, Vermont, *Chairman*

DIANNE FEINSTEIN, California
CHUCK SCHUMER, New York
DICK DURBIN, Illinois
SHELDON WHITEHOUSE, Rhode Island
AMY KLOBUCHAR, Minnesota
AL FRANKEN, Minnesota
CHRISTOPHER A. COONS, Delaware
RICHARD BLUMENTHAL, Connecticut
MAZIE HIRONO, Hawaii

CHUCK GRASSLEY, Iowa, *Ranking Member*
ORRIN G. HATCH, Utah
JEFF SESSIONS, Alabama
LINDSEY GRAHAM, South Carolina
JOHN CORNYN, Texas
MICHAEL S. LEE, Utah
TED CRUZ, Texas
JEFF FLAKE, Arizona

KRISTINE LUCIUS, *Chief Counsel and Staff Director*
KOLAN DAVIS, *Republican Chief Counsel and Staff Director*

CONTENTS

SEPTEMBER 17, 2014, 10:34 A.M.

STATEMENTS OF COMMITTEE MEMBERS

WITNESSES

QUESTIONS

ANSWERS

WHY NET NEUTRALITY MATTERS: PROTECTING CONSUMERS AND COMPETITION THROUGH MEANINGFUL OPEN INTERNET RULES

WEDNESDAY, SEPTEMBER 17, 2014,

UNITED STATES SENATE,
COMMITTEE ON THE JUDICIARY,
Washington, DC.

The Committee met, pursuant to notice, at 10:34 a.m., in Room SH–216, Hart Senate Office Building, Hon. Patrick J. Leahy, presiding.

Present: Senators Whitehouse, Klobuchar, Franken, Blumenthal, Hirono, Grassley, Hatch, Lee, Cruz, and Flake.

OPENING STATEMENT OF HON. PATRICK J. LEAHY, A U.S. SENATOR FROM THE STATE OF VERMONT

Chairman LEAHY. Senator Grassley is on his way, we will begin with my opening statement and I will yield to him when he gets here. Senator Lee is here, Senator Whitehouse, Senator Klobuchar, Senator Franken, and Senator Hirono.

I appreciate the number of people who are here. I also appreciate the almost overwhelming number of people who have emailed me or contacted me about this hearing.

On Monday, the Federal Communications Commission closed the public comment period on its proposed rules to protect an open Internet. I was not surprised by the number of emails and calls I got in my office because the FCC got 3.7 million—Americans made their voices heard. The issue is critical to consumers and businesses. An overwhelming number of the comments called on the FCC to enact meaningful rules that will protect consumers and preserve competition online. I should note I agree, and I believe the FCC should heed their call.

This is the second hearing the Judiciary Committee has convened on this issue. The first hearing, which I chaired in Vermont this summer, was an important opportunity to hear voices outside of the Beltway. Vermont-based small businesses now have a reach they only dreamed of thanks to the transforming power of the Internet. For the Vermont Country Store—it has long operated two retail outlets and a mail order business, the Internet now accounts for a remarkable 40 percent of its business, one third of its employees and they hire several hundred people. Logic Supply is based entirely online and sells industrial computers to consumers around the world.

They both were very honest and said they have reached a point and size that they could pay extra to jump over other people, but they do not want it to be that way. They said they never would have been able to start in the first place had they had to face that kind of obstacle. Their testimony was simple, keep the Internet an open playing field for small businesses so that they can launch and thrive. Cabot Orton from the Vermont Country Store said, "All the small business community asks is simply to preserve and protect Internet commerce as it exists today, which has served all businesses remarkably well." He could not be more right.

Martha Reid, the Vermont State Librarian, testified about the important role that libraries play in communities throughout the country, particularly those in underserved areas. She said, "All Americans, including the most disenfranchised citizens who would have no way to access the Internet without the library, need to be able to use Internet resources equally."

So this testimony and the testimony we will hear today will underscore the importance of why net neutrality matters. It matters for our economic growth and competitiveness. I believe the Internet is an equalizer. It can help break a lot of cycles of unemployment and poverty. It matters because the online world is the ultimate tool for free expression and democracy—a tool so powerful that it has helped topple totalitarian governments. Think about that. I mean this is something even a few years ago, none of us could even imagine. If you have the Internet become a two-tiered system of "haves" and "have-nots," controlled by a small number of corporate gatekeepers, it destroys everything that has made it one of the greatest innovations, certainly in history. The FCC must act in a meaningful way to protect its openness.

Meaningful rules would stop so-called "paid prioritization" deals that would allow large corporations to drown out smaller competitors. I introduced legislation with Congresswoman Doris Matsui of California that would require the FCC to develop rules to stop these deals. Regardless of whether our bill passes or not, the FCC should act to block this kind of behavior. You have to have rules that go beyond the antitrust laws, which play an important role as a backstop but alone are not enough to promote and preserve free speech and innovation online.

The FCC's action will determine whether the Internet as we know it stays open, vibrant, and competitive, or whether it is going to become a place where only the most powerful have a say. I know the outcome the people in Vermont want.

I thank the witnesses for coming today on Constitution Day. We have extra copies if anybody wants it.

Before I start, one of my friends of decades in the U.S. Senate, Senator Grassley of Iowa—today is his birthday. So let us all wish him a happy birthday.

Senator GRASSLEY. Thank you.

Chairman LEAHY. That faked you out; did it not?

OPENING STATEMENT OF HON. CHUCK GRASSLEY, A U.S. SENATOR FROM THE STATE OF IOWA

Senator GRASSLEY. Yes. Thank you all. Thanks to everybody in the audience who is here. Most importantly, the witnesses who have prepared for this and our experts in this area. It is very important that you have a hearing like this, I think a complex topic, and I am glad the committee can hear from all sides of the debate. I believe that many, if not all of us, share similar goals with respect to the Internet. We all want the Internet to grow. We want it to prosper. We all want faster and cheaper Internet access. We all want more deployment of broadband technologies, particularly the areas that remain without access. We all want more innovations and new avenues by which we can access that information. We all want consumers to have more choice and options.

The FCC is in the process of considering whether to adopt rules that would regulate the Internet. Chairman Wheeler claims that there is not enough competition in the highspeed broadband marketplace. There are some that dispute that. Rather, these people say that we have competitive dynamic Internet right now and the push for new regulations is a solution in search of a problem.

Is the Internet really broken? Broadband and Internet technologies are advancing every day. New products are constantly entering the market. Overall, broadband deployment and speeds, both wired and wireless, are estimated to reach 98 percent of the American households with broadband speeds of 10 megabytes or faster. 82 percent of those households have access to broadband speeds of 50 megabytes or faster.

The overall broadband industry—cable, telco, satellite and wireless—has invested over $1.2 trillion in infrastructure, $60 billion a year recently. Further, it is estimated that broadband speeds double every 2 to 3 years.

So many contend that the FCC and others are just speculating about future harms and there is no need to deviate from the current policies that have generated Internet phenomenal growth. Morever, many—including this Senator—are highly skeptical about the prospects of expansive FCC regulation over every aspect of the Internet. The Internet has been successful precisely because of a hands-off approach.

I note that this policy was first implemented under President Clinton. The lack of government intervention has allowed competition to flourish beyond wildest imaginations.

We all want more deployment of technology and infrastructure. In fact, I would like to see more broadband growth and options take place in rural America where I live and where the Chairman proudly says that he resides. However, it is more likely that we will see improvements in this area as a result of innovation and investment and not more regulation.

Because of the fast changing Internet market, rules and regulations could just end up impeding the development and adoption of new technologies and services. In fact, they could threaten investment in network upgrades, generate legal and marketplace uncertainty, and ultimately cost jobs, harming the economy.

It is doubtful that creating an expansive regulatory regime will increase broadband deployments, spur innovation and ensure better quality services and consumer satisfaction.

Supporters of net neutrality do contend that new rules will restore Internet protections and ensure the vitality of the Internet. If anything, I am concerned that the imposition of such regulations and in particular, expansion of 80 year-old rules designed to regulate old telephone monopolies under Title II might have the exact opposite effect.

There are legitimate concerns about making sure Internet competition and consumers are protected from bad actors. I know about them and hear about them quite often.

No I do not support monopolistic, anti-competitive or predatory practices in the Internet marketplace or anywhere for that matter, but rather than allow the FCC to impose regulations on an industry that has been so successful under a hands-off regime, antitrust and consumer protection laws may provide a better option to ensure consumers and businesses are not harmed by anti-competitive conduct in the modern Internet ecosphere. I have been a strong supporter of vigorous enforcement of antitrust laws by the Justice Department and the Federal Trade Commission to ensure a fair playing field in many sectors of our economy—just recently got somewhat of a modification in the meat-packing industry of such a merger to make sure that that would take place. So you know that I am active in the enforcement of the antitrust laws. I hope that these people, the Federal Trade Commission and the Justice Department, will be paying close attention to this market as well. So in conclusion, because the Internet is so important to con- sumers and to our economy, we should proceed with caution. No one wants to undermine the Internet. It is a complex policy debate and I look forward to today's testimony. And who knows? You could change my mind.

Chairman LEAHY. It has been known to happen.

Senator GRASSLEY. Not often enough.

Chairman LEAHY. Not often enough.

[Laughter.]

Chairman LEAHY. I was showing some of you the picture in rural Vermont where I live and the Senator from Iowa has a similar picture of his home in rural Iowa where he lives. An open Internet in a rural area is critical. It is similar to what my grandparents would tell me about when—in Vermont—they got rural electricity, rural telephone, the difference it made. It is something we all take for granted today.

Our first witness is Brad Burnham. He is a cofounder and managing partner of Union Square Ventures, a New York based venture capital firm. He has invested in companies like Twitter, Etsy and Kickstarter. Obviously, you know where to invest.

He previously worked at AT&T in a variety of sales, marketing and business development roles. He also worked at AT&T Ventures, the venture capital group.

Mr. Burnham, please go ahead.

STATEMENT OF BRADFORD BURNHAM, MANAGING PARTNER, UNION SQUARE VENTURES, LLC, NEW YORK, NEW YORK

Mr. BURNHAM. Thank you, Senator Leahy for the opportunity.

As you said, my perspective has been shaped by a career spent on both sides of the issue, first as a telecommunications executive at AT&T and a partner at AT&T Ventures and then later as a founding partner of Union Square Ventures.

I believe we are at a crossroads. The rules the FCC is now considering will shape the Internet ecosystem for many years to come and could have a profound effect on our economy, our place in the world and ultimately on the nature of our society. Almost everyone has benefited from the phenomenal innovation enabled by the Internet, but few of us have stopped to think about how all of this happened.

The Internet we know is the direct result of two key characteristics. First, the Internet separates applications from infrastructure, making it possible to create a networked application without knowing anything about the underlying network. Second, every applications is immediately available to every consumer. These two characteristics radically lowered the cost of building and distributing Internet applications, opening the market to a much larger and more diverse pool of creators.

For the first time, people without money, connections, or corporate backing could create an application and reach a global audience. Facebook was created in a dorm room. Foursquare spent $25,000 to reach their first 100,000 users. These companies and thousands more started from scratch and grew to reach global audiences. They have since gone on to empower hundreds of millions of others—independent craftspeople setting up shop on Etsy, filmmakers raising millions of dollars on Kickstarter, and journalists reaching a global audience on Twitter.

This incredible explosion of innovation happened because it became so cheap to create and distribute an application on the Internet that innovators no longer required permission from a boss, a network operator, or an investor to launch a business. If you could imagine an application like Instagram, you could build it yourself and get it into the hands of thousands or millions of consumers almost overnight. Later, once you had a large audience, you could approach investors from a position of strength to raise money to grow your business. This is the model of innovation that powered the growth of the Internet, and all of this is about to change.

Until recently, Internet access providers could not tell if you were watching Netflix, playing Angry Birds, or posting on Facebook. By default, access to the Internet was open. They have now deployed technology that allows them to see what services you are using. This will make it possible for the cable and telephone companies we use to get to the Internet to charge application developers for faster delivery of packets, slow traffic they decide is less important and even block traffic altogether.

Even as Internet access providers increase their ability to treat applications differently, the Internet has remained a relatively level playing field because of a combination of FCC enforcement actions and Comcast's acceptance of net neutrality principles as a condition of their merger with NBC. Today, those agreements are nearing expiration, and the FCC's ability to enforce open Internet principles has been sharply curtailed by the DC Circuit Court's decision in the Verizon case.

Unfortunately, the FCC, in search of a compromise, is not proposing to reclassify Internet access. Instead, they are proposing rules that would explicitly allow cable and telephone companies to treat Internet applications differently for a variety of business and network management reasons. The combination of access provider's new technical abilities and the FCC's proposed rules will dramatically increase the cost of creating and distributing Internet applications. Applications developers will have to consider the network management strategies and even the business interests of cable and telephone companies when they design their applications. They will also have to change the way they approach investors.

Every web application developer knows speed is a feature. They all work to shave milliseconds off the time it takes to load a page. Start-ups will need to raise money up front to buy access to the fast lane to succeed, making it impossible to launch first as Tumbler and Foursquare did and then raise money later. No new application will be created in a dorm room. The applications like video and voice that compete with cable and telephone companies will find it especially hard to raise money.

It may seem like I am overstating my case, but ask yourself how comfortable would you be investing in a company creating a new air conditioner if the company that delivered power to that device could single it out and throttle its power during busy periods while delivering full power to their own air conditioners. What if the power company zero-rated their air conditioners, powering them for free?

It seems obvious that allowing electric utilities to discriminate between different applications—technically or financially—would distort the market for applications. The companies that provide access to the Internet are asking to be able to do just these things. Lobbyists for cable and telephone companies like to jump on this analogy to suggest that advocates for the open Internet are fuzzy headed liberals who want the Internet regulated as a public utility. This is a cynical, but effective misdirection. I am a capitalist. I believe in markets. If anything, like many investors, I lean libertarian. I am not suggesting the Internet should be regulated. I am suggesting the telecommunications networks we use to get to the Internet not be allowed to exploit that bottleneck position to distort the market for Internet applications.

This is not some dangerous new government intervention into a free market. We have always recognized that telecommunications services were essential services because they are the connective tissue of our entire economy. In fact, until 2004, there was no question that Internet access was a telecommunications service. It was only then that cable companies convinced the FCC to treat Internet access as an information service. That was a fiction then, and it is still a fiction.

How many of us use our cable or telephone company for anything other than access to the Internet? The vast majority of applications we use come from independent developers. Many were created on a shoestring budget in the last couple of years. I understand why cable and telephone companies would like to change that. I understand why it is in their business interests to leverage their ability to control access to consumers to advantage their own applications or to get paid to advantage other providers' applications. I do not understand why anyone other than the access providers or the shareholders of the access providers would think this a good idea.

There is a way to preserve the key characteristics that enabled the emergence of the applications on the Internet. It is possible to keep the cost of developing and distributing Internet application within the reach of anyone with a computer and a little programming knowledge. All we have to do is admit what we all know, that access to the Internet is an essential services. Classify that service as a telecommunication service and then immediately forbear most of the regulatory overhead of the current telecommunications regulation. This would give the FCC sound legal authority to adopt the rules we need to protect innovation and investment on the Internet—rules against blocking? rules against prohibiting application-specific discrimination and rules banning access fees. This simple, clear, solution is the lightest weight approach possible. Not only is it not overbearing government regulation, it is the only way to prevent the distortion of the market for Internet applications which would ultimately require much more heavy-handed intervention.

Chairman LEAHY. Thank you very much, Mr. Burnham. Incidently, everybody's statement will be placed in the record in full. We are going to have to try to keep closer to our time, only because I know we are going to have votes on the floor and we will be losing Members when that happens.

[The prepared statement of Bradford Burnham appears as a submission for the record.]

Chairman LEAHY. Ruth Livier is writer, independent producer and actress. She created the award-winning bilingual web series, Ylse, and she is the first member of the Writers Guild of America West to join that union solely for work in new media.

Please go ahead.

STATEMENT OF RUTH LIVIER, WRITER, INDEPENDENT PRODUCER, AND ACTRESS, PACIFIC PALISADES, CALIFORNIA

Ms. LIVIER. Thank you, Chairman Leahy.

I am here as a Union actress and as the first person to join the Writers Guild of America West via my work in digital Media to share about how net neutrality changed my life.

Minority communities have historically lacked equitable and balanced representation in traditional media. UCLA's Dr. Darnell Hunt, a media diversity expert, testified that business as usual in the industry is wholly inadequate for addressing the stagnation in Hollywood diversity. A new paradigm is Needed that goes beyond symbolic pronouncements and token gestures. This is where net neutrality, or the open Internet comes in.

As an American Latina, I got tired of seeing the disproportionate amount of negative stereotypes about my community in traditional media. So, in 2000, I wrote Ylse as a TV pilot. It is a bicultural dramedy about a modern Latina.

At a conference designed to nurture Latino talent, I approached an executive for advice who said, "Who are you for anyone to produce your show?" Others asked, "Who's going to watch this?" Their comments were not based on my writing. They had not read a single word. Their immediate objections were based entirely on the concept of a Latina-driven show written by someone with no track record.

Who was I to think that anyone would take me seriously? And how was I supposed to prove there was a market for my content? There was no way in so, I filed the script away.

Then, years later, everything changed. Technology advanced. Camera equipment was no longer cost prohibitive. The Internet suddenly put worldwide distribution at our fingertips. It all seemed too good to be true, but, it was. And it changed everything.

We independent artists suddenly had unprecedented access to create, produce and distribute our content. In this exciting new frontier, anyone, regardless of ethnicity or socio-economic standing, could finally tell their stories from our points of view without getting discouraged, derailed or having our visions diluted by corporate gatekeepers.

So in 2008, I took that old script and reconceived it into the award-winning web series, Ylse.net. Our global audience was even broader than expected. Our indie series provided jobs for a diverse work force in front of and behind cameras. Our minority directors earned points toward becoming members of the Directors Guild of America and I earned points toward becoming a Writers Guild of America member via digital Media. This meant that the open Internet was a viable alternative way to build a career and diversify the talent pool of professional writers. It also meant that programming on the web was not up to the same few gatekeepers who controlled traditional media where, by all accounts, by every study, minorities are still under-represented in the writers' rooms, Executive positions, and in front of cameras. And Latinos are the most under-represented relative to our share of the US population.

But, with an open Internet, low-budgets and no connections does not mean there was no way in. Never again could we be disregarded by anyone who essentially asks, "Who are you to have your story be told?" We all deserve to have our stories told. We all deserve to be heard, to be acknowledged, and to not have to sit in the shadows until someone else decides that our lives are worthy of being reflected in the media and to have to wait for someone else to get it done. We could now take the reigns in our hands and take responsibility for our own destinies.

The open Internet has given the rest of us an opportunity to improve our crafts, provide jobs and a creative outlet for a more diverse work force, define ourselves by creating more varied, complex, positive and balanced portrayals of our demos. It has given us instant access to information and reputable data to prove our markets and connect with our global audiences. It has empowered and motivated historically marginalized communities to take the reigns in our own hands and create content, knowing there is a distribution outlet for it.

This communication platform must not go the way of traditional media, since through it diverse voices can finally partake in the national conversation at all levels. But the same companies that distribute traditional media control Internet service and they are advancing an agenda of unenforceable rules that would allow them to be the gatekeepers and decide what content is available online and on what terms. We cannot allow this to happen. That is why the FCC must institute strong rules that ban unjust and unreasonable discrimination by Internet service providers.

I join with the millions who have commented on the FCC's proposed rules to call on the Commission to reclassify Internet service as a telecommunications service, that it may, once and for all, permanently protect Internet openness. Make no mistake, this is a civil rights issue and it is my hope that for future generations of minority and low-income youth having a platform where they can express themselves on an equal-playing field will be nothing out of the ordinary because for us it has been nothing short of revolutionary. Thank you. Chairman Leahy. Thank you very much. I do appreciate that.

[The prepared statement of Ruth Livier appears as a submission for the record.]

Chairman LEAHY. Our next witness is Robert McDowell who served as a member of the Federal Communications Commission from 2006 to 2013. Last week he joined the law firm Wiley Rein as a partner. Prior to serving at the FCC, Mr. McDowell worked for 10 years at Comptel. It is an association of competitive communication service providers.

Please go ahead.

STATEMENT OF HON. ROBERT M. MCDOWELL, FORMER COMMISSIONER, FEDERAL COMMUNICATIONS COMMISSION, AND PARTNER, WILEY REIN LLP, WASHINGTON, DC

Mr. MCDOWELL. Thank you, Mr. Chairman, Ranking Member Grassley and all Members of the Committee. It is an honor to be here before you today and thank you for pointing out the resume. I will cut that out of my testimony right now.

I did start at Wiley Rein just last week. Nonetheless, the opinions I will give today are strictly my own and not those of any clients of Wiley Rein. I have to say that to make sure I have a job when I get back to the office later this afternoon.

As was the case during my 7 years on the FCC, my hope is that the Internet remains open and freedom-enhancing as it has been since its inception, since it was privatized in the mid-1990s.

As the Net migrated further away from government control, it grew beautifully, growing from just under 90 thousand users in the late 1980s to approximately 3 billion globally today. Its success as the fastest growing disruptive technology in human history was the direct result of the Clinton Administration's bipartisan policy to keep the government's hands, largely, off of the Internet sector. The Clinton Administration was expressly vigilant about resisting attempts to regulate the Net like an old phone monopoly, as some net neutrality proponents desire today. In short, the Internet is the greatest deregulatory success story of all time.

While serving on the FCC, I saw many, many different iterations of the net neutrality debate. Without a doubt, the definition of the term "net neutrality" keeps morphing by the day. Years ago, new rules were offered up, ostensively, to prevent Internet service providers from blocking or degrading the content and applications consumers seek to use.

Since then, the term has become a sort of Rorschach inkblot to mean anything anyone can envision regarding the Internet to benefit their agenda and their interests. For instance, net neutrality has evolved from being about the last mile ISPs to the middle mile.

And for the first time this year, it has grown to include ideas for regulation of the Internet backbone. The FCC's record even contains comments calling for the Commission to have general regulatory over the Internet, including not only networks like those built by cable and phone companies, but content and application providers at the so-called "edge" as well. At the end of the day, some are attempting to use public policy to essentially regulate their business rivals.

I have opposed new rules for many reasons, including, but not limited to, these five: (1) nothing is broken in the Internet access market that needs fixing; (2) no government agency has conducted a bona fide, peer-reviewed market study that has diagnosed any alleged systemic illness; (3) if systemic market failure were to come to light, ample laws already exist to remedy the problem, while current laws provide a deterrent against anti-competitive behavior; (4) retrofitting Title II of an 80-year old statute designed for the now-extent dinosaur phone monopolies of the early 20th century would be devastating to the entire Internet ecosphere and should not be held out as America's cutting edge 21st century tech policy for the world to emulate; and (5) expansion of the government's reach into the operations of the Net is providing cover and encouragement to regimes such as those in China, Iran, and Russia to push for multi-lateral, intergovernmental, or as Vladimir Putin said 3 years ago, "international control of the Internet."

At this critical crossroads, two disturbing trends are emerging at the FCC. The first is to subject the Internet to antiquated phone monopoly regulations known as Title II. The second is to suffocate the competitive, dynamic, vibrant and world-leading wireless industry with new and unnecessary rules. Some technology companies that are pushing for classification of Internet access as a telecommunication service under Title II should be careful what they wish for.

This section of the Communications Act is not only antiquated, but it is particularly powerful, prescriptive, far-reaching and it has over 1000 requirements. As market forces cause the technical architecture of tech and telecom—as we used to call them—companies to converge, companies that today are calling for the regulation of their rivals and think they will not get swept up in Title II regulation themselves could wake up 1 day having to live under its mandates.

As a technical matter and business matter, transmission services and information services are quickly becoming indistinguishable. It would be impossible to parse the difference between broadband service providers and other tech companies that combine transmission with information processing or storage such as content delivery networks or E-reader services.

Accordingly, across the globe, content and application companies are falling under the purview of more and more regulations and court orders. The FCC has the potential to stoke a contagion of international Internet regulation.

This scenario becomes even more nettlesome and discouraging when it comes to wireless broadband. Since its inception, American wireless companies have spent nearly $400 billion on infrastructure. Investment grew more than 40 percent between 2009 and

2013, and may add up to $1.2 trillion in new economic activity by 2017.

Over 90 percent of Americans have a choice of four mobile broadband providers. Furthermore, America leads the world in 4G build-out and adoption. The wireless market is clearly working and consumers are benefiting from it like no other time in human history.

Most importantly, though, wireless is different. As a matter of physics, wireless networks operate far differently from fiber or co-axial cable and require unique management. Subjecting wireless to new, unnecessary and one-size-fits-all rules will inject uncertainty into a thriving marketplace. Such government action could undermine American global competitiveness as the mobile Internet of everything comes over the horizon to change our world. Brace yourselves, it is coming.

In conclusion, whether creating new rules or foisting antiquated and obsolete laws on new technologies, the end result would be unnecessary and counterproductive while creating uncertainty and unintended consequences. A better path if we all share the same goal of freedom and choice and openness on the Internet, would be to rely on time-tested anti-trust and consumer protection laws that have helped make the American economy the strongest and most innovative in the world.

Thank you for the opportunity to testify today and I look forward to your questions.

Chairman LEAHY. Thank you very much.

[The prepared statement of Hon. Robert M. McDowell appears as a submission for the record.]

Chairman LEAHY. Dr. Jeffrey Eisenach is a visiting scholar at the American Enterprise Institute. He directs the Center for Internet, Communications and Technology Policy. He serves as executive editor of Tech Policy Daily.com. He writes on a wide range of issues, including industrial organization, communications policy, the Internet, government regulations, labor economics, and public finance. In his spare time, he comes and testifies here before the Congress.

Go ahead, Doctor.

STATEMENT OF JEFFREY A. EISENACH, PH.D., VISITING SCHOLAR, AMERICAN ENTERPRISE INSTITUTE CENTER FOR INTERNET, COMMUNICATIONS AND TECHNOLOGY POLICY, WASHINGTON, DC

Mr. EISENACH. Jack of all trades, master of none, perhaps. Thank you for your introduction.

Chairman Leahy, Ranking Member Grassley, and Members of the Committee, thank you for the opportunity to appear before you to present my views on net neutrality regulation. I do want to say that while I am here in my capacity as a visiting scholar at the American Enterprise Institute, the views I express are my own and should not be contributed to any of the organizations with which I am affiliated.

My testimony today advances three main points. First, net neutrality would not improve consumer welfare or protect the public interest. Rather, it is best understood as an effort by one set of pri-

vate interests to enrich itself by using the power of the state to obtain free services from another, a classic example of what economists term "rent-seeking." Second, the potential costs of net neutrality regulation are both sweeping and severe, and extend far beyond a simple transfer of wealth from one group to another. Third,
legitimate policy concerns can be addressed through existing antitrust and consumer protection laws.

To begin, let us be clear what we mean by net neutrality regulation. The rules favored by net neutrality advocates would ban or
restrict payments from one type of business, edge providers, to another type of business, broadband ISPS. Now it is easy to see why
edge providers would lobby for such rules, but difficult to understand how they would benefit consumers or the economy generally.

Net neutrality advocates offer a variety of justifications starting
with the idea that broadband ISPs have monopoly power. But the
monopoly argument has several fatal flaws. First, as the FCC has
repeatedly noted, broadband ISPs are investing billions of dollars to
upgrade their networks, prices are falling at a rapid pace and
broadband speeds are increasing—Senator Leahy, as I think you
mentioned—at 30 percent or more every year. That sort of performance is not consistent with the "cozy duopoly" theory advanced by
net neutrality advocates. Indeed, the broadband market is less concentrated than other Internet markets like search engines, social
networks, and personal computer operating systems.

Another variant of the market power argument suggests that
while big, established edge providers might be able to fend for
themselves against the ISPs, we need to look out for the little guys,
the new entrants who may be strangled in the crib as a result of
discriminatory access fees. But what no one can explain, however,
is why ISPs would want to discriminate against start-up edge providers which pose no competitive threat and which create the applications and content that draw consumers to subscribe to the
broadband in the first place. Indeed, historically, they have not
done so.

The FCC's case for net neutrality regulation is mostly not based
on concerns about monopoly power. Instead, its main theory is that
in the two-sided market in which broadband ISPs operate—with
edge providers on one side and consumers on the other—edge providers generate so much innovation that they deserve to be subsidized by consumers through a rule that forces consumers to pay
100 percent of the cost of the network while edge providers pay
zero. Now, this is a fine theory, but there is not a scintilla of empirical evidence to support it.

Finally, some argue net neutrality regulations are needed to protect freedom of speech. There are numerous problems with this argument as well, not the least of which is that giving Netflix the
right to distribute "Orange Is the New Black" over Comcast
broadband network for free, has nothing to do with protecting political speech or dissenting views.

When these erroneous arguments are stripped away, what is left
is the obvious—edge providers big and small and those who fund
them and profit from their success have a powerful economic interest in getting the government to guarantee them free access to the

ISP's networks. Occam's razor applies, the simplest explanation tends to be the correct one and net neutrality is no exception.

Now if all that were at issue here were a transfer of wealth from consumers and ISPs to edge providers and venture capitalists, that would be bad enough. But much more is at risk. The regulations being considered by the FCC, especially Title II, would replace the current dynamic pragmatic business and engineering approach to operating the Internet with a static, bureaucratic, politicized regulatory regime.

Ironically, common carrier regulation would not prevent price discrimination, but instead can actually require that rates vary across different types of services and customers just as postal rates do today. Under a Title II regime, the FCC could easily find itself overseeing rate proceedings that look a lot like the perennial scrum between first, second and third class mailers over who will pay how much for junk mail, magazines, and so forth. That is not the future of the Internet any of us want to see.

Finally, adoption of net neutrality regulation would harm the cause of Internet freedom worldwide. By embracing the idea of state-control of the Internet, the adoption of net neutrality rules in the U.S. would legitimize the efforts of tyrants everywhere to impose far-more repressive forms of statist intervention.

To conclude, it is true that the economic characteristics of high-tech markets throughout the Internet ecosystem result in many firms having a form of market power and that such market power creates the potential for anti-competitive acts. But these characteristics are not unique to broadband markets or broadband ISPs and they cannot justify discriminatory regulation. The appropriate remedy is vigilant, nondiscriminatory enforcement of the anti-trust laws.

Mr. Chairman and Members of the Committee, this completes my testimony and I look forward to answering any questions.

Chairman LEAHY. Thank you very much.

[The prepared statement of Jeffrey A. Eisenach, Ph.D., appears as a submission for the record.]

Chairman LEAHY. Our next witness, the last one, Ms. Nuala O'Connor. She is the president and CEO for the Center for Democracy and Technology, and an internationally recognized expert in Internet and technology policy.

Prior to joining CDT, she held a number of positions in the public and private sector, including as the first Chief Privacy Officer at the Department of Homeland Security, senior positions at General Electric and Amazon.com. She was born in Belfast, Northern Ireland. And I—with a certain amount of pride—mention she is a graduate of Georgetown University Law Center many, many, many years after I graduated from there.

Please go ahead.

STATEMENT OF NUALA O'CONNOR, PRESIDENT AND CHIEF EXECUTIVE OFFICER, CENTER FOR DEMOCRACY AND TECHNOLOGY, WASHINGTON, DC

Ms. O'CONNOR. Thank you, Chairman Leahy, Senator Grassley, distinguished Members of the Committee, my esteemed colleagues on the panel—I thank you.

I am honored to be here today to represent the Center for Democracy and Technology. For over 20 years, CDT has worked to promote and sustain public policy that protect a free and open Internet. Above all, we are dedicated to advancing the individual's interest in a digital world that supports free expression, freedom of association, personal privacy, and innovation.

Both the technology and the policy architectures of the Internet must support these individual rights and freedoms while also fostering innovation and the free flow of information—not only within the United States, but around the world. The Internet, at just over two decades old, is still in its infancy. Sound technical and policy choices have brought about an Internet that has supported robust expression, creativity and innovation.

While it is an appropriate time to strengthen the rules governing our rights in the digital world, we must be thoughtful about the consequences. We must seek to protect an individual's profound need to fully engage in the digital world as speakers, as creators, as recipients of rich and diverse ideas at reasonable costs and effective speeds. We must remain dedicated to growth and innovation that supports these goals in both public and private policies.

The Center for Democracy and Technology strongly supports the concept of net neutrality. We believe that the Internet is an enabler of knowledge, of community, and of Democracy around the world. We encourage the FCC to take decisive action to establish clear and strong rules that will create a level playing field for consumers.

We seek new rules that are undergirded by principles of fairness and Internet openness and we believe that all options should be on the table for the FCC to consider. When the FCC's open Internet rules were adopted in 2010, there was, in fact, even far less agreement on net neutrality than there is today. Most now agree that we need strong, open Internet rules that provide clarity for consumers and for businesses alike. Ultimately, strong rules should make it clear that the open and free nature of the Internet cannot and would not be changed.

We advocate for a principled and a pragmatic approach to the new rules with the following principles guiding any decision: (1) there must be no blocking, no censorship allowed; (2) we must have transparency about the services and the practices offered; (3) there should be low barriers to entry to the market on the Internet not only for individuals, but for start-up companies as well, which means we must have baseline nondiscriminatory rules; (4) we must encourage open technical standards while still allowing for reasonable network management.

It is through the lens of these principles that we should consider all of the options on the table and be open to new ones that we have not even considered yet.

In our comments to the FCC and our written testimony for today's hearing record, CDT has provided a detailed examination of the pros and cons of a number of the authorities on which the FCC could base its oversight, including both Title II and Section 706. We also explored a number of hybrid proposals that had been suggested.

While all of these are real options, we remain concerned about the limitations inherent in the structure and enforcement of any of these solutions and the challenges to speedy and effective implementation.

Over 3 million comments have been submitted to the FCC in the course of this rulemaking process. The vast majority of which call for strong rules that protect and preserve an open Internet. While the details of these comments vary, citizens have weighed in on this issue as never before, largely through online filings and emails showing the very nature of the Internet as a vehicle for political speech and openness. Many of these comments call for Title II reclassification and all agree that the Internet is a valuable resource and a platform and essential to our daily lives.

While there are some procedural concerns and hurdles that Title II must overcome, it nevertheless remains a very significant option for the FCC to consider. Other options are also possible.

A number of companies have called for hybrid proposals involving Title II applied to edge providers and Section 706 to end users. Others have suggested that prioritization might be acceptable if it is a choice made by the individual end user herself.

All of these proposals reflect thought and effort and creativity and deserve the time and attention of the FCC in crafting a new and innovative policy framework, one that matches the speed and the innovation and the impact of the Internet on our economy, our institutions, and our private lives.

The Center for Technology and Democracy believes that any regulatory framework adopted by the Federal Communications Commission must promote access, free expression, and the civil rights that will enable the greatest number of individuals to fully engage in the digital world. Whatever path the FCC chooses to take, it must act swiftly to create policy certainty that protects the individual and promotes the future growth and innovation.

Thank you.

Chairman LEAHY. Thank you very much.

[The prepared statement of Nuala O'Connor appears as a submission for the record.]

Chairman LEAHY. Let me ask a few questions here and then yield to Senator Grassley. I have to go back to the floor. I am going to ask Senator Hirono to take the gavel after that.

Mr. Burnham, when you talked about why a free and open Internet is crucial for the businesses that are flourishing online—others have raised concerns that if you have strong net neutrality protection, it is going to come at the cost of investment in broadband networks. You worked at a large telecommunications provider. You have seen what happens.

How do you respond to the concerns that net neutrality will come at the cost of investment in broadband networks?

Mr. BURNHAM. First of all, I think that all of us would like to see more investment, particularly anyone who lives in any sort of rural community would like to see a lot more investment in broadband capacity. I think that the important thing to remember is that nobody I know in the community that advocates strong network neutrality rules would object to any provider of access to the Internet charging whatever they felt they needed to charge in order to be able to build out the network. I think consumers would make that trade. They would pay more for more speed.

The problem with allowing access providers to sort of vertically integrate up into the applications layer and extract new profits from the applications layer in order to fund a build-out is that it actually perverts the incentives. If they are going to create fast lanes, the incentive is to actually have the rest of the Internet be fairly slow to create a market for their fast lanes.

So I think that in order to see investment, we need to separate the infrastructure of the Internet, the actual wires, from the applications layer and we need to manage them separately and regulate them separately. So I do think that it is absolutely possible to see investment in the network and investment on the network without having this vertical integration.

Chairman LEAHY. Thank you.

Ms. Livier, we have had a lot of hearings on this. I was struck by the fact that you are the first one who has spoken of it as a civil rights issue. I am going to ask you the same question I asked a number of businesses and others in Vermont when I had my hearing. Could you have launched your own series if the Internet had been operating under fast lanes and slow lanes?

Ms. LIVIER. No, sir. I could have not. I do not have deep pockets. I would not be able to pay for a fast lane, so there is no way that I would be able to distribute my show. There is no way that I would have been able to find an audience or prove my market if that existed.

Chairman LEAHY. Well, now of course, you can have others come in and compete against you. Do you want them to have the same opportunity you have?

Ms. LIVIER. Everyone should have the same opportunity. Everyone everywhere should have the same opportunity to do it.

Chairman LEAHY. You know it is interesting because I asked that question at our hearing up in Vermont. We had a couple of companies there doing extremely well now. They started off as startups and were happy they did not have to pay for a fast lane.

They all said they could easily pay for a fast lane today because they have grown so large, but they do not want it.

Ms. LIVIER. No. It is not fair.

Chairman LEAHY. Okay. Well, thank you.

Ms. LIVIER. Thank you.

Chairman LEAHY. Obviously, you preach to the converted.

[Laughter.]

Ms. LIVIER. Thank you.

Chairman LEAHY. Ms. O'Connor, more than 3.5 million Americans filed comments with the FCC. I think that sets a record. I know the comments I have received have just been enormous.

So I share your belief that the FCC has to adopt strong and clear rules to protect the open Internet. What is the best approach to do that?

Ms. O'CONNOR. We are open to not only the Title II approach, but the hybrid approaches that have been proposed in a number of the filings as well as what is called a Section 706 heavy approach. We do think Title II is one of the clearest and most direct paths to deal with the issues raised in the overturning of the prior rules, but there are a number of policy innovations on the table. We think the FCC should consider all of them fully before making a decision. I am sensitive to—having worked in the Internet industry for many years—concern about heavy-handed regulation, but the time is now for the FCC to take action and to settle the playing field. I think Mr. Burnham's comments are quite right when he says market certainty will actually help in many ways here.

So we are really asking for the FCC to take decisive action based on the principles of openness and focus on that as their goal.

Chairman LEAHY. Dr. Eisenach, I know in your testimony you said that in a paid prioritization world, the ISPs have an incentive to give start-ups a lowest cost access, but what if those start-ups are competing with products or services that are being provided by those who are paying the higher price? Are they going to have a conflict there?

Mr. EISENACH. Well, certainly, I am glad you asked. I think this is precisely where the antitrust laws come into play. A case that we are all familiar with and remember—Senator Hatch and I talked about this at the time—was a Microsoft case.

In that circumstance, you had a monopolist which exercised its market power to disadvantage a new entrant, Netscape, also JAVA at the time, and the antitrust laws were brought to bear successfully. So I think it was always hard to figure out what to do with Microsoft when you caught them, but we did finally catch them and deterred that behavior and we have not seen it since.

So that is an example of how the antitrust laws can come to bear in precisely the circumstance you are talking about. That is a legitimate concern.

Chairman LEAHY. Mr. Burnham, how do you feel about that?

Mr. BURNHAM. That is a very difficult way to solve the problem for a start-up. The start-ups in the Internet world come and go in a matter of years for sure, but perhaps months. So by the time an antitrust procedure works its way through the courts or even an FCC 706 procedure, I think that it would be irrelevant for most start-ups.

I think you need clear bright-line rules that start-ups can rely on so that they can build their business without having to hire a lawyer and represent themselves either in front of the Department of Justice or the FCC.

Chairman LEAHY. Thank you very much.

Senator Grassley.

Senator GRASSLEY. Thank you very much.

Chairman LEAHY. I would note for everybody, I kept within my 5 minutes.

Senator GRASSLEY. All right. I am going to ask Mr. McDowell to comment on something that was in Mr. Burnham's testimony about Title II reclassification and the fact that—not concerned about the impact on investment in the Internet marketplace. Do you agree with that position? Is there any problem in that area?

Mr. McDOWELL. No. I do not agree with that position and actually, other analysts do not as well. For instance just this Monday, Robert Kaminski from Capital Alpha Partners—investment analysts called Title II classification the nuclear option. Back in 2010, when the FCC examined this issue last, Credit Suisse's Jonathan

Chaplin said, "But while it is business as usual now, capital investment will come down if Title II becomes a reality."

So the investment community has a variety of concerns and like
a lot of things, where you stand is a matter of where you sit, perhaps.

Senator GRASSLEY. To you, Dr. Eisenach and Commissioner
McDowell—both of you do not have to answer this, but if you want
to—I want an answer on the claim that rural communities will be
hit especially hard if there is no new net neutrality rules. Do you
agree and should I—coming from a rural state—have any concern?

Mr. EISENACH. You absolutely should have concern that net neutrality regulation would deter investment in rural broadband networks. That is precisely what would happen and that is something
that even the advocates of net neutrality acknowledge. I am quoting
Tim Wu when I say that, "The impact of net neutrality reg- ulations,
an open question whether in subsidizing one side of the market
content the welfare gains would be as great as consumers would
enjoy or the benefit of expanding broadband service to new
consumers." So in subsidizing edge providers, we are explicitly taxing consumers and the ISPs who we want to be building out rural
broadband service.

Senator GRASSLEY. Yes. Do you have anything to add? If you do
not want to, I will go on.

Mr. McDOWELL. I would like to go back, actually to something
Mr. Burnham said earlier, a common misconception that somehow
before 2004, broadband access was classified as common carriage.
That is simply not the case. If you look in the attachment to my
voluminous testimony, there is a May 2010 letter to Congressman
Waxman which outlines this.

But you can go back to the 1996 act and also the 1998—what
was called the Stevens' Report, named for Senator Stevens—to
Congress from the FCC where the Clinton era FCC Chairman
Kennard issued a report to Congress saying, "Internet access services are appropriately classified as information rather than telecommunication services. The provision of Internet access services
offers end-users information service capabilities inextricably intertwined with data transport. As such, we conclude that it is appropriately classified as information service."

They have never, ever been classified under Title II, those services.

Senator GRASSLEY. All right. Mr. McDowell and Mr. Eisenach, it
has been argued that antitrust analysis is purely a numbers game
that does not take into account important non-economic values. Do
you agree, but more importantly, does an antitrust analysis only
consider financial and economic values, or can it, in fact, constitute
a broader consumer welfare-based analysis that looks at other consumer values?

Mr. McDOWELL. There is antitrust. There is also consumer protection laws, in general, as well as breach of contract and the Trial
Lawyers Bar, others who would have a field day if Internet service
providers, indeed, were to act in anti-competitive way that harms
consumers.

But when you have robustly competitive markets that actually
makes a rising tide that floats all boats, not just economically, but

socially as well—so let us just take a look back at what has made the Internet so fantastically successful. It has been this incredible area of freedom that has benefited society in more ways than we ever could have imagined 15 years ago.

Mr. EISENACH. I would just add that we are all very strong supporters of the social benefits that have been created by the Internet both here and abroad and those benefits have been created under an unregulated regime. The concerns that—those of us who have concerns about net neutrality is that bringing regulation into the mix will harm rather than benefit those benefits in the future.

Senator GRASSLEY. Then for the two of you again—and this will be my last question—in your opinion, has there been any widespread anti-competitive behavior within the Internet ecosystem that would warrant a prescriptive regulator solution imposed by the FCC?

Mr. MCDOWELL. The answer is no. I have long advocated for years that the Government do a peer-reviewed market study that would be put out for public comment. The last time the Government looked at this was in 2007, the Federal Trade Commission. It was not a peer-reviewed market study, but they unanimously on a bipartisan basis found there was no market failure and they warned against the unintended consequences of new rules.

Mr. EISENACH. Yes. I think what we have seen is some occasional accusations, but the accusations have not been borne out. Most recently, Netflix—I think—has been making wild accusations with respect to Comcast and other ISPs. In a current filing at the Federal Communications Commission in the past few days, it has acknowledged that it was the one that was throttling traffic and then turned around and used the slow delivery of some of its traffic to some of its customers as an excuse to try to seek regulation of the ISPs.

So I think there is the potential for lots of back and forth. That is what we are worried about. But there have not been any bonafide antitrust problems that we know of.

Senator GRASSLEY. Thank you. Those are all my questions, but I have some materials I would like to enter into the record.

Senator HIRONO. Certainly, without objection.

[The information referred to appears as submissions for the record.]

Senator HIRONO. Senator Klobuchar.

Senator KLOBUCHAR. Thank you very much, Madam Chair. Thank you for holding this important hearing to Senator Leahy, Senator Grassley.

The open and equal nature of the Internet has been incredibly important for economic development in the U.S. and I do not think people always think of it that way, but it has been.

In our state of Minnesota where Senator Franken and I serve, online sales represented more than 36 billion in revenue for local businesses just last year. And in the wake of recent court decisions, it has become clear that the FCC needs to pursue new rules.

The record three million comments received by the FCC—I believe the website went down a number of times—are proof that Americans recognize the impact of these decisions and the importance of our careful deliberation.

Legitimate concerns have been raised about the FCC's May 2014 rulemaking proposal regarding what authority the agency is seeking to use and what regulations may include or what types of business arrangements would be allowed.

As Chairman of the Senate Judiciary Antitrust Competition Policy and Consumer Rights Subcommittee, I have a strong interest in ensuring robust competition for all users of the Internet. And as I wrote the FCC earlier this summer, antitrust law alone is not sufficient to regulate the Internet. We need a clear set of rules for a fair playing field.

Mr. Burnham, one of the most central elements of the Internet is its ability to foster new and creative developments like Yahoo and Google, Facebook, they have all resulted from literally students using the open and free Internet to create billion dollar companies. As a venture capitalist in this field, what is the most important idea for encouraging this type of innovation, how will investment in tech and Internet companies change if FCC rules do not sufficiently protect and promote the open Internet and competition?

Mr. BURNHAM. It will change. And so we are really debating here investment in the Internet or in the infrastructure that delivers the Internet and investment on the Internet.

The problem with investing on the Internet, you know, the opportunity that we have had is to invest in any idea that could reach any consumer in a completely free and open way with no discrimination. The minute you begin to allow the infrastructure, the wires that deliver that service to consumers to reach up into that layer and either manage it for network management purposes or extract some kind of rents from that layer, it distorts that market. And so we as investors would have to then consider what kind of relationship they had with a provider.

If you want to get a hint of what this looks like, think back to all of the applications that were created and distributed by cell phone operators on their cell phone before the iPhone. How many of those actually became businesses? How many of those did you actually use?

Those services were controlled by the carriers and distributed by the carriers. And you had to get permission of the carrier to launch that service. Once we opened that up, the world changed.

Senator KLOBUCHAR. Right. Exactly. Mr. Eisenach, do you not you think this paid prioritization could affect this investment that I was just discussing with Mr. Burnham?

Mr. EISENACH. Well, two points. The first point is that he is right. This is a question over who will pay for the network. And the proposal, as Mr. Burnham said very clearly is that consumers pay 100 percent of the cost of the network and rich venture capital firms like Mr. Burnham's and their companies that they invest in pay zero.

Now, there is no shortage of investment going into Internet startup companies. Mr. Burnham's company has invested hundreds of millions of dollars and returned billions of dollars on those investments, and that is in the absence of net neutrality regulation. There is simply no basis for thinking net neutrality regulation is needed.

This is my second point, the phenomenon Mr. Burnham just described which is the death of vertically integrated cell phone applications and the rise of this very vibrant mobile applications economy happened in the absence of any kind of net neutrality regulation. It happened through the free market.

Senator KLOBUCHAR. Can I go to Ms. O'Connor because you have heard Ms. McDowell and Dr. Eisenach talking about how antitrust laws could be used effectively and I want to know what you think. Do you believe that antitrust law is sufficient to address potential Internet distribution issues, the things that would harm competition and consumers and what do you think needs to be done?

Ms. O'CONNOR. Well, the short answer to that question is no. After almost 20 years of practicing law, I have seen few areas of the bar short of their ability to solve the problem than the antitrust bar, maybe second only to the telecom bar. But I do not think it works in this context.

First of all the analysis is largely economic and commercial, but it is also ex post. So it would not solve for the issue Mr. Burnham has raised, and that is a very real one, the ability of a small independent start-up or an individual user to get online absent interference. To ask those individuals to apply for antitrust relief after the fact would basically prevent individual freedom and opportunity in getting into the Internet economy, into the Internet space, into the digital world. So it is not an effective and it is not a complete solution to the problem we are facing of a truly open and vibrant digital life.

Senator KLOBUCHAR. Thank you.

Senator HIRONO. Senator Lee.

Senator LEE. Thank you, Madam Chair, and thanks to each of you for being here today and for your thoughtful testimony. The issue of an open Internet has attracted a lot of attention from a lot of Americans. A considerable amount of public attention. Now, regardless of where any American stands on this issue, whether someone views herself as in support of or against what is commonly known as net neutrality, Americans are sending a consistent message which is, do not break the Internet. Do not mess with it. Do not mess with the most vibrant, expansive, even explosive area of our economy because it has worked and it has worked well, and it has brought enormous benefits in terms of economic growth to our great country and it has played an important role in bringing more information, more education, more entertainment, more opportunities generally to people not only throughout our great country, but throughout the world.

Subjecting the Internet to heavy-handed regulations, the type of regulations that were designed to regulate the railroad industry in the 19th century and designed to regulate Ma Bell in the 20th century could threaten to do precisely that.

Unwise regulation in this area would do nothing, I fear, but stifle much-needed innovation in Internet service and would, in the process, make it harder in the long run for consumers to be able to secure better service and ultimately have a real choice, more choices than they currently have about who delivers their Internet service. Anyone who has ever had an hour-long frustrating phone call with their cable company's customer service representative knows that consumers certainly could use more choices rather than fewer choices, particularly in this area. The proposed regulations of the sort that we are talking about today, would, I fear, do nothing to make the underlying problem better, but instead, I fear, would make it much, much worse.

So I have a few questions. I would like to talk to you first, Dr. Eisenach. Rent-seeking is often defined as a process in which someone devotes money and other resources to lobbying government so that they can take in a greater share of wealth that is already been produced without actually generating wealth on their own. Would you agree basically with that definition?

Mr. EISENACH. I think that is correct.

Senator LEE. Do you think we should be concerned about the possibility that the sort of FCC regulation that we are talking about today will lead to more rent-seeking behavior than it would solve the problems for which it was purportedly designed to solve?

Mr. EISENACH. Absolutely. The FCC has a long history and an unfortunate history in the rent-seeking department. Ronald Coase who won a Nobel Prize for helping to develop the theory of rent-seeking won it in part for an article titled "The Federal Communications Commission" which was about the lobbying and political influence that went into the allocation of broadcast licenses back during the 1950s and 1960s. That same kind of activity, and I spent an unfortunate amount of my time in and around the Federal Communications Commission and a tremendous amount of activity, as Rob knows better than anyone, goes into precisely that sort of lobbying and everyone who is paying a lobbyist to be there on all sides of the argument is there defending the interests—their economic interests—in these arguments. Senator Lee. So when government gets involved in picking winners and losers in the marketplace, the winners end up being not necessarily those who provide the best service at the best price to consumers, but rather those with the most effective context perhaps with the best relationships to government decisionmakers. I would like to ask you briefly about a point that was made earlier, I believe, by Mr. Burnham. An analogy was made to an air conditioner. Let us take that analogy a step further, let us explore it a little bit more. Let us suppose that someone installed a particular type of air conditioner that consumed an extraordinary amount of electric power, so much power that it made it very difficult for the electric utility in question to supply adequate electricity to other customers in the area. Would there be anything extraordinary about the electric power company perhaps charging a higher rate for that consumer who chose to use that particular air conditioning system?

Mr. EISENACH. No, nor would there be anything wrong with the electric company turning around and saying to manufacturers of air conditioners, you know, our network, our ability to serve our customers efficiently depends on your making more efficient air conditioners. We would like to give incentives for you to use less energy in the air conditioners that you manufacture. Both of those would be good things and would result in more efficient markets.

Senator LEE. And one follow-up to that. If the electric utility company in question decided to get into the business of providing its own air conditioning equipment to its rate payers, if it did that

and then engaged in practices that favored its own system as com‐
pared to others, would not antitrust laws be equipped to handle
that? And so too here, to the extent that we have Internet service
providers that start to compete with content providers, if they use
their position in the marketplace in an anti‐competitive manner,
are our antitrust laws not there for that very reason?

Mr. EISENACH. Absolutely. That story is called Microsoft and
Netscape. And one can easily imagine that story replaying itself in
this environment. And one can easily imagine the antitrust laws
being responsive to that.

One point very quickly on the speed with which regulation
versus antitrust can be brought to bear. We are a decade into the
net neutrality saga. We do not have enforceable rules. Whatever
the FCC does, we will not have enforceable rules for three to 5
years while this round of regulatory gamesmanship plays itself out
in the courts. In the meantime we could have had five rounds of
antitrust cases.

So the notion that regulation is a faster way of getting to the
right end I think is upside down.

Senator LEE. Okay. Thank you, sir.

I see my time is expired, Madam Chair, thank you.

Senator HIRONO. Thank you. Senator Franken.

Senator FRANKEN. Thank you, Madam Chair.

I think there is a fundamental misunderstanding here. Net neu‐
trality is not about regulating the Internet. Net neutrality is about
preserving the Internet as it is. Net neutrality has been the archi‐
tecture of the Internet from the very beginning.

Innovation has not just happened while net neutrality has been
in place. It has happened because net neutrality is in place. Let me
just talk about one example so everybody who is listening and
watching can hear.

Before YouTube there was a thing called Google Video. It was
not very good. The guys who started YouTube did it over a pizza
place in San Mateo, California. It was superior to Google Video.
And because it was allowed to travel at the same speed, people pre‐
ferred it and it replaced Google Video as the medium that people
watched videos on. And Google ended up buying it for $1.6 billion.
This is about innovation that has taken place because of net neu‐
trality. What the FCC has proposed, paid prioritization—that rep‐
resents a change. That is why 3.5 million people have commented—
because they understand this. This is not about new regulation;
this is about preserving the structure that we have had. The
Occam's razor here is do not change what we have.

Ms. O'Connor, can you speak to that?

Ms. O'CONNOR. Thank you so much, Senator Franken and thank
you so much for your leadership on this issue. That is exactly right,
there has always not only been rules and regulation, but there has
been the specter of enforcement by the FCC and the FTC for the
entire lifetime of the Internet.

We are looking at it not only obviously as an economic empower‐
ment issue and as an opportunity for growth and innovation, and
small business empowerment, we are looking at it as a need of the
individual to engage in digital life in every aspect of their world:

in their communications with their spouses, with their employers, with their schools, with each other.

The example that Jeff gave about antitrust law versus net neutrality regulation I think actually proves the point. In the case he cited, *Microsoft v. Netscape*, millions of dollars of legal fees were spent on both sides. No small business is going to have the resources to engage in that kind of fight. But 3.5 million individual citizens of this country were able to comment on this proceeding at the FCC. That proves the point that regulation is a more democratic opportunity here, and this is the path we need the FCC to take.

Senator FRANKEN. And it is just preserving the way it has been the whole time. So all this innovation you have cited, all this investment you have cited has happened while there has been net neutrality.

Mr. Burnham, I have met with some small businesses in Minnesota and start-ups who tell me that net neutrality is just crucial for them. They are making applications to do all kinds of things ranging from a company called "thisCLICKS," which helps companies manage their employees' time sheets. That is in St. Paul. A Minnesota company called "Sport Ngin," which is now employing about 300 people, has tripled their number of people in the last year, connecting people who want to join recreational sports leagues.

Now these companies are growing and they are innovating and there are thousands and thousands of companies like them. Now, if under pay prioritization they were made to compete with bigger, deep-pocketed entities, they could not do that, but let us say they did. Let us say they got on, they paid for pay prioritization. What they told me is that the apps that they use—the software that they use to run their app—unless those subcontractors pay for pay prioritization, their thing would not work. Is this not all about these pay prioritizations? Is this not about squelching the kind of innovation that we have all been celebrating, all five witnesses? Is that not the way it has been and aren't these pay prioritization lanes going to squelch that? Is that not a huge change?

Mr. BURNHAM. It is a huge change. And as I pointed out in my testimony, it is only in the last few years that the Internet access providers have even had the technology to figure out what you are doing online and therefore to be able to discriminate between that. So not only do we have the threat of FCC enforcement, but we also had the lack of technology in place. That is what has changed. The technology is in place and the FCC has proposed a new set of rules.

You bring up a very interesting point which is, it is not just the application that you see that matters, it is all the applications that they use. So, for instance Tumblr runs their application in their own data center, but they store all of their images at Amazon. And so in order to load a Tumblr page, you go to the Tumblr data center, but you also send a call out to the Amazon data center. If Amazon is not paying for paid prioritization, that page will not load. So there is a whole ecosystem of services that are built on top—or rather underneath—the services that you see that would also be affected.

Senator FRANKEN. Well, speaking of Amazon, all the companies that are like Amazon: DropBox, eBay, Facebook, Google, Microsoft, Netflix, Reddit, Tumblr, Twitter—they are all saying we need this. These are the innovators. And I just want everybody to understand that this is about preserving the Internet the way it is. That is what net neutrality is about.

Thank you, Madam Chair.

Senator HIRONO. Senator Hatch.

Senator HATCH. Well, thank you, Madam Chairperson. Net neutrality is not a new issue. Congress has been debating this issue for year. As Chairman of the Senate Republican High Tech Task Force I co-authored a Wall Street Journal op-ed in the fall of 2009 when then FCC Chairman Julius Genachowski and his Democratic colleagues first proposed their net neutrality rules. My op-ed entitled "Who is Going to Build the Information Superhighway" is just as applicable today as it was then.

Here is what I wrote in 2009. "If there is any sector of our economy where competition is so fierce, and where the pace of innovation is so rapid that government interference would only get in the way, it is the Internet and telecommunications market. The Internet has grown because of the virtuous and mutually beneficial circle.

"Network operator provide ever-increasing speed and bandwidth. Content providers one-up each other with game changing innovations and consumers adapt and adopt at lightning speed. Yet despite an overwhelming record of innovation and customer satisfaction Washington wants to replace the judgment of consumers with that of politicians and bureaucrats. Net neutrality may sound like fairness, but it is actually the opposite. Bandwidth is finite like the finite number of lanes on a highway network providers must innovate in order to accommodate the burgeoning traffic. As they invest billions of private dollars in new and improved networks they should right expect to set prices and manage those networks as they see fit.

"If the FCC takes control of the Internet, we will have the inevitable result of all poorly designed regulations, business decisions prejudiced by politicians and political decisions prejudiced by corporations. Keep in mind we are talking about the most competitive, efficient, and consumer-driven industry in the global economy."

Now, I did not write those words 5 days ago, but 5 years ago. I ask unanimous consent to enter the entire Wall Street Journal op-ed into the record at this point?

Senator HIRONO. Without objection.

[The op-ed referred to appears as a submission for the record.]

Senator HATCH. Although 5 years have past, those statements are just as true today. We have been the recipients of an explosion of apps, products, and services that directly result from broadband and Internet growth.

Without government regulation the Internet is growing. So what is the problem? What is broken? What is it that needs to be fixed?

An unregulated Internet has spurred innovation and economic growth all around the world. Yet despite all these successes, some argue we need to regulate the Internet. I cannot disagree more.

Let me just ask Mr. McDowell and Mr. Eisenach to answer a simple question. If so, what is it that needs to be fixed here? If you could answer that question.

Mr. MCDOWELL. Senator, you raise an excellent point which is nothing is broken that needs fixing. And we have the open and freedom enhancing explosive and amazingly bountiful Internet today precisely because of market forces and the laws that already existed before there were any formal net neutrality rules which really did not even start happening until 2008. We had Facebook, eBay, all those great companies had already blossomed into giants.

Senator HATCH. They did not do that because of net neutrality rules.

Mr. MCDOWELL. It was long before then.

Senator HATCH. Right. Mr. Eisenach.

Mr. EISENACH. Well, Senator, absolutely. So what you have in the Internet echo system is you have lots of firms who are creating value and they share in the creation of that value. So edge providers and networks and applications providers all have to get together. They get together on the screen of your iPhone to produce something of tremendous value and they fight about how they are going to share that value creation. All right. Every day on the Internet is a battle over who is going to——

Senator HATCH. I want to keep that fight going.

Mr. EISENACH. And that fight should happen between private companies in private bargaining as opposed to being a complaint before the Federal Communications Commission every time two parties disagree.

Senator HATCH. Well, let me ask you both again, do you think that the Internet today would be characterized by the current level of innovation if it had been subject to common carrier regulation? Mr.

MCDOWELL. No, sir. What folks are calling for is what is called ex-ante regulation, before the fact, or what some call "Moth- er May I," which is that then starts to prompt companies that may have thousands of miles of fiber optics and servers and routers that offer voice, video, and data services, those could be tech start-ups. Those are going to be tech companies, not what we think of as cable or phone companies.

Senator HATCH. Let me ask you——

Mr. MCDOWELL. They would have to file petitions for declaratory ruling at the FCC for permission to innovate.

Senator HATCH. Sure. Now, what will be the global impact if the FCC reclassifies the Internet as a utility under Title II of the Communications Act?

Mr. EISENACH. The International Telecommunications Union has been trying to get its hands on the Internet since the mid-1990s when the Clinton administration said no. And that is precisely what would happen. They would ultimately be successful in doing what they would like to do which is regulate the Internet as a public utility internationally.

Senator HATCH. One last question and this just needs a yes or no from both of you. In your view would investment and innovation increase or decrease if the FCC subjects broadband services to common carrier regulation?

Mr. MCDOWELL. I think the right answer is decrease, not yes or no, but, yes, decrease.

Mr. EISENACH. Technological innovation would decrease; lobbying innovation, however, would grow.

Senator HATCH. What are we talking about here. I mean, to me, I cannot understand why my friends on the other side love this type of regulation so much when I think it will wind up really fowling up the whole Internet.

Well, thank you, Madam Chairman.

Senator HIRONO. Thank you.

We have heard a lot about the antitrust laws as being adequate to provide consumer protection in this area. I am curious to know from either Mr. Burnham or Ms. O'Connor who I assume you have practiced in this area, you understand antitrust law. So, Ms. Livier has said that if we did not have net neutrality it would be highly unlikely that you would have been able to get your show on the Internet. So I am curious to know what kind of—in her situation looking at that kind of start-up, Mr. Burnham or Ms. O'Connor, what kind of antitrust claim would lie that she could pursue? Are we talking about price fixing? Are we talking about time? What are we talking about? What would she be able to proceed under to go forward?

Mr. BURNHAM. Well, I am not a lawyer and I am not practiced in antitrust law, so I am going to turn it over to Ms. O'Connor.

Ms. O'CONNOR. Having been in the Internet law and policy space again my entire career almost working in front of the Federal Trade Commission and in this area, there would be precious few remedies available under antitrust law. Your point is incredibly well taken. The limitations for a small individual artist or start-up company or individual end user to avail themselves of redress under the law would be quite limited. And the phrase that keeps coming to mind is, your antitrust law is not good enough for my Internet. It is just not comprehensive enough to protect the needs of the individual end user, the rights of the citizen.

Again, it is a fallacy to say the Internet has not been regulated. I was at a company in the late 1990s that had not only an FTC investigation, but 21 class actions, 12 attorney general investigations, a slew of regulatory oversight for the idea—the scintilla of an idea about a data matching project. It is wrong to say the Internet has not been regulated by the FCC and the FTC for years.

To not act right now would actually be the change. Senator Franken is right, to not act would be the absence of the playing field that is open and accessible to the individual end user.

Senator HIRONO. Thank you. I appreciate, Mr. Burnham, your pointing out that the technology has changed, so now our providers can figure out what the consumers are accessing. I think that is a very powerful piece of information for providers. And this is why I believe that the landscape is changing and why we are here today.

Now, Ms. O'Connor, you mentioned that—and several of you mentioned Title II is really probably not terribly applicable because Title II is a public utility. And we regulate public utilities up the kazoo. So this is not necessarily where we want to go.

You also mentioned that maybe we should look at Section 706. But that may not fit either. So my question to either Mr. Burnham, or you, Ms. O'Connor, is should we be talking about a new title? Ms. O'CONNOR. We would welcome that kind of policy innovation from Congress or from the Federal Communications Commission. The Internet is a precious and valuable space for the individual and for the end user and for small business innovation. And I am sympathetic to those claims that these are old titles that were based in historical parts of the economy that are very different. And we do not want to slow down the speed of the Internet economy and growth. But given the options on the table, we encourage the FCC to explore all of the options, all of the opportunities. And we have seen some very creative hybrid approaches proposed by policy groups and by companies, things that would combine 706 and Title II to get the enforcement abilities of both. And we encourage the FCC to consider those.

Senator HIRONO. Well, possibly in the best of all worlds that we would be coming up with a very clear new title, but in the absence of that happening, which will very likely be the case, that you are saying that the FCC—and I assume that Mr. Burnham agrees—that they have the authority to proceed under either Section 706 or Title II——

Ms. O'CONNOR. Yes.

Senator HIRONO [continuing]. To protect consumers?

I mean, clearly consumers feel that net neutrality is important because all of us have heard from hundreds, and hundreds, and hundreds of our constituents who have said, make sure that we are not going to create an environment where they are going to have to pay differential rates for access to the Internet.

So my time is fast expiring and I would like to—well, Senator Flake.

Senator FLAKE. I will go quickly. I find it interesting, I heard one of my colleagues say that the purpose of these net neutrality rules is to maintain the Internet as it is. Imagine if any tech company said, we are going to succeed by maintaining our company as it is. If Apple prior to launching iPhone 6 or the Apple watch said, we are just going to maintain as it is. I do not think if the Internet stays as it is, that it will be prepared for the future innovations that we are going to need to advance.

I hear the same kind of arguments with regard to pharmaceuticals or drug companies. I think with regulation we can make current drugs cheaper. You can, but you do not get the innovation you need to grow and progress and to go into other areas. So, I am always wary when we want to maintain something as it is especially something as dynamic as the Internet.

But just one question. I know we have votes going on. Dr. Eisenach, you have done some work in this area, can you discuss the University of Pennsylvania, Professor Chris Hugh's work on Europe and investment in broadband and Internet compared where they have regulatory regime perhaps similar to what we would be moving to here compared to what we have here? What is the difference between investment there and in the United States?

Mr. EISENACH. Thank you, Senator Flake. As Christopher Hugh has written as Richard Bennett at the American Enterprise Institute has written in a new study available from the TechPolicyDaily.com. The Europeans have followed a much more regulatory course than the U.S. and five or 10 years ago there was a debate about how wise a course that was. There was a debate about whether the U.S. was ahead or behind in broadband infrastructure. There is no debate today. The Europeans have recognized that the U.S. course was the wiser course. There is almost no fiber availability, virtually no fiber availability from telephone companies and very little from cable companies in Europe. The Europeans are a generation behind now on wireless broadband access, LTE only covers about a quarter of the population of Europe versus virtually 100 percent of the U.S.

So the regulatory course proved to be disastrous for Europe. And I think has the potential—we talked about leaving things the same versus changing them. The Internet has not been regulated. Net neutrality is a proposal to regulate it, I think it is that simple.

Senator HIRONO. We need to vote now, so I would like to call a brief recess and ask the witnesses to remain until I return. And I am also expecting Senator Blumenthal to return so he can pose his questions.

Recess.

[Whereupon at 12:08 p.m., the Committee recessed.]

[Whereupon at 12:15 p.m., the Committee reconvened.]

Senator BLUMENTHAL. We are now back in session. Thank you very much for being so patient. I was going to apologize for voting, but we should not be apologizing for voting. We should be applauded for moving forward. Thank you.

Let me ask, I have a few questions and then I understand Senator Cruz is coming back. Mr. Burnham, as you know better than anyone, the Internet's incredible economic success has been made possible because it is an open platform where anyone with a good idea can connect and consumers across the globe can compete on a level playing field for their business. And it is the relevance of an entrepreneur's product, the consumers are not sort of their sweetheart deals with large broadband providers that determine success. After launching their business start-ups frequently come to you, they want to be financed. They need capital. And they pitch their ideas to secure additional funding that would take their ideas to the next level.

Without net neutrality start-ups may not even be able to launch their products without turning to you for funding first. And it seems like to be successful in a paid priority context, you would want to know whether they have a deal with Comcast or AT&T. They would have to come to you with that sort of sweetheart deal first. Can you tell me how the content of start-up pitches would change in a world without the net neutrality rules? How do your criteria as an investor change?

Mr. BURNHAM. Well, we would need to understand the relationship between what they were doing and the interests of the companies that they depended on for distribution. And so that would—you know, we would stop focusing on the innovation and start focusing on the deal that they had struck. And that would make it very difficult.

I think, you know, contrary to what Mr. Eisenach has said about venture capital, this actually is not so bad for venture capital. If we end up in a paid prioritization regime because every start-up would now have to come to us first. They would have no negotiating leverage and we could extract a fairly big chunk of the company in exchange for taking the risk to fund them in this new riskier environment.

The way the world works today, start-ups launch, they get to scale, and they have real engagement with users, real traction, and then they farm out, you know, they basically shop that opportunity and venture capitalist compete with each other to do that deal because they have already proven that it works. That is a much better situation for entrepreneurs and start-up and any creator. It is not so great for venture capital, but we would prefer to see the world favoring entrepreneurs.

Senator BLUMENTHAL. So it might be better for some of the sources of financing, but worse for the start-ups, worse for the entrepreneurs?

Mr. BURNHAM. Yes.

Senator BLUMENTHAL. Ms. O'Connor, the antitrust laws are intended to prohibit business practices that unreasonably deprive consumers of the benefits of competition and that result in higher prices for goods and services. These important laws are crucial to America's success today by prohibiting collusion, conspiracy, monopoly power, and they evaluate combinations and agreements to preserve competition. But really what is at stake here is more than just questions of the economic benefit, it has also harmed the customers and freedom of speech. It is the speech that is made possible as a core component of our democracy.

In a world of pay prioritization, for example, NBC's website could tap into its affiliation with Comcast to make sure that its news reaches Comcast subscribers faster than Fox's website. Or we could see one Presidential candidate pay a broadband provider so that content on his or her website loads faster than the other candidates. Consumers and content providers alike would be affected. And these are effects in noneconomic ways. So my belief is that to safeguard free speech in the 21st century and the infrastructure that prevents interference with free speech, we ought to make sure that net neutrality is preserved. And maybe you can tell us a little bit more about how net neutrality affects those values of free speech?

Ms. O'CONNOR. Senator Blumenthal thank you so much for raising what we think is the fundamental question. It is important to address the antitrust laws and the appropriate authorities the FCC should consider. But it is the voices of the individual citizen, the voices of the artists like Ruth. The voices of the entrepreneur, the start-up technology who has the tiny kernel of an idea. Those are the voices we are concerned about, not only in the United States, but around the world.

And the concern, first of all, internationally that by taking some action we will be sending the wrong signal to the rest of the world, we are concerned about that too at CDT, but we think the signal we would be sending is that free speech is a fundamental right. It is the most important right, and the Internet is the greatest engine and the greatest platform that history has known for the individual's voice to be heard.

An independent artist like Ruth can suddenly reach millions of viewers overnight. A small company like the ones Senator Leahy talked about can suddenly reach customers all around the world. Without strong open Internet protections, those voices will go to the back of the line. This is simply unacceptable and undemocratic. It is the fundamental reason I am here today.

Thank you.

Senator BLUMENTHAL. Well, thank you for that strong statement. I agree completely with you because it highlights the non-economic benefits, but those non-economic benefits in turn produce enormous value throughout our society. It is the reason that entrepreneurs want to come here. And scientists want to invent and that great writers want to be here. The value of free speech is what distinguishes America, our protections for free speech.

Let me ask Commissioner McDowell, you know, I know from what I have been told that you have spoken about the efficiency and effectiveness of the market and competition apart from the net neutrality rules. Two weeks ago FCC Chairman Wheeler said, and I am quoting, "Meaningful competition for high speed, wired broadband is lacking and Americans need more competitive choices for faster and better Internet connections." He went on to say that "between three-quarters and 82 percent of consumers lack choice depending on the service."

Why do you believe that broadband is a competitive market that will correct itself in light of what Chairman Wheeler has said?

Mr. McDOWELL. Thank you, Senator, and it is a privilege to be before you today. Excellent question. I think the Commission is looking at the broadband market too myopically. We have wireless broadband. We also have unlicensed wireless. Senator Klobuchar and I have worked very closely together on the proliferation of that.

If you look at market data, I also look at my children, my young kids, the number one screen now is becoming the mobile screen. And that is causing a wonderfully disruptive element to the marketplace. So that is, I think, disrupting things in a way we could not have imagined 10 years ago.

Back to your Comcast and NBC analogy though, there are a number of complaints, thinking as a lawyer, that could be brought, not just in the antitrust context that would prevent that from happening or deter that from happening like exclusionary conduct and raising rivals' costs, but also breach of contract and tortious interference with contract and state attorneys general of which you were one, would have a field day if that type of behavior were to happen. That is also a deterrent, I think, in the marketplace.

Senator BLUMENTHAL. Thank you. Well, I want to thank all of you for giving us the benefit of your wisdom and insight on this very, very important issue. It has been very valuable testimony. I am going to turn back to Senator Hirono if she has additional questions. And, again, many thanks for being here.

Senator HIRONO. Thank you. I understand that Senator Cruz is on his way back. So I would like to give him the opportunity to come back in time to ask his questions. So that being the case I have a question for Ms. O'Connor.

Chairman Wheeler has proposed evaluating certain practices of broadband providers under a commercially reasonable standard. Can you explain your concerns with that standard and why it would be a poor fit for preserving open Internet?

Ms. O'CONNOR. Thank you so much, Senator. The commercially reasonable standard was only a relatively recent creation of the Federal Communications Commission and it certainly goes to the commercial qualities of any agreement between various providers on the Internet. But we think it misses the mark in an open Internet proceeding that is, we wish, to protect the interests of the individual end user and the entrant to the market, not the established players. We seek a standard that looks more like something that protects the qualities of an open Internet or does not degrade services to the individual. So we think that not only the language, but kind of the theory underpinning commercially reasonable, while perhaps and completely applicable in other contexts under FCC jurisdiction is not the right standard for a rulemaking proposal that seeks to protect the qualities of a flat Internet structure that allows for low barriers to entry and a free market—and a market that is open to all.

Senator HIRONO. Thank you. Mr. McDowell, you have testified that the antitrust laws would be adequate to protect the consumers. So there has been discussion about the antitrust laws as basically protecting an economic argument. So if the Internet providers now know what customers are accessing, it would be a way for them to determine without net neutrality rules in place that they would want to have differential pricing based on what the consumer is accessing. So in that kind of circumstance, do you think that the antitrust laws are adequate to protect the consumers' right to access whatever programming and applications the consumer wants to access?

Mr. McDOWELL. I do. And as I explained in greater length in the appendices to my testimony more about that. But not just the antitrust laws, but general consumer protection laws, Section 5 of the Federal Trade Commission Act, for instance, you have state laws and other Federal laws. As I was explaining to Senator Blumenthal, breach of contract, tortious interference with contract. You have to remember that every major ISP has in their terms of service, their contracts essentially, with their customers these types of protections. If they were to breach them, the plaintiffs' bar would have a field day. That is a huge deterrent right there. But let us look at what has worked. What has worked in this country to have a wonderfully, you know, blossoming Internet ecosystem are the laws that are in place, that were in place before net neutrality came about as a government action which was only 2008. You know, the iPhone came about in 2007. And the ap community started to—the ap industry started to explode.

So that is what has made it wonderful is the marketplace, market forces, and these general, flexible, more nimble rules that are in place that, as Nuala pointed out before, in the 1990s she was at a company or knew of a company that was investigated by the Federal Trade Commission, state attorneys general, and all the rest. What is better than creating a new body of law which would create uncertainty and years of litigation, as Dr. Eisenach pointed out, would be for the Government to sit down and sort of assemble a war council. I called for this for years. You could have the Federal Trade Commission, you could have the FCC, you could have the Department of Justice, state attorneys general, consumer groups, the plaintiffs' bar, all sit down and say, hey look, any of you, whether you are ISPs, or you are search engine giants, if you act in an anti-competitive way that harms consumers, then we are going to come down on you. We are going to launch this avalanche of rules.

But I also agree and wanted to speak to the fact that we sorely need to rewrite the Communications Act of 1934. We need to start over and look at all of this through the lens of consumer protection, knock down the silos that regulate based on your technology whether it is copper, or coaxial cable, or fiber, or wireless. All those are regulated differently. From the consumers' perspective, they just want their stuff when they want it and generate it, right? So they do not really care what the laws are behind the scenes. They are antiquated, they need to be rewritten. I hope in the next Congress we can get that done.

Senator HIRONO. I see our witnesses nodding their heads. So there seems to be general agreement that we probably should amend the 1934 law so that it is up with the times. So pretty much you agree? Well, maybe we can work on that.

I see that Senator—I am sorry, Ms. O'Connor, did you want to say something?

Ms. O'CONNOR. I could not agree more that consumers want what they want when they want it. And they do not really differentiate how they get their Internet whether it is on their mobile device, or on their home computer, or in the air.

And I would like us to consider banning the phrase "Internet of things." This is not the Internet of things. This is the Internet of people. So we want what we want when we want it, but we also want a level playing field to get in the game.

Senator HIRONO. Thank you. Senator Cruz.

Senator CRUZ. Thank you, Madam Chairman. And I want to thank each of the witnesses for being here today to discuss a critical issue that impacts the desire of all of us to keep the Internet free and open, a marketplace of competition and an oasis that historically has been beyond the unnecessary reach of government regulators.

This is by no means the first time the issue of so-called net neutrality has been raised. And every time it stirs up an interesting debate between government regulation versus to some the terrifying freedom of the Internet. I think the American people do not find that freedom all that terrifying at all.

The FCC's latest adventure in net neutrality in my view would only serve to stifle innovation, and would potentially subject the Internet to nanny state regulation from Washington.

Internet freedom has produced robust free speech for billions across the world. And a wide open incubator for entrepreneurs to generate jobs and to expand opportunity.

Back in May, FCC Commissioner Ajit Pai said this is, "not for us five unelected individuals to decide. Instead it should be resolved by the people's elected representatives, those who choose the direction of the Government and those whom the American people can hold accountable for their choice." I could not agree more. Although in Washington there are a lot of folks in Congress who are fans of pushing difficult decisions off to unelected members of our Government to insulate themselves from accountability at the voting booth.

And I fully agree with Commissioner Pai that a five-member government panel should not be dictating how Internet services will be provided to millions of Americans. More than $1.2 trillion has already been invested in broadband infrastructure since 1996. And that has led to an explosion of new content, applications, and Internet accessibility.

The FCC should not be endangering future investments by needlessly stifling growth in the online sector which remains one of the few bright spots in an economy that is otherwise struggling.

Net neutrality is a wolf in sheep's clothing. It is a set of government directives disguised, as they always are, as concerns about consumers and competition. That is the justification for nanny state regulations over and over again, whether it is the Mayor of New York telling us that our glass of Coke is too big, or the FCC deciding here is how the Internet should be governed.

We must keep in mind that when government imposes new regulations, inevitably the cost of them is easily absorbed by the large dominant companies, by the major players, and those who bear the brunt of it, those who are fatally strangled so often by these regulations are the little guys or the start-ups or the "mom and pops." The Internet has grown and flourished in ways we never could have imagined from back in the days when Al Gore invented the Internet.

And a big part of the reason has been that Washington has left the Internet alone.

Now, that used to be a bipartisan commitment. Back in 1996, President Clinton said, "Governments can have a profound effect on the growth of electronic commerce. By their actions they can facilitate electronic trade or inhibit it."

Government officials should respect the unique nature of the medium and recognize that widespread competition and increased consumer choice should be the defining features of the new digital marketplace.

We are seeing this growth in nanny state regulation in many contexts. One is net neutrality and the push to bring Washington into the day-to-day, online world. Another is a bill that Congress is considering and that I fear Congress will try to push through in the lame duck session and that is, namely, extending an Internet sales tax to millions of "moms and pops" who are selling their goods online who are starting small businesses and who if Congress has its way will be forced to collect taxes for 9600 jurisdictions nationwide. The big guys will be benefited by that. But the little guys, the young people, the Hispanics, the African Americans, the single moms, the people just filled with hopes and dreams wanting the American dream will find their lives made harder if we begin taxing the Internet, if we begin regulating the Internet. Instead, I believe we should protect the freedom of the Internet. And that should be something that brings us together across partisan lines, across the country, keep the Internet free that protects our speech. It protects our economy, and most importantly it protects opportunity for those who are struggling and want a better life.

Thank you, Madam Chairman.

Senator HIRONO. Thank you, Senator Cruz. Thank you to our witnesses. This hearing is adjourned and the record will stay open for 1 week.

[Whereupon, at 12:36 p.m., the Committee was adjourned.]

[Additional material submitted for the record follows.]

A P P E N D I X

ADDITIONAL MATERIAL SUBMITTED FOR THE RECORD

Witness List

Hearing before the
Senate Committee on the Judiciary

On

"Why Net Neutrality Matters: Protecting Consumers and Competition Through Meaningful
Open Internet Rules"

Wednesday, September 17, 2014
Hart Senate Office Building, Room 216
10:30 a.m.

Brad Burnham
Managing Partner
Union Square Ventures
New York, NY

Ruth Livier
Writer, Independent Producer, and Actress
Pacific Palisades, CA

The Honorable Robert M. McDowell
Former Commissioner, Federal Communications Commission
Partner, Wiley Rein LLP
Washington, DC

Dr. Jeffrey A. Eisenach
Visiting Scholar
American Enterprise Institute Center for Internet, Communications and Technology Policy
Washington, DC

Nuala O'Connor
President and CEO
Center for Democracy & Technology
Washington, DC

38

STATEMENT OF BRADFORD BURNHAM,

MANAGING PARTNER,

UNION SQUARE VENTURES, LLC

HEARING:

WHY NET NEUTRALITY MATTERS: PROTECTING CONSUMERS AND COMPETITION THROUGH MEANINGFUL OPEN INTERNET RULES

UNITED STATES SENATE

COMMITTEE ON THE JUDICIARY

SEPTEMBER 17, 2014

Thank you Chairman Leahy for the invitation to participate in this hearing to address the vitally important question of how make sure the Internet remains an engine of innovation and economic growth.

My perspective has been shaped by a career spent on both sides of the issue, first as a telecommunications executive at AT&T and Partner at AT&T Ventures, where I worked with or invested in the infrastructure of the Internet, and now at Union Square Ventures where we invest exclusively in applications layer services like Twitter, Tumblr, Kickstarter, Etsy, and Lending Club.

I believe we are at a crossroads. The rules the FCC is now considering will shape the Internet ecosystem for many years to come and could have a profound effect on our economy, our place in the world and ultimately on the nature of our society.

Almost everyone has benefited from the phenomenal innovation enabled by the Internet -- whether you are playing Words with Friends with your grandchild, or collaborating with other scientists across continents or finding validation and support in an online community - but few of us have stopped to think about how all this happened. The rich, dynamic, emergent innovation we have witnessed happened because of two two key characteristics of the Internet's architecture. First, the underlying protocols of the Internet separated applications from infrastructure, making it possible to create a networked application without knowing anything about, or seeking permission from, the underlying network. Second, developers could create applications, confident they could reach the millions of consumers who had already paid to be connected to the Internet. These two characteristics radically lowered the cost of building and distributing Internet applications, opening the market to a much larger and more diverse pool of creators.

For the first time, people without money, connections, or corporate backing could create an application and reach a global audience. Facebook was created in a dorm room. Foursquare spent $25,000 to reach their first 100,000 users. When Tumblr had 100,000 users, they were two employees, a part time designer and a couple of desks tucked away in the corner of another startup. Each of these companies -- and thousands more -- started from scratch and grew to reach global audiences. And they have since gone on to empower hundreds of millions of others: independent craftspeople setting up shop on Etsy, filmmakers raising millions of dollars on Kickstarter, journalists reaching global audiences on Twitter, musicians launching careers on Soundcloud, and so on.

This incredible explosion of innovation and democratization of opportunity happened because it became so cheap to create and distribute an application on the Internet that innovators no longer required permission from a boss, a network operator, or an investor to launch a business. If you could imagine a service like Instagram or Pinterest you could build it yourself and get it into the hands of thousands or millions of consumers almost overnight. Later, once you had a large audience, you could approach investors from a position of strength to raise the money needed to grow your business. This is the model of innovation that powered the growth of the Internet. And all of this is about to change.

Until recently, internet access providers could not tell if you were watching Netflix, playing Angry Birds, or posting on Facebook — by default, access to the internet was "open". They have now deployed "deep packet inspection" technology that allows them to see what services you are using. Because they can now figure out which packets are which, access providers can now charge application developers for faster delivery of packets, slow traffic they decide is less important, and even block traffic altogether.

As the cable and telephone companies deployed equipment to identify which packets came from which applications, the FCC undertook a number of actions to keep the Internet a level playing field, culminating in the formal adoption of network neutrality principles in 2010. For the last several years, one of the biggest providers of broadband Internet access, Comcast, has been operating under network neutrality principles they agreed to as a condition of their merger with NBC. Because, of all of these factors, Internet access providers have not exploited their powerful market position, and the Internet has remained relatively open.

Today, those merger agreements are near expiration, and the FCC's ability to enforce open internet principles has been sharply curtailed by the DC Circuit Court's decision in the Verizon case, which supported the FCC's policy goals, but ruled that the FCC couldn't legally pursue them without reclassifying internet access providers as "telecommunications services" rather than "information services".

Unfortunately, the FCC, in search of a compromise, is not proposing to reclassify Internet access. Instead, they are proposing rules that would explicitly allow cable and telephone companies to treat internet applications differently for a variety of business and network management reasons.

The combination of these new technical abilities and these proposed rules will dramatically increase the cost of creating and distributing Internet applications. Applications developers will have to think about the network management strategies and even the business interests of cable and telephone companies when they design their applications. They will also have to change the way they approach investors.

Every web service developer knows speed is a feature. They all work to shave milliseconds off the time it takes to load a page. Startups will need to raise the money up front to buy access to the fastlane to succeed, making it impossible to launch first -- as Tumblr and Foursquare did -- and then raise money to fund the growth of a proven concept. No new service will be created in a dorm room. And services like video, voice, and payment services that compete with the applications layer ambitions of the cable and telephone companies will find it especially hard to raise money.

It may seem like I am overstating my case but ask yourself how comfortable you would be investing in a new electric appliance if the company that delivered power to that device were able to throttle or cut off that power while delivering full power to their own devices or the devices of their business partners. What if your new device had to compete with a device that got electricity for free. If electric utilities were able to do these things, consumers could no longer shop for appliances without knowing what deal the manufacturer had with the utility. Investors would not be able to support promising new ideas without negotiating access to electricity up front. It seems obvious that allowing electric utilities to discriminate between different appliances technically or financially would distort the market for appliances. The companies that provide access to the Internet are asking to be able to do all these things.

Lobbyists for the cable and telephone companies like to jump on this analogy to suggest that advocates for the open Internet are fuzzy headed liberals who want the Internet regulated as a public utility. This is a cynical but effective misdirection. I am a capitalist. I believe in markets. If anything, like many investors, I lean libertarian. I am not suggesting the Internet should be regulated. I am suggesting the telecommunications networks -- that are, for the foreseeable future, the only practical way any of us will get to the Internet -- be required not to exploit that privileged position to distort the vibrant market for Internet applications.

This is not some dangerous new government intervention into a free market. We have always recognized that telecommunications services were essential services because they are the connective tissue of our entire economy. In fact, until 2004, there was no question that Internet access was a telecommunications service. It was only then cable companies convinced the FCC to treat Internet access as an information service. That was a fiction then, and it is still a fiction. How many of us, use any information service from our Internet access provider. Most of us spend our time on the Internet on a service created on a shoestring just a few years ago. I understand why cable and telephone companies would like to change that. I understand why it is in their business interest to leverage their powerful market position to advantage their own applications layer services or get paid to advantage other providers services. I don't understand why anyone other than the access providers and their shareholders would think this a good idea.

There is a way to preserve the key characteristics that enabled the emergence of the rich profusion of applications on the Internet. It is possible to keep the cost of developing and distributing an Internet application within the reach of anyone with a computer and a little programming experience. All we have to do is call a spade a spade, classify last mile broadband access as a telecommunications service and then immediately forbear most of the regulatory overhead of current telecommunications regulation. This would give the FCC sound legal authority to adopt the kind of open internet rules we need to protect innovation and investment on the Internet: rules against blocking; rules prohibiting application-specific discrimination; and rules banning access fees.

This simple, clear, solution is the lightest-weight approach possible. Not only is it not overbearing government regulation, it is the only way to prevent the distortion of the market for Internet applications which would ultimately require much more heavy handed intervention We can preserve the freedom to innovate on the Internet. We can align incentives to encourage investment in both the infrastructure layer and the applications layer. We can have fast, robust networks and the decentralized, emergent innovation at the applications layer that is the Internet as we know it. We are at a crossroad. We just have to choose the right road forward.

Testimony of Ruth Livier

Before the

United States Senate Committee on the Judiciary

At a Hearing Entitled

" Why Net Neutrality Matters: Protecting Consumers and Competition Through Meaningful Open Internet Rules."

Thank you, Senator Leahy. My name is Ruth Livier. I'm here today as a Union actress and as the first person to join the Writers Guild of America West via my work in digital Media to share about how net neutrality has changed my life.

Countless studies have shown that minority communities have historically lacked equitable and balanced representation in traditional media. UCLA's Dr. Darnell Hunt, a media diversity expert, testified "that business as usual in the industry is wholly inadequate for addressing the stagnation in Hollywood diversity…. A new paradigm is needed…". [That goes] "…beyond symbolic pronouncements and token gestures". [1]

This is where Net Neutrality, or the Open Internet comes in.

As an American Latina, I got tired of seeing the disproportionate amount of negative stereotypes about my community in traditional media. So, in 2000, I wrote *Ylse* as a TV pilot. It's a bicultural dramedy about a modern Latina: Someone with big dreams fighting thru other people's low expectations; juggling career, a not-so-successful love life and a family who sometimes doesn't understand her progressive American ways.

At a conference designed to nurture Latino talent, I approached a traditional media executive for advice on how to get my show produced who said, "Who are you for anyone to produce your show?" Others asked, "Who's going to watch *this?*" Their comments were not based on my writing. They had not read a single word. Their immediate objections were based entirely on the concept of a Latina-driven show

---

1 http://judiciary.house.gov/_files/hearings/pdf/Hunt100607.pdf

written by someone with no track record. Who was I to think that anyone would take me seriously? How was I supposed to prove there was a market for my content? There was no way in so, I filed the script away.

Then, a few years later, everything changed. Technology advanced. Camera equipment was no longer cost prohibitive. The Internet suddenly put worldwide distribution at our fingertips. It all seemed too good to be true. But, it was good. And, it was true. And, it changed *everything*. We independent artists suddenly had unprecedented access to create, produce and distribute our content. In this exciting new frontier of an open Internet, anyone, regardless of ethnicity or socio-economic standing, could finally tell their stories from their points of view without getting discouraged, derailed or having their visions diluted by corporate gatekeepers.

So in 2008, I took that old TV script and reconceived it into the award-winning web series, www.Ylse.net. Our global audience was even broader than expected. Our independent low-budget series provided jobs for a diverse workforce in front of and behind the cameras. And, because we were a union signatory, our minority directors earned points towards their Directors Guild of America membership and I earned points towards becoming the first person to join the Writer's Guild of America via work in digital Media.

Joining the WGAw through this medium was significant because it meant that Digital Media was in fact a viable alternative way to build a career and diversify the talent pool of professional writers. It also meant that programming on the web was not up to the same few gatekeepers who control traditional media where, by all accounts, minorities are still underrepresented in the writers rooms, Executive positions, and in front of the camera. And Latinos are the most underrepresented relative to our share of the US population.

But, in the unprecedented world of an open, non-discriminatory Internet, no longer did low-budgets and no connections mean there was no way in. Never again could we be disregarded by anyone who essentially asks, "Who are *you* to have your story be told?" We all deserve to have our stories told. We all deserve to be heard, to be acknowledged, and to not have to sit in the shadows until someone else decides that our lives are worthy of being reflected in the media and have to wait for someone else to get it done. We could now take the reigns in our hands and take responsibility for our own destinies.

The open Internet has given the rest of us an opportunity to:

-Improve our crafts

-Provide jobs and a creative outlet for a more diverse workforce.

-Define ourselves by creating more varied, complex, positive and balanced portrayals of our demos.

-Instantly access information and reputable data to prove our markets.

-Connect with our global audiences, again, proving our markets.

-Empower and motivate historically marginalized communities to take the reigns in our own hands and create content, knowing there is a distribution outlet for it.

As long as this revolutionary platform does not go the way of traditional media, diverse voices can finally partake in the national conversation at all levels.

Unfortunately, not everyone wants the Internet to remain open and free of gatekeepers. The same companies that distribute traditional media control Internet service, and they are advancing an agenda of weak rules that would allow them to be the gatekeepers and decide what content is available online as well and on what terms. We cannot allow this to happen. That's why the FCC must institute strong open Internet rules that ban unjust and unreasonable discrimination by Internet service providers. I join with the majority of Americans who have commented on the FCC's proposed rules to call on the Commission to reclassify Internet service as a telecommunications service, so that it may, once and for all, *permanently* protect Internet openness.

The Open Internet may just be that "effective mechanism" Dr. Hunt alluded to in his testimony "for an industry truly committed to catching up with a changing America".

It's a civil rights issue. And, it is my hope that, for future generations of minority and low-income youth, having a platform where they can express themselves on an equal playing field will be nothing out of the ordinary because, for us, it has been nothing short of revolutionary.

Thank you.

STATEMENT
OF
THE HON. ROBERT M. MCDOWELL
PARTNER
WILEY REIN, LLP

"WHY NET NEUTRALITY MATTERS: PROTECTING CONSUMERS AND COMPETITION
THROUGH MEANINGFUL OPEN INTERNET RULES"

BEFORE THE
UNITED STATES SENATE
COMMITTEE ON THE JUDICIARY

SEPTEMBER 17, 2014

WILEY REIN, LLP
1776 K STREET, N.W.
WASHINGTON, D.C. 20006
WWW.WILEYREIN.COM

TABLE OF CONTENTS

APPENDIX A: STATEMENT OF THE HON. ROBERT M. MCDOWELL BEFORE THE U.S. HOUSE COMMITTEE ON THE JUDICIARY SUBCOMMITTEE ON REGULATORY REFORM, COMMERCIAL AND ANTITRUST LAW, JUNE 20, 2014

APPENDIX B: SELECTED PUBLICATIONS

INTRODUCTION

Chairman Leahy, Ranking Member Grassley and distinguished Members of the Committee, thank you for having me testify before you today. My name is Robert McDowell. Until last year, I served as a Commissioner of the Federal Communications Commission (FCC) for seven years. Last week, I joined the internationally recognized communications law firm of Wiley Rein, LLP as a partner. Nonetheless, I am not testifying today on behalf of any client of Wiley Rein, and the opinions I express today are strictly my own.

I have always supported policies that promote an open and freedom-enhancing Internet. That is what the American private sector built as the result of long-standing and bipartisan public policy that insulated the Net from unnecessary regulation.

During my tenure at the FCC, the issue of government regulation of Internet network management, or "net neutrality," came before me several times in a variety of contexts. I am deeply familiar with the arguments for and against new regulations in this area. I voted against the Commission's first two attempts to issue new rules for many reasons, and I oppose the FCC's current attempt to regulate in this space, because:

1) Nothing is broken in the Internet access market that needs fixing;

2) The FCC has not conducted a *bona fide*, peer-reviewed market study to diagnose any alleged "illness" before issuing a "cure" in the form of new rules;

3) If a systemic market failure were to come to light, ample laws already exist to remedy the problem;

4) I do not believe that Congress has given the FCC the authority to issue the rules it has proposed;

5) If the FCC overreaches again, it will likely lose in court for a third time;

6) Fabricating a new and untested body of law, even using a "skinny" version of Title II, will create uncertainty and perverse unintended consequences that will spread beyond the ostensible regulatory target of network operators, like phone and cable companies, to the entirety of the Internet ecosystem, such as content, applications and content delivery networks (CDNs);

7) Expansion of the government's reach into the operations of the Internet is only providing cover and encouragement to foreign governments, as well as multilateral and intergovernmental institutions, that want to have, as Vladimir Putin said, "international control of the Internet;"[1] and

8) Government regulation of Internet network management violates the First Amendment of the U.S. Constitution.

Over the years, I have had many other concerns too. For the Committee's convenience and the sake of brevity, I have included as part of my testimony today previous statements, dissents, testimony and opinion-editorials I have written on this subject.

The appellate courts largely rejected most of the Commission's two attempts to regulate by viewing the FCC's actions as an overreach.[2] Recognizing the FCC's lack of statutory authority to issue net neutrality rules, some Members of the 110th Congress tried, but failed, to pass legislation that would have granted the Commission the power to do so.[3]

Apparently undeterred by its two previous defeats in court, the Commission is trying yet again to expand its reach into the Internet's affairs. As the Commission deliberates, two disturbing ideas are emerging. First, the Commission is again considering classifying—for the

---

[1] Vladimir Putin, Prime Minister of the Russian Federation, Working Day, *Prime Minister Vladimir Putin Meets with Secretary General of the International Telecommunications Union Hamadoun Touré*, GOV'T OF THE RUSSIAN FED'N (June 15, 2011), http://premier.gov.ru/eng/events/news/15601/.

[2] *Verizon v. FCC*, 740 F.3d 623 (D.C. Cir. 2014); *Comcast Corp. v. FCC*, 600 F.3d 642 (D.C. Cir. 2010).

[3] *See, e.g.*, Internet Freedom Preservation Act of 2008, H.R. 5353, 110th Cong. (2008).

first time—broadband as a common carrier service under Title II of the Communications Act of

1934. This effort has been reported in the media as treating the Internet like a "utility." The

other troubling idea is to expand new network management rules to wireless broadband. Each is

unnecessary and would be highly counterproductive.

I.   **CLASSIFYING BROADBAND AS A "UTILITY" –STYLE COMMON CARRIER UNDER TITLE II OF THE COMMUNICATIONS ACT OF 1934 WOULD GENERATE UNCERTAINTY, CAUSE UNINTENDED CONSEQUENCES AND UNDERMINE GROWTH IN THE ENTIRE INTERNET ECOSYSTEM.**

First, the notion that retrofitting Title II, an antiquated—but powerful—80-year-old

statute designed for the copper-based, analog, voice-only phone monopolies of the early 20th

Century, would somehow be good for the dynamic and ever-evolving Internet ecosystem is just

plain wrong. During my 24 year career in the telecommunications space I have become quite

familiar with Title II. Proponents of regulating the Internet under Title II argue that doing so

would prevent two-sided markets, usage-based pricing and "discrimination"[4] of Internet traffic.

In fact, the exact opposite is true.

Not only does Title II allow usage-based pricing, that is exactly what it is designed to

regulate.[5] Not only does it allow for the "reasonable" discrimination of traffic, it mandates that

similarly situated producers of traffic can be charged similar rates if those rates are "just or

---

[4] The term "discrimination" is often misused in the net neutrality debate. Discrimination can have many meanings. To a network engineer, discrimination is absolutely necessary and means having the ability to manage Internet Protocol networks. For instance, consumers downloading movies want those video bits to arrive on their screens quickly and without interference from other Internet traffic such as email or voice over Internet protocol (VoIP) communications. Similarly, a caller using VoIP in an emergency wants his/her call to 911 to take priority over Internet traffic carrying a cat video. Another example is Internet traffic carrying heart monitoring data from a patient to his/her doctor. During a medical crisis, the patient will want discrimination thus allowing life-saving data to reach the doctor as quickly as possible and ahead of other traffic. This is also known as "prioritization," something net neutrality proponents oppose. Treating all Internet traffic "equally," as many net neutrality proponents want, would undermine the beneficial aspects of allowing the freedom to innovate through the ability to discriminate in the engineering context. What should *not* be permitted, and is prohibited under existing antitrust and consumer protection laws, is discrimination that has an anticompetitive effect that harms consumers. Boiling the net neutrality debate down to the bumper sticker of "treat all Internet traffic equally" may have popular appeal, but it is a misleading slogan that will likely have dangerous implications if it is codified as public policy.

[5] 47 U.S.C. §§ 201-202.

reasonable."[6] Title II would not prevent network operators from charging some content and application—or "edge"—providers to carry their Internet traffic. Indeed, Title II would allow for a "sending party pays"[7] construct that some American edge providers and network operators are battling against *together* in international regulatory arenas.

At the consumer level, industry analysts have concluded that new utility-like economic regulation of the Internet would likely "have the perverse effect of raising prices to all users" and some users would likely see the end of their service entirely.[8]

Finally, a Title II framework would lay a broad-based legal foundation for the Commission eventually to regulate the entire Internet ecosystem. Such is the goal of the influential godfather of the movement, the man who coined the term "net neutrality," Columbia law professor, Timothy Wu. This is not merely theoretical. He testified to such alongside me at a House Judiciary Committee hearing on net neutrality this past June.[9] Furthermore, Professor Wu has tremendous influence at the FCC having authored the first-ever net neutrality merger conditions during the Commission's approval of the AT&T/BellSouth transaction in 2006.[10]

---

[6] *Id.* § 202(a).

[7] *Revisions of the International Telecommunications Regulations – Proposals for High Level Principles to be Introduced in the ITRs*, ETNO, CWG-WCIT12 Contribution 109, at 2 (2012), http://www.itu.int/md/T09-CWG.WCIT12-C-0109/en.

[8] Howard Buskirk, *Investors, Analysts Uneasy About FCC Direction on Net Neutrality*, COMM. DAILY, Oct. 2, 2009, at 2; *see also* National Cable & Telecommunications Association Comments at 19 and Verizon and Verizon Wireless Reply Comments at 17–18 to *Preserving the Open Internet*, GN Docket No. 09-191; *Street Talk*, CableFAX, June 14, 2010 ("But while it's business as usual now, capital investment will come down if Title II becomes a reality, said Credit Suisse telecom services dir[ector] Jonathan Chaplin. He said the next place companies would look to capture some of the return is costs, which would mean jobs.").

[9] *See* House Judiciary Subcommittee on Regulatory Reform, Commercial and Antitrust Law, *Net Neutrality: Is Antitrust Law More Effective than Regulation in Protecting Consumers and Innovation?*, 113th Congress, 2nd sess., 2014 (testimony of Timothy Wu), at http://judiciary.house.gov/_cache/files/bcecca84-4169-4a47-a202-5e90c83ae876/wu-testimony.pdf.

[10] Spencer E. Ante, *Tim Wu, Freedom Fighter*, BUS. WK., Nov. 8, 2007, available at http://www.businessweek.com/stories/2007-11-08/tim-wu-freedom-fighterbusinessweek-business-news-stock-market-and-financial-advice; Robert M. McDowell, *This is Why the Government Should Never Control the Internet*, WASH. POST, July 14, 2014, http://www.washingtonpost.com/posteverything/wp/2014/07/14/this-is-why-the-government-should-never-control-the-internet/.

In sum, it would be impossible to draw a principled line between broadband service providers and other entities that combine transmission with information processing or storage, such as the content delivery networks that give us Netflix movies or YouTube videos. As Robert Litan recently explained, "[t]here is a very slippery slope from having designated ISPs as being subject to common carriage regulation to having to include other forms of Internet transmissions as well because they arguably use 'telecommunications services', the legal hook in Title II for its application."[11]

In other words, as part of providing their "information" services, many tech companies also provide transmission services. For example, many application and content providers, CDNs, and providers of services offered through connected devices, provide transmission service as a component of their information service. The same is true for search engines that connect an advertising network to a search request, and for email providers and social networks that enable chat or messaging sessions.

Also caught in the Title II dragnet would be tech companies that sell other services, such as e-reader services, but which buy wireless access on a wholesale basis to deliver their content. Such synergistic deals would be complicated—at best—under Title II because the e-reader service provider would be considered a reseller of telecommunications services under Commission precedent.

II. WIRELESS BROADBAND IS DIFFERENT FROM WIRELINE INTERNET SERVICES AND SHOULD NOT BE SUBJECT TO NET NEUTRALITY RULES.

The FCC is also poised to impose new net neutrality regulations on the wireless industry. In the Commission's 2010 net neutrality order, it was the bipartisan and unanimous consensus of

---

[11] *See* Robert E. Litan, *Regulating Internet Access as a Public Utility: A Boomerang on Tech If It Happens*, Economic Studies at Brookings, at 2 (June 2, 2014).

the FCC that the heart of new net neutrality rules not be applied to wireless broadband services.[12] The primary reason for treating wireless and wireline differently is that mobile broadband technologies use shared networks. Wireless consumers may not realize it, but they are sharing bandwidth with their neighbors. The sharing of wireless bandwidth creates a host of technical and operational challenges associated with the availability of capacity, the lack of predictability about consumer demand and the scarcity of spectrum. As such, the intricate art of network management of wireless networks is far different from that of fiber or coaxial-based networks.[13] Applying one-size-fits-all regulations to mobile broadband would tie the hands of engineers trying to maximize network efficiency for consumers as they are forced to live under new "Mother-may-I" government supervision. Innovation, investment and consumer well-being would be at risk as new rules would create uncertainty and spark a counterproductive regulation/litigation cycle.[14] Thankfully, in Title III, Congress wisely prohibited the FCC from regulating wireless services as a common carrier utility under Title II.[15]

The American wireless industry has been a crown jewel of the American economy for over 30 years. In fact, since its inception, the domestic wireless industry has invested nearly $400 billion in infrastructure.[16] The White House Office of Science and Technology has noted

---

[12] *Preserving the Open Internet*, GN Docket No. 09-191, WC Docket No. 07-52, Report and Order, 25 FCC Rcd 17905 at ¶¶ 80-92 (2010).

[13] For instance, according to CTIA, the Wireless Association, "a single fiber strand can carry 1,000 times more bits per second than a 10 GHz radio channel." Reply Comments of CTIA—The Wireless Association, GN Docket Nos. 14-28, 10-127, at 3 (filed Sept. 15, 2014). Wireless technologies are, indeed, different and highly complex, and should not be burdened by new "one-size-fits-all" regulation.

[14] *See* Robert Litan and Hal Singer, *The Best Path Forward on Net Neutrality*, Progressive Policy Institute, at 8 (Sept. 4, 2014) (noting that "a heavy-handed Title II approach could risk substantial core investment without generating any offsetting incremental investment at the edge").

[15] 47 U.S.C. § 332.

[16] CTIA—The Wireless Association, *CTIA's Wireless Industry Summary Report: Year-End 2013 Results* (2014), available at http://www.ctia.org/docs/default-source/Facts-Stats/ctia_survey_ye_2013_graphics-final.pdf?sfvrsn=2.

that "[a]nnual investment in U.S. wireless networks grew more than 40% between 2009 and 2012, from $21 billion to $30 billion, and exceeds investment by the major oil and gas or auto companies."[17] Additionally, mobile broadband is the fastest growing segment of the broadband market.[18]

Analysts' projections estimate that between 2013 and 2017 wireless infrastructure investment will generate as much as $1.2 trillion in economic growth and create (directly and indirectly) up to 1.2 million new jobs.[19] This will result in an estimated $85 to $87 billion of economic growth *each year* from 2013 through 2017, giving a 2.2% boost in GDP by 2017.[20] Furthermore, unlicensed spectrum, like Wi-Fi, generates an estimated $62 billion a year for the U.S. economy.[21]

Wireless carriers are investing in the world's best infrastructure because competition is fierce. According to the FCC, as of late 2012, 92 percent of the U.S. population had access to at least three mobile broadband providers, while "82 percent…lived in areas with coverage by at least four mobile broadband providers"[22] Robust competition is providing a check against anti-competitive behavior. Accordingly, the long-standing and bipartisan consensus regarding public policy in the wireless space has been to allow competition to obviate the need for command-and-

---

[17] Federal Communications Commission, *Fact Sheet: Internet Growth and Development* (2014), available at https://apps.fcc.gov/edocs_public/attachmatch/DOC-325653A1.pdf.

[18] International Telecommunication Union, *Measuring the Information Society* (2013), available at http://www.itu.int/en/ITU-D/Statistics/Documents/publications/mis2013/MIS2013_without_Annex_4.pdf.

[19] Alan Pearce, J. Richard Carlson & Michael Pagano, *Wireless Broadband Infrastructure: A Catalyst for GDP and Job Growth 2013-2017 (2013)*, available at http://www.pcia.com/images/IAE_Infrastructure_and_Economy_Fall_2013.PDF.

[20] *Id.*

[21] See Consumer Electronics Association, *Unlicensed Spectrum and the American Economy: Quantifying the Market Size and Diversity of Unlicensed Devices* (2014), available at http://www.ce.org/CorporateSite/media/gla/CEA UnlicensedSpectrumWhitePaper-FINAL-052814.pdf (estimating the "unlicensed spectrum generates $62 billion per year in incremental retail sales value").

[22] *Implementation of Section 6002(b) of the Omnibus Budget Reconciliation Act of 1993; Annual Report and Analysis of Competitive Mobile Conditions with Respect to Commercial Mobile Services,* Sixteenth Report, WT Docket No. 11-186, ¶ 48 (rel. Mar. 21, 2013).

control regulation and industrial policy. As the statistics reveal, this hands-off approach has produced a brilliant explosion of entrepreneurial brilliance which is benefiting consumers. Now is not the time to put our gains at risk by injecting unnecessary regulations into a thriving competitive market.

Furthermore, America is *leading the world* in 4G, or LTE. U.S. consumers account for nearly 50 percent of the world's LTE subscribers even though America is home to less than five percent of the world's population.[23] In addition, while only two percent of connections in the European Union (EU) were on LTE networks at the end of 2013, almost 30 percent of all U.S. connections were on LTE networks.[24]

Dominance in 4G penetration and adoption is giving America a decisive advantage in the highly competitive global marketplace. We didn't get here through government mandates, however. Investment in new wireless technologies, unfettered by unnecessary government regulation, is producing faster mobile data connection speeds with the U.S. being 75 percent faster than the EU average.[25] Best of all, that gap is expected to grow. As the "Internet of Everything" explodes to connect billions more devices to the Net through mobile technologies— from cars to health monitoring equipment to inventory control technologies—it will transform the global economy and America will have an advantage over our economic rivals.

But new government policies could inhibit investment and innovation and America could lose her competitive advantage in the mobile space if we extend new rules to the wireless industry. As I illustrate in the attachments to this testimony, consumers are more than

---

[23] CTIA—The Wireless Association, *U.S. Investment in Wireless Leads the World* (2014), available at http://www.ctia.org/docs/default-source/default-document-library/031014-wireless-value-and-contributions.pdf.

[24] *Id.*

[25] Erik Bohlin, Kevin W. Caves & Jeffrey A. Eisenach, *Mobile Wireless Performance in the EU & the US (2013)*, available at http://www.gsmamobilewirelessperformance.com/GSMA_Mobile_Wireless_Performance_May2013.pdf.

adequately protected under existing laws. The Internet ecosphere is blossoming beautifully, resulting in the most positive and constructive transformation of the human condition in history. Let's learn from what has worked and not jeopardize the future with the uncertainty of a new regulatory regime.

Thank you for the opportunity to testify and I look forward to your questions.

##

APPENDIX A

STATEMENT OF THE HON. ROBERT M. MCDOWELL BEFORE THE U.S. HOUSE COMMITTEE ON THE JUDICIARY SUBCOMMITTEE ON REGULATORY REFORM, COMMERCIAL AND ANTITRUST LAW, JUNE 20, 2014

AVAILABLE AT:

http://judiciary.house.gov/_cache/files/cc1ccc99-2711-459f-9e70-67cb8dff7536/mcdowell-testimony.pdf

61

APPENDIX **B**

S**ELECTED** P**UBLICATIONS**

OPINION

Net Neutrality Vs. Free Speech

Cable interests are trying to drag Internet 'edge' providers down with them into the regulatory abyss.

By ROBERT M. MCDOWELL

Aug. 28, 2014 7:43 p.m. ET

As the Federal Communications Commission's Sept. 15 deadline for public comment on its new net-neutrality rules approaches, the "open Internet" movement has taken an unexpected turn toward undermining free speech. Net-neutrality activists have long tried to sell the public on the need to protect people from Internet service providers blocking or degrading consumer access to websites and online applications. Now the cable industry has jumped on the net-neutrality bandwagon.

Historically, cable companies vehemently opposed new rules governing Internet network management. Why? Because nothing is broken in the Internet-access market that needs fixing, and existing laws could prevent or fix any future problems. Also, new net-neutrality rules would politicize business and engineering decisions and slow down lightning fast developments in the Internet space to the sclerotic crawl of Washington bureaucrats.

Federal Communications Commission (FCC) Chairman Tom Wheeler *European Pressphoto Agency*

Now, however, as a third misguided FCC attempt to implement net neutrality gains momentum, Time Warner Cable and the National Cable and Telecommunications Association are trying to drag Internet "edge" providers—including the websites of local broadcasters airing ABC, CBS, NBC and Fox—down with them into the regulatory abyss.

The "edge" of the Internet is where consumers go to get content such as movies from Amazon, streaming online TV shows from broadcasters and apps from companies like Uber. Thousands of start-ups sprout each year while billions in private risk capital is being plowed into a new economy that is providing unprecedented consumer freedom and benefits. Today's Internet blossomed precisely because the government kept its hands off of it.

Until now.

The FCC's attempt to turn the Internet into what amounts to a federally regulated public utility—all in the name of protecting consumers—has produced tortured logic among cable interests: If Internet service providers are going to be regulated, then websites that their subscribers watch—especially broadcasters' sites—should be regulated too.

According to comments filed with the FCC by Time Warner Cable and the National Cable and Telecommunications Association, broadcasters should not be allowed to take down or withhold the content they produce and own from online distribution even if subscribers have not paid for it—as a matter of federal law. In other words, edge providers should be forced to stream their online content no matter what. Such an overreach, of course, would lay waste to the economics of the Internet. It would also violate the First Amendment's prohibition against state-mandated, or forced, speech—the flip side of censorship.

It is possible that the cable companies figure that subjecting powerful broadcasters to anti-free speech rules will shift the political momentum in the FCC and among the public away from net neutrality. But cable's anti-free speech arguments play right into the hands of the net-neutrality crowd. They want to place the entire Internet ecosystem, physical networks, content and apps, in the hands of federal bureaucrats.

For instance, Columbia law professor Tim Wu, the architect of the movement who coined the term "net neutrality," testified before Congress in June that new rules should "capture" "media policy, social policy" and even FCC "oversight of the political process." His goal, and that of his myriad followers, is to have "FCC oversight of the Internet." Period.

Mr. Wu has outsize influence over regulators. He penned the first-ever net-neutrality conditions that were part of the FCC's approval of the AT&T -BellSouth merger in 2006. And he now appears to have a powerful industry ally, albeit perhaps unwittingly, in cable.

But America's cable companies should be careful what they wish for. History teaches us that once you invite regulators into your neighborhood to regulate your rival, it won't stop at the house across the street. Having cable argue for dragging edge-based content providers, like broadcasters or anyone else, into the morass only adds momentum to the net-neutrality effort.

Instead of sympathizing with its captors and helping to expand the dragnet of unnecessary regulations to every corner of the Internet, cable should flatly oppose new rules. The FCC has an unsuccessful track record in court after two similar power grabs in 2010 and this past January, so there's good reason to believe a hat trick of losses is in the making. Now is not the time to panic; it is the hour to persist in favor of a free Internet, and to begin preparing court appeals.

Mr. McDowell, a former commissioner of the Federal Communications Commission, is a visiting fellow at the Hudson Institute.

This is why the government should never control the internet

Tomorrow is the deadline for the public to comment on the Federal Communications Commission's (FCC) attempt to regulate the Internet under the seemingly innocuous moniker of "net neutrality." The architect of this movement, and the man who coined the term "net neutrality," is Columbia law professor Tim Wu. Unfortunately, he has proved to be immensely influential among regulators.

Net neutrality rules have been sold for a decade as a way to keep the Internet "open and free" by keeping Internet service providers (ISPs), such as phone and cable companies, from blocking or degrading Web sites. Its advocates have argued that ISPs have an economic incentive to act anti-competitively toward consumers and competitors. In a common hypothetical they cite, ISPs would slow — or buffer — traffic for Netflix unless it unfairly pays for more access points, or "off ramps," and better quality of service.

In truth, however, market failures like these have never happened, and nothing is broken that needs fixing. If consumers were being harmed by ISPs, ample antitrust, competition and consumer protection laws already exist to fix the problem. And major broadband providers have pledged, in their terms of service, to keep the Net open and freedom-enhancing. Why? Because it is good business to do so.

Additionally, Netflix produces upwards of 34 percent of the Net's traffic at peak times. It can clog any pipe it touches. That torrent of traffic imposes delivery costs that Netflix would prefer to pass on to others. But the market is sorting out these growing pains as the open Net grows, just as it has successfully from the beginning. (My views on this subject long predate my affiliation with the Hudson Institute, but in the interests of full disclosure: Hudson receives financial support from media, technology and telecom companies, as well as foundations, including those on both sides of the net neutrality debate.)

The Net *has been* open since it was privatized by the Clinton administration. It proliferated globally as it migrated farther away from government control — bringing freedom and prosperity to billions. It grew from a mere 88,000 users in the late 1980s, to more than 3 billion today. Cisco estimates that the exploding "Internet of Everything" (that is, machines talking to one another online, such as your car and your tablet) will generate more than $14 trillion in global economic growth by 2022. In short, the Internet is the greatest deregulatory success story of all time — a simple fact that vexes those seeking new and unnecessary rules.

In refreshingly honest congressional testimony, Wu has crystalized the net neutrality movement's goal: "FCC oversight of the Internet." His simple statement acts as a dog whistle to regulators, telling them to sweep everything about the Internet under the government-controlled net neutrality umbrella— technical operations, business decisions, content and *speech.* State manipulation of the Net would shape "not merely economic policy, not merely competition policy, but also media policy, social policy" and "oversight of the political process," according to Wu's testimony. Current regulations simply do not "capture" the Net the way more government powers would through powerful new rules, he argued.

Without contesting the adequacy of existing laws to protect consumers and preserve the free flow of information over the Net, Wu asserted that only "the FCC is equipped to deal with issues like regionalism, like localism, like diversity, which ... aren't captured" by other agencies. These words were likely not selected randomly: They have legal significance at the FCC in regulating speech and go far beyond net neutrality's original sales pitch.

Wu's vision of more government "capture" strongly resembles old broadcast regulations spurred by a "scarcity" of outlets in the mid-20th century — the legal rationale for government regulation of speech over the airwaves, which would never be tolerated by, say, newspapers. Even in today's competitive and digitized media markets, broadcasters must adhere to strict rules dictating speech, or risk losing their licenses. This Supreme Court-blessed government speech control operates under aliases such as "regionalism" and "localism" as invoked by Wu. These rules compel broadcasters to tailor their content to serve properly (in the eyes of regulators) their "communities of license." That could include mandates ranging from sufficient local news, sports and weather, to a minimum amount of programming for children.

Broadcast regulations have also controlled political speech. The most infamous FCC effort to exert "oversight over the political process," in Wu's words, was known as the "Fairness Doctrine." For decades, it allowed the government to censor political speech by justifying its purpose as "balancing" competing points of view in the name of "diversity," serving the "public interest" and, most cynically, *protecting freedom of expression*. That meant the state muted some political voices while amplifying others. Although the Reagan-era FCC correctly scrapped the Fairness Doctrine, vestiges of it remain, such as the confusingly similar "equal time rule," which, for example, curtailed the airing of old Reagan movies when he ran for office. FCC "oversight of the political process" through more Internet regulations sounds eerily like political speech controls. Will new FCC rules lay down a slippery slope toward those kinds of controls?

While some tech companies have been inspired by Wu as they try to "regulate their rivals," phone and cable companies, they may be forging their own regulatory chains, link by link. During my seven years as a FCC commissioner, I lived through several iterations of the net neutrality debate. Its proponents have broadened the term's definition each time to serve their own growing purposes, both here and abroad. Wu's vision, which goes far beyond the Netflix scenario, shows how their ostensible goal could continue to morph into a regulatory regime for the entire Internet ecosystem, affecting far more than ISPs. Inviting regulators into your neighborhood is likely to embolden them to control not only your neighbor but you, too. Wu's supporters should be careful what they wish for.

OPINION

A Victory for an Unfettered Internet

After another court loss, the FCC should abandon its 'net neutrality' regulation goal.

By ROBERT MCDOWELL

Jan. 14, 2014 7:09 p.m. ET

A federal appeals court in Washington slapped the Federal Communications Commission on Tuesday for overstepping its legal authority by trying to regulate Internet access. The FCC is now a two-time loser in court in its net-neutrality efforts. Has the government learned its lesson, or will the agency take a third stab at regulating the Internet? The answer to that question will affect the Internet's growth in the 21st century.

The FCC's quest to regulate the Internet began in 2010, when the commission first promulgated rules for net neutrality. The rules, proponents argue, are needed to police Internet "on-ramps" (Internet service providers) ostensibly to ensure that they stay "open." To accomplish this, some want the FCC to subject the Internet to ancient communications laws designed for extinct phone and railroad monopolies.

Related Video

Former FCC Commissioner Robert McDowell on why a federal appeals court decision against net-neutrality rules is a win for free access to the Internet. Photos: Getty Images

But the trouble is, nothing needs fixing. The Internet has remained open and accessible without FCC micromanagement since it entered public life in the 1990s. And more regulation could produce harmful results, such as reduced infrastructure investment, stunted innovation, slower speeds and higher prices for consumers. The FCC never bothered to study the impact that such intervention might have on the broadband market before leaping to regulate. Nor did it consider the ample consumer-protection laws that already exist. The government's meddling has been driven more by ideology and a 2008 campaign promise by then-Sen. Barack Obama than by reality.

Further FCC attempts to regulate the Internet could trigger global regulation of the Internet by the International Telecommunication Union, a treaty-based organization under the U.N.'s control. Russian President Vladimir Putin and his allies have been working for a decade to upend a 1988 agreement—forged by delegates from 114 countries—to leave the Internet unfettered. The U.S. has so far been opposed to applying new international rules for the Internet. In October, 193 countries will gather again for talks to conclude a new treaty that will decide the Internet's fate. Proponents hope to build off

67

victories won last year at International Telecommunication Union talks in Dubai that gave the agency narrow authority to regulate. The goal is to achieve what Mr. Putin summarized in 2011 as "international control of the Internet."

The prospect of multilateral regulation makes the FCC's next move all the more important, as it will set the standard for what happens in the next round of negotiations in South Korea. The U.S. argument that regulation of the Internet at home is a good idea but a bad one internationally is eroding American credibility. The U.S. attempt to have it both ways has inspired scorn from other countries, as I personally experienced during official meetings in Dubai in 2012.

Which is why the FCC should drop its pursuit of net-neutrality rules altogether. The regulations are a bad idea for many reasons, but especially because they radically depart from—and endanger—the highly successful, nongovernmental, private-sector-led, "multi-stakeholder" process for resolving the Internet's technical challenges. Under this loose structure, engineers, academics and users from all over the world work individually to keep a borderless "network of networks" open and thriving. The flat and dispersed architecture of the Internet defies centralized and top-down control: No government is capable of keeping up with the Web's warp-speed evolution. The nimble multi-stakeholder structure of Internet governance, which enjoyed broad bipartisan and international support during the Clinton and Bush administrations, has made the Internet the greatest deregulatory success story of all time.

As a result of this framework for innovation, Internet usage has penetrated faster than any technology in history. Rapid adoption of Internet-enabled mobile devices is profoundly improving the lives of billions of people, especially in the developing world. It is also helping to change their political expectations as it strengthens the sovereignty of the individual by providing fast and inexpensive access to the world's information. Authoritarian regimes feel threatened by unfettered Internet access. That's why they've embarked on a patient diplomatic strategy to accrue power over its on-ramps.

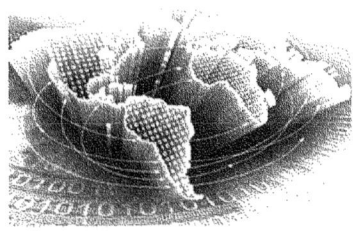

Getty Images

Pursuing an expanded U.S. government role into the Internet's affairs foolishly plays into the hands of these pro-regulation regimes. At a minimum, new American rules provide them with political cover and the veneer of a rational argument to use for their own nefarious ends. Especially in light of current concerns about National Security Agency surveillance, it should be obvious that the problem of too much state interference with the Internet will not be cured by even more government meddling, either domestically or internationally. Now is a chance to turn back the tide of state encroachment.

The U.S. government must reverse course immediately. First, the FCC should abandon any further legal appeals of its case. Next, the FCC should unequivocally restate its commitment to the multi-stakeholder model of resolving network-management challenges and Internet governance. Then, the commission should work with antitrust and consumer-protection agencies to take an inventory of all existing laws that could either prevent or cure anticompetitive conduct in the Internet sphere, instead of making new rules. This will be essential to the International Telecommunication Union negotiations in the fall, as proponents of global rules just need a simple majority of the 193 to impose their agenda.

In short, governments could have a seat at the multi-stakeholder Internet-governance table, they just shouldn't own the table. The existing paradigm has produced positive and constructive results and will continue to do so if governments stay out of the way.

Otherwise, the consequences of multilateral control of the Internet could cause a radical disruption of the digital economy that would harm tomorrow's Internet users in the developing world the most. It is not too late to turn back these assaults on Internet freedom, but we are running out of time.

Mr. McDowell is a former commissioner of the Federal Communications Commission and a visiting fellow at the Hudson Institute.

 **American Enterprise Institute**
for Public Policy Research

Statement before the Senate Committee on the Judiciary
On "Why Net Neutrality Matters: Protecting Consumers and Competition Through
Meaningful Open Internet Rules"

Testimony of Jeffrey A. Eisenach, Ph.D.

Visiting Scholar
American Enterprise Institute

September 17, 2014

TESTIMONY

OF

JEFFREY A. EISENACH, PH.D.

BEFORE THE

COMMITTEE ON THE JUDICIARY

UNITED STATES SENATE

September 17, 2014

Mr. Chairman and Members of the Committee, thank you for the opportunity to appear before you at today's hearing on "Why Net Neutrality Matters: Protecting Consumers and Competition through Meaningful Open Internet Rules."

I have had the opportunity to study communications, media and Internet policy issues over the course of many years and in several capacities, including in my current positions as Director of the American Enterprise Institute's Center for Internet, Communications and Technology Policy, Executive Editor of TechPolicyDaily.com, Co-Chair of NERA Economic Consulting's Communications, Media and Internet Practice, and adjunct professor at George Mason University Law School, where I teach the course on regulated industries. I should note that while my academic studies and my consulting practice often involve issues relating to Internet and communications policies, I am appearing today solely on my own behalf, and the views and opinions I express should not be attributed to any of the organizations with which I am affiliated.

My testimony today advances three main points. First, net neutrality regulation cannot be justified on grounds of enhancing consumer welfare or protecting the public interest. Rather, it is best understood as an effort by one set of private interests to enrich itself by using the power of the state to obtain free services from another – a classic example of what economists term "rent seeking." Second, the potential costs of net neutrality regulation are both sweeping and severe, and extend far beyond a simple transfer of wealth from one group to another. Third, legitimate policy concerns about the potential use of market power to disadvantage rivals or harm consumers can best be addressed through existing antitrust and consumer protection laws and regulations.

To begin, net neutrality regulation cannot be justified as a means of enhancing consumer welfare or advancing or protecting the public interest, and instead is best understood as a classic example of rent seeking.[1] This is particularly true of the more extreme flavors of net neutrality regulation advanced by companies like Netflix, which would ban payments from companies like Netflix to Internet Service Providers (ISPs) like AT&T.[2]

---

[1] For a general discussion of the economic theory of rent seeking, see George J. Stigler, "The Theory of Economic Regulation," *The Bell Journal of Economics and Management Science* 2;1 (Spring 1971) 3-21.

[2] For clarity, I will refer to this type of regulation as a "zero price rule," as distinct from the less extreme versions put forward in the FCC's Open Internet Notice of Proposed Rulemaking, which would allow such payments so long

As a general matter, government intervention in the marketplace can enhance economic welfare only in cases of market failure, which may occur under two primary sets of circumstances: (a) when a firm or group of firms can exercise monopoly power to raise prices, reduce quality or prevent entry by rivals; or (b) when markets are characterized by externalities (such as pollution) or public goods (such as national defense).[3]

Looking first at the monopoly power rationale for intervention, there is no basis for believing – nor does the FCC assert – that net neutrality regulation can be justified by concerns about traditional monopoly power.[4] Indeed, the Commission's Notice of Proposed Rulemaking waxes eloquent about the strong performance of the broadband marketplace, citing the billions of dollars invested each year and the rapid increases in performance that have come about as a result.[5] Such performance is not consistent with the "cozy duopoly" characterizations sometimes advanced by net neutrality advocates. Nor is the structure of the broadband market a cause for concern. Indeed, the broadband market is, if anything, less concentrated than many markets that make up the Internet ecosystem: one need only think of the markets for search engines, social networks and personal computer operating systems to realize that such markets are typically served – at any given time – by a few firms rather than by the atomistic structures imagined in introductory economics texts.

To be sure, broadband ISPs, like virtually all other firms in the Internet ecosystem, do possess a certain type of market power, which is the power, derived from successful product differentiation, to charge prices above marginal costs.[6] But the existence of such market power is hardly cause for pervasive regulation – rather, as the courts have recognized, it is both the incentive to innovate and the reward for doing so, and hence the motive force behind growth and prosperity in a modern economy.[7] And while this sort of market power – combined with the

---

as they are "non-discriminatory" or "commercially reasonable." I refer to this milder form of proposal as a "non-discrimination rule."

[3] These are necessary conditions for government intervention to improve welfare, not sufficient ones. In addition, it must be the case that it is possible to design and implement policies that, on net, create greater benefits than costs.

[4] See Jerry Brito, et al, "Net Neutrality: The Economic Evidence" (April 12, 2010) (available at http://papers.ssrn.com/sol3/papers.cfm?abstract_id=1587058) (expert declaration before the FCC of 21 economists and communications policy experts).

[5] See Federal Communications Commission, *In the Matter of Protecting and Promoting the Open Internet, Notice of Proposed Rulemaking*, GN Docket 14-28 (May 15, 2014) at ¶30.

[6] Given the fundamental economic characteristics of high-tech markets in general and the markets that comprise the Internet ecosystem in particular, the only firms we observe in the marketplace are those that have successfully differentiated their products and thus have the capacity to charge prices above marginal costs; without such power, they would be unable to earn a return on the large and risky typically needed to participate. Such investments may take the form of R&D (e.g., developing software for a new application), producing content (e.g., making a movie or creating a content aggregation service), or investing in infrastructure (e.g., building a broadband distribution system). In each case, companies incur high fixed costs but, having done so, are able to produce additional units of outcome at low marginal cost. See generally Jeffrey A. Eisenach, *Broadband Competition in the Internet Ecosystem*, American Enterprise Institute (October 2012). For a layman's explanation of the same phenomenon, see Peter Theil, "Competition is for Losers," *Wall Street Journal* (September 13-14, 2014) at C1.

[7] See e.g., *Novell, Inc. v. Microsoft Corp.*, 731 F.3d 1064, 1073 (10th Cir.2013) ("If the law were to make a habit of forcing monopolists to help competitors by keeping prices high, sharing their property, or declining to expand their own operations, courts would paradoxically risk encouraging collusion between rivals and dampened price competition—themselves paradigmatic antitrust wrongs, injuries to consumers and the competitive process alike. Forcing firms to help one another would also risk reducing the incentive both sides have to innovate, invest, and

need for firms to collaborate with one another to create value – can create the incentive for firms to deny access to their platforms as a means of obtaining or maintaining market power (as the courts found Microsoft did in the case of Netscape and Java), such incentives are not unique to broadband markets, and thus cannot justify discriminatory regulation of ISPs.

Another variant of the market power argument suggests that while big, established edge providers might be able to fend for themselves against the ISPs, we need to look out for the little guys, the new entrants who may be strangled in the crib as a result of discriminatory access fees. What no one can explain, however, is why ISPs would want to discriminate against start-up edge providers – the very firms that create the applications and content that draw consumers to subscribe to broadband service in the first place. The reality is that to the extent ISPs engage in efficient price discrimination, basic economic theory predicts they will offer startups – those most sensitive to price – the lowest prices rather than the highest ones.[8]

Rather than being motivated by worries about market power, the FCC (like some other net neutrality advocates) justifies its proposed regulations on the existence of externalities in the Internet ecosystem.[9] Specifically, the theory goes, innovation "at the edge" generates benefits that are not reflected in the price system, and therefore deserving of subsidization – either in the form of a zero price rule granting them free access to ISP's services, or through a non-discrimination rule designed to shift value away from ISPs and in favor of edge providers by preventing broadband ISPs from engaging in efficient price discrimination.

Like other firms in the Internet ecosystem, broadband ISPs operate in what economists call a "two-sided market." On one side are consumers, who value Internet access; on the other are providers of complementary products, like content, devices and applications, who value the ability to use the network to reach their ultimate customers. Such markets are not unusual: newspapers, for example, serve both advertisers and subscribers. The challenge for such firms is to set prices for each customer group in such a way as to attract the optimal mix: Newspapers need just enough advertisers to allow them to keep subscription prices low, but not so many as to annoy readers and drive down subscribership.

The FCC's primary theory of net neutrality regulation (embraced by the DC Circuit in *Verizon v. FCC*) is that one side of the two-sided market served by ISPs (the "edge providers") generates so

---

expand—again results inconsistent with the goals of antitrust. The monopolist might be deterred from investing, innovating, or expanding (or even entering a market in the first place) with the knowledge anything it creates it could be forced to share; the smaller company might be deterred, too, knowing it could just demand the right to piggyback on its larger rival.") For a discussion, see Jeffrey A. Eisenach and Ilene Knable Gotts, "In Search of a Coetition Doctrine for Information Technology Markets: Recent Antitrust Developments in the Online Sector," in *Communications and Competition Law: Key Issues in the Telecoms, Media and Technology Sectors* (Alphen aan den Rijn, The Netherlands: Kluwer Law International/International Bar Association series, forthcoming 2014).

[8] Indeed, small/start-up edge providers – who have not yet achieved the scale necessary to justify building their own content delivery systems – are most likely to benefit from the ability to purchase high quality delivery services from ISPs. On the economic basis for – and beneficial effects of – competitive price discrimination, see e.g., David B. Audretsch, William J. Baumol and Andrew E. Burke, "Competition Policy in Dynamic Markets," *International Journal of Industrial Organization* 19 (2001) 613-634 and Jonathan B. Baker, "Competitive Price Discrimination: The Exercise of Market Power without Anticompetitive Effects (Comment on Klein and Wiley)," *Antitrust Law Journal* 70 (2003), 643-654.

[9] See NRPM at ¶43.

much innovation and other "external" benefits that it should be subsidized by the other side (that is, by consumers) through a rule that forces consumers to pay 100 percent of the costs of the network while edge providers pay zero. This is a fine theory – but there is not a scintilla of empirical evidence to support it. Indeed, a strong argument can be – and often is – made that the external benefits generated by investment in broadband infrastructures are at least as great as if not greater than the benefits associated with innovation at the edge.[10] In short, the edge-provider-innovation-externality rationale for net neutrality regulation is a naked emperor of an argument if ever there was one.

Finally, some argue net neutrality regulation is needed to protect freedom of speech – that without it, "alternative, non-profit and dissenting voices" will be consigned to "Internet slow lanes."[11] There are at least three problems with this theory. First, there is virtually no evidence that ISPs have (or have incentives) to stifle dissenting or alternative views; indeed, as explained above, the availability of diverse content on the Internet is what makes it valuable and causes people to want to pay ISPs for broadband access in the first place. Second, to the extent "censorship" is an issue, it implicates other types of Internet firms at least as much as (and likely more than) ISPs. Third, and finally, it is simply not apparent that giving Netflix free use of Comcast's network has anything to do with protecting political speech.

When these rationales are stripped away, what is left is the obvious: Edge providers, big and small, and those who fund them and profit from their success, have a powerful economic interest in getting the government to guarantee them free access to the ISPs' networks. Occam's Razor applies: when it doubt, the simplest explanation tends to be the correct one, and net neutrality is no exception.

At this point in my testimony, I want to be emphatically clear that, in suggesting that net neutrality is a battle over the allocation of economic rents, I am not impugning the integrity of anyone involved in the process. Government intervention in markets – whether justified or otherwise – invariably results in the redistribution of wealth, and the affected parties have every right – even, arguably, an obligation – to look out for their own interests.[12] That is the way our democracy works and, to paraphrase Churchill, it is a terrible system...except when compared to

---

[10] This point is acknowledged even by the strongest supporters of net neutrality regulation. See e.g., Robin S. Lee and Tim Wu, "Subsidizing Creativity through Network Design: Zero-Pricing and Net Neutrality," *Journal of Economic Perspectives* 23;3 (Summer 2009) 61–76 at 67 ("Of course, for a given price level, subsidizing content comes at the expense of not subsidizing users, and subsidizing users could also lead to greater consumer adoption of broadband. *It is an open question whether, in subsidizing content, the welfare gains from the invention of the next killer app or the addition of new content offset the price reductions consumers might otherwise enjoy or the benefit of expanding service to new users*.")(emphasis added). For a summary of more recent research indicating that net neutrality regulation is likely to harm consumer welfare, see Comments of Justin (Gus) Hurwitz, Assistant Professor of Law,University of Nebraska College of Law, GN Docket 14-28 (

[11] See e.g., Testimony of Michael Copps Before the Committee on the Judiciary, July 1, 2014 at 12.

[12] Nobel Prize winner Ronald Coase described the political dynamics of regulatory intervention in the market in his famous 1959 article on the FCC's approach to the allocation of broadcast licenses. See R.H. Coase, "The Federal Communications Commission," *Journal of Law and Economics* 2 (October 1959) 1-40 at 35-36 ("That [efforts to exercise political influence over licensing decisions] should be happening is hardly surprising. When rights, worth millions of dollars, are awarded to one businessman and denied to others, it is no wonder if some applicants become overanxious and attempt to use whatever influence they have (political and otherwise), particularly as they can never be sure what pressure the other applicants may be exerting.").

the alternatives. Nor do I mean any disrespect to the heartfelt views of those across the political spectrum who worry about the need to protect free speech on the Internet and elsewhere. I share their ultimate goals and objectives, even though I may not fully share their assessment of the nature of the challenge, or the appropriate response.

But while there is nothing illegal or even immoral about private entities seeking to advance their interests through the use of state power, the results can prove highly damaging, and ultimately can be far more harmful than a simple transfer of wealth from one group to another. In the case of net neutrality, the risk is that the intensely dynamic, pragmatic, business-and-engineering-driven approach to building and running the most important "general purpose" technology in history – the approach that has facilitated the remarkable growth of the Internet over the past two decades – could be replaced by a static, bureaucratic, politicized regulatory regime, not only in the U.S. but around the world.

There is no economic basis for a general rule forcing one side of the market, consumers, to bear 100 percent of network costs while the other side, the firms that benefit from the ability to deliver content over the network, pay zero. Indeed, as the types and volumes of traffic carried over the web change, one would expect pricing structures and other contractual terms to adjust accordingly – as has been the case with peering and transit arrangements, which have adjusted dynamically to the explosive growth of the Internet without regulatory intervention for nearly two decades. Net neutrality regulation would at best inhibit, or at worst prohibit altogether, the market's ability to achieve such adjustments.

The costs of net neutrality regulation are directly related to the substantive standards imposed, the extent of their application, and the means by which they are enacted and enforced. For example, a rule that presumptively bans all forms of differentiated service offers could literally cripple the ability of the Internet to adjust to the continued growth in the amount and types of traffic, especially if it were extended to wireless ISP services, where differentiation is especially important due to inherent limitations on bandwidth and other engineering concerns.

The specter of common carriage regulation is of particular concern. As others have noted, Title II regulation would not ban price discrimination by ISPs. To the contrary, Title II specifically envisions that prices should vary across different types of services and different types of customers, just as – for example – postal rates do today. It may seem difficult to imagine imposing on the Internet a public-utility-style rate setting process akin the Postal Regulatory Commission; but can anyone doubt that if broadband were declared a Title II service, it would not be long before the Commission would take comments on whether some types of services should bear more of the costs of the network than others, leading inevitably to something closely resembling the perennial scrum between first, second and third class mailers over who will pay how much for junk mail, magazines, and so forth?

Even less intrusive approaches could have serious costs. Consider, for example, the comments filed with the FCC by startup firm Syntonic, which develops innovative technologies that allow content providers to make their content available to consumers over mobile networks without charge. Such "sponsored data" plans shift the cost of bandwidth from consumers – especially those less able to afford high-end data plans – to mobile wireless carriers and content providers, and are increasingly popular in both the U.S. and, to an even greater extent, in developing countries.[13]   As Syntonic explains in its comments, "despite the fact that these alternative business models increase consumer choice and help bring consumers the content they desire more efficiently ... opponents can use stringent net neutrality rules to impose homogeneity on broadband markets and destroy even the most consumer-friendly alternatives to the status quo ... [showing] the danger of structural rules designed to protect edge providers rather than consumers."[14]

Adopting net neutrality regulation would also harm the cause of Internet freedom worldwide. The Internet the most powerful and disruptive force for freedom in the world, threatening the power of the state and setting literally billions of people free to learn, think, and decide for themselves. It represents a fundamental threat to repressive, authoritarian regimes from Moscow to Tehran, from Beijing to Caracas. By embracing the idea of state control of the Internet – both economic and political – the adoption of net neutrality regulation by the U.S. would legitimize the efforts of tyrants everywhere to impose far more repressive forms of statist intervention.

My last point, which I will make briefly because it has been so thoroughly addressed elsewhere, is that legitimate concerns about the exercise of market power by ISPs (and other firms in the Internet ecosystem) can readily be addressed through existing laws, including specifically the Sherman Act, the Clayton Act and the Federal Trade Commission Act.[15]   These laws have protected competition and consumers for well over a century, and have developed into a dynamic and sophisticated body of economic doctrine and legal jurisprudence that is fully capable of addressing the threat that Internet firms, whether ISPs or others, will use the market power signified by their persistence in the marketplace for harmful purposes. Antitrust is not perfect, but it is by far the best approach to addressing concerns about the business practices of broadband ISPs.

* * *

Mr. Chairman and Members of the Committee, this completes my testimony. I look forward to answering any questions you may have.

---

[13] See Roslyn Layton, "IGF Highlights How Developing Countries Use Zero Rating Programs to Drive Internet Adoption," *TechPolicyDaily.com* (September 4, 2014) (available at
http://www.techpolicydaily.com/communications/igf-zero-rating-programs/)
[14] See Reply Comments of Syntonic, Inc., GN Docket No. 14-28 (September 3, 2014) at 12-13.
[15] See for a discussion see e.g., Brito *et al* and Eisenach and Gotts.

ATTACHMENT I TO PREPARED STATEMENT OF JEFFREY A. EISENACH, PH.D.

**Before the
Federal Communications Commission
Washington, D.C. 20554**

In the Matter of	)	
	)	
Preserving the Open Internet	)	GN Docket No. 09-191
	)	
Broadband Industry Practices	)	WC Docket No. 07-52

NET NEUTRALITY REGULATION: THE ECONOMIC EVIDENCE

APRIL 12, 2010

CONTENTS

I. INTRODUCTION

1.   As economic scholars, professors and practitioners who have studied, taught, and written about regulation of telecommunications, the Internet, and broadband networks in general, and about net neutrality regulation in particular, we are submitting this declaration to provide the Commission with our shared assessment of the economic evidence as it relates to the "net neutrality" regulations proposed in Commission's *Notice of Proposed Rulemaking Regarding Preserving the Open Internet and Broadband Industry Practices* (the "NPRM"). [1]

2.   In our shared opinion, the economic evidence does not support the proposed regulations; to the contrary, it strongly suggests that the regulations, if adopted, would reduce consumer welfare in both the short and long run. We base this opinion on three overarching conclusions.

> *First,* as a general matter, regulation can improve economic welfare only in the face of market imperfections, such as market power, externalities, or information asymmetries. While the markets at issue in this proceeding are characterized by product differentiation, high fixed costs and other deviations from the textbook model of "perfect competition," the evidence provides no support for the existence of market failure sufficient to warrant *ex ante* regulation of the type proposed by the Commission.

> *Second,* the practices that would be banned under the NPRM are likely, in most circumstances, to be welfare-enhancing. While it is possible to construct theoretical models in which economic welfare *might* be harmed, there is virtually no empirical evidence that such harm has occurred or is likely to occur in the future. Thus, it is extremely likely that the regulations proposed in the NRPM would harm consumers and competition and reduce economic welfare.

---

[1] Federal Communications Commission, *In the Matter of Preserving the Open Internet and Broadband Industry Practices, Notice of Proposed Rulemaking* (GN Docket No. 09-191; WC Docket No. 07-52, October 2009) (hereafter "*NPRM*"). Each of us shares the overall views and primary conclusions expressed herein even though as individuals we might characterize particular points somewhat differently. Dr. Eisenach, whose effort in coordinating its preparation was supported by Verizon Communications, is the only signatory who was compensated for participating in this declaration.

Third, to the extent potentially welfare-reducing conduct does emerge, such practices are amenable to a variety of case-by-case remedies under existing law and regulation. There is no need, in other words, for the Commission to throw the welfare-enhancing baby out with the anticompetitive bathwater.

3. The remainder of this declaration is organized as follows. In Section II we summarize the economic evidence as it relates to market failure in the markets at issue, and explain why none of the theories advanced in the NPRM (or any other theories of which we are aware) constitute a valid basis for the proposed rules. In Section III, we summarize the primary ways in which the proposed rules would reduce economic welfare by banning beneficial practices. In Section IV, we briefly explain the basis for our opinion that a case-by-case approach, based on empirical economic analysis of the consumer welfare consequences of specific practices in particular circumstances, is superior to the *ex ante* regulation proposed in the NPRM. Section V presents a brief summary of our conclusions.

II. THE ECONOMIC EVIDENCE DOES NOT SUPPORT A FINDING OF SYSTEMATIC MARKET FAILURE

4. The NPRM proposes that broadband Internet access service providers ("broadband ISPs") be prohibited from preventing users from (i) "sending or receiving the lawful content of the user's choice," (ii) "running the lawful applications or using the lawful services of the user's choice," (iii) "connecting to and using on its network the user's choice of lawful devices;" or, (iv) "depriv[ing] any of its users of the user's entitlement to competition among network providers, application providers, service providers, and content providers;"[2] and, further, that they be required to (v) "treat lawful content, applications, and services in a

---

[2] NPRM at ¶92. As we discuss further below, each of these requirements would be is "subject to reasonable network management;" "subject to exceptions for the needs of law enforcement, public safety, national and homeland security authorities;" and, subject to an exemption for "managed services."

nondiscriminatory manner."[3] By "nondiscriminatory," the Commission means "that a broadband Internet access service provider may not charge a content, application, or service provider for enhanced or prioritized access to the subscribers of the broadband Internet access service provider [but] this rule would not prevent a broadband Internet access service provider from charging subscribers different prices for different services."[4]

5.   In support of these restrictions, the NPRM advances two primary theories of market failure. First, it implies (but does not conclude) that broadband ISPs may have market power, which could cause them to discriminate in their pricing among or between providers of content and applications, or simply to restrict output or charge supra-competitive prices. Second, it posits that network externalities or "spillover effects" might distort ISPs' incentives, causing them to charge higher-than-optimal fees to content or applications providers.[5]

6.   The economic evidence demonstrates that the proposed regulations are not justified under either set of theories. With respect to market power, the evidence demonstrates that broadband markets are highly competitive and rivalrous, and hence not generally susceptible to the types of anticompetitive conduct discussed in the NPRM.[6] As for theories associated with network externalities and spillover effects, the underlying literature is, at best, highly stylized, speculative, and heavily dependent on assumptions for which there is no empirical basis.

---

[3] NPRM at ¶105.

[4] NPRM at ¶106. The NPRM also proposes a sixth "transparency" principle (see NPRM at ¶¶118-132). Our comments focus on the first five principles and, in particular, the non-discrimination principle. This should not be taken as an indication, however, that we believe the economic evidence necessarily supports "transparency" regulation.

[5] See generally NPRM at ¶¶7-8.

[6] The relevant geographic market for broadband markets depends on the issue being addressed. For purposes of foreclosure analysis, for example, the appropriate market definition may be either national or international, while in other contexts the relevant geographic market is likely local (see, e.g., Federal Trade Commission, *Broadband Connectivity and Competition Policy, FTC Staff Report* (June 2007) at 156 (hereafter *FTC Report*).

A. Regulation Is Not Justified on the Basis of Market Power

7. The NPRM describes three discrete theories of harm based on market power: (i) broadband ISPs with market power "may have an incentive to <u>raise prices</u> charged to content, application, and service providers and end users;"[7] (ii) broadband ISPs, "particularly [those] with market power, may have the incentive and ability to <u>reduce or fail to increase transmission capacity</u> ... in order to increase the revenues obtained from content application, and service providers or individual users who desire a higher quality of service;"[8] and, (iii) broadband ISPs with market power which are vertically integrated might "<u>make it more difficult or expensive for end users to access services competing with those offered by the network operator or its affiliates</u>."[9]

8. As a preliminary matter, it is noteworthy that the NPRM's first two theories of harm (i.e., that broadband ISPs with market power might harm economic welfare by raising prices and/or restricting output) do not appear to distinguish between upstream and downstream market power – that is, they postulate that broadband ISPs might raise prices or restrict output with respect to either consumers, on the one hand, or content, applications and service providers, on the other. Yet, the proposed regulations would do nothing to restrain downstream pricing since, under the proposed non-discrimination rule, both differential and discriminatory pricing to "subscribers" apparently is permitted.[10]

---

[7] NPRM at ¶70 (emphasis added).

[8] NPRM at ¶71 (emphasis added).

[9] NPRM at ¶63 (emphasis added); see also n. 146.

[10] We define differential pricing as charging different prices for different services, e.g., charging one price for "Internet access service" and a different price for "Premium Internet access service." We define "price discrimination" as charging different prices to different consumers for the same service. See e.g., Dennis Weisman and Robert Kulick, "Price Discrimination, Two-Sided Markets and Net Neutrality Regulation," (March 2010) (available at http://papers.ssrn.com/sol3/papers.cfm?abstract_id=1582972).

9.   It is also striking that the NPRM *never concludes* that broadband ISPs have

market power, and, indeed, only once strongly implies it: At paragraph 7, the Commission

finds that "In many parts of the United States, customers have limited options for high-speed

broadband Internet access service;"[11] and, at paragraph 73, it implies there is a terminating

access monopoly issue, such that "even if there is competition among broadband Internet access

service providers, once an end-user customer has chosen to subscribe to a particular broadband

Internet access service provider, this may give that broadband Internet access service provider

the ability, at least in theory, to favor or disfavor any traffic destined for that subscriber."[12] In

all other cases, the Commission's references to ISP market power are purely hypothetical.

10.   The NPRM's failure to examine empirically whether broadband ISPs have

market power is difficult to understand, since the issue of market power is central to any

meaningful assessment of the impact of the proposed rules.[13] For example, if broadband ISPs

do not possess significant power over prices, they cannot set prices above cost or constrain

output to either upstream or downstream consumers. If they do not possess the ability to

exclude rivals, they cannot plausibly protect or extend their "monopolies" in neighboring

markets by raising their rivals' costs through discrimination. Moreover, as we discuss below,

many of the stylized empirical models cited by the Commission for the existence of network

externalities or spillover effects assume the existence of monopoly (or, at least, Cournot-

behaving duopoly) in the broadband market. Thus, the existence of market power is, in our

---

[11] NPRM at ¶7 (emphasis added).

[12] NPRM at ¶73. The NPRM does not use the words "terminating monopoly." Indeed, the word "monopoly" appears only once, at ¶25, in a reference to "the era of monopoly-provided telephone service."

[13] See e.g., Robert Hahn, Robert Litan and Hal Singer, "Addressing the Next Wave of Internet Regulation: The Case For Equal Opportunity," Georgetown Center for Business and Public Policy (January 2010) at 19 ("Perhaps the most jarring comment in the NPRM is the notion that market power and vertical integration (that is, affiliation with content providers) would merely exacerbate the alleged anticompetitive effects of allowing such contracting; these factors are not considered by the Commission to be necessary conditions for the challenged conduct (charging a positive price for QoS) to generate anticompetitive effects.")

opinion, a necessary (but not sufficient) condition for concluding that the proposed regulations would benefit consumers or contribute to economic efficiency.[14]

11.   The evidence before the Commission, however, demonstrates that broadband ISPs, in general, do not possess significant market power vis-à-vis pricing or exclusion, nor do they behave like Cournot duopolists.

12.   First, as a preliminary matter, the modern market for broadband services is a far cry from the statutory monopoly that formed the basis for the *Carterphone* regulations, which some net neutrality supporters see as a precedent for the regulations proposed in the NPRM.[15] Indeed, there is a widespread consensus today that broadband service in most areas of the United States is not a natural monopoly. As the Justice Department concluded in an *ex parte* filing in this matter:

> Between the ongoing deployment of wireline broadband networks, the geographic expansion of wireless broadband services (hopefully spurred by the availability of additional spectrum to broadband wireless services), and increased transparency, the Department is hopeful that the vast majority of American households will benefit from significant competition in their local broadband markets. Put differently, *most regions of the United States do not appear to be natural monopolies for broadband service.*[16]

---

[14] See, e.g., Jon M. Peha, "The Benefits and Risks of Mandating Network Neutrality, and the Quest for a Balanced Policy," *International Journal of Communication* 1 (2007), 644-668, at 652 ("The previous section showed that the technologies for discrimination … can be beneficial to users. In this section, we show how a network operator has incentive to use the same technologies to the detriment of users, *if and only if it has sufficient market power*.") (emphasis added).

[15] See NPRM at ¶25.

[16] U.S. Department of Justice, Ex Parte Submission, *In the Matter of Economic Issues in Broadband Competition and A National Broadband Plan for Our Future,* GN 09-51 (January 5, 2010) at 28 (emphasis added) (hereafter *DOJ Ex Parte*). See also Declaration of Marius Schwartz, Exhibit 3 to *Comments of AT&T,* GN Docket 09-191 and WC Docket 07-52 (January 14, 2010) (hereafter Schwartz Declaration) at 28 ("First, economic logic implies that a broadband provider's incentive to engage in anticompetitive discrimination is much weaker than was true for the monopoly Bell system. It is well known that the type of price regulation applied to the Bell system will bias a monopolist to integrate into adjacent services that require access to the core monopoly service and stifle competition in those services. The vertically integrated AT&T was very tightly regulated in its prices for the monopoly local phone service (which reportedly were close to marginal cost or lower), but less so for its long-distance and other services. That created strong incentives to restrict competitors' access to the monopoly service in

13. Further, the fact that the number of broadband ISPs in each market falls short of the textbook idea of atomistic competition is not an indication of market failure, and certainly does not constitute a basis for regulation. As the Department of Justice's *ex parte* filing explains,

> In markets such as this, with differentiated products subject to large economies of scale (relative to the size of the market), the Department does not expect to see a large number of suppliers. Nor do we expect prices to be equated with incremental costs. If they were, suppliers could not earn a normal, risk-adjusted rate of return on their investments in R&D and infrastructure.[17]

Thus, there is no basis for concluding, simply based on industry structure, that the broadband ISP market is in any way deficient or amenable to improvement by regulation.

14. In fact, the evidence demonstrates that the vast majority of consumers have two or more choices of broadband ISPs,[18] that broadband ISPs engage in intense rivalry to capture and retain consumers,[19] that levels of innovation and technological innovation are high, and that new entry is occurring in the form of both fixed and mobile wireless services.[20] Similarly,

---

order to boost its own sales of those adjacent services. Such strong foreclosure incentives cannot be extrapolated to today's broadband carriers.")

[17] *DOJ Ex Parte* at 7.

[18] See, e.g., Declaration of Michael D. Topper, Attachment C to *Comments of Verizon Communications and Verizon Wireless*, GN Docket 09-191 and WC Docket 07-52 (January 14, 2010), at Attachment B (hereafter Topper Declaration) (showing that 97 percent of households in Verizon's service territory have both Verizon broadband and cable modem service available).

[19] See, e.g., Schwartz Declaration at 32 (providing examples of comparative advertising claims by broadband ISPs); at 33 (providing examples of technology upgrades in response to competitors); at 34 (providing examples of price competition and customer switching behavior). See also Jeffrey A. Eisenach, "Broadband in the U.S. – Myths and Facts," in *Australia's Broadband Future: Four Doors to Greater Competition* (Melbourne: Committee for Economic Development of Australia, 2008) 48-59 at 53-54 (providing examples of competition-induced innovation).

[20] See, e.g., Robert C. Atkinson and Ivy E. Schultz, *Broadband in America*, Columbia Institute for Tele-Information (November 2009) (hereafter *CITI Report*) at 7 (Finding that, by 2013-14, "In addition to several wireless broadband choices, the majority of American homes will have the choice of two wired broadband services."); see also *FTC Report* at 9 ("There is evidence that the broadband Internet access industry is moving in the direction of more, not less, competition, including fast growth, declining prices for higher-quality service, and the current market-leading technology (i.e., cable modem) losing share to the more recently deregulated major alternative (i.e., DSL)."); see also Declaration of Gary S. Becker and Dennis W. Carlton, Attachment A to

recent research has failed to find the existence of supra-competitive profits by broadband ISPs;[21] to the contrary, by standard measures of profitability, applications, content and service providers are far more profitable than cable and telephone companies.[22]

15.   Most recently, based on an analysis of Form 477 data, the Commission found in its National Broadband Plan that facilities-based broadband ISPs compete on the basis of investment and service quality,[23] and that while data limitations prevent a robust conclusion, there is some evidence that "monthly prices are lower when more wireline providers are in a census tract."[24]

16.   Thus, virtually all of the available evidence suggests that broadband ISPs do not have significant market power in most markets.[25] Moreover, the evidence demonstrates that

---

Comments of Verizon Communications and Verizon Wireless Comments of Verizon Communications and Verizon Wireless, GN Docket 09-191 and WC Docket 07-52 (January 14, 2010) at 5 ("[A]vailable evidence suggests that there is substantial and growing competition in the provision of broadband access services. As discussed below, data indicate that (i) multiple broadband Internet access providers are available in nearly all geographic areas; and (ii) a variety of firms are in the process of deploying new broadband access services.")

[21] Thomas W. Hazlett and Dennis L. Weisman, "Market Power in U.S. Broadband Services," George Mason University Law and Economics Research Paper Series 09-69 (November 2009) at 31 ("We find no credible basis to believe that broadband providers, despite their relatively few numbers, are currently exercising market power.")

[22] See Larry F. Darby, "Facts About Market Power and Profits in the Internet Space," American Consumer Institute (October 8, 2009) ("Readers will be interested in different comparisons, but the data make clear that, according to each of these measures, operators of broadband networks (Comcast, Time Warner, AT&T and Verizon) earn relatively modest returns compared to other major companies both inside and outside the Internet sector. Indeed, in each case, returns are below the average for firms in the S&P 500 index and substantially below those posted by other firms in the Internet Value Cluster. For example, Google's profit margin is 2-3 times greater than earned by network providers and twice the average rate for S&P 500 firms.") (available at http://www.theamericanconsumer.org/2009/10/08/facts-about-market-power-and-profits-in-the-internet-space/).

[23] Federal Communications Commission, *Connecting America: The National Broadband Plan* (March 2010) at 38 ("The presence of a facilities-based competitor impacts investment. Indeed, broadband providers appear to invest more heavily in network upgrades in areas where they face competition.... So, for example, available cable speeds are higher in areas in which cable competes with DSL or fiber than in areas where cable is the only option. DSL and fiber show similar results. Available speeds are even higher where three wireline providers compete (e.g., where a cable over-builder is also present)."). Hereafter, *National Broadband Plan.*

[24] *National Broadband Plan* at 39.

[25] We do not exclude the possibility that broadband ISPs could possess market power in certain geographic markets, and recommend that the Commission (or other enforcement authority) include a finding of market power as a key element in a case-by-case approach to policing anticompetitive behavior in Internet-related markets. However, as we discuss below, localized market power would not in general create the potential for exclusionary behavior by broadband ISPs relative to content and applications providers.

broadband markets are becoming more, not less competitive, suggesting that any residual market power which may exist in the market for broadband ISP services is transitory.[26]

17.   The NPRM also suggests that broadband ISPs may have the ability to raise rivals' costs or otherwise deter entry and, in cases where they are vertically integrated into content, applications and/or services, might have incentives to discriminate against competing content, applications or service providers.   Again, however, there is virtually no empirical evidence that broadband ISPs possess such market power, or that they would have an incentive to use it. Indeed, market power in the access market is a necessary (but not sufficient) condition for the ability to engage successfully in such anticompetitive practices.[27]

18.   Similarly, the NPRM's concern about a terminating access monopoly problem is entirely hypothetical. While it is conceivable that a broadband ISP could seek to raise prices to content, applications and service providers above the competitive level, a competing broadband ISP would have incentives to undercut those prices, and as a result, offer a broader array of content which would allow them to attract more customers.[28] Moreover, at least some of the

---

[26] See, e.g., *National Broadband Plan* at 41 ("The ongoing upgrade of the wireless infrastructure is promising because of its potential to be a closer competitor to wireline broadband, especially at lower speeds. For example, if wireless providers begin to advertise, say, 4 Mbps home broadband service, wireline providers may be forced to respond by lowering prices of their broadband offerings. This could be true even if wireless services are more expensive, especially if the service is also mobile.")

[27] See e.g., Hahn, Litan and Singer at 11-12 ("In the absence of significant market power in the access market, it is unlikely that a BSP would have the ability to engage in anticompetitive discrimination. Indeed, a necessary condition for adverse welfare effects in nearly every economic model of vertical foreclosure is that the firm in question has market power—that is, the ability to raise price above competitive levels or exclude rivals. When a firm lacks market power, vertical restraints cannot in theory be motivated by anticompetitive reasons, and are therefore more likely motivated for efficiency reasons.") See also Schwartz Declaration at n. 51 ("[I]t is far from evident that any individual broadband provider could, even if it tried, have any realistic chance of monopolizing a market for content or applications."); see also C. Scott Hemphill, "Network Neutrality and the False Promise of Zero-Price Regulation, *Yale Journal on Regulation* (2008) 135-179, at 156-7 ("As a general matter, then, a content provider is not very vulnerable to exclusion by an access provider that controls only a small part of the content provider's audience. That strategy can no more succeed than if a single computer manufacturer, such as Dell, had tried to shut down Netscape by refusing to carry the Netscape browser.")

[28] See Topper Declaration at 62 ("As evidenced by the high churn rates of wireline and wireless broadband providers, consumers can and do switch providers when faced with more attractive options, and this competitive discipline deters providers from charging 'inefficiently high' prices.")

institutional characteristics of the market for traditional telephone services (including retail price regulation) that resulted in concerns about the terminating access monopoly are not present in the market for broadband.[29] As of now, broadband ISPs do not charge terminating access charges, and there is no basis for believing, in the absence of any empirical data whatsoever, that the terminating monopoly problem would lead to access charges above the efficient level.

19.   In summary, the proposed regulations cannot be justified on the basis of market power in the market for broadband ISP services. As we explain further below, even if market power exists in some geographic markets, or if there is a potential for exclusionary conduct in some particular instances of vertical integration, these situations would best be addressed through a case-by-case approach, rather than through sweeping *ex ante* bans on conduct that is likely, in most cases, to be welfare enhancing.[30]

B.   Regulation Is Not Justified on the Basis of Network Externalities or "Spillover Effects" in the Markets for Content, Applications or Services

20.   The second set of market failure theories advanced by the NPRM relates to network externalities and spillover effects, i.e., to the proposition that Internet technologies generate economic benefits which are not fully internalized by the price system, and that charges on providers of content, applications and/or services would lead to under-production of these products and services.[31] In general, these theories rely on a two-sided markets analysis, and suggest that broadband ISPs might have incentives to set fees on content, applications, or

---

[29] See Jerry Brito and Jerry Ellig, "A Tale of Two Commissions: Net Neutrality and Regulatory Analysis," *CommLaw Conspectus* 16;2 (2007) at 26-31.
[30] See, e.g., *FTC Report* at 7 ("The balance between competing incentives on the part of broadband providers to engage in, and the potential benefits and harms from, discrimination and differentiation in the broadband area raise complex empirical questions and may call for substantial additional study of the market generally, of local markets, or of particular transactions. Again, further evidence of particular conduct would be useful for assessing both the likelihood and severity of any potential harm from such conduct.")
[31] A related thesis is that the Internet is a "general purpose technology," which produces external benefits which are not captured by private market actors. See NPRM at ¶64.

service providers "too high" relative to the socially optimally level, while setting prices to downstream consumers "too low." In support of these theories, the NPRM cites articles by Nicholas Economides,[32] Robin S. Lee and Tim Wu,[33] and Barbara van Schewick.[34] In addition, as part of its comments in this proceeding, Google submitted two declarations, one by Professor Economides[35] expanding on his prior work, and citing a co-authored paper with Joacim Tåg,[36] and a second by Christiaan Hogendorn.[37]

21. The existing literature on network externalities, spillovers and two-sided markets does not provide support for the proposed rules, for two primary reasons. First, the economic literature on these topics is in a very early stage of development,[38] and is therefore speculative, highly abstract and theoretical, and lacking in empirical support.[39] Second, the limited empirical research that is available suggests there is a stronger basis for believing the proposed regulations would harm consumer welfare than for believing they would improve it.

---

[32] Nicholas Economides, "'Net Neutrality,' Non-discrimination and Digital Distribution of Content Through the Internet," *I/S: A Journal of Law and Policy for the Information Society* 4;2 (2008) 209-233.

[33] Robin S. Lee and Tim Wu, "Subsidizing Creativity Through Network Design: Zero-Pricing and Net Neutrality," *Journal of Economic Perspectives* 23;3 (Summer 2009) 61–76.

[34] Barbara van Schewick, "Towards an Economic Framework for Network Neutrality Regulation," *Journal on Telecommunications and High Technology Law* 5 (2007) at 385-86 (discussing the Internet as a "general purpose technology" and concluding that "measures that reduce the amount of application-level innovation have the potential to significantly harm social welfare by significantly limiting economic growth.")

[35] Nicholas Economides, "Why Imposing New Tolls on Third-Party Content and Applications Threatens Innovation and Will Not Improve Broadband Providers' Investment," Appendix A to *Comments of Google Inc.* GN Docket 09-191 and WC Docket 07-52 (January 14, 2010).

[36] Nicholas Economides and Joacim Tåg, "Net Neutrality on the Internet: A Two-Sided Market Analysis" (Rev. May 2009) (available at http://papers.ssrn.com/sol3/papers.cfm?abstract_id=1019121).

[37] See Christiaan Hogendorn, "Spillovers and Network Neutrality," Appendix B to *Comments of Google Inc.* GN Docket 09-191 and WC Docket 07-52 (January 14, 2010).

[38] This point is conceded even by net neutrality supporters. See, e.g., Economides and Tåg at 6 ("Despite a considerable literature discussing the rights and legal issues of net neutrality and its abolition, the literature on economic analysis of this issue is thin.") and at 32 ("[T]he economics literature on net neutrality regulation is still in its early stages.").

[39] See, e.g., Christopher S. Yoo, "Network Neutrality, Consumers, and Innovation," *The University of Chicago Legal Forum* (2008) at 184-5 ("[T]he stylized nature of the assumptions on which exemplifying theories tend to be based limit them to identifying what can happen and prevent them from providing any insight into the likelihood that the effects they identify will actually come to pass. Absent empirical support, exemplifying theory cannot provide the broad policy inferences needed to support ex ante categorical prohibitions. In other words, the mere fact that a particular practice may be harmful under certain circumstances does not justify banning that practice categorically.")

22.   The existing literature consists primarily of two types of research: (i) stylized, abstract theoretical models that do not closely resemble real-world markets; and (ii) speculative "discussion papers" that proffer hypotheses and suggestions for potential research, but do not contain rigorous analysis. Neither of these types of studies provides a basis for concluding that the proposed rules, or any similar rules, would have a net positive effect on consumer welfare, either in the short run or the long run.

23.   The existing theoretical literature on network and spillover effects in two-sided markets represents a preliminary effort to isolate and understand the effects of particular market characteristics or policy parameters, holding other factors constant, as a *first step* towards a more complete understanding of real world markets that exhibit these characteristics.

24.   Because of their highly stylized nature, the predictions of such theoretical models are extremely sensitive to underlying assumptions, in two senses. First, such models are, by nature, based on simplifying assumptions that abstract from the institutional complexities of the actual marketplace. Indeed, one purpose of theoretical modeling is to explore the robustness of various models to underlying assumptions (i.e., to assess the extent to which a model's predictions are sensitive to the application of alternative, "more realistic," assumptions), so as eventually to develop models that capture as many of the salient characteristics of the real world as mathematical technique and human comprehension will permit, and which, ideally, are amenable to meaningful empirical assessment.

25.   The theoretical literature on network and spillover effects in two-sided markets has not reached this stage. For example, the leading theoretical paper cited by Professor Economides in his declaration is Economides and Tåg, which presents a model of network effects in two-sided markets based on a large number of simplifying assumptions, including (for

example) (i) that content providers' revenues are strictly proportional to their number of visitors, (ii) that there is neither innovation nor competition in the market for content provision, and (iii) that the value of the network to consumers is a strict multiple of the number of content providers from which they can choose. None of these assumptions is realistic: Content providers' revenues are a function of many factors other than the number of visitors, the Internet content market is nothing if not competitive and innovative, and the value of an additional content web site to consumers is almost surely decreasing in the number of web sites.[40]

26.   Moreover, the Economides and Tåg model depends on the imposition of arbitrary constraints on the model's structure. For example, in order to be able to achieve a unique mathematical solution, the authors impose conditions which (as Caves demonstrates) imply that the profits of platform providers (i.e., phone and cable companies) significantly exceed the profits of content and applications providers (i.e., search engines, online merchants, etc.), an assumption for which there is no apparent empirical basis.[41]

27.   Moreover, the model does not appear to have been tested for its robustness to these assumptions. Hence, even if the model showed an unambiguous gain from the imposition of net neutrality regulation (and, as discussed below, it does not), the only thing the Commission could reasonably infer from that finding is that net neutrality regulation would

---

[40] This list is by no means exhaustive; as in any theoretical model, the model is designed to capture only a few aspects of "the real world," with the rest being captured by "simplifying assumptions." Two other noteworthy aspects in which the Economides and Tåg model differs from reality are (a) it assumes that broadband ISPs are either monopolists or Cournot duopolists and (b) it assumes that regulation takes the form of prohibiting ISPs from charging content providers *any* access fees, whereas the proposed rules appear to ban only fees on "enhanced or prioritized" access. See NPRM at ¶106. Arguably, however, the distinction is one of degree: The effect of the proposed non-discrimination rule would be to impose a zero-price rule (for upstream prices) on all ISP services except "basic Internet access."

[41] Specifically, under conditions that Economides and Tåg impose on their model, it can be shown that the ratio of content provider profits under net neutrality to platform operator profits under net neutrality must be strictly less than 0.4. See Kevin W. Caves, "Modeling the Welfare Effects of Net Neutrality Regulation: A Comment on Economides and Tåg" (March 2010) (available at http://papers.ssrn.com/sol3/papers.cfm?abstract_id=1585254).

increase economic welfare in the imaginary world of the Economides and Tåg model – not in the real world.

28. A second way in which such models rely on assumptions is in their choice of parameter values. In general, economic models involving price discrimination (including models of two-sided markets) do not generate unambiguous results: Discrimination is not, in general, "always harmful" or "always beneficial."[42] The same holds for models of two-sided markets, where the welfare effects of different outcomes typically depend on the values assumed for various parameters, such as the magnitudes of upstream and downstream demand elasticities, and the size and nature of network effects.[43]

29. Again, the Economides and Tåg paper provides an instructive example. As the authors forthrightly admit, the paper's key results – that net neutrality regulation might improve social welfare – hold only "for some parameter values."[44] Specifically, for net neutrality regulation to be welfare enhancing, it must be true that "a content provider values an additional consumer more than a consumer values an additional content provider"[45] – but, as Caves points out, not more than five times as much.[46] In addition, it must true that consumers and content providers are "jointly...sufficiently differentiated," meaning that the product of a variable describing the degree of the differentiation in consumers' valuation of Internet access, and another variable describing the degree of differentiation in content providers' fixed start up

---

[42] See, e.g., Hal R. Varian, "Price Discrimination and Social Welfare," *American Economic Review* 75;4 (September 1985) 870-875 (demonstrating, in general, that price discrimination increases economic welfare when it results in increased output).

[43] See e.g., Weisman and Kulick.

[44] See Economides and Tåg at 1 ("When access is monopolized, for reasonable parameter ranges, net neutrality regulation (requiring zero fees to content providers) increases the total industry surplus as compared to the fully private optimum at which the monopoly platform imposes positive fees on content providers. However, *there are also parameter ranges for which total industry surplus is reduced.*") (emphasis added).

[45] See Economides and Tåg at 14.

[46] See Caves at 6.

costs, must fall within a certain range, which in turn depends on other parameters of the model.[47] The problem with such assumptions is not just that there is no empirical basis for choosing particular numerical values, but that the variables themselves lack any clear empirical analog in the real world.[48]

30.   Indeed, as even strong proponents of net neutrality regulation acknowledge,[49] the results of virtually all of the various theoretical models of net neutrality are dependent on assumptions about parameter values for which there is little or no empirical basis. The lack of an empirical foundation is nowhere more clear than with respect to the argument that imposing fees on content providers should be prohibited since the result might be to reduce investment and innovation in content – irrespective of the acknowledged fact that doing so could both reduce investment in networks and result in higher prices to downstream consumers (and hence lower broadband adoption). Lee and Wu, for example, who make the case for net neutrality regulation based on the benefits of "subsidizing content," concede that

> Of course, for a given price level, subsidizing content comes at the expense of not subsidizing users, and subsidizing users could also lead to greater consumer adoption of broadband. *It is an open question whether, in subsidizing content, the welfare gains from the invention of the next killer app or the addition of new content offset the price reductions consumers might otherwise enjoy or the benefit of expanding service to new users.*[50]

31.   Just as striking (and admirable) is the candor of Harvard economist Glen Weyl, whose authoritative paper on two-sided markets has won plaudits even prior to formal publication. In response to an email query from Commission staff, Weyl responded:

---

[47] See Caves at 6; see also Economides and Tåg at 15 (Assumption 2).

[48] See Caves at 6 ("[I]t is quite difficult to imagine how one might quantify this differentiation empirically, let alone establish that it is sufficiently large, either in absolute or relative terms.")

[49] See Economides and Tåg at 6-8, summarizing the results of several models yielding "ambiguous" results.

[50] See Lee and Wu at 67 (emphasis added).

> I don't know how much of a help I can be in answering your query [whether content providers paying for access will maintain their current quality of content] *as I really have no empirical data to support any assertion I make*, but perhaps I can provide a little bit of conceptual clarity about what elasticities are likely to matter, *even if I don't know their magnitudes.*[51]

Having "no empirical data" to support "any assertion I make" is fine for an academic, especially when he or she is forthright in identifying what follows as academic theorizing rather than demonstrated results. For the Commission to impose regulations on the basis of such theorizing, of course, is a different matter.[52]

32.   This brings us to the second primary class of existing research on net neutrality, network externalities and spillover effects, which consists of "discussion papers" (published or otherwise) that raise various issues and pose various hypotheses for further research, but do not apply rigorous methods (theoretical or otherwise) to achieve conclusive results.   One example is the paper is by Lee and Wu, which is cited by the Commission for the proposition that broadband ISPs might be better off collectively if they did not charge content providers for access to subscribers, but that each broadband ISP acting individually might nevertheless have an incentive to levy fees, thus making things worse for all ISPs (and reducing economic

---

[51] Memorandum from Chuck Needy to Marlene Dortch, February 12, 2010, *Ex Parte Submission in Docket 09-191* (Email from Glen Weyl to Chuck Needy, January 29, 2010) (emphasis added). Weyl's email goes on to identify some key empirical estimates and suggests that "it would be feasible with a little hard work to get a sense of them." See also E. Glen Weyl, "A Price Theory of Multi-Sided Platforms" (October 2009; forthcoming, *American Economic Review*) (available at http://papers.ssrn.com/sol3/papers.cfm?abstract_id=1324415) at 35 ("On the theoretical side, much remains to be done to understand pricing in networks more generally. For example my approach so far allow only extremely stylized models of competition of limited direct empirical relevance.")

[52] See Weisman and Kulick at 26-28 (reviewing the literature on two-sided market structures and concluding that "There is no basis for presuming that regulatory intervention to alter the price structure in such markets would prove to be welfare-enhancing. Put differently, regulatory intervention that alters the relative prices paid by the upstream and downstream sides of the market cannot be justified on grounds that it enhances economic welfare."); see also Schwartz Declaration at 21-23 (providing further examples of the stylized assumptions typical of the two-sided markets literature and concluding, "In sum, the theoretical analysis of two-sided markets — while offering insights — is not yet settled, is quite complex, and the results are highly sensitive to conditions about which regulators are likely to have highly imperfect information.")

welfare).[53] This is an intriguing notion, which may well be worthy of both more rigorous theoretical modeling and, if testable hypotheses, an appropriate methodology, and the necessary data can be identified, empirical investigation. As researchers, we appreciate the value of intriguing theories, and hope that this one (and many others associated with this topic) will be fully pursued in the academic arena. Again, however, from the perspective of public policy, we do not believe that the Commission should make public policy decisions on the basis of imaginative theories that have not yet been formally modeled, let alone empirically demonstrated.[54]

33.   Similarly, the Economides and Hogendorn declarations, and the Van Schewick article (as it relates to the spillover effect of "general purpose technologies"),[55] as well as the bulk of the advocacy literature on these topics, are lacking in both theoretical rigor and

---

[53] NPRM at ¶¶68-9 (citing Lee and Wu, and stating "This dynamic raises a collective action problem: Although it might be in the collective interest of competing broadband Internet access service providers to refrain from charging access or prioritization fees to content, application, and service providers, it is in the interest of each individual access provider to charge a fee, and given multiple providers, it is unlikely that access providers could tacitly agree not to charge such fees.")

[54] See Lee and Wu at 70-71. The authors state that "it *seems implausible* that Internet service providers have appropriate incentives to price according to the social optimum," and describe several reasons why they believe this to be the case, including that "it *might* be individually optimal for one provider to defect and charge positive fees to content providers, although if all content providers charged such fees, the outcome would be worse than had all providers refrained from doing so." (Emphasis added.) On the implications of this thesis, see also Hahn, Litan and Singer at 17 (suggesting that "[t]he Commission appears to be proposing a regulatory 'work-around' for BSPs to escape antitrust scrutiny. According to its logic, if BSPs could somehow coordinate in the setting of prices for QoS, they would choose a zero price according to the NPRM; yet competition among BSPs drives them to set an inefficiently positive price. (Of course, if the jointly profit - maximizing price for QoS were zero, and if net neutrality allowed BSPs to achieve that allegedly optimal solution, then BSPs would favor net neutrality regulation! Alas, they do not.) Again, this basis for intervention is purely theoretical and is not recognized in regulatory economics as a solid basis for intervention.") See also See Schwartz Declaration at 25 ("But no evidence has been offered that the supply of Internet content is deficient relative to that of broadband infrastructure, nor are there strong reasons to believe that this pattern would hold if charges to content providers were implemented.")

[55] See also Frischmann and Van Schewick at 423-6, and n. 168 for a discussion of general purpose technologies ("GPTs"). GPTs are technologies which generate externalities associated with their ability to increase productivity across industries. There is a theoretical argument for subsidizing research in and/or deployment of such technologies (though the practical obstacles to doing so effectively are formidable). Further, it is plausible that the Internet is a GPT. (See, e.g., *National Broadband Plan* at 29.) However, *even if* the Internet is a GPT, and *even if* the practical obstacles to creating efficient subsidy programs could be overcome, what would still not be clear is why it would make sense to subsidize some aspects of the Internet value chain (content, applications, etc.) at the expense of others (e.g., infrastructure).

empirical support.[56] For the most part, these contributions contain the appropriate caveats, arguing that net neutrality regulation "might" improve social welfare "if" certain criteria are satisfied, or (alternatively) that unregulated markets "may" experience various forms of market failure.[57] Again, as researchers we value these and similar contributions, as the proffering of hypotheses and expression of informed opinion is an important part of the process of gaining a better understanding of these complex markets – even if we disagree with most or all of their hypothesized conclusions. The important point, however, is that the Commission should not mistake speculation, conjecture, hypothesis and argument for rigorous analysis, empirical evidence, or proof.

34. Finally, and perhaps most important, for all of the hypothesizing and discussion of how models based on network externalities and spillover effects provide support for net neutrality regulation, there is *at least* as much support for the opposite proposition.[58] It is

---

[56] For another example, see Inimai M. Chettiar and J. Scott Holladay, *Free to Invest: The Economic Benefits of Preserving Net Neutrality*, New York University Institute for Policy Integrity, Report No. 4 (2010), at 9-10. As Weisman and Kulick point out (at 19), "The authors of this study fail to account for the fact that in two-sided markets with network externalities, price discrimination actually would serve to mitigate the market failure that creates this positive network externality.")

[57] See, e.g, Hogendorn Declaration at 12 ("ISPs were to prioritize or degrade service for certain applications, certain websites, etc., there could be a reduction in both types of network effects. The question is whether an individual ISP would have incentives that do not align with social incentives. There are two reasons this *might* happen.") (emphasis added); see also Van Schewick at 329 ("This paper also highlights important limitations of the 'one monopoly rent' argument, demonstrating previously unidentified exceptions that *may* be quite common in the Internet context, showing how exclusion *may* be a profitable strategy even if the excluding actor does not manage to drive its competitors from the complementary market, and proving that competition in the primary market *may* be insufficient to remove the ability and incentive to engage in exclusionary conduct.") (emphasis added); see also Economides Declaration at 1 ("Broadband providers insist that imposing these new charges will greatly improve network investment, and thus these charges are beneficial. I argue that this is not the case. Possible higher revenues from discrimination *may* simply be returned to shareholders and not invested.") (emphasis added).

[58] For example, Economides and Tåg (at 7) acknowledge that models that use different assumptions yield different results. For example, they note that a paper by Cheng, Bandyopadhyay and Guo finds that consumer surplus may increase when content providers pay access fees, and explain that "The reason why the consumer surplus may increase is that it is always the more profitable content provider that pays for access and hence, gets preferential treatment. This benefits consumers of the more profitable content provider because congestion is reduced. However, it means a loss for consumers of the less profitable content provider that does not pay for preferential access, since there is an increase in the congestion costs."); see also Mark A. Jamison and Janice A. Hauge, "Getting What You Pay For: Analyzing the Net Neutrality Debate," (April 2008) (available at http://papers.ssrn.com/sol3/papers.cfm?abstract_id=1081690) at 2 ("When only a single transmission speed is

remarkable, for example, that the only robust result of the Economides and Tåg model – the only result that applies under all parameter values – is that consumers are *always* made worse off by net neutrality regulation.[59]

35. To summarize, the evidence before the Commission demonstrates that broadband ISPs do not have generalized market power, and thus provides no support for the proposed regulations based on any traditional theory of market failure. Moreover, the speculative theories and stylized models put forth as potential justifications for regulation in the absence of market power provide no empirical – that is, no *real world* – foundation for concluding that the proposed regulations would increase rather than harm consumer welfare.

36. In 2007, the FTC declared that, "to date we are unaware of any significant market failure or demonstrated consumer harm from conduct by broadband providers."[60] In our opinion, it remains the case there is no evidence, empirical, theoretical, or otherwise, to contradict this finding. If anything, the market for broadband services has continued to exhibit rapid innovation and increasing competition. Accordingly, there is no economic basis for a finding of market failure in the markets at issue.

---

offered by the network provider, some low-value content providers choose to not produce because their potential advertising revenue would not cover their content production costs and their fixed costs. However, when a premium transmission speed is offered, some low-value sites that did not produce under the single speed scenario find it profitable to purchase the premium speed and so choose to enter the market. This results in an increase in the amount and diversity of content available for consumers. We consider this increase in the variety of content on the network to constitute innovation on the edges, which raises the value of the network.").

[59] See Economides and Tåg at 31 ("Comparisons between outcomes under the private equilibrium with two-sided pricing and the private equilibrium under net neutrality regulation indicated that a removal of net neutrality regulation would lead to a lower subscription price for consumers, but less content available due to an increase in fees to content providers. Content providers are worse off in the aggregate, while consumers are better off.").

[60] See *FTC Report* at 11. See also e.g., Gerald R. Faulhaber and David J. Farber, "The Open Internet: A Customer-Centric Framework," Exhibit 1 to *Comments of AT&T, Inc.* in GN Docket Nos. 09-157, 09-51 (September 2009) at 1 ("Despite many colorful predictions about what evil doings ISPs might do in the future, we find that during ten years of experience without network neutrality regulations, there are just two incidents (the tiresomely familiar Madison River and Comcast cases) of any *actual* misbehavior by broadband ISPs. Two incidents – both remedied without the prescriptive rules proposed here - is not empirical evidence, nor are the many lurid but unrealized nightmare scenarios."); see also Schwartz Declaration at 4 ("Beyond these *a priori* objections, and perhaps most important, is the striking lack of evidence for the postulated harms.")

III. THE PROPOSED REGULATIONS WOULD BAN BENEFICIAL PRACTICES AND OTHERWISE HARM ECONOMIC WELFARE

37.   While there is no evidence of systematic market failures that might be remedied or ameliorated by the proposed rules, there is substantial basis for believing that the proposed regulations would harm competition, slow innovation, and reduce consumer welfare.[61] These likely harms are a function of the facts that (i) many of the practices that would be banned by the proposed regulations are presumptively welfare enhancing, (ii) the proposed "carve outs" for reasonable network management and "managed services" do not provide a basis for distinguishing between beneficial practices and harmful ones; and (iii) the litigation and regulatory uncertainty created by the regulations would slow innovation and have other unintended consequences.

A.   Most of the Conduct that Would Be Prohibited Is Presumptively Welfare Enhancing

38.   Given the vagueness of the proposed "reasonable network management" and "managed services" exceptions, it is somewhat difficult to predict precisely which forms of conduct would be prohibited under the proposed regulations. However, one effect of the proposed non-discrimination rule is predictable and clear: To the extent the rule prohibits broadband ISPs from levying positive fees on upstream customers such as content providers, the

---

[61] See, e.g., *FTC Report* at 11 ("Policy makers also should carefully consider the potentially adverse and unintended effects of regulation in the area of broadband Internet access before enacting any such regulation. Industry-wide regulatory schemes – particularly those imposing general, one-size-fits-all restraints on business conduct – may well have adverse effects on consumer welfare, despite the good intentions of their proponents. Even if regulation does not have adverse effects on consumer welfare in the short term, it may nonetheless be welfare-reducing in the long term, particularly in terms of product and service innovation. Further, such regulatory schemes inevitably will have unintended consequences, some of which may not be known until far into the future. Once a regulatory regime is in place, moreover, it may be difficult or impossible to undo its effects."); see also Michael L. Katz, "Maximizing Consumer Benefits from Broadband," Attachment B to *Comments of Verizon Communications and Verizon Wireless Comments of Verizon Communications and Verizon Wireless,* GN Docket 09-191 and WC Docket 07-52 (January 14, 2010) (hereafter Katz Declaration) at 15 (providing examples of the unintended negative consequences of regulation and concluding "It is well documented that even well-intentioned regulations can impose significant costs and often have harmful unintended consequences.")

upshot would be to raise prices to downstream subscribers and ultimately reduce broadband

adoption – precisely the opposite of what the Commission is seeking to accomplish through its

National Broadband Plan.[62] Unlike the conjectural benefits of "subsidizing content," the

substantial economic benefits of increased broadband adoption have been demonstrated in

numerous empirical studies.[63]

39.   In addition to the direct effect of raising prices for broadband access above

competitive levels, the proposed regulations would limit or proscribe (to a somewhat

unpredictable degree) a variety of business practices that presumptively contribute to economic

efficiency,[64] promote competition,[65] foster innovation,[66] increase investment,[67] promote product

---

[62] See, e.g., Hemphill at 171-173 (discussing consumer benefits of positive pricing by network providers; see also Schwartz Declaration at 3 ("[P]ositive fees to content providers would result in lower prices to broadband consumers, advancing the Commission's goal of expanding broadband penetration and use especially among economically disadvantaged groups.")

[63] See e.g., Robert W. Crandall and Hal J. Singer, "The Economic Impact of Broadband Investment," (February 2010); see also Mark Dutz, Jonathan Orszag, and Robert Willig, *The Substantial Consumer Benefits of Broadband Connectivity For U.S. Households*, Internet Innovation Alliance, (July 2009); Robert Crandall, William Lehr, and Robert Litan, "The Effects of Broadband Deployment on Output and Employment: A Cross-sectional Analysis of U.S. Data," *The Brookings Institution: Issues in Economic Policy No. 6* (2007); Robert E. Litan, *Great Expectations: Potential Economic Benefits to the Nation From Accelerated Broadband Deployment to Older Americans and Americans with Disabilities*, New Millennium Research Council (2005); and, Austan Goolsbee, "The Value of Broadband and the Deadweight Loss of Taxing New Technology," *Contributions to Economic Analysis & Policy* 5;1 (2006). By contrast, we are not aware of any rigorous empirical analyses of the benefits of "subsidizing content."

[64] See, e.g., Schwartz Declaration at 12-13 (noting that upstream pricing of QoS may be efficient because "[a] content provider is likely to be in a much better position than end users to know what performance requirements are needed for its service to work well [and] the transactions costs of contracting for such arrangements are likely to be much lower when dealing with a content provider than with a host of end users.")

[65] See e.g. Jamison and Hauge at 2.

[66] See e.g., Crandall and Singer (2010) at 51-53 (discussing negative impact of net neutrality regulation on innovation and investment in both networks and Internet content); see also Schwartz Declaration at 2 ("Such payments can enable valuable and mutually beneficial arrangements, for example, by allocating scarce network capacity efficiently and avoiding the need for costly overbuilding, and by funding network enhancements desired by particular content providers."); see also Katz Declaration at 13-15 (noting that the rules would, by design, freeze the current structure of the Internet in place and concluding that "it would not be in consumers' interest to ossify the Internet.") and at 30 ("[A] policy that triggered capacity investment in lieu of capacity management would be inefficient. Because a managed network can provide greater levels of service for a given amount of investment in physical infrastructure than can an unmanaged network, a managed network provides services at a lower unit cost. A second fundamental flaw with the argument that a policy that blocks network management can promote investment is that such a policy might actually reduce the overall amount of capacity investment. Restrictions on an operator's management of its network will prevent the operator from producing as much output as possible from any given amount of physical plant and equipment. Because the physical plant cannot be used efficiently, the cost

differentiation and consumer choice,[68] and enhance consumer welfare.[69] Yet, depending on how they are enforced, the proposed rules could, for example, inhibit content providers' ability to enter into mutually beneficial (and economically efficient) exchanges with broadband ISPs; and, more broadly, limit the ability of all firms in the Internet value chain to engage in unilateral conduct, or to enter into contracts that would contribute to economic efficiency by reducing risk, lowering transactions costs, creating disincentives to opportunistic behavior, ensuring product quality, or creating consumer choice through product differentiation.[70]

B. The Reasonable Network Management and "Managed Services" Criteria Would Not Protect Consumer Welfare

40. The proposed rules would allow broadband ISPs to engage in "reasonable network management,"[71] and create an exception for "managed services."[72] While any relief

---

of capacity per unit of output is higher. These higher costs reduce the operator's net return on investment and, consequently, the operator may invest less in physical capacity.")

[67] See Larry F. Darby, "The Informed Policy Maker's Guide to Regulatory Impacts on Broadband Network Investment," American Consumer Institute (2009) at 2 ("There is no reasoned, factual and analytical basis for concluding that network neutrality rules will not impact the rate of investment in existing broadband networks. Some rules will have more impact than others, but any rule that constrains the ability of firms to pursue business activities that may increase shareholder value will almost certainly affect their allocation of cash to different uses, including domestic network investment."); see also Schwartz Declaration at 20 ("Claims that charges to content providers should be opposed because they would reduce incentives to invest in the edge either expressly or implicitly minimize the importance of incentives for investment in network infrastructure with no justification."); see also Katz Declaration at 59 ("Free Press recently released a report in which the author claims to demonstrate that network neutrality regulations do not meaningfully harm investment incentives. Scrutiny of the study, however, reveals that it is fatally flawed and offers no such demonstration.").

[68] See e.g., Benjamin E. Hermalin and Michael L. Katz, "The Economics of Product-Line Restrictions with an Application to the Network Neutrality Debate," *Information Economics and Policy* 19;2 (2007) 215-248, at 236 ("[C]onsumers have fewer applications available to them as a consequence [of net neutrality regulation]."); see also Everett M. Ehrlich, Jeffrey A. Eisenach, and Wayne A. Leighton, "The Impact of Regulation on Innovation and Choice in Wireless Communications," *Review of Network Economics* 9;1 (2010).

[69] See e.g., Katz Declaration at 11, describing the direct consumer benefits of traffic prioritization ("The fact that customers pay for the ability to differentiate between traffic in managing their own internal networks demonstrates that users want and value such differentiation.")

[70] See generally Christopher S. Yoo, "Beyond Network Neutrality," *Harvard Journal of Law and Technology* 19;1 (Fall 2005) 1-77; see also Ehrlich, Eisenach and Leighton at 48 ("By making it more difficult to manage the risk of innovation and entry, prohibitions on network management would ... slow innovation and reduce consumer choice, the opposite of what proponents of such regulation say they desire.").

[71] NPRM at ¶135 ff.

[72] NPRM at ¶148 ff.

from otherwise harmful regulations is better than none, these criteria are not founded in sound economic analysis and would not ensure that consumer welfare is protected.

41. Network management – i.e., traffic prioritization – benefits consumers and enhances economic efficiency by allowing ISPs to ensure the quality of Internet applications that require faster and more reliable delivery, such as video conferencing, interactive online gaming, and remote health care. Regulations that limit the ability of broadband providers to engage in such network management, without producing compensating benefits, would reduce economic efficiency and consumer welfare.

42. The regulations as proposed do not contain a consumer welfare standard, but instead offer a vague and ultimately circular definition, in which "reasonable network management" is defined as "reasonable steps to maintain the proper functioning of their networks."[73] Such ambiguity is neither necessary nor constructive: Broadband ISPs should be permitted to engage in business practices generally, and network management practices in particular, that do not harm consumer welfare. Further, the burden of proof, in competitive markets such as the ones at issue here, should be on the Commission to demonstrate that a particular network management practice would harm economic welfare, not on broadband ISPs to prove it is beneficial.

---

[73] See NPRM at ¶140 ("Finally, we propose that broadband Internet access service providers may take other reasonable steps to maintain the proper functioning of their networks. We include this catch-all for two reasons. First, we do not presume to know now everything that providers may need to do to provide robust, safe, and secure Internet access to their subscribers, much less everything they may need to do as technologies and usage patterns change in the future. Second, we believe that additional flexibility to engage in reasonable network management provides network operators with an important tool to experiment and innovate as user needs change."); see also Katz Declaration at 4 ("Network management can facilitate more efficient use of capacity and can protect consumers from harmful traffic and applications. However, the proposed rules would create an uncertain regulatory environment that would discourage efficient network management. For example, the proposed rules allow for 'reasonable' practices without defining reasonable. Moreover, any definition of reasonable would almost certainly either be vague or would draw bright lines that in important instances lead to outcomes that harmed consumer welfare....").

43.   Similarly, the NPRM's discussion of managed services contains no suggestion that any exceptions to the proposed regulations for such services (however they ultimately are defined) would be tied to a substantive economic welfare standard. Indeed, there is no basis for believing that the exceptions suggested in the NPRM – for telemedicine, smart grid applications and eLearning – are based on any type of either technical or economic analysis.[74] Thus, the managed-services exemption, as proposed in the NPRM, is completely untethered from any concept of consumer welfare or economic efficiency. Indeed, to the extent the managed-services exemption served as a regulatory safe harbor for "nascent" services, it risks actually discouraging the widespread adoption and commercialization of new and innovative services – which, by the very virtue of their success, would grow out of the regulatory safe harbor that made them possible in the first place, and hence find themselves subjected to costly or even prohibitive regulation.[75]

C.   Enacting the Proposed Regulations Would Raise Regulatory Risk and Harm Investment and Innovation

44.   The proposed regulations are ambiguous and poorly drafted. As noted above, the NPRM provides no practical guidance as to what the Commission would consider to be "reasonable" network management, or what services would be deemed to fall within the "managed services" exception,[76] but these are only two of many uncertainties companies would face if the rules were adopted. For example, the proposed regulations fail to provide a practical

---

[74] See NPRM at ¶150. It is not at all clear why eLearning applications, for example, would be more likely to "require or benefit from enhanced quality of service rather than traditional best-effort Internet delivery" than, say, online gaming or corporate video conferencing.

[75] See Katz Declaration at 44 ("Even if the Commission does create a managed services exception, there is a very real danger that this policy will impose service qualifications that result in the rules' becoming a form of success tax.")

[76] See Katz Declaration at 4 ("Although it is vital to the promotion of consumer welfare that network providers continue to be permitted to develop and offer their own services that may be thought of as managed or specialized, the NRPM's managed services exception is vague and unworkable. Moreover, it cannot reasonably be expected to substitute for the sound analysis that is missing from the NPRM.")

means of distinguishing between content, applications and service providers, on the one hand, and "subscribers" (many of whom also generate content), on the other.[77] To the extent regulatory uncertainty prevents parties from engaging in efficiency-enhancing conduct, or entering into efficiency-enhancing contracts, or increases the risks that such conduct or contracts will be voided (or even penalized) by subsequent Commission decisions, firms are less likely to engage in the investment or innovation that such conduct and contracts would otherwise have enabled.[78]

IV. CASE-BY-CASE APPLICATION OF EXISTING STANDARDS IS THE BEST APPROACH

45. In paragraph 103 of the NPRM, the Commission identifies the challenge before it with respect to banning discrimination as follows: "The key issue we face is distinguishing socially beneficial discrimination from socially harmful discrimination in a workable manner."[79] In the accompanying footnote 226, the Commission suggests that, by "workable," it means a rule that would "limit how network operators can discriminate in a manner that [1] prevents them from fully exploiting market power in ways that seriously harm users, and [2] does not prevent them from using discrimination in ways that greatly benefit users."[80] Based on these passages, the Commission appears to recognize the tension between what economists refer to as "Type I" and "Type II" error (i.e., between a rule that deters too little

---

[77] See Katz Declaration at 41 ("What if a broadband Internet access service provider required content, application, or service providers to become subscribers in order to receive enhanced or prioritized access? Would the broadband Internet access service provider then be allowed to charge them different prices for different services? If not, whom could it charge?")

[78] See, e.g., *FTC Report* at 11 ("Industry-wide regulatory schemes – particularly those imposing general, one-size-fits-all restraints on business conduct – may well have adverse effects on consumer welfare, despite the good intentions of their proponents. Even if regulation does not have adverse effects on consumer welfare in the short term, it may nonetheless be welfare-reducing in the long term, particularly in terms of product and service innovation.")

[79] See NPRM at ¶103.

[80] See NPRM at n. 226 (citing Peha at 645). Note the reference in this quotation to market power, the existence of which, as noted above, the Commission neither asserts nor demonstrates, and which, as we explained above, does not generally exist in the markets at issue.

harmful behavior, and one that deters too much beneficial behavior); and, further, to acknowledge (correctly) that the ultimate objective is to minimize the combined welfare losses associated with both types of errors.

46.   The Commission proposes further to adjudicate the key question of which practices constitute "reasonable network management" (and are hence permitted) through a "case-by-case" approach, stating that "the novelty of Internet access and traffic management questions, the complex nature of the Internet, and a general policy of restraint in setting policy for Internet access service providers weigh in favor of a case-by-case approach."[81] This approach, too, is sensible, as it suggests that the Commission recognizes that distinguishing between beneficial behaviors and harmful ones is likely to be both analytically difficult and factually complex.

47.   However, the Commission proposes to apply its case-by-case approach in a prohibitive rather than permissive fashion: That is, all "discriminatory" behavior that is not found to be permitted (on a case-by-case basis) would be banned. As we have explained above, the conduct potentially covered by the proposed regulations is far more likely to be beneficial than harmful. Accordingly, the Commission's proposed approach is precisely the reverse of what the economic evidence supports, and virtually guarantees far more Type II error than is consistent with economic efficiency and consumer welfare.[82]

---

[81] See NPRM at ¶134.

[82] See, e.g., Weisman and Kulick at 22 ("There are two strong reasons to believe that, at this point in time, specific regulation of vertical integration by ISPs into the Internet content space will be subject to substantial Type I error. First, monopoly power in one market is a necessary condition for anticompetitive effects in almost all models of anticompetitive vertical integration. As discussed above, competition is becoming increasingly intense in the ISP market and there is scant evidence that, as a general matter, broadband providers possess true monopoly power. Second, ISPs generally serve regional markets whereas content markets are often national or international…. On the other hand, at this point in time, there is little risk of Type II error.")

48.   While we agree that a case-by-case approach to enforcement is appropriate for the conduct and issues addressed in the NPRM,[83] the Commission should adopt a permissive rather than a prohibitive approach: Conduct should be considered permitted unless, after a case-specific adjudication of the facts, it can be shown to be harmful, on net, to economic efficiency and consumer welfare.[84]   That is, rather than being presumptively unlawful, network management practices and other "discriminatory" behavior should be presumptively lawful.

49.   In assessing the lawfulness of specific conduct, the Commission should apply existing, generally agreed-upon standards for the evaluation of market power, market failure, and consumer welfare – standards such as those implicit in the FTC-Department of Justice *Merger Guidelines*,[85] the Office of Management and Budget's Circular A-4, [86] the FTC's Policy Statements on and Deception[87] and Unfairness,[88] and, more broadly, the pro-competition, pro-consumer doctrines that have developed under the Sherman Act and other antitrust statutes.[89]

---

[83] See Katz Declaration at 36 ("Case-by-case application of antitrust laws is the best way to deal with concerns that, in some circumstances, network management can be used to harm competition. Such an approach is the only way to block the use of these practices when they harm competition and consumers while at the same time ensuring that service providers can engage in these practices in the many instances where they benefit consumers and promote competition and the achievement of other public-interest goals.")

[84] See Ehrlich, Eisenach and Leighton at 48 ("On their face, the existing proposals would presumptively prohibit a wide range of business practices. Indeed, taken at face value, they would appear to prohibit a wide variety of practices about which even regulation advocates have expressed no concerns. Moreover, the only limiting principle regulation advocates concede is technical feasibility, a standard which effectively precludes a weighing of benefits against costs to maximize consumer welfare.")

[85] See U.S. Department of Justice and Federal Trade Commission, *Horizontal Merger Guidelines* (rev. April 8, 1997) (available at http://www.justice.gov/atr/public/guidelines/horiz_book/hmg1.html).

[86] See Office of Management and Budget, Circular A-4, *Regulatory Analysis* (September 17, 2003) (available at http://www.whitehouse.gov/omb/circulars/a004/a-4.pdf).

[87] See Federal Trade Commission, *FTC Policy Statement On Deception, Appended to Cliffdale Associates, Inc.*, 103 F.T.C. 110, 174 (1984) (available at http://www.ftc.gov/bcp/policystmt/ad-decept.htm).

[88] Federal Trade Commission, *FTC Policy Statement On Unfairness, Appended to International Harvester Co.*, 104 F.T.C. 949, 1070 (1984) (available at http://www.ftc.gov/bcp/policystmt/ad-unfair.htm) see also 15 U.S.C. § 45(n).

[89] See generally Brito and Ellig at 7-37; see also Joseph Farrell and Philip J. Weiser, "Modularity, Vertical Integration, and Open Access Policies: Towards a Convergence of Antitrust and Regulation in the Internet Age," *Harvard Journal of Law and Technology* 17;1 (Fall 2003) at 134 ("In developing its regulatory strategy for new environments such as broadband where price regulation is absent, *the FCC should define more clearly when to restrict a firm's conduct — for instance, only after exclusionary conduct is demonstrated, where it seems probable, or where it would do the most harm. Antitrust enforcers normally address exclusionary conduct by a single firm*

50.   Beyond recommending that the Commission give weight to these general substantive standards, we do not make specific recommendations for how the Commission should go about implementing a case-by-case approach.[90] We do note, however, that a number of parties have recommended various aspects of such approaches. For example, Professor Neuchterlein (among many others) recommends application of antitrust law by the traditional antitrust enforcement agencies;[91] Drs. Hahn, Litan and Singer suggest applying "existing FCC procedures for resolving discrimination in other contexts";[92] and, Google and Verizon jointly recommend creation of technical advisory committees to ensure the Commission's assessments of individual business practices are grounded in a sound technical understanding.[93] Others have pointed out that any concerns about the adequacy of competition can best be addressed by taking steps to promote competition (e.g., by increasing the amount of spectrum available for licensed use).[94] We offer these examples not because we have concluded any of them represent the best or only approach supported by the economic evidence, but rather as a demonstration that there are viable alternatives to the prohibitive *ex ante* regulations proposed in the NPRM.

---

only ex post, once such conduct has been proven. Regulators, by contrast, often act to avoid vertical competitive harms before they occur, but do not always explain how their actions fit with ICE or antitrust policy more generally. The FCC must provide such an explanation if it decides to impose an open access requirement on broadband platforms.") (emphasis added).

[90] Professor Kahn qualifies his approval of the case we make here for non- or de-regulation of Internet access by emphasizing the principle that forbearance from direct economic regulation transfers responsibility for the public interest to competition protected by the antitrust laws. In particular, in the present context, he would emphasize the prohibition of unfair methods of competition (or unfairly exclusionary practices) as defined in Section 5 of the Federal Trade Commission Act, preferably exercised in cooperation with the antitrust agencies.

[91] See Jonathan E. Nuechterlein, "Antitrust Oversight of an Antitrust Dispute: An Institutional Perspective on the Net Neutrality Debate," *Journal on Telecommunications and High Technology Law* 7 (2009) 20-65.

[92] See Hahn, Litan and Singer at 20.

[93] *Google and Verizon Joint Submission on the Open Internet*, GN Docket No. 09-191; WC Docket No. 07-52 (January 14, 2010). As the Commission notes in the National Broadband Plan, evaluating competition in application and content markets is particularly challenging. See *National Broadband Plan* at 52 ("Applications, content and the services they enable are bundled, sold, priced and monetized in many different ways. The nature and intensity of competition in applications and content varies tremendously and must be evaluated on a case-by-case basis.")

[94] See, e.g., Faulhaber and Farber at 33.

V. CONCLUSION

51. The regulations proposed in the NRPM are unsupported by the economic evidence. There is no economic evidence, even in the abstract, of generalized market power or systematic market failure in the markets at issue. There is no economic basis for believing the practices at issue are reducing economic efficiency or consumer welfare. There is no empirical evidence whatsoever that consumers have been harmed in the past.

52. There is strong economic evidence that the regulations would inhibit, or prohibit, efficiency enhancing conduct, thereby reducing competition, slowing innovation, deterring investment and ultimately reducing consumer welfare.

53. To the extent the types of conduct addressed in the NPRM may, in isolated circumstances, have the potential to harm competition or consumers, the Commission and other regulatory bodies, including the Federal Trade Commission, have the ability to deter or prohibit such conduct on a case-by-case basis, through the application of existing doctrines and procedures. Hence, the approach advocated in the NPRM is not necessary to achieve whatever economic benefits may be associated with prohibiting harmful discrimination on the Internet.

107

Respectfully submitted,

Jerry Brito, J.D.
Mercatus Center, George Mason University

Martin Cave, D.Phil.
Warwick Business School, University of Warwick

Robert W. Crandall, Ph.D.
The Brookings Institution

Larry F. Darby, Ph.D.
American Consumer Institute and George Mason University Law School

Everett M. Ehrlich, Ph.D.
ESC Company

Jeffrey A. Eisenach, Ph.D.
Navigant Economics LLC and George Mason University Law School

Jerry Ellig, Ph.D.
Mercatus Center, George Mason University

Henry Ergas
Economist

David Farber
Carnegie Mellon University

Gerald R. Faulhaber, Ph.D.
Wharton School, University of Pennsylvania

Robert W. Hahn, Ph.D.
University of Manchester and University of Oxford

Alfred E. Kahn, Ph.D.
National Economic Research Associates

Wayne A. Leighton, Ph.D.
Francisco Marroquin University

Robert Litan, Ph.D.
The Brookings Institution and the Kaufman Foundation

Glen O. Robinson, J.D.
University of Virginia

Hal J. Singer, Ph.D.
Navigant Economics LLC and Georgetown University School of Business

Vernon L. Smith, Ph.D.
Chapman University, Economic Science Institute

William Taylor, Ph.D.
National Economic Research Associates

Timothy J. Tardiff, Ph.D.
Advanced Analytical Consulting Group

Leonard Waverman, Ph.D.
Haskayne School of Business, University of Calgary

Dennis L. Weisman, Ph.D.
Kansas State University

*Affiliations listed for identification purposes only.

BROADBAND COMPETITION
IN THE INTERNET ECOSYSTEM

JEFFREY A. EISENACH

October 2012

AMERICAN ENTERPRISE INSTITUTE

109

AEI Economic Studies

Broadband Competition in the Internet Ecosystem

Jeffrey A. Eisenach

October 2012

AMERICAN ENTERPRISE INSTITUTE

Acknowledgments

I am grateful for comments and suggestions from Rob Atkinson, Patrick Brogan, Kevin Caves, Larry Downes, Everett Ehrlich, Joseph Fuhr, Shane Greenstein, Robert Kulick, Jonathan Sallet, Nick Schulz, Howard Shelanski, Hal Singer, Scott Wallsten, Dennis Weisman, and several anonymous commenters. Partial support for an earlier version of this paper was provided by Verizon Communications. All views expressed, and any remaining errors, are solely the responsibility of the author.

Foreword

In this paper, Jeff Eisenach tackles the important and timely debate surrounding the regulation of Internet-based communications. Broadband service providers are currently treated differently from other information technology industries in that they are subject to increasing levels of ex ante regulation by the Federal Communications Commission (FCC). Other Internet sectors are subject to ex post treatment under standard antitrust laws. The discrepancy is justified by claims that broadband is somehow crucially different from the remainder of the Internet ecosystem and as a result requires special regulatory practices.

The FCC outlined its rationale in the December 2010 Open Internet Order; however, its authority to implement the order is currently being challenged in court. Verizon Wireless appealed FCC's "data roaming" rules, which would impose new open-access regulations on broadband service providers, and last month the FCC presented oral arguments defending its rules.

In a similar case, the DC Court of Appeals will pass judgment next year on the "net neutrality" rules, which would prohibit broadband providers from engaging in business practices that are both common and legal in other industries. The outcomes of these cases will help answer the question at the heart of the issue: will more regulation improve broadband networks?

The case for heavier government regulation is often justified on the grounds that competition in broadband markets operates differently from competition in other Internet markets. Many believe that broadband is a monopoly, but in this paper, Eisenach argues the other side and makes a convincing case that this assumption is simply not true. He analyzes the core characteristics of broadband networks—dynamism, modularity, network effects, and multisidedness—which are remarkably similar to other information technology industries. His analysis effectively dismantles the claim that broadband deserves asymmetric regulatory treatment and suggests that modern antitrust principles should be applied instead.

Applying the proper regulatory framework is crucial since a failure to do so can stifle the incentives to innovate with broad implications for the entire economy. It is my hope that this paper will help identify the appropriate policies that will encourage competition among broadband service providers.

—Aparna Mathur, AEI Economic Studies Editor

Executive Summary

Like the other information technology (IT) markets that comprise the Internet ecosystem, broadband communications services are characterized by rapid innovation, declining costs, product differentiation, competitive price discrimination, network effects, and "multisidedness." Broadband Internet service providers (ISPs) make large sunk cost investments and seek to differentiate their products so that they can earn economic returns on those investments. They seek to assemble or participate in systems that create value for consumers and do so by choosing both the platforms they join and the products with which they interconnect. They experience both supply-side economies of scale and scope and demand-side externalities that create powerful incentives to increase volumes by maximizing system openness, but as with other IT firms, these incentives do not always outweigh the costs of interoperability. In short, like other IT markets, broadband (1) is characterized by rapid innovation, high sunk costs, and declining average costs (*dynamism*); (2) functions as a complementary component in modular platforms (*modularity*); and (3) is subject to demand-side economies of scope and scale (*network effects*).

Despite these similarities, broadband is treated differently from other IT industries when it comes to competition policy: competition in the rest of the IT sector is subject to scrutiny under antitrust laws, while broadband is regulated by the Federal Communications Commission (FCC). Indeed, the FCC is currently in court defending its authority to impose "net neutrality" regulations prohibiting broadband ISPs from engaging in business practices that are both presumptively legal and commonplace in other industries. In the wireless arena, the FCC asserts its authority over the electromagnetic spectrum to impose economic regulation on wireless ISPs. And

the commission's recent decision to extend the $9 billion "universal service" program (heretofore limited to telephone services) to broadband promises to impose de facto price controls on broadband ISPs that participate. In short, while other elements of the "Internet ecosystem"—applications, content and devices—receive ex post treatment under the antitrust laws, broadband ISPs are subject to ex ante regulation.

Broadband is regulated differently from other IT markets in part because it is analyzed differently. Although important unsettled questions remain about how best to police competition in such markets, it is generally agreed that analysis of such markets should deemphasize the traditional "structure-conduct-performance" paradigm and assess the consequences of potentially harmful conduct on a case-by-case basis. Thus, high levels of concentration in IT markets such as handsets, operating systems, search engines, and social networks are not regarded as signals of market power (or at least not market power sufficient to justify ex ante regulation), but the FCC often still utilizes anachronistic measures of concentration to justify regulation of broadband markets.

One asserted rationale for asymmetric treatment is the notion that broadband networks are uniquely at the "core" of the Internet while content, applications and devices are at the "edge." This metaphor is at best misleading, and in any case does not justify differential policy treatment. To the contrary, for purposes of competition analysis, it is no longer possible to distinguish meaningfully between the competitive characteristics of broadband markets and other IT markets, and accordingly, there is no basis for asymmetric regulatory treatment. Accordingly, ex ante oversight of competition by the FCC should be replaced by the same ex post enforcement framework that applies to the rest of the Internet ecosystem.

1

Introduction

It is increasingly apparent that markets for broad-band communications services share many of the "high-tech" characteristics found in other information technology (IT) markets, including rapid innovation, declining costs, product differentiation and competitive price discrimination, network effects, and "multi-sidedness."[1] These characteristics have important implications for competition analysis, including the need for increased focus on market dynamism and vertical relationships among market participants, a reduced emphasis on traditional structural presumptions, and increased reliance on case-by-case analysis.

Some scholars suggest competition in IT markets is so naturally intense, or that the risks of policy error are sufficiently high, that enforcers should apply a reduced level of antitrust scrutiny.[2] Others argue that IT markets are in some respects more prone to market failure than more traditional markets and hence deserve enhanced scrutiny.[3] The Federal Communications Commission's (FCC's) December 2010 Open Internet Order seems to endorse an extreme form of the latter view.[4] While the FCC presented a cursory "structural" assessment of the broadband market,[5] it ultimately concluded that the conduct it sought to deter does "not depend upon broadband providers having market power with respect to end users"[6] and, in fact, that the "broad purposes of this rule . . . cannot be achieved by preventing only those practices that are demonstrably anticompetitive or harmful to consumers."[7] Instead, the FCC determined that ex ante regulation of broadband providers' conduct in the "Internet ecosystem"[8] was justified based on arguments associated with network effects and multisidedness—theories that, it concluded, suggest that broadband Internet service providers (ISPs) might "set inefficiently high fees to edge providers"[9] or "withhold or decline to expand capacity."[10]

The FCC's acknowledgement that broadband markets have become integrated with the overall Internet ecosystem is reflective of a rapidly emerging consensus.[11] However, its decision to impose price controls and preemptively ban certain conduct, and to do so without finding that the conduct at issue was harmful to consumers, is not easily squared with mainstream academic opinion, which widely agrees that competition oversight of IT markets should be case-specific, narrowly tailored, and grounded in a concern for consumer welfare.[12]

As this is written, the FCC's authority to implement the Open Internet Order is being challenged in litigation before the US Court of Appeals for the DC Circuit.[13] Even if the challenge is successful, however, the FCC might assert its authority to impose ex ante rules on broadband services through a variety of means. For example, the agency imposes various regulations on wireless ISPs, based at least in part on its authority over the electromagnetic spectrum,[14] and, its recent expansion of the Federal Universal Service Fund—heretofore limited to supporting voice communications services—would subject broadband ISPs receiving support from the new Connect America Fund to de facto price regulation.[15] Moreover, even if the Open Internet Order is overturned, the FCC might well attempt to revisit its prior decisions declaring that broadband is not a telecommunications service and hence not subject to the FCC's core authority over common carriers. As recently as 2010, the FCC's general counsel issued a memorandum stating that it could declare broadband a Title II "communications service," subject to the full array of common carrier rules designed for monopoly providers of traditional telephone service.[16]

The central thesis here is that the expansion of ex ante FCC regulation over broadband markets is inconsistent with both academic consensus and market reality. To the contrary, the convergence of broadband with other IT markets argues for a convergence at the policy level as well: if it is no longer possible to distinguish meaningfully between the competitive characteristics of broadband markets and other IT markets, the basis for asymmetric regulatory treatment—for ex ante regulation of broadband services and ex post antitrust scrutiny of other IT markets—is impossible to sustain. Further, if the choice is between applying modern competition principles to broadband and subjecting the rest of the Internet ecosystem to FCC-style regulation, the former course is far superior to the latter.

In this context, this paper examines the market for broadband services through the lens of the literature on competition in IT markets. I conclude that the competitive dynamics[17] of broadband markets are now substantially similar to those in other sectors of the Internet ecosystem and that competition oversight of broadband markets should therefore be brought into conformity with the ex post, case-specific approach applied to other IT markets. This discussion is organized around three sets of characteristics that distinguish competition in IT markets from competition in more traditional ones: dynamism, modularity, and network effects.

By *dynamism*, I refer to what is sometimes called "innovation competition" or "Schumpeterian competition." It is the idea that firms compete primarily by creating new and better products, as opposed to "static competition," in which firms compete to charge the lowest price for a homogenous and unchanging commodity. Markets characterized by rapid innovation are often associated with high rates of capital spending (for R&D and capital expenditures), economies of scale and scope, "competitive price discrimination," and product differentiation.

Modularity refers to what some have called "mix and match" competition: the ability to assemble bundles of complementary products from different suppliers, and the interoperability (for example, the existence of standards or of a technology "platform") that makes it possible to do so. Providers of complementary products in such markets must cooperate to make their products work together, but they also compete for the economic rents generated by a successful platform, including by seeking to become "customer facing."

Third, *network effects* are present in markets where the value of a product or service to each customer is affected by the number of other customers who use it, as with telephones and fax machines, for example. Multisided markets represent a particular form of network effects, in which some types of consumers attach value to the presence of other customer types, such as when stock exchanges compete for both listings and investors or newspapers compete for both readers and advertisers. Both phenomena represent what can also be referred to as demand-side complementarities or, to be more specific, demand-side economies of scale (network effects) and demand-side economies of scope (multisidedness).

Taken together, these characteristics cause the competitive dynamics of IT markets to differ from the competitive dynamics of more traditional ones. They help to explain, for example, why IT markets are often relatively concentrated yet typically exhibit high levels of rivalry and strong performance. All three sets of characteristics are present in broadband markets, which despite being relatively concentrated, evidence falling prices, rising output, rapid innovation, and few apparent instances of anticompetitive conduct.

The remainder of this paper is organized as follows. Section 2 briefly discusses the "structure-performance paradox," finding that, like many other IT markets, the broadband market exhibits both (a) relatively high levels of concentration by traditional metrics, and (b) strong performance in terms of output expansion, innovation, and other metrics. Section 3 describes the broadband market from the perspective of the three themes I described—dynamism, modularity, and network effects—and shows how the economic phenomena associated with these concepts affect the competitive dynamics of broadband markets, causing them to behave like IT markets. Section 4 outlines some specific implications of this analysis for competition oversight of broadband markets, concluding overall that the dynamism and complexity of broadband markets, and their interrelatedness with other elements of the Internet ecosystem, argue strongly against the sort of industrial policy–oriented, ex ante regulation practiced by the FCC. Section 5 provides a brief conclusion.

2

Broadband Competition:
The Structure-Performance Paradox

In a 1999 article on competition in the computer industry, Tim Bresnahan took note of an interesting paradox arising out of Andy Grove's description of the computer industry.[18] In *Only the Paranoid Survive* (1995), Grove had argued that the industry had shifted from a "vertical" to a "horizontal" structure comprised of independent competitors at each of several layers (for example, Dell and Hewlett-Packard selling computers and Microsoft and Apple selling operating systems).[19] Moreover, Grove said, competition in this new "mix and match" model, was more intense than in the old vertically integrated structure in which firms like IBM and DEC competed to sell the entire "stack" of complementary products and services. Bresnahan noted that Grove's assessment was widely shared: "Almost all market participants characterize the 'Silicon Valley' style of industry organization as more competitive than the 'IBM style.'"[20]

For economists, Bresnahan pointed out, Grove's conclusions presented something of a puzzle:

> The puzzle arises when one looks at [the new horizontal structure] with an industrial organization economist's eyes, especially with an antitrust economist's eyes. Several of these 'competitive' horizontal layers have very concentrated structures, typically suggesting a dominant firm and fringe model. . . . [A]n elementary structural analysis shows a puzzle. How can this be so competitive?[21]

As Bresnahan said in 1999, "Resolving the puzzle is the key to understanding computer industry competition."[22] The same is true for broadband markets today.

The Structural Presumption

Although recent developments have begun to shift the focus of competition analysis away from structural presumptions,[23] both the antitrust agencies and the telecommunications regulatory agencies—the FCC and state public utility commissions—continue in many cases to base their analyses largely on traditional concepts of market definition and concentration. While rebuttable, the "structural presumption" is that, other things equal, highly concentrated markets are more likely than unconcentrated ones to be subject to the exercise of market power.[24]

Market power takes two basic forms. First, firms may possess traditional market power: the ability to raise price above the competitive level, reduce quality, or otherwise deprive consumers of the benefits of competition (for example, by slowing innovation). Traditional market power is manifested through either coordinated effects (explicit or tacit collusion)[25] or unilateral effects; the latter is typically associated with some form of locational market power[26] resulting from geography or product differentiation, which allows a firm to raise prices (or lower quality) to a subset of consumers without having to fear that they will switch to competitors in sufficient numbers to make the price increase unprofitable.[27] Second, firms may possess exclusionary market power: the ability to deprive competitors or potential competitors of inputs or access to markets or to raise their costs, reducing competition in the long run.

Traditional analysis invariably concludes that markets for broadband service are relatively concentrated: as illustrated in figure 1, there typically are two wireline suppliers and three wireless providers serving each community. Moreover, although many think that the next generation of 4G wireless services

FIGURE 1
US RESIDENTIAL BROADBAND AVAILABILITY BY MODALITY, 2009

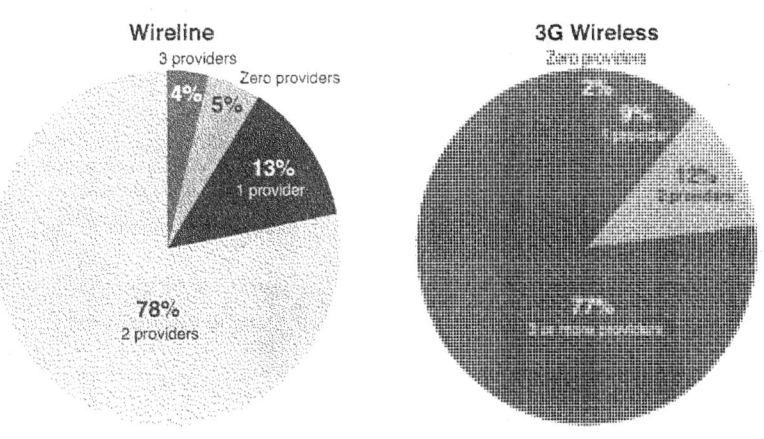

SOURCE: Federal Communications Commission, Office of Broadband Initiatives, *Connecting America: The National Broadband Plan* (March 2010).

(based on LTE or WiMAX technology) will serve as an economic substitute for wireline broadband, there is not yet a consensus that that moment has arrived; hence, the wireline and wireless markets are often considered separately.[28] Finally, it would seem that entry barriers in wireline service are high enough to make new entry unlikely, and even in wireless, some argue that the costs of acquiring spectrum and building out a network limit the likelihood of entry.[29]

In its Open Internet Order, the FCC summed up the structural evidence as follows:

(1) The wireline broadband market is highly concentrated, with most consumers served by at most two providers; (2) the prospects for additional wireline competition are dim due to the high fixed and sunk costs required to provide wireline broadband service; and (3) the extent to which mobile wireless offerings will compete with wireline offerings is unknown.[30]

As noted above, the FCC ultimately refused to base its net neutrality rules on a finding that broadband

ISPs had traditional market power.[31] In other contexts, however, it has not hesitated to rely on structural evidence as a basis for findings of market power. In its 2010 Qwest Forbearance Order, for example, the FCC conducted a "traditional market power analysis,"[32] determined that "the retail mass market for wireline services in Phoenix remains highly concentrated with two dominant providers, Qwest and Cox,"[33] and was "unable to find that Qwest is subject to effective competition in the Phoenix MSA."[34]

Similar findings frequently play important roles in the FCC's analyses of wireless competition. In its recent Data Roaming Order, it justified the new rules in part on grounds that they would "promot[e] competitive choice in broadband services."[35] Similarly, the FCC cited the desire to increase the number of wireless broadband providers in its decision granting a wireless license transfer from Skyterra Communications to Harbinger Capital Partners Funds.[36] In 2010, for the first time in many years, the FCC failed to find the wireless market "effectively competitive," at least in part as a result of concerns about "continued industry concentration."[37] In 2011, the Department of Justice sued to block the acquisition of AT&T by T-Mobile in part because "the proposed merger would result in an HHI [Herfindahl-Hirschman Index] of more than 3,100 for mobile wireless telecommunications services, an increase of nearly 700 points. These numbers substantially exceed the thresholds at which mergers are presumed to be likely to enhance market power."[38]

More broadly, the structuralist approach has been a touchstone of groups advocating increased regulation, which have frequently characterized the wireline broadband market as a "cozy duopoly"[39] and argued that even the wireless market has an insufficient number of competitors to achieve a competitive result.[40] According to Cooper,

> Most communications markets have a small number of competitors. In the high speed Internet market, there are now two main competitors and the one with the dominant market share has a substantially superior technology. When or whether there will be a third, and how well it will be able to compete, is unclear. This situation is simply not sufficient to sustain a competitive outcome.[41]

For structural purists, a market with even six competitors would not be sufficiently unconcentrated to produce competitive results.[42]

The predicted consequences of high concentration, according to the structuralists, include high prices; reduced output; retarded innovation; and frequent, successful exclusionary conduct. In a joint 2007 filing at the FCC, for example, the Consumer Federation of America, Consumers Union, and Free Press argued that, as a result of high concentration and insufficient regulation, US hroadband connections were "slow, expensive, and not universally available."[43] Pointing to inadequate competition in the wireless market and the failure of the FCC to impose network neutrality regulation, the groups complained that wireless broadband networks "actively block the use of unapproved equipment," that "certain applications and services are prohibited

(e.g., VoIP)," and that network operators were seeking to turn wireless services into "a proprietary network of 'walled garden' content and services."[44]

The Performance Paradox

The broadband industry has consistently confounded structuralist predictions of poor performance, thus presenting precisely the same type of paradox Bresnahan identified in Grove's analysis of the "new" computer industry. Despite (or perhaps because of) high concentration, broadband output is rising, prices are falling, quality is increasing, firms are making large investments in new technologies and infrastructures, rivalry is intense, and there are few significant instances (some would say none) of demonstrated anticompetitive conduct.

While a complete discussion of the performance of US broadband markets is beyond the scope of this paper, a lengthy treatment is hardly necessary to reject the "cozy duopoly" hypothesis. Indeed, the evidence that broadband markets are performing well can be found in the FCC's own reports, beginning with the 2010 *National Broadband Plan* (NBP) report, which concluded, "Due in large part to private investment and market-driven innovation, broadband in America has improved considerably in the last decade. More Americans are online at faster speeds than ever before."[45] Research performed for the FCC in conjunction with the NBP report found that real wireline broadband prices fell at a 5 percent annual rate between 2004 and 2009,[46] while evidence reported by the FCC in its regular *CMRS Competition Reports* shows rapid declines in prices for both mobile voice and data.[47]

Quality-adjusted broadband prices have declined primarily as a result of higher speeds, which in turn reflect the deployment of more capable infrastructure. The NBP report surveyed deployment plans of new broadband infrastructures by major broadband providers. As shown in figure 2, it found that both telephone companies (deploying either fiber-to-the-premises [FTTP] or advanced DSL infrastructures)

FIGURE 2
SELECTED FIXED BROADBAND INFRASTRUCTURE UPGRADES

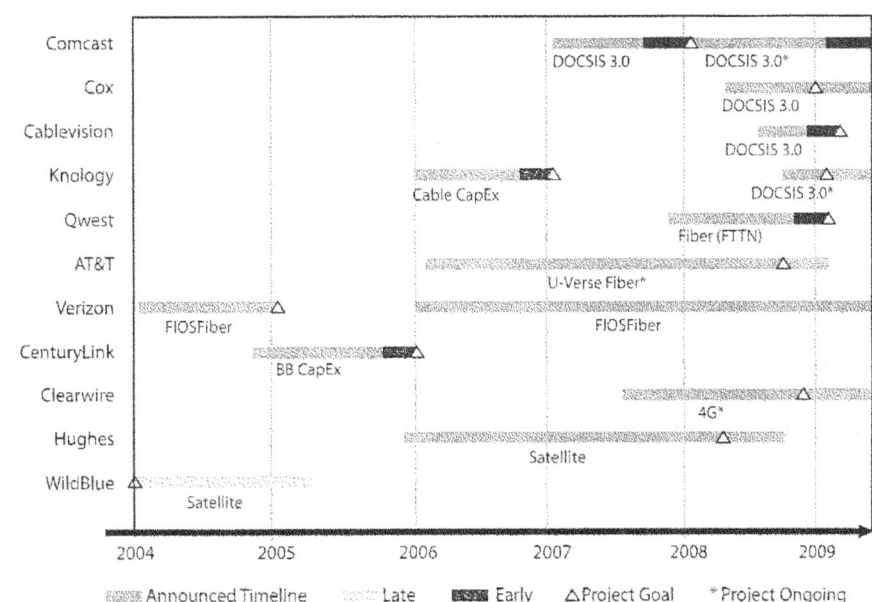

SOURCE: Federal Communications Commission, Omnibus Broadband Initiative, *Connecting America: The National Broadband Plan* (March 2010), 39.

and cable companies (rolling out third-generation DOCSIS 3.0 infrastructure) were in the process of completing upgrades to their networks and that Clearwire had begun rolling out a nationwide 4G network based on WiMAX technology. Separately, the report noted that several wireless carriers had announced plans to roll out 4G wireless networks based on LTE technology, including Verizon, which had committed to upgrading its entire 3G infrastructure to 4G by 2013.[48]

In another report prepared in conjunction with the NBP, Atkinson and Schulz surveyed the capital expenditures of major US communications companies, estimating investments for 2008 through 2015 based on actual spending and announced plans, concluding that cumulative private-sector investment in broadband infrastructure over the eight-year period would total $244 billion.[49] The NBP report specifically

concludes that high levels of investment are the result of competition among network operators.[50]

Declining prices, improving quality, and increasing availability have led to increased adoption and output. In a report released in February 2011, the National Telecommunications and Information Administration found that broadband penetration increased to 68.2 percent in October 2010 from 63.5 percent a year earlier and just 19.9 percent in 2003. Broadband is the fastest-propagating technology in history, and mobile broadband is propagating even more rapidly than wireline.[51]

There is no evidence that countries that have taken a more regulatory approach have achieved superior performance as a result. Despite entreaties from advocates of increased regulation to conclude that the United States was "falling behind" other nations,[52] the NBP report refused to weigh in, concluding only that "each country's experiences and challenges have critical differences."[53] In fact, US markets appear to be performing well on a variety of metrics, including the deployment of fiber-to-the-premises and of 4G wireless, where the United States has a clear lead.[54] A recent Nielsen report found that among nine Western nations, America was second only to Switzerland in broadband connection speeds.[55]

In addition to strong performance, other metrics are also inconsistent with the structuralist hypothesis. First, no credible evidence exists that broadband ISPs earn above-market returns. For example, Hazlett and Weisman analyze financial market valuations of telephone and cable companies and find no evidence of market power,[56] while Darby presents evidence that broadband providers earn lower returns than the Standard and Poor's average and significantly lower returns than many high-tech firms.[57]

Second, it is worth noting that despite the sunk costs associated with entry, new broadband providers have entered the market, and further entry is likely. In the mobile arena, Clearwire represents a recent case of new entry, and Dish is seeking government permission to acquire the spectrum necessary to enter. Moreover, in an important sense, *all* wireless broadband providers are recent entrants into the market for 3G services, and either new or aspiring entrants into the market for 4G.[58] On the wireline side, infrastructure upgrades undertaken by wireline carriers have allowed them to enter and compete in new product markets (for example, cable companies in telephony, telephone companies in video).[59] Such behavior is not consistent with the structuralist prediction that "cozy duopolists" would refuse to enter one another's markets.

Third, structuralist predictions of exclusionary conduct and stifled innovation have not been borne out by experience. To the contrary, whereas the structuralists predicted that wireline providers would seek to emulate the "walled garden" of the early wireless marketplace—in which carriers chose equipment, limited access to outside content and applications, and so forth—the opposite has occurred: the advent of 3G wireless led to the opening up of the "wireless ecosystem," with content, application, device, and companies like Apple, Google, Microsoft, and Samsung taking the lead in defining the wireless value proposition.[60] Rather than limiting the devices and applications on their networks, mobile providers are now competing on the basis of the types and number of third-party applications available through their phones and devices.[61] Nor is innovation limited to the wireless sphere. "Over-the-top" video services such as Netflix now account for the bulk of Internet traffic, and broadband ISPs are responding by offering such services such as TV Everywhere and applications that allow customers to watch live television programming on their iPads using home Wi-Fi connections.[62] On the other hand, the FCC's Open Internet Order could cite only two adjudicated instances of anticompetitive conduct (one of which, Comcast's alleged discrimination against BitTorrent, has since been overturned in the courts) and none since 2007.[63]

The fact that the broadband market outperforms structuralist predictions is not surprising in the context of modern competition analysis, which recognizes that large numbers of competitors are not necessary to achieve competitive results. As the NBP report noted,

> The lack of a large number of wireline, facilities-based providers does not necessarily mean competition among broadband providers is inadequate. While older economic models of competition emphasized the danger of tacit collusion with a small number of rivals, economists today recognize that coordination is possible but not inevitable under such circumstances. Moreover, modern analyses find that markets with a small number of participants can perform competitively.[64]

"The critical question," the report continued (quoting from the Department of Justice's ex parte comments), "is not 'some abstract notion of whether or not broadband markets are 'competitive' but rather 'whether there are policy levers that can be used to produce superior outcomes.'"[65] Before turning to that question, we first seek a better understanding of the competitive dynamics of the Internet ecosystem generally and modern broadband markets in particular.

3

The Competitive Dynamics of Broadband

Bresnahan began his 1999 article on the computer industry by explaining that, for an industry economist, "the first task is to understand how competition works in the industry, and how structure influences and is influenced by competition. Only when that task is done can we reasonably hope to say what kinds of industry structures public policy should favor and how."[66] In the same spirit, this section describes how competition works in the modern broadband industry. The conclusion, to summarize, is that competition in the broadband industry is shaped by the same forces as in the rest of the Internet ecosystem, like the markets for computers, content, applications, software, and so forth. As I have explained, those characteristics can be thought of as falling into three broad categories: dynamism, modularity, and network effects.

First, because broadband markets are dynamic, the primary focal points of competition are innovation and product differentiation. Broadband ISPs, like other Internet firms, seek to outpace their rivals, and earn economic rents, by developing superior products and services. To do so, they make large, nonrecoverable investments in R&D, equipment, and other fixed assets. To recover these costs (which must be recovered, at least in expectation, or the investments would not be made), ISPs must charge at least some customers prices in excess of marginal cost, which is to say they must price discriminate or, as some prefer to say, engage in "differential pricing."[67] To price discriminate, they must differentiate their products. This causal chain (or, more accurately, causal circle)—invest, innovate, differentiate, price discriminate, invest, and so forth—is central to the competitive dynamics of all IT markets, including broadband. (See figure 3.)

Second, broadband products serve as complementary inputs in larger systems. The ability to assemble different types of inputs into value-producing systems is referred to as modularity, which is made possible, in turn, by the existence of standards or "platforms." Competition may occur both within platforms (intraplatform competition) and between them (interplatform competition). As I will discuss, broadband services are one of four types of modules (along with applications, content, and devices) that comprise Internet platforms. (See figure 4.)

Third, broadband markets are, like other IT markets, subject to both demand-side economies of scale (network effects) and demand-side economies of scope (multisidedness). Markets are said to be subject to network effects if the value attached to a product or service by each consumer is a function of how many other consumers use it. In multisided markets, some types of consumers (for example, content and application providers) value the presence of other types of consumers (for example, subscribers). (See figure 5.)

Network effects and multi-sidedness typically go hand in hand. For example, a vertically integrated content and application aggregator and device manufacturer (for example, Apple) may place a higher value on distributing its products through a broadband ISP with many customers than one with fewer customers, not only because it will sell more iPhones, but also because doing so increases its own value to the content and applications providers (the other participants in its platform) on which it depends for complements.

It is worth noting that the term *platform* is used to describe both modularity (referring to institutions that facilitate the exploitation of complementarities between products) and multisidedness (institutions that facilitate complementarities between economic actors). Thus, both the Windows/Intel ("Wintel") computer environment (facilitating interaction between complementary

FIGURE 3
CYCLE OF DYNAMIC INNOVATION

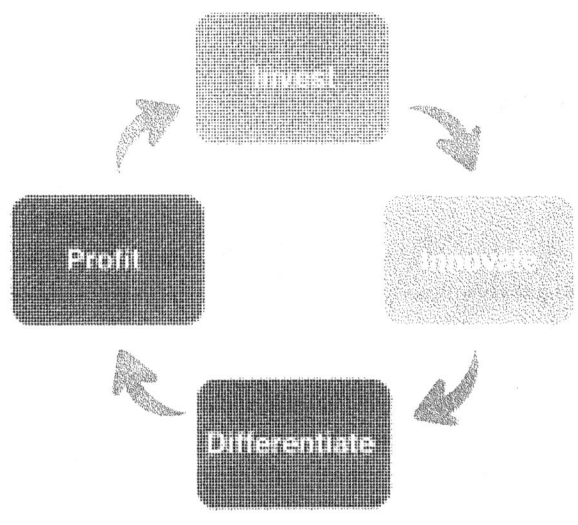

SOURCE: Author.

FIGURE 4
ELEMENTS OF AN INTERNET ECOSYSTEM PLATFORM

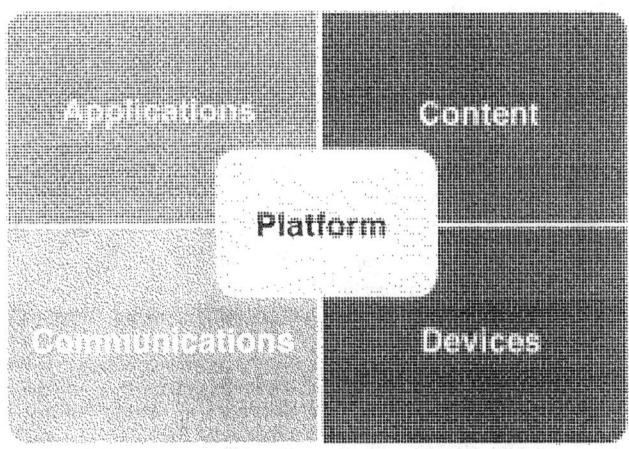

SOURCE: Author.

124

FIGURE 5
THE ROLE OF ISPS IN A TWO-SIDED MARKET

SOURCE: Author.

computer products) and the local newspaper (facilitating interactions between advertisers and readers) are referred to as "platforms."[68]

We now turn to a more extensive examination of how these characteristics manifest themselves in broadband markets.

Dynamism

Markets characterized by rapid technological change are often referred to as "dynamic." Market structures may change rapidly, and firms must innovate and adapt just to keep up; today's dominant firm may be seeking bankruptcy protection tomorrow. But technological change does not happen of its own accord: innovation demands investment, not only to invent new products (R&D), but also to bring them to market (capital expenditures). Such investments tend to be both sunk (unrecoverable) and fixed (insensitive to output). As a result, industries characterized by

rapid technological change are generally subject to economies of scale and engage in efficient price discrimination, enabled by product differentiation, to earn back past investments and attract the capital needed to make new ones.[69]

In innovation markets, firms compete not only by seeking to offer the best products at the lowest prices, but also—and primarily—by making investments intended to create entire new categories of products or substantially reduce the costs of making existing ones. According to Baumol, "Innovation has replaced price as the name of the game in a number of important industries. The computer industry is only the most obvious example, whose new and improved models appear constantly, each manufacturer battling to stay ahead of its rivals."[70] Innovation competition plays a central role in economic progress[71] and likely contributes far more to long-run economic prosperity than the static efficiency gains associated with achieving the competitive result in traditional models.[72]

Telecommunications markets were not traditionally thought of as "innovative" in this sense, but the convergence of telecommunications with digital computing has accelerated the pace of change. Mobile wireless markets are the most obvious example, with new technologies now being introduced roughly every five years as the market progresses from 3G to 4G wireless standards (WiMAX and LTE).[73] However, wireline networks are also evolving rapidly: current fiberoptic networks deliver speeds four times as fast as those initially introduced in the early 2000s[74]; techniques developed in just the past few years (known as vectoring and pair bonding) now allow even legacy copper networks to deliver broadband speeds up to 100 Mbps.[75]

One important characteristic of innovation competition is its riskiness: innovation markets have a win-or-lose aspect, where the firms that innovate successfully are rewarded with high margins, while those that do not die off.[76] The leading exponent of dynamic competition, Joseph Schumpeter, famously coined the phrase "creative destruction" to describe it. As Schumpeter put it, innovation competition "strikes not at the margins of the profits and the outputs of the existing firms but at their foundations and their very lives."[77]

Again, telecommunications markets were not traditionally thought of in such terms; for decades, AT&T was the prototypical safe investment, and telephone companies enjoyed the steady returns associated with rate-of-return regulation until the mid-1990s.[78] But investors in firms such as Clearwire, with its bet-the-firm commitment to WiMAX technology—or for that matter, in Verizon, with its arguably even more audacious bet on fiber-to-the-home—can have little doubt that everything is at risk. Firms that bet wrong do, in fact, cease to exist: AT&T, which made losing bets on everything from cell phones (it sold, then bought) to cable companies (it bought, then sold), survives today in name only.

Dynamism has several important implications for competition analysis. First, and perhaps most obviously, rapid technological change places a burden on antitrust enforcers to take a forward-looking approach to the assessment of market power. Katz and Shapiro, for example, note that "under the Schumpeterian view that competition consists of repeated waves of innovation that sweep aside 'dominant' incumbents, current product-market shares may indicate very little about the future of the industry or about whether any given firm will possess significant market power."[79] Similarly, Posner, writing in 2001, concluded, "Because of the extraordinary pace of innovation, not only in computers but in communications technology . . . the networks that have emerged in the new economy do not seem particularly secure against competition."[80] The US Department of Justice made essentially the same point in a 2010 filing before the FCC:

> In any industry subject to significant technological change, it is important that the evaluation of competition be forward-looking rather than based on static definitions of products and services. Insight can best be gained by looking at product life cycles, the replacement of older technologies by newer ones, and the barriers facing suppliers that offer those newer technologies. In the case of broadband services, it is clear that the market is shifting generally in the direction of faster speeds and additional mobility.[81]

In one respect, at least, the FCC seems to have taken this advice to heart: Looking at potential future technological developments in the broadband market, the NBP report concluded today's telephone companies—dominant firms, in the eyes of many—are at risk of obsolescence if they are not able to find a way effectively to compete with cable's cost-effective DOCSIS 3.0 technology.[82]

The extent to which dynamism erodes market power, and perhaps reduces the need for antitrust enforcement in general, is a matter of contention.[83] However, many agree on a narrower point: that the traditional presumption against market concentration does not carry over to innovation markets. As Katz and Shelanski explain:

A proper understanding of innovation-based competition means that, in some markets, antitrust enforcement cannot rely on its long-established presumptions that increased concentration or market power will reduce innovation or harm consumer welfare. A merger from four to three firms, or even from three to two, while raising a presumption of increased short-run power over price and output, does not so easily raise a presumption of reduced development and deployment of new technology.[84]

In other words, to the extent market performance is measured by the pace of innovation, there is simply no basis for presuming an inverse relationship between concentration and performance.

Another important implication of dynamism in IT markets is the importance of economies of scale, which lead ultimately to competitive price discrimination. As Baumol notes, innovative industries spend substantial proportions of their revenues on fixed costs such as research and development. He observes, "These outlays [on R&D and other innovative activities] are substantial, amounting to more than 10 percent of total annual revenue in industries such as communications and pharmaceuticals. In the computer software industry they may well be higher."[85] Such costs can be recouped only through high margins. As Shapiro explains:

Since R&D costs often do not vary with the scale of output, such fixed costs are common in innovative industries. In my experience it is common in the technology sector for firms to follow a rule of thumb that involves investing some percentage of revenues into R&D; hence, long-term viability requires sufficient margins to fund ongoing R&D efforts. Fixed costs also are very common in industries that create informational content. Indeed, in some of these markets, such as those for movies or music, that involves (sic) "hits" and "duds," it is well understood that the large margins earned

on the "hits" are necessary to compensate for the larger number of "duds" that are inevitable.

For all of these reasons, competitive prices are often above marginal cost in innovative industries, and sometimes far above marginal cost.[86]

The problem of defraying fixed costs in industries with economies of scale is a familiar one, especially to students of regulated industries (like traditional telecommunications), who recognize it as the central challenge posed by natural monopoly. Economic efficiency requires that prices be set equal to marginal cost, but marginal cost is always below average cost in industries with downward-sloping average cost curves over the relevant range of output; thus, setting price equal to marginal cost ensures the firm earns negative returns and, having anticipated the problem, never enters the market in the first place. As Varian explains:

Many important industries involve technologies that exhibit increasing returns to scale, large fixed and sunk costs, and significant economies of scope. Two important examples of such industries are telecommunications services and information services. In each of these cases the relevant technologies involve high fixed costs, significant joint costs and low, or even zero, marginal costs. Setting prices equal to marginal cost will generally not recoup sufficient revenue to cover the fixed costs and the standard economic recommendation of "price at marginal cost" is not economically viable. Some other mechanism for achieving efficient allocation of resources must be found.[87]

The efficient solution is price discrimination. As Wallsten explains in the context of broadband, "Because [broadband] carriers must recover the high fixed costs of investment, average prices must exceed marginal costs if providers are to continue investing in their networks. The most efficient way to recover those fixed costs is to charge different types of consumers different prices."[88] Such price discrimination is efficient to the extent that it reflects Ramsey pricing principles: when price-cost margins are set in inverse proportion to the elasticities of demand of different customer groups so that the least price-sensitive customers shoulder the fixed costs by paying prices above average cost, while the most price-sensitive are offered prices at or near marginal cost (below average cost).

For many years, economists believed that price discrimination was impossible in competitive markets, since competitors would always have an incentive to undercut ("cream skim") above-cost prices. Indeed, the expectation that competition would make price discrimination impossible led economists for many years to suppose that the presence of price discrimination was a certain indicator of market power. As it turns out, neither proposition is true: competition does not preclude price discrimination, and price discrimination does not imply market power.[89]

Indeed, recent work by Baumol and others has led to a growing recognition of the ubiquity and significance of the practice, especially in IT markets.[90] As Baumol and Swanson explain in an important 2003 article, competitive price discrimination is not just *desirable* in markets with high fixed costs and heterogeneous consumers, but also *necessary* and *inevitable*. Moreover, the prices charged are generally efficient (reflecting Ramsey pricing), and so long as the market is sufficiently competitive, the price-discriminating firms earn only competitive returns.[91]

The economic imperative to differentiate products has a profound impact on competition in the Internet ecosystem: it means that individual firms compete to create new products and new product attributes that serve as effective differentiators—attributes that create sufficient added value to cause some cohort of consumers to be willing to pay a price greater than marginal cost.[92] Thus, broadband service providers seek to differentiate both their wireline (FiOS vs. U-Verse vs. DOCSIS 3.0) and wireless (LTE vs. HSPA+ vs. WiMAX) communications offerings.[93] At least equally important, they also compete by seeking to assemble the most compelling combinations of products for consumers (those that generate

the most value for at least some subsets of consumers).[94] Thus, at the same time that they are innovating internally, broadband ISPs are also collaborating with suppliers of complementary inputs (mobile wireless devices, high-capacity DVRs, video applications for iPads, TV Everywhere services, and so forth) to generate compelling bundles of products and services that differentiate them from their competitors.

To reiterate, what I have described is a causal chain with direct implications for both the competitive dynamics of broadband markets and the challenges faced by competition authorities in evaluating them. High rates of innovation (dynamism) imply large sunk costs, which must be recouped through price discrimination, but price discrimination is possible only if products can be sufficiently differentiated to allow for higher margins on at least some sales.[95] Thus, firms are constantly engaged in a search for product-differentiating attributes in their own products; in markets characterized by modularity, in the complementary products produced by others; or, in multisided markets, in the types of customers to whom they cater.

Modularity

In its FCC filing on the *National Broadband Plan*, the Department of Justice concluded that "Broadband services are one part of a wider information technology ecosystem that ultimately delivers value to consumers."[96] The statement rings true, but an economist cannot help but ask: precisely what does it mean to be "part of an ecosystem"?

The answer lies in the related concepts of modularity (an engineering term) and complementarity (an economic one). Modularity refers to standards (or "platforms") that allow different products (or "modules") to interoperate, while complementarity refers to the fact that the products generate greater benefits if used together than if used independently.[97] In IT markets, it is commonplace for modules to be perfect complements, meaning that they generate no value at all unless used in conjunction with other modules as part of a platform (a personal computer, an operating system, and one or more types of applications software).[98] Thus, to say that a product or service is part of the Internet ecosystem is to say that it is one of the complementary modules operating together on one of the many platforms that comprise the "platform of platforms"[99] called the Internet.

It is conventional to classify the modules that make up Internet platforms into four categories: applications, communications (broadband), content, and devices.[100] Further, an Internet platform can be defined as a system that contains at least one of each type of module, without which it would be unable to function; that is, the term "Internet platform" can sensibly be defined such that the four types of modules are perfect complements.

The recognition that broadband comprises just one of four equally necessary components of all Internet platforms has important implications for how we think about the competitive dynamics of the Internet ecosystem. In particular, it becomes clear from this perspective that one of the central metaphors in the policy discussion about broadband regulation—the notion that broadband networks are at the "core" of the Internet while content, applications, and devices are at the "edge"[101]—is fundamentally misleading and economically incorrect. Although it is certainly understandable that the modern telecommunications intelligentsia would see broadband as the center of the Internet ecosystem (just as pre-Copernican astronomers, seeing the universe from their earthbound perspective, mistakenly believed the Earth was the center of the universe), it is not. For purposes of competition analysis, at least, broadband is a complement among complements, a module among modules.

This realization does not end the debate about appropriate competition policy for broadband and other Internet services, but it does reframe it. First, it explains why it is incorrect to argue, as the FCC does in the Open Internet Order, that broadband ISPs differ from "edge" providers because they "control access to the Internet for their subscribers and for anyone

wishing to reach those subscribers" and, on this basis alone, to "find broadband providers distinguishable from other participants in the Internet market-place."[102] The same could be said for the providers (collectively) of any essential input to Internet platforms, including operating systems, browsers, Internet access devices, and so forth. (For example, it is equally true that operating system providers "control access to the Internet for their subscribers and for anyone wishing to reach those subscribers.") Going further, the ability to cut off access to the entire Internet is hardly necessary to raise competition issues: it may be sufficient, in theory, for a device manufacturer to restrict interoperability with a software program, or for a search engine operator to decline to show results from a competitor's sites. Nothing is unique, in other words, about the ability of broadband ISPs to affect— for competitive reasons or otherwise—how various modules interoperate, or fail to interoperate, on Internet platforms.[103]

To understand the competitive dynamics of broadband markets, it is necessary to dispense altogether with the edge versus core metaphor and focus instead on the roles played by broadband ISPs in two types of competition: competition between producers of modules within platforms (intraplatform competition) and competition between platforms (interplatform competition).[104] I will discuss both types of competition in this section and the following one.

To begin, the central economic function of a platform is to strike the optimal balance between the benefits and costs of modularity (in this context, interoperability) on one hand and the benefits and costs of integration on the other.[105] The primary benefit of modularity is that it allows firms (and the platform or platforms in which they participate) to capture both the benefits of specialization (of specializing in the production of one or a few modules) while still benefiting from the economies of scale and scope made possible by participation in a widely distributed platform.[106] But modularity also imposes costs. Most obviously, the design and engineering costs of achieving interoperability across different products (porting costs) may outweigh the benefits.[107]

Modularity can also interfere with the ability of entrepreneurs to appropriate returns on investment,[108] or (in cases of complementary monopoly products) inhibit efforts to avoid "double marginalization" through vertical integration.[109] Successful platforms achieve a mix of interoperability and integration that maximizes overall value, given the technical and economic context of the market in question and are capable, over time, of adjusting to change.

Given the obvious complexity of this balancing exercise, it might seem that the challenge of creating and maintaining a stable interface would best be solved through centralized decision making. That is, regardless of whether the platform operator opts for relative modularity (like Android) or a more integrated approach (like Apple), intuition suggests that there will generally be a single "platform czar" calling the shots. This intuition, however, turns out to be wrong—or, to be more precise, true only as a special case.[110] In general, platform participants compete to control the direction of a platform and, by doing so, to affect how current and future economic rents are divided. Indeed, intraplatform competition is commonplace in the computer sector and in the broadband ISP sector as well.[111]

In a 1999 article, Bresnahan and Greenstein coined the term "divided technical leadership" to describe "a structure in which a number of firms possess the capability to supply key platform components."[112] As Bresnahan explains:

> Under divided technical leadership, there is no single vertically integrated firm with control over direction of a platform. Instead, a number of firms supply, in the short run, and invent, in the long run, platform components. Frequently, different firms will have positions of dominance in different layers. These firms must cooperate in the short run to serve their customers. They find themselves, however, in competition when it comes to invention.[113]

According to Bresnahan and Greenstein, divided technical leadership was the "inevitable" consequence of the emergence of client/server architectures, which "necessarily have divided technical leadership because they re-use components from other platforms," requiring an "aspiring client/server platform steerer" to "make progress on each component at or near the technical level of the leader of that component," an "extraordinarily difficult feat."[114]

Modularization has had the same effect in the Internet ecosystem, permitting the reuse of components across platforms, making it difficult or impossible for a single firm to steer the technological development of every module or component, and leading to divided technical leadership (intraplatform competition).[115] As Bresnahan puts it, intraplatform competition results in part from the fact that "a firm in one layer [of the platform] has every incentive to grab the rents of a firm in another layer."[116] Consider the following example, offered by Sallet:

> A consumer who buys a book from Amazon on her iPad using the AT&T wireless network engages in three separate transactions with three separate revenue streams, three price points, and three consumer relationships. But, and this is the critical point, the transactions are interdependent, and this interdependence—the shared value arising from the use of a package of complementary products—is what firms can bargain over. The bargaining may involve specific terms of a contractual relationship, such as exclusivity rights. It may involve payment from one firm to another for the ability to gain access to the package. It may be the purchase or subsidization of another firm's product for the ability to engage in joint marketing.[117]

Firms in the Internet ecosystem compete over rents by seeking to develop better products or superior brand images, or by leveraging control of some key input or attribute like intellectual property. For example, a recent study by Dedrick, Kraemer, and Linden analyzes the intraplatform competition for the rents generated by smartphones:

FIGURE 6
RETURN ON ASSETS FROM "ICONIC" SMARTPHONES

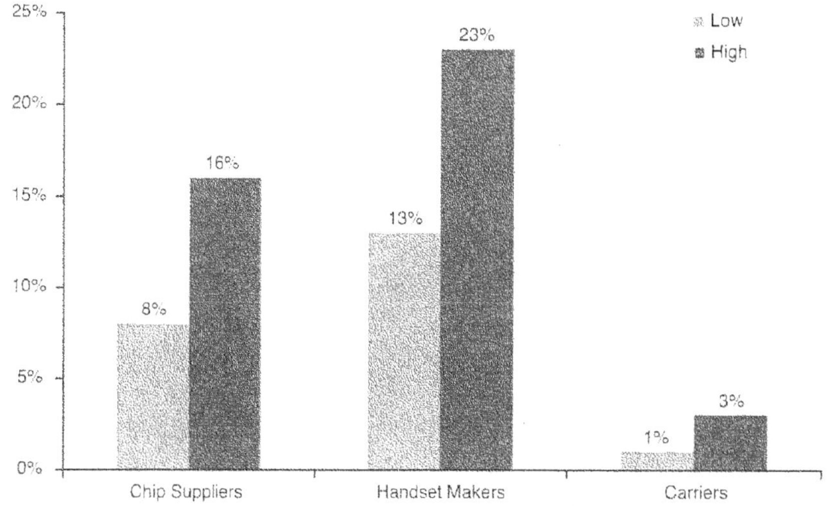

SOURCE: Table 4 in Jason Dedrick, Kenneth L. Kraemer, and Greg Linden, "The Distribution of Value in the Mobile Phone Supply Chain," *Telecommunications Policy* 35 (2011): 505–21.

In the smartphone market, carriers and handset makers each try to increase their leverage. Handset makers can accomplish this in part by building brand image with consumers. An excellent recent example of this is Apple's iPhone. Well regarded by consumers based on its hit line of iPod music players, Apple was reportedly able to negotiate a share of monthly iPhone subscriber revenue from AT&T.[118]

As shown in figure 6, Dedrick, Kraemer, and Linden examined the division of profits between chipset suppliers, handset makers, and wireless carriers and found that both chipset suppliers and handset makers earned far higher returns on assets than the carriers, who earned just 1–3 percent, largely as a result of the high capital costs incurred in creating and maintaining their networks.[119]

Based on their findings, Dedrick and colleagues conclude that "value-adding complementary goods

and services" are "shifting the key level of competition toward platforms based on operating systems, including those provided by software makers such as Google and Microsoft or by the handset makers such as Apple."[120]

The FCC has acknowledged the growing role of complementary goods in broadband competition, at least in the wireless market. For example, in its 2011 report on competition in the commercial mobile radio services market, it concluded:

In addition to network quality and advertising, a third component of non-price rivalry among mobile wireless service providers is the differentiation of the downstream products that they offer or that rely on their networks, including handsets/devices, operating systems, and mobile applications. . . . As mobile operating systems, and the functionalities and application stores they enable, play a more prominent role in a consumer's mobile wireless experience, consumers are showing an increasing loyalty to particular operating systems or device platforms.[121]

Although this acknowledgement is certainly a step in the right direction, it remains—in the spirit of the FCC's continuing adherence to the core-edge metaphor—carrier-centric. That is, differentiation is portrayed not as competition among platforms, but rather as "rivalry among mobile wireless service providers." Indeed, the discussion is contained in a section of the report labeled "Provider Conduct," implicitly suggesting that applications, content, and device providers are passive players in the competitive dynamics of wireless communications markets, rather than active participants in the competition within and among ecosystems.

In fact, platform competition takes place along virtually every dimension of product differentiation and involves all types of platform participants.[122] Broadband platforms compete to offer the most compelling content (like music and apps in wireless and access to video-on-demand or compelling sports programming in wireline), to provide the most compelling devices and applications software,[123] and to build and protect the most valuable intellectual property portfolios.[124] They also compete for brand recognition and the ability to be "customer facing."[125] Although broadband providers are often portrayed as customer facing, Sallet notes this is not always the case.[126] For example, a broadband ISP may play a visible but secondary role, as when a satellite TV company (for example, DirecTV) sells a triple-play package in which the wireline broadband service is provided by a phone company. In still other instances, the broadband provider may be completely "upstream" from the customer, such as when a consumer purchases a Kindle packaged with connectivity from a provider (originally Sprint, now AT&T) whose identity the consumer may not even know.

The role of modularity in modern broadband markets is perhaps best illustrated by the recent travails of formerly dominant cell phone supplier Nokia. As

Sallet points out, in February 2011, Nokia's CEO sent a memorandum to employees describing the firm's strategic challenge and "telling the tale of value creation"[127] in the Internet ecosystem:

> The battle of devices has now become a war of ecosystems, where ecosystems include not only the hardware and software of the device, but developers, applications, ecommerce, advertising, search, social applications, location-based services, unified communications and many other things. Our competitors aren't taking our market share with devices; they are taking our market share with an entire ecosystem. This means we're going to have to decide how we either build, catalyze or join an ecosystem.[128]

Three days later, Nokia announced its decision to enter a strategic alliance with Microsoft, in the hope of creating a new ecosystem capable of competing successfully with the likes of Apple; Android; and another formerly dominant but now fading provider, Research in Motion. The first major result of that collaboration—the Nokia Lumia 900, a 4G smartphone using the Windows operating system—rolled out in Spring 2012.[129] It was available exclusively on the AT&T network.[130]

Network Effects and Multisidedness

The third set of characteristics that distinguish IT markets from traditional ones is the presence of network effects and multisidedness. Network effects are demand-side economies of scale, meaning that the value of a product or service to consumers is a function of how many other consumers use it.[131] Multisided markets, by contrast, involve demand-side economies of scope: that is, participants in multisided markets are assumed to be heterogeneous and to value diversity rather than numbers.[132] A telephone network with identical subscribers evidences network effects, as its value is an increasing function of the number of subscribers. A telephone network to which businesses as well as consumers subscribe is also multisided, assuming both groups value the presence of the other type of subscriber.[133]

The competition literature on network effects has two main themes. One theme focuses on "tipping" and "lock-in" effects. Tipping means that if the value of a network increases with the number of subscribers, then (a) in equilibrium, there will only be one network, and (b) once one network establishes a lead, the balance of competition must "tip" in its favor, perhaps even if it is in other respects inferior.[134] Moreover, subscribers, recognizing that they will to some extent be "locked in" to their choices by the investments they make to join a network (in software, hardware, or learning), will tend to join the networks they expect to prevail, even if those networks would not otherwise be their first choice. Tipping and lock-in, in other words, suggest not only that network effects create a tendency toward monopolies, but that the resulting monopolies may be as much the result of chance as of merit.[135]

The second theme relates to the nature of competition in markets where tipping has not occurred. In this case, network effects tend to intensify competition, since the effects of changes in product characteristics (price, quality, availability of complements) are magnified by demand-side complementarities.[136]

Importantly, the tendency of network effects to result in monopoly is often counterbalanced by offsetting factors, including declining returns to scale and the presence of heterogeneous consumer tastes. As Weiser explains:

> The claim that network markets will invariably tip to a single standard . . . overlooks important reasons why network competition can occur. Significantly, the tipping prediction does not take account of the likely scenario where a network effect (the value of additional customers) declines at some point in time because the network size has reached critical mass or where a rival network is able to overcome the first mover's initial advantage. In markets where the critical mass is small

enough to accommodate multiple providers of a particular product or service, multiple firms will compete at the platform level, as they currently do in the market for video game consoles and cell phones. Moreover, it is quite clear that consumers' demand for variety can compensate for a lack of a strong network effect.[137]

Moreover, tipping is an issue only in the case of incompatible standards—Betamax versus VHS, QWERTY versus Dvorak, Apple versus Wintel, and so forth. If platforms are interoperable or, to use Rohlf's term, interlinked, then network effects are tied to total industry output—that is, to the size of all interlinked platforms, rather than to the size of any one platform.

It is noteworthy that broadband communications networks have been characterized by voluntary peering and transit arrangements (voluntary interconnection). For example, Economides notes that "dire predictions" that network effects would lead to the emergence of a dominant Internet backbone provider which would "degrade interconnection with a targeted rival" have not been borne out by experience; instead, "on the Internet we have observed a trend in the opposite direction (toward interconnection and full compatibility)."[138]

Despite universal interconnection of their communications functions, broadband networks experience indirect network effects by virtue of their participation in both "upstream" platforms associated with competing network architectures (for example, DOCSIS 3.0, FTTP/GPON, LTE, WiMAX) and "downstream" platforms associated with competing consumer platforms (for example, Android, iOS, Windows Phone).[139] In each case, ISPs benefit from belonging to larger platforms—and suffer, as seems to be the case with Sprint-Nextel's choice of WiMAX for its 4G standard, from choosing smaller ones. The value of a broadband ISP to an Internet platform can also be a function of indirect network effects. A device maker (like Nokia) may value distributing its devices through a larger broadband ISP not because its devices will be able to communicate with more customers (which, because of interlinking, is not the case), but because the larger ISP may have a larger customer base or more sales outlets and thus contribute to more sales of the device, in turn contributing to the value of the Nokia platform (for example, to suppliers of applications and content).

The presence of network effects, combined with the multisided nature of the market, provides an important constraint on downstream pricing power. For example, a broadband ISP that raises prices to downstream consumers has to take into account not just the lost revenues from consumers who switch to other providers, but also the resulting reduction in its value to producers of complements. And the feedback loop does not stop there: as customers flee to competitors, the competitors' value grows. As Rysman explains:

> If there are multiple competing market intermediaries, the effect of participation of one side on the other has even more bite. Consider two competing platforms pricing to consumers and sellers. As without competition, the consumer price depends on consumer demand, consumer cost, and the mark-up to sellers. But now, lowering the consumer price attracts consumers from the competing platform, which degrades the value of the competitor to buyers, and hence leads to a larger increase in buyer interest in the original platform. Hence, the "two-sidedness" of pricing can be more pronounced in competitive markets.[140]

Network effects intensify interplatform competition in nonprice dimensions as well. As Weiser notes, "standards competitions" create strong incentives for innovation:

> Standards competitions often will enable consumers to benefit from a more dynamic product market that includes more choices, enhanced products, and lower prices. To be sure, a head start or an installed base from a related technology is important to influencing the ultimate outcome of such a battle, but, regardless of the outcome, it seems clear that competition to control the standard will push companies to develop superior technology in the hope of establishing their preferred standard.[141]

Thus, network effects intensify both intra- and interplatform competition, while creating strong incentives for interoperability.[142] As Weiser explains, "where a firm sponsoring a platform standard faces competition, it is likely to provide open access to its platform in order to attract complementary products even without regulatory requirements that it do so,"[143] promoting competition within platforms and facilitating the entry of "independent" modules.[144]

Efforts to promote development of complements can also have more direct effects on competition in other layers. For example, Intel's decision to invest billions of dollars in wireless broadband ISP Clearwire was driven by its desire to catalyze growth in the WiMAX platform, of which Intel is the lead sponsor,[145] and Google's desire to foster development of a platform around its Android operating system was a driving force behind its decision to enter the device business.[146]

Multisidedness can intensify competition in the same way as network effects. Indeed, the two often go hand in hand: as explained above, for example, the downstream pricing power of a broadband ISP is attenuated by the combination of network effects and multisidedness, which together tie its value to upstream complementers to the volume of downstream customers. In addition, three other consequences of multisidedness have important consequences for broadband competition.

First, efficiency in two-sided markets demands price discrimination, in the sense that the very purpose of a two-sided platform is to set relative prices so as to achieve the optimal mix between the two types of participants (or, more broadly, the optimal mix between multiple participant groups).[147] Thus, in general, advertisers will be charged one price and readers a different one, and so forth. Moreover, to the extent customers on one or both sides of the market are heterogeneous, the case for price discrimination within customer groups is strengthened—since efficient price discrimination can lower prices to marginal consumers, bringing more of them to the platform and creating "external" benefits for customers on the other side.[148]

Second, multisided markets are also associated with the notion of "terminating monopoly": the notion that a platform operator (for example, a broadband ISP) might be able to exercise upstream market power by virtue of the fact that its downstream consumers "single home," or subscribe to only one broadband ISP.[149] As Rysman explains, the question of "multi-homing" vs. "single-homing" matters because

> The intermediary can be viewed as a monopolist over access to members that do not use other intermediaries. Hence, firms compete aggressively on the side that uses a single network in order to charge monopoly prices to the other side that is trying to reach them. As a result, competition between platforms can have large price effects on the side of the market that uses a single platform and little or no effect on the side that uses multiple platforms.[150]

As intuition suggests, however, the terminating monopoly problem is premised on the assumption that downstream consumers do not value the ability to access multiple upstream providers (they do not value diversity), so that the platform operator can threaten to exclude upstream providers without lowering the value of its platform to consumers.[151] This assumption is not valid in the market for broadband access, where consumers place a high value on the diversity of available applications, content, and devices.

Third, it is worth emphasizing that the literature on two-sided markets is in an early phase of development. The theoretical models are highly stylized (they fail to capture salient attributes of actual markets), and to the extent that they have been used to predict either the efficiency consequences or distributional implications of various policy proposals (for example, net neutrality), the predictions typically depend on strong assumptions both about the structure of the models and the values of various parameters.[152]

How Broadband Competition Works

To summarize, broadband markets are now characterized, like markets in the rest of the IT sector, by dynamism, modularity, network effects, and multisidedness. The competitive dynamics of such markets are shaped by complex interactions between market-specific factors on both the demand and supply sides, but the central tendencies are straightforward. Dynamism is shorthand for a causal circle in which firms compete by investing to create new products and, by succeeding, differentiate themselves sufficiently to earn an economic return on their investments, which attracts the capital needed to repeat the cycle. Modularity allows this process of innovation and differentiation to exploit the specialized capabilities of multiple firms to generate complementary products; it places producers of complementary goods in competition with one another over the current rents and future directions of the platforms in which they participate; and it creates a new type of competitor, competitive platforms, composed of loose and fluid alliances of complementers that may themselves belong to multiple platforms. Network effects and multisidedness function in many respects as competition "superchargers"—they magnify the effects of competitive choices through demand-side complementarities of scale and scope.

For purposes of competition analysis, broadband markets share all the key characteristics of other IT markets, including, specifically, the markets for Internet applications, content, and devices. Like other IT firms, broadband ISPs make large sunk cost investments. For many IT firms, such investments primarily take the form of intellectual property; for broadband ISPs, they are primarily telecommunications infrastructures. From an economic perspective, however, the effect is the same: in each case, firms invest to create products that are sufficiently unique and highly valued (by at least some consumers) to command prices that generate returns sufficient to compensate for not only the capital invested but also the risk of failure. Put simply, there is no economic difference between the risky investments made by companies like Sprint Nextel (in WiMAX) and Verizon (in FiOS) and the similarly risky investments made by companies like Facebook (in Instagram) or Intel (in WiMAX). In other words, broadband markets, like other IT markets, are characterized by dynamic competition.

Similarly, broadband ISPs, like other IT-sector firms, seek to assemble or participate in systems that create new value for at least some types of consumers, and they do so by choosing both the platforms they interoperate with and, when they function as platform leaders, the complementors they admit. Their decisions regarding interoperability are affected by both supply-side and demand-side economies of scale and scope, which create powerful incentives to increase volumes by maximizing system openness and capturing the benefits of modularity, but these incentives do not always overcome the costs of interoperability.[153]

Because of both supply- and demand-side economies of scale, broadband markets, like other IT-sector markets, are relatively concentrated. Moreover, as in other IT markets, firm-level entry may involve sector-specific costs (for example, patents and copyrights, access to content and distribution networks, a new semiconductor fabrication plant, the need to procure spectrum licenses). Yet the rapid pace of innovation associated with all of these markets forces incumbents to constantly reinvest, whether in intellectual property or in new network equipment, diluting the advantages of incumbency.[154]

4

Implications for Regulation and Competition Policy

The emergence of the Internet ecosystem has accelerated innovation, enhanced economic growth, and increased consumer welfare. The challenge for public policy is to develop and maintain a legal and regulatory framework that facilitates its continued development, including a framework for preventing anticompetitive conduct that harms consumers without stifling rivalry and entrepreneurship. In this section, I will begin by explaining why ex post antitrust oversight would be superior to ex ante regulation for broadband markets and close by discussing some of the broader implications for competition analysis and regulatory policy of the theory of broadband competition I have presented.

Replacing Regulation with Antitrust

Competition policy seeks to preserve competition and enhance consumer welfare while avoiding the temptation to protect or promote particular competitors, industries, or technologies. In a world of imperfect information, this must necessarily involve weighing benefits and costs, including the benefits and costs of waiting to intervene (weighing "Type I" against "Type II" error).[155] In general, the balancing of benefits and costs places a high value on the recognition that, absent clear evidence of market failure, competition provides powerful incentives for the efficient allocation of resources to their highest valued uses,[156] and it recognizes that the exercise of government authority is itself not without costs, including the incentives it creates for "rent seeking" or "taxation by regulation."

With these principles in mind, competition policy in the United States has generally relied upon ex post antitrust enforcement over ex ante regulation. The exceptions have included, and to some extent still include, markets thought to be subject to natural monopoly (for example, electricity, pipelines, railroads, and telecommunications), as well as markets where, correctly or not, policymakers perceived a unique, compelling need for government intervention (for example, airlines and broadcasting).

The legacy of traditional communications regulation—in the form of the FCC and the fifty-state public utility commissions—remains in place. Until fairly recently, it had appeared that these legacy regulators would limit themselves primarily to traditional communications services—primarily to voice telephony (Title II of the Communications Act for landline service; Title III for mobile wireless) and to traditional broadcast (Title III) and cable (Title VI) video platforms—and not extend ex ante regulation to the Internet. As these traditional services were gradually subsumed into the Internet ecosystem, many believed, legacy regulatory structures would become less relevant.[157]

Two factors now suggest otherwise. First, the FCC's foray into "net neutrality" regulation—beginning in 2005 with its decision to adopt four "Open Internet Principles" (which it later sought to enforce in the Comcast-BitTorrent Order), and most recently with its issuance of the Open Internet Order—indicates the agency believes it is "compel[led] to protect and promote the Internet" and has "broad authority to promote competition, investment, transparency, and an open Internet."[158] Second, as noted above, both the FCC and state regulators continue to intensively regulate traditional communications services, promulgating and enforcing various forms of prescriptive regulations, including price controls, universal service programs, interconnection mandates, and open-access policies, the effects of which increasingly are spilling over onto the Internet.[159] At the same time, of course, most of the Internet ecosystem remains subject to traditional antitrust enforcement,[160] which is quite different both in operation (ex post vs. ex ante) and substance (antitrust being far less prescriptive and, because it develops over time through precedent, more evolutionary, than regulation).

The most obvious risk of this duplicative approach to competition regulation is the potential for confusion and inconsistency, and the obvious remedy is for policymakers to facilitate development of coherent, integrated approach to the regulation of all IT-sector markets, broadband included. This conclusion is not new and should not be controversial. As Farrell and Weiser put it in 2003,

> As the Internet, computer software, and telecommunications ("New Economy") industries converge, affected firms will increasingly seek clear and consistent legal rules. Moreover, courts reviewing the FCC's decisions in this area are increasingly pressuring the Commission to devise a regulatory regime more compatible with economic theory and antitrust policy.[161]

The factors that led Farrell and Weiser to this conclusion have only intensified in the intervening years, yet there is little apparent progress towards the integration they urged. Indeed, the incompatibilities between FCC regulatory policies on the one hand and economic theory and antitrust policy on the other continue to be significant.

Second, arguably the most fundamental distinction between antitrust and regulation is that the former is inherently reactive while the latter seeks to be proactive. As the Antitrust Modernization Commission explained:

> Antitrust law in the United States is not industrial policy; the law does not authorize the government (or any private party) to seek to "improve" competition. Instead, antitrust enforcement seeks to deter or eliminate anti-competitive restraints. Rather than create a

regulatory scheme, antitrust laws establish a law enforcement framework that prohibits private (and, sometimes, governmental) restraints that frustrate the operation of free-market competition.[162]

The same cannot be said for communications regulation: while the question of the FCC's authority over broadband is yet to be fully litigated, its role in traditional communications markets goes beyond simply protecting competition to shaping the industry's form and structure in "the public interest."[163] In short, the FCC is charged—at least, with respect to its regulation of traditional telecommunication services—with executing the very sort of "industrial policy" the antitrust laws reject.[164] The potential costs of such an approach are especially high in environments, like the Internet ecosystem, where technologies and industry structures are rapidly evolving. That is, in an environment with a technologically stable telecommunications industry, policies that bias the level of investment away from the efficient optimum are presumably less harmful than they might be in a more fluid environment where policy biases risk tipping the competitive outcome in favor of a less efficient technology or structure.[165] As Renda notes,

> Asymmetries in the regulatory treatment of players located at different layers of the value chain may result in distortions of platform competition, and should thus be avoided unless they are justified by the need to remove sources of egregious, irreversible market power, or refusals to supply truly indispensable assets.[166]

A third, and related, principle is that a less concentrated industry structure, in and of itself, should not be an objective of competition policy when it comes to broadband. More broadly, policymakers should dispense with the structural presumption in favor of the far more nuanced approach embodied in modern antitrust doctrine. For all the reasons I have described, relatively high levels of concentration are to be expected in IT sector markets, including broadband, and do not signal market dysfunction or indicate policy opportunities to improve competitive outcomes. Concentration, when it occurs, is usually efficient, often transitory, seldom if ever leads to collusion, and does not imply the ability to earn monopoly rents; to the contrary, even "monopolists" in platform industries are subject to market forces that often dictate welfare-maximizing outcomes.

Ultimately, it is not sufficient simply to deemphasize the role of structuralism in as a policy objective (for example, in formulating spectrum policy); rather, policymakers should recognize that the role of competition policy, in broadband as in other industries, should be to *protect* competition, not *promote* it. In today's converged broadband market, there is no more basis for proactive policies designed to increase the number of broadband ISPs, per se, than for policies designed to increase the number of search engines, operating systems, or social networks.[167]

Fourth, prescriptive regulation should be avoided in favor of ex post enforcement of more broadly defined tenets. This principle emerges, first, from the rapidly changing nature of Internet markets and technologies—dynamism in the narrow sense, that is, of fluidity.[168] As the *National Broadband Plan* concludes, "Technologies, costs and consumer preferences are changing too quickly in this dynamic part of the economy to make accurate predictions."[169] While some worry that ex post enforcement is by nature "too slow" to keep up with rapidly changing markets,[170] markets are often self-correcting (the purported anticompetitive outcome is remedied—for example, by entry—before government action of any kind can take effect).[171] As Shapiro and Varian conclude,

> We believe a cautious approach toward antitrust policy and enforcement is called for in high-technology industries, in part because technological change does tend to erode monopoly power and in part because much of the conduct at issue has at least some claim on increasing consumer welfare.[172]

Even when government action is required, it is far from clear that ex ante regulation is a more expeditious remedy: in this context, the main difference between prescriptive rules and ex post enforcement is the time required to write the rules, and resolve the inevitable litigation that follows, before enforcement can even begin. Moreover, experience has shown that, once a rule is in place, it can take at least as long to modify or repeal it as it took to pass it in the first place, creating the possibility that rules designed to address an ephemeral problem persist long after the problem is resolved—and so are transformed from cure to disease.[173]

Another rationale for avoiding prescriptive rules is that, in an economic environment in which similar conduct (even the very same conduct) can have both positive and negative consequences, banning entire classes of conduct risks throwing "the welfare-enhancing baby out with the anticompetitive bathwater."[174] Broad rules are more likely to do harm than good when the competitive effects of particular types of conduct are fact-dependent and when, as is certainly the case with Internet platforms, economic science has not yet arrived at the kinds of established, broad findings that underlie, for example, the per se rule against horizontal collusion.[175]

Finally, the presumption against prescriptive regulation is further strengthened by the tendency of regulatory agencies to engage in cross-subsidization and, in so doing, create a marketplace for rent seeking. As Shapiro and Varian point out, "We also must note that regulation brings its own dangers: a regulatory structure created to control monopoly power can easily be used to serve other purposes, in particular, to support a system of cross-subsidization."[176] It is noteworthy, in this regard, that one of the rationales proffered for net neutrality rules is the desirability of subsidizing "edge" providers, even at the cost of disadvantaging infrastructure providers.[177]

Thus, to summarize, we have at least four reasons to replace ex ante regulation of broadband with ex post antitrust enforcement. First, doing so is necessary to harmonize competition policy across the various sectors of the Internet ecosystem. Second, ex ante regulation invites counterproductive "industrial policy" efforts to shape the evolution of a highly dynamic marketplace. Third, there is no basis for efforts to "increase competition" by increasing the number of competitors (and thus reducing measures of industry concentration), and thus no need for ex ante regulation to pursue this objective. Fourth, by its nature, ex ante regulation is inferior to ex post enforcement because it is less accurate in discriminating between welfare-enhancing and welfare-reducing conduct, is cumbersome to implement, and often leads to rent seeking and politicization.

Toward a Pro-Competition Policy for Broadband

The task of replacing today's legacy regulatory framework with a pro-competition, antitrust-based approach to broadband competition is complex and will not happen overnight. Moreover, our understanding of how to apply ex post antitrust principles to high-tech markets is far from perfect and still evolving. Thus, the objective is to replace an imperfect regulatory model with a *less imperfect* enforcement approach. Even so, the analysis I have presented has some clear and immediate implications for how we should regulate, or not regulate, broadband markets.

First, blanket bans on vertical restraints and discriminatory pricing should be avoided in broadband markets as they are in other IT markets.[178] Although such conduct can pose difficult issues for competition analysis in IT markets as elsewhere (because it often generates both benefits and costs), broad consensus exists that ex ante prohibitions on vertical restraints are not justified. For example, Carl Shapiro, who has written that exclusive dealing arrangements are more likely to be problematic in network industries than in traditional ones, nevertheless opposes blanket bans:

Of course, exclusive dealing and exclusive membership rules need not be anticompetitive, even in network industries. These contractual

forms can serve to differentiate products and networks, to encourage investment in these networks, and to overcome free riding. I am certainly not proposing a *per se* rule against exclusivity in a network context.[179]

Similarly, Jonathan Baker, who opposes blanket approval of price discrimination, also opposes a blanket ban:

So long as entry is easy, and the practices facilitating price discrimination do not harm competition, as by raising entry barriers or otherwise reducing competition by excluding actual or potential rivals, price discrimination is competitive, and not a harmful practice.[180]

As Renda emphasizes, the arguments in favor of vertical restraints and differential pricing are at least as powerful in broadband markets as in other parts of the Internet ecosystem.

When looking at the economics of complex and interconnected system goods, there seems to be very little room to differentiate between ISPs and gateway players located at higher layers. In both cases, players have an incentive to secure a share of the value created by the system by engaging in some form of differential pricing or price discrimination from their supply side, and in preferential agreements on the demand side.[181]

Renda also notes that the case against ex ante regulation of vertical restraints is further strengthened by the fact that the optimal balance between integration and interoperability often shifts over time, with closed systems often being more efficient (or even necessary) for the development of new platforms, which later evolve towards more open models.

As often happened in the past few years, the need to create successful business models and to ensure security will initially call for some degree of proprietary-ness (as in the case of the App store), and later give leeway to a significant degree of commoditization of lower platform layers. In other words, market forces, rather than a regulator, are likely to solve the problem by pushing for interoperability once the market becomes more mature.[182]

Because exclusivity is often more beneficial to new business models than old ones, blanket bans are likely to have the perverse effect of discriminating against innovation and, by extension, against entry.

A pro-competitive presumption for vertical restraints in broadband markets would have profound implications for regulation. First, and most obviously, the proscription of entire classes of vertical restraints imposed by the Open Internet Order represents precisely the sort of blanket ban rejected by Baker and Shapiro in the context of other high-tech markets. Net neutrality would thus be the first and most obvious regulation to fall.[183] But the effects extend much further, to virtually all forms of vertical "open-access" regulation, existing and proposed, including those governing Internet access devices (the CableCARD and AllVid rules)[184] and wireless handsets,[185] as well as legacy rules governing wireline consumer premises equipment and wireless service (which require wireless service to be offered separately from devices on a nondiscriminatory basis).[186]

Acknowledging the convergence of broadband with the Internet ecosystem also has important implications for horizontal issues, including interconnection and "unbundling." As discussed above, the competitive dynamics of the IT sector, where incentives for innovation are of paramount importance and network effects provide strong incentives (short of tipping) for voluntary interconnection, mitigate strongly against horizontal open-access mandates.

Much of the economic analysis of these issues in the IT sector has been in the context of intellectual property law, where a patent or copyright can give a platform operator de facto exclusive control. The policy questions are when, if ever, the government should impose a compulsory license (the equivalent

of unbundling in the telecommunications environment) or mandate "open interfaces" with competing platforms (the equivalent of mandatory interconnection). As Weiser explains, the balance tips in favor of encouraging competition between platforms rather than mandating interconnection:

A central tenet of the competitive platforms model is that, even if the industry structure will ultimately rely on a single standard, competition policy should still err on the proprietary side of the line, allowing rival standards to battle it out in the marketplace.[187]

The rationale is straightforward: platform competition promotes increased output, product enhancement, and new product innovation.

By encouraging competition between rival platforms, intellectual property law can advance three critical goals: forcing companies to compete to build a valuable customer base, requiring all companies to continue to enhance their products and bring new ones to market more quickly for fear of being displaced by a new killer application, and driving companies to innovate and develop superior technologies. By contrast, providing open access to a single standard that would otherwise face viable platform competition undermines the achievement of each of these benefits.[188]

For these reasons, content, applications, and device manufacturers are seldom forced to engage in compulsory licensing, except in the context of targeted, typically time-limited, remedies in cases of merger or monopolization.[189] In telecommunications, by contrast, mandated interconnection requirements are commonplace—resulting, as Hovenkamp notes, in reduced incentives for investment:

Antitrust together with intellectual property is often a better vehicle for addressing such problems as 'interconnection' and the lack of neutrality in networked communications. Regulatory solutions have tended to go too far, requiring interconnection and sharing even when doing so inefficiently diminishes investment incentives.[190]

Ultimately, as Renda explains, the effect of open-access regulation is to systematically disadvantage broadband ISPs relative to other Internet ecosystem competitors:

> Being a dominant network operator and internet service provider today means being clearly handicapped in the race to become a dominant IP-based platform, since it entails being subject to a series of open access obligations that other players in the value chain do not have.[191]

Heretofore, regulators have mostly limited horizontal unbundling and interconnection regulations to traditional telecommunications platforms and services, but both national and international regulators are now considering extending such rules to broadband.[192] The convergence of broadband into the Internet ecosystem argues against both unbundling (for example, data-roaming requirements on wireless carriers) and mandatory interconnection regimes.[193]

Lastly, the characteristics of IT markets, including broadband markets, have important implications for merger analysis. For reasons explained above, measures of market concentration have little or no saliency in such markets, yet antitrust authorities in general, and the FCC in particular, continue to focus on such metrics, at least as triggers for further review. More recently, antitrust authorities have begun to rely on "upward pricing pressure" models designed to estimate the unilateral effects of mergers in differentiated product markets.[194] The ability of these models accurately to predict the consumer welfare effects of mergers is directly limited in the presence of multisidedness and other IT market characteristics.[195]

5

Conclusions

The notion that broadband services have been "converging" with other aspects of the IT sector is neither new nor controversial. Indeed, convergence seems to be universally recognized, including by telecommunications regulators, who routinely refer to broadband services as part of the "Internet ecosystem." Yet, despite the fact that broadband markets are now essentially indistinguishable from other IT markets from the perspective of competition analysis, they remain subject to a starkly different and increasingly anachronistic regulatory regime.

The application of modern antitrust principles to the Internet ecosystem is and will remain as much art as science, and both doctrinal and episodic errors will no doubt be made. Such errors are likely to be far smaller, however, than the consequences of continuing to apply nineteenth century regulatory policies and principles to a twenty-first century marketplace.

Notes

1. The idea that telecommunications has converged with other "new economy" sectors such as the Internet and computer software is, of course, not new. See, for example, Joseph Farrell and Philip J. Weiser, "Modularity, Vertical Integration, and Open Access Policies: Towards a Convergence of Antitrust and Regulation in the Internet Age," *Harvard Journal of Law & Technology* 17, no. 1 (Fall 2003): 85–134, at 87: "As the Internet, computer software, and telecommunications ('New Economy') industries converge, affected firms will increasingly seek clear and consistent legal rules"; Michael K. Powell, "The Great Digital Broadband Migration," in *Communications Deregulation and FCC Reform: Finishing the Job*, ed. J. A. Eisenach and R. J. May (Kluwer Academic Publishers, 2001), 11–21, at 15–16: "Computer systems working in parity with communications have spawned the Internet and the advanced networks we see today that fully integrate satellites, telephones, wireless devices, broadcasting and cable over fiberoptic, broadband, and wireless networks. The result is what we now call convergence"; and Richard A. Posner, "Antitrust in the New Economy," *Antitrust Law Journal* 68 (2001): 925–43, at 925: "I shall use the term the 'new economy' to denote three distinct though related industries. The first is the manufacture of computer software. The second consists of the Internet-based businesses (Internet access providers, Internet service providers, Internet content providers), such as AOL and Amazon. And the third consists of communications services and equipment designed to support the first two markets."

2. See, e.g., Geoffrey A. Manne and Joshua D. Wright, "Innovation and the Limits of Antitrust," *Journal of Competition Law & Economics* 6, no. 1 (2010): 153–202; Robert W. Crandall and Clifford Winston, "Does Antitrust Policy Improve Consumer Welfare? Assessing the Evidence," *Journal of Economic Perspectives* 17, no. 4 (Fall 2003): 3–26; and Daniel F. Spulber, "Unlocking Technology: Antitrust and Innovation," *Journal of Competition Law & Economics* 4,

no. 4 (2008): 915–66. For a brief summary of the debate, see David Evans, "The Middle Way on Applying Antitrust to Information Technology Industries," *Competition Policy International* (November 2009), www.techpolicyinstitute .org/files/evansnov-09.pdf (accessed October 9, 2012).

3. See, e.g., Carl Shapiro, "Exclusivity in Network Industries," *George Mason Law Review* 7 (Spring 1999): 673–82; F. M. Scherer, *Technological Innovation and Monopolization* (John F. Kennedy School of Government, October 2007), http://ssrn.com/abstract=1019023 (accessed September 27, 2012); and Mark Cooper, "The Importance of Open Networks in Sustaining the Digital Revolution," in *Net Neutrality or Net Neutering: Should Broadband Internet Service Be Regulated?*, ed. T. M. Lenard and R. J. May (Progress & Freedom Foundation, 2006), 107–61, especially 126–32.

4. See Federal Communications Commission, *In the Matter of Preserving the Open Internet and Broadband Industry Practices, Report and Order*, GN Docket No. 09-191, WC Docket No. 07-52 (December 23, 2010) (hereafter, Open Internet Order). See also Federal Communications Commission, *In the Matter of Preserving the Open Internet and Broadband Industry Practices, Notice of Proposed Rulemaking*, GN Docket No. 09-191, WC Docket No. 07-52 (October 22, 2009).

5. FCC, Open Internet Order, ¶32–34.

6. Ibid., ¶32.

7. Ibid., ¶78.

8. Ibid., ¶53: "Promoting competition throughout the Internet ecosystem is a central purpose of these rules."

9. Ibid., at ¶25; see generally ¶¶24–28.

10. Ibid., ¶29; see generally ¶¶29–30. While rejecting a traditional market power analysis, the FCC did embrace a theory of exclusionary market power based on based on raising rivals' costs. See ¶¶21–23.

11. For example, the *National Broadband Plan* specifically concludes that broadband markets are part of a "broadband

ecosystem." See Federal Communications Commission, Omnibus Broadband Initiative, *Connecting America: The National Broadband Plan* (March 2010; hereafter, NBP Report), www.broadband.gov/download-plan/ (accessed September 28, 2012), xi: "Policymakers, including the FCC, have a broad set of tools to protect and encourage competition in the markets that make up the broadband ecosystem: network services, devices, applications and content."); see also 15.

12. See, e.g., Jerry Brito et al., *Net Neutrality Regulation: The Economic Evidence* (April 12, 2010), http://ssrn.com/abstract=1587058 (accessed September 28, 2012).

13. *Verizon v. FCC, Notice of Appeal*, US Court of Appeals, DC Circuit, Case No. 11-1355 (October 2, 2011), www.fhhlaw.com/VerizonNoticeofAppeal.netneutrality.2011.09.30.PDF (accessed September 28, 2012).

14. For a recent statement of the FCC's view of its authority to regulate wireless broadband providers, see its brief in Verizon's challenge of data roaming order: *Cellco Partnership d/b/a Verizon Wireless, v. Federal Communications Commission, Brief for Respondents*, US Court of Appeals, DC Circuit, Case No. 11-1135 (January 9, 2012), www.fcc.gov/document/cellco-partnership-v-fcc-usa-no-11-1135-and-1136-dc-cir (accessed September 28, 2012).

15. See Federal Communications Commission, *In the Matter of Connect America Fund, Report and Order and Further Notice of Proposed Rulemaking*, WT Docket 10-90 (November 18, 2011), ¶¶113–4.

16. See Federal Communications Commission, *In the Matter of Framework for Broadband Internet Services, Notice of Inquiry*, GN Docket No. 10-127 (June 17, 2010).

17. I use the term "competitive dynamics" to refer broadly to how competition works—to the ways in which technology, institutions, demand conditions, and other salient market characteristics are related to industry structure, competitive outcomes, and market performance.

18. See Timothy F. Bresnahan, "New Modes of Competition: Implications for the Future Structure of the Computer Industry," in *Competition, Innovation and the Microsoft Monopoly: Antitrust in the Digital Marketplace* ed. J. Eisenach and T. Lenard (Kluwer Academic Press, 1999), 155–208.

19. For a refresher in graphic form, see www.refresher.com/!paranoid.html.

20. Ibid., 157.

21. Ibid., 157.

22. Ibid., 159.

23. See e.g., Antitrust Modernization Commission, *Report and Recommendations* (April 2007), 2–3: "To be competitive, markets need not conform to the economic ideal in which many firms compete and no firm has control over price. In fact, the real world contains very few such markets. Rather, competition generally 'refers to a state of affairs in which prices are sufficient to cover a firm's costs, but not excessively higher, and firms are given the correct set of incentives to innovate.' Experience has shown that intense competition can take place in a wide variety of market circumstances. Some factors—such as many sellers and buyers, small market shares, homogeneous products, and easy entry into a market—may suggest competitive behavior is likely. The absence of those factors, however, 'does not necessarily prevent a market from behaving competitively.'" [Internal quotations from H. Hovenkamp, *The Antitrust Enterprise* (2005), 13, and E. Gellhorn, *Antitrust Law and Economics* (2004), 72; other internal citations omitted.]

24. See, e.g., US Department of Justice and Federal Trade Commission, *Horizontal Merger Guidelines* (August 19, 2010), at 3: "Mergers that cause a significant increase in concentration and result in highly concentrated markets are presumed to be likely to enhance market power, but this presumption can be rebutted by persuasive evidence showing that the merger is unlikely to enhance market power." (hereafter, 2010 Merger Guidelines). The courts continue to embrace the structural presumption in one form or another. See, e.g., *FTC v. H.J. Heinz* 246 F.R. 3d 708 (2001) and *US v. H&R Block* 789 F.Sup. 2d.74 (2011), both of which reiterate the Supreme Court's embrace of market share as an indicator of market power in *United States v. Philadelphia Nat'l Bank*, 374 U.S. 321.

25. See 2010 Merger Guidelines, 24–27.

26. I use the term "locational pricing power" to refer to the ability of firms in differentiated product markets to price above marginal cost even in the presence of free entry.

27. See 2010 Merger Guidelines, 20–24.

28. Interestingly, Timothy Wu, a leading proponent of net neutrality regulation, testified before Congress in early 2012 that "it is clear that 4G to the home is a cable *replacement*, not a complement," apparently contradicting a decade or more of argument by regulation proponents that

wireless is a complement, not a substitute, for wireline and should not be considered as part of the relevant product market. See page 5 of Tim Wu, "Creeping Duopoly?," Testimony before the Senate Judiciary Committee, Subcommittee on Antitrust, Competition Policy, and Consumer Rights, March 21, 2012, www.judiciary.senate.gov/pdf/12-3-21WuTestimony.pdf (accessed October 9, 2012).

29. See Federal Communications Commission, *Annual Report and Analysis of Competitive Market Conditions with Respect to Mobile Wireless, Including Commercial Mobile Services*, WT Docket 10-33 (June 27, 2011), ¶¶55–66 (hereafter, Fifteenth Report).

30. FCC, Open Internet Order, n. 143, summarizing Department of Justice submission. The apparent implication is that broadband may evolve into two separate antitrust markets, a wireline market and a wireless market, each relatively concentrated, and each exercising little or no competitive discipline upon the other.

31. Ibid., n. 87: "Because broadband providers have the ability to act as gatekeepers even in the absence of market power with respect to end users, we need not conduct a market power analysis." The FCC did conclude, however, that market power, if it did exist, would exacerbate its concerns, and averred that "the risk of market power is highest in markets with few competitors, and most residential end users today have only one or two choices for wireline broadband Internet access service." See Open Internet Order, ¶32.

32. See *Petition of Qwest Corporation for Forbearance Pursuant to 47 U.S.C. § 160(c) in the Phoenix, Arizona Metropolitan Statistical Area*, WC Docket No. 09-135, *Memorandum Opinion and Order* (June 22, 2010), ¶82.

33. Ibid., ¶80.

34. Ibid., ¶86. The FCC also examined potential competition and the likelihood of entry. See generally ¶¶80–86.

35. See *Reexamination of Roaming Obligations of Commercial Mobile Radio Service Providers and Other Providers of Mobile Data Services*, WT Docket No. 05-265, *Second Report and Order* (April 7, 2011), ¶16.

36. See *SkyTerra Communications, Inc., Transferor, and Harbinger Capital Partners Funds, Transferee*, IB Docket No. 08-184, *Memorandum Opinion and Order and Declaratory Ruling*, 25 FCC Rcd 3059 (March 26, 2010) at ¶60–61: "Large portions of the country are served by three or fewer

providers of mobile broadband service. . . . Harbinger could have a beneficial impact on competition."

37. See Federal Communications Commission, *Annual Report and Analysis of Competitive Market Conditions with Respect to Mobile Wireless, Including Commercial Mobile Services, Fourteenth Report*, WT Docket No. 09-66 (May 20, 2010), Section III.C (hereafter, Fourteenth Report), a finding repeated in the Fifteenth Report (see, e.g., ¶2).

38. US Department of Justice, Complaint, *United States of America vs. AT&T Inc.* (August 31, 2011), ¶25. For a full explication of the FCC's assessment of the proposed merger, see also Federal Communications Commission, *Staff Analysis and Findings* (WT Docket No. 11-65), especially ¶¶12–122.

39. See, e.g., *Comments of the Consumer Federation of America, Consumers Union and Free Press, In the Matter of Broadband Industry Practices*, WC Docket No. 07-52, Federal Communications Commission (June 15, 2007), 11, http://apps.fcc.gov/ecfs/document/view?id=6519529519 (accessed October 9, 2012; hereafter, 2007 Consumer Group Comments).

40. See, e.g., Ad Hoc Public Interest Spectrum Coalition, *Comments in Skype Communications S.A.R.L., Petition to Confirm a Consumer's Right to Use Internet Communications Software and Attach Devices to Wireless Networks*, RM-11361, Federal Communications Commission (April 30, 2007).

41. Mark Cooper, "The Public Interest in Open Communications Networks," Consumer Federation of America (July 2004), 47, http://fjallfoss.fcc.gov/ecfs/document/view?id=6516283898 (accessed September 28, 2012).

42. See, e.g., Texas Office of Public Utility Counsel, Consumer Federation of America, Consumers Union, *Comments in Inquiry Concerning High Speed Access to the Internet Over Cable and Other Facilities*, GN Docket No. 00-185 (January 11, 2001), 44: "While six [competitors] is a clear danger sign, theoretical and empirical evidence indicates that many more than six firms are necessary for competition—perhaps as many as fifty firms are necessary."

43. 2007 Consumer Group Comments, 74.

44. Ibid., 25. Consumer groups are not alone in pressing concerns based on structuralist models. For example, in 2009, Senator Herb Kohl wrote to Assistant Attorney General Varney and FCC Chairman Genachowski warning that "four [wireless] carriers control over 90% of the cell phone

market" and expressing concern that "the concentrated state of the cell phone marketplace could lead to future price increases." Letter from Senator Herb Kohl (July 6, 2009), 1.

45. NBP Report, 3.

46. Shane Greenstein and Ryan McDevitt, "Evidence of a Modest Price Decline in US Broadband Services," *Information Economics and Policy* 23, no. 2 (2011): 200–11. (The authors emphasize that prices have declined even more rapidly for products like computers and integrated circuits.)

47. See e.g., Fifteenth Report, ¶191 and ¶194: "AT&T's estimated price per MB for data traffic . . . has declined from $1.21 in 2008 to $0.35 in 2009 to $0.17 in 2010." See also Everett Ehrlich, Jeffrey A. Eisenach, and Wayne A. Leighton, "The Impact of Regulation on Innovation and Choice in Wireless Communications," *Review of Network Economics* 9, no. 1 (2010): 1–49 (especially 17); and Gerald R. Faulhaber, Robert W. Hahn, and Hal J. Singer, "Assessing Competition in US Wireless Markets: Review of the FCC's Competition Reports," *Federal Communications Law Journal* 64, no. 2 (March 2012): 319–69.

48. See NBP Report, 77; see also Fifteenth Report, ¶¶108–15.

49. Robert C. Atkinson and Ivy E. Schultz, *Broadband in America: Where It Is and Where It Is Going* (Columbia Institute of Tele-Information, November 2009).

50. See NBP Report, 38: "Indeed, competition appears to have induced broadband providers to invest in network upgrades."

51. See Mary Meeker (Morgan Stanley), *Internet Trends* (Presented at the CM Summit, New York City, June 7, 2010), slide 4, http://bbh-labs.com/internet-trends-2010-by-morgan-stanleys-mary-meeker (accessed September 28, 2012).

52. See Berkman Center for Internet and Society, Harvard University, *Next Generation Connectivity: A Review of Broadband Internet Transitions and Policy from Around the World* (2010), http://cyber.law.harvard.edu/publications/2010/Next_Generation_Connectivity (accessed September 28, 2012). For a rebuttal, see Robert W. Crandall, Jeffrey A. Eisenach, and Allan T. Ingraham, *The Long-Run Effects of Copper Unbundling and the Implications for Fiber* (March 2012), http://papers.ssrn.com/sol3/papers.cfm?abstract_id=2018929 (accessed September 28, 2012); and Jeffrey

A. Eisenach, "Broadband in the U.S.—Myths and Facts," in *Australia's Broadband Future: Four Doors to Greater Competition* (Melbourne: Committee for Economic Development of Australia, 2008), 48–59.

53. NBP Report, 4. In May 2011, the commission's International Bureau issued a report which found that "data sources on international broadband are incomplete and generally challenging to compare. . . . As a result, we are limited in the conclusions we can draw from the data." See Federal Communications Commission, *In the Matter of International Comparison Requirements Pursuant to the Broadband Data Improvement Act International Broadband Data Report*, IB Docket No. 10-171, *Second Report* (May 20, 2011), ¶1.

54. See, e.g., Meeker, *Internet Trends*, slide 19: "U.S. is the global leader in mobile users and innovation."

55. See "Swiss Lead in Speed: Comparing Global Internet Connections," Nielsen Wire, April 1, 2011, http://blog.nielsen.com/nielsenwire/global/swiss-lead-in-speed-comparing-global-internet-connections (accessed September 28, 2012). Historically, US broadband speeds have doubled approximately every 18–24 months (at approximately the same pace as dictated by Moore's Law). See J. Eisenach, C. Eldering, and M. Sylla, "Is There a Moore's Law for Bandwidth?" *IEEE Communications Magazine* (October 1999): 117–21; and, for an update, Michael Turk, "Broadband Speed and Moore's Law," CableTechTalk, August 14, 2008, www.cabletechtalk.com/tech-discussions/2008/08/14/broadband-speed-and-moores-law-a-response-to-robb-topolski/ (accessed September 28, 2012).

56. See Thomas W. Hazlett and Dennis L. Weisman, "Market Power in U.S. Broadband Services," *Review of Industrial Organization* 38, no. 2 (March 2011): 151–71.

57. See Larry F. Darby, "The Informed Policy Maker's Guide to Regulatory Impacts on Broadband Network Investment" (American Consumer Institute, November 2009), 10: "Using two of the most common indicators of profitability—net profit margin reflecting deduction of all costs from revenue and return on total capital—the data indicate that broadband access providers are earning less than the S&P average and substantially less than Google."

58. As discussed in note 85, Baumol points out that in industries characterized by rapid innovation, incumbents are required to make continuing investments to remain

competitive. When incumbents and entrants alike face large capital costs, they are not properly considered barriers to entry. See George J. Stigler, *The Organization of Industry* (Chicago: University of Chicago Press, 1968), 67–70.

59. Wireline entry has also occurred in geographic markets where competition is perceived as producing insufficient results, including dozens of instances of municipal entry as well as Google's recent announcement that it will deploy a gigabit fiber network in Kansas City, Kansas.

60. See generally Ehrlich et al., "The Impact of Regulation"; and NBP Report, 75: "Mobile broadband represents the convergence of the last two great disruptive technologies— Internet computing and mobile communications—and may be more transformative than either of these previous breakthroughs. Mobile broadband is scaling faster and presents a bigger opportunity. This revolution is being led not only by domestic wireless carriers, who are investing billions in network upgrades, but also by American companies such as Amazon, Apple, Intel, Google, Qualcomm and numerous entrepreneurial enterprises that export innovation globally."

61. See, e.g., Fifteenth Report, ¶¶151–4.

62. For a more complete treatment of innovation in both wireline and wireless telecommunications networks, see Larry F. Darby and Joseph P. Fuhr, *Innovation and National Broadband Policies* (American Consumer Institute, March 2010); and Jonathan Sallet, *The Creation of Value: The Broadband Value Circle and Evolving Market Structures* (April 4, 2011), www.annenberglab.com/adminfiles/files/BroadbandValueCircle_Sallet.pdf (accessed September 28, 2012).

63. Open Internet Order, ¶35.

64. NBP Report, 37 (citations omitted). See also Fifteenth Report, ¶10: "Market performance metrics provide more direct evidence of competitive outcomes and the strength of competitive rivalry than market structure factors, such as concentration measures.")

65. NBP Report, 37, quoting *Ex Parte Submission of the United States Department of Justice, In the Matter of Economic Issues in Broadband Competition, A National Broadband Plan for Our Future*, GN Docket No. 09.51 (January 4, 2010), 11.

66. See Bresnaban, "New Modes of Competition," 155.

67. For a useful discussion of the economic distinctions between price discrimination and price differentiation, see Denis L. Weisman and Robert B. Kulick, "Price Discrimination, Two-Sided Markets and Net Neutrality Regulation," *Tulane Journal of Technology and Intellectual Property* 13 (Fall 2010): 81–102.

68. See, e.g., Bresnahan, "New Modes of Competition," 159: "A platform is a shared, stable set of hardware, software and networking technologies on which users build and run computer applications."; and Mark Rysman, "The Economics of Two-Sided Markets," *Journal of Economic Perspectives* 23, no. 3 (Summer 2009): 125–43, at 128: "Newspapers are a canonical two-sided market, where the newspaper provides a platform for communication from advertisers to consumers" and 129: "Many papers that study operating systems identify themselves with network effects rather than two-sided markets so perhaps this example is less canonical, but . . . the two literatures have a lot in common." Rysman (132–3) presents the distinction between supply-side and demand-side complementarity slightly differently from the distinction used here. He characterizes interoperability as a strategic decision made by the ("monopolist") operator of a multisided platform. My focus on modularity as a distinct concept facilitates a richer exploration of the interaction between platform participants.

69. For an overview of various approaches to innovation in antitrust doctrine, see Robert D. Atkinson and David B. Audretsch, "Economic Doctrines and Approaches to Antitrust" (Information Technology & Innovation Foundation, January 2011), distinguishing an "innovation economics" approach to antitrust that focuses on the importance of innovation and productivity growth as policy objectives.

70. William J. Baumol, *The Free Market Innovation Machine: Analyzing the Growth Miracle of Capitalism* (Princeton, NJ: Princeton University Press, 2002), 4.

71. The seminal work is Robert Solow, "Technical Change and the Aggregate Production Function," *Review of Economic Studies* 39 (August 1957): 312–20, finding that 87.5 percent of the increase in nonfarm output in the United States between 1909 and 1949 was due to technological progress. See also Atkinson and Audretsch, "Economic Doctrines," 13–14.

72. See e.g., David B. Audretsch, William J. Baumol, and Andrew E. Burke, "Competition Policy in Dynamic Markets," *International Journal of Industrial Organization* 19, no. 5 (2001): 613–34.

73. See Federal Communications Commission, Omnibus Broadband Initiative, *Technical Paper No. 6: Mobile Broadband* (October 2010), 15. See also Robert Hahn and Hal J. Singer, "Why the iPhone Won't Last Forever and What the Government Should Do to Promote Its Successor," *Journal on Telecommunications and High Technology Law* 8, no. 2 (2010): 313–50, especially 317–30.

74. See "GPON FTTH Market and Technology Overview," PMC, April 2006, www.pmc-sierra.com /ftth-pon/ftth_overview.html (accessed October 3, 2012).

75. Analysys Mason, "'Up to a Point Copper': Quantifying the Reach of Accelerated DSL," January 26, 2012, www.analysysmason.com/About-Us/News/Insight /Insight_Accelerated_DSL_Jan2012/ (accessed September 28, 2012).

76. Evans, "The Middle Way," 2: "Dynamic competition is important in many parts of the information technology sector. Some firms compete to create a new market—or a new category. We forget about the many, many firms that competed to create social networks, video sharing sites, computer operating systems, and so forth—and then died off."

77. Joseph Schumpeter, *Capitalism, Socialism and Democracy* (New York: Harper & Brothers, 1942), 84.

78. See Jean-Jacques Laffont and Jean Tirole, *Competition in Telecommunications* (Cambridge, MA: MIT Press, 2000), 4. Some rural companies are still subject to rate-of-return regulation.

79. Michael L. Katz and Howard A. Shelanski, "'Schumpeterian' Competition and Antitrust Policy in High-Tech Markets," *Competition* 14 (2005), 10, http://papers.ssrn .com/sol3/papers.cfm?abstract_id=925707 (accessed September 28, 2012).

80. See Posner, "Antitrust in the New Economy," 930.

81. *Ex Parte Submission of the US Department of Justice*, 4; see also Carl Shapiro, *Antitrust, Innovation, and Intellectual Property* (Testimony before the Antitrust Modernization Commission, November 8, 2005), 2: "In such 'innovative industries,' antitrust must pay careful attention to the incentives and obstacles facing firms seeking to develop and commercialize new technologies, and antitrust must very explicitly recognize that market conditions, business strategies, and industry structure can be highly dynamic."

82. NBP Report, 42: "Thus, in areas that include 75% of the population, consumers will likely have only one service provider (cable companies with DOCSIS 3.0-enabled infrastructure) that can offer very high peak download speeds." Such predictions have often proved inaccurate or even embarrassing. The US Federal Trade Commission, for example, justified imposing significant conditions on the merger of American Online and Time Warner Inc. with its finding that "AOL is the leading provider of narrowband internet access, with a share of approximately 50 percent of narrowband subscribers. AOL is positioned and likely to become the leading provider of broadband internet access as well." See US Federal Trade Commission, *In the Matter of America Online, Inc. and Time Warner Inc.*, Docket No. C-2989, Complaint (December 14, 2000), 3.

83. For arguments against this proposition, see Jonathan B. Baker, "Beyond Schumpeter vs. Arrow: How Antitrust Fosters Innovation," *Antitrust Law Journal* 74 (2007) 575–602 (arguing that antitrust enforcement promotes innovation); Cooper, "The Public Interest," 47–48: "The theory supporting Schumpeterian rents appears to be particularly ill-suited to several layers of the digital communications platform. It breaks down if a monopoly is not transitory, a likely outcome in the physical layer. In the physical layer, with its high capital costs and other barriers to entry, monopoly is more likely to quickly lead to anti-competitive practices that leverage the monopoly power over bottleneck facilities into other layers of the platform"; and J. Gregory Sidak and David J. Teece, "Dynamic Competition in Antitrust Law," *Journal of Competition Law & Economics* 5, no. 4 (2009) 581–631, at 618: "The evolutionary and behavioral economics approaches outlined here would not abandon antitrust enforcement or even necessarily restrict it."

84. Katz and Shelanski, 19. See also Shapiro, *Antitrust, Innovation, and Intellectual Property*, 11–12: "However, there is no consensus among industrial organization economists about the general relationship between concentration and innovation competition." See also Sidak and Teece, "Dynamic Competition in Antitrust Law," 588: "Despite 50 years of research, economists do not appear to have found much evidence that market concentration has a statistically significant impact on innovation."

85. William J. Baumol, *The Free Market Innovation Machine: Analyzing the Growth Miracle of Capitalism* (Princeton, NJ: Princeton University Press, 2002), 165 (citation

omitted). Importantly, as Baumol explains elsewhere, such costs do not constitute barriers to entry. See William J. Baumol, "Regulation Misled by Misread Theory" (AEI-Brookings Joint Center for Regulatory Studies, 2006), 23: "The sunk costs that traditional theory says do not matter for an incumbent firm's decisions are the once-and-for-all expenditures made in the past and not repeated thereafter. They are the ancient history that no current decision can change, whereas the sunk outlays that the firm must be expected to recoup are those that are incurred currently and will continue into the foreseeable future. These expectable and recurring sunk outlays most directly drive the firm to discriminatory pricing. And it is crucial to recognize that they are not barriers to entry in Stigler's (1968) pertinent sense because they are equal burdens for the entrants and the incumbents—that is, they offer no substantial competitive advantage and, hence, no monopoly power to an incumbent firm."

86. Shapiro, *Antitrust, Innovation, and Intellectual Property*, 7.

87. Hal R. Varian, "Differential Pricing and Efficiency," *First Monday* 1, no. 2 (August 1996): 2.

88. See page 3 of Scott Wallsten and Colleen Mallahan, "Residential Broadband Competition in the United States" (March 2010), http://papers.ssrn.com/sol3/papers.cfm?abstract_id=1684236 (accessed October 1, 2012).

89. Arguably, the seminal article on competitive price discrimination is Robert H. Frank, "When Are Price Differentials Discriminatory?" *Journal of Policy Analysis and Management* 2, no. 2 (1983): 238–55. For other early contributions, see Michael E. Levine, "Price Discrimination without Market Power," *Yale Journal on Regulation* 19 (Winter 2002): 1–35, at 25–26: "In the same way, high speed Internet access subscribers are charged on a monthly basis by the data transfer rate they wish to purchase, even though the 'cost' (other than the modem) of serving them is the same. The result of all this segmentation is the ability to support large networks with relatively ubiquitous service, offering some very low prices and some very high prices and many prices in between"; and Mark Armstrong and John Vickers, "Competitive Price Discrimination," *Rand Journal of Economics* 32, no. 4 (Winter 2001): 579–605.

90. See, e.g., Jonathan B. Baker, "Competitive Price Discrimination: The Exercise of Market Power without

Anticompetitive Effects (Comment on Klein and Wiley)," *Antitrust Law Journal* 70, no. 3 (2003): 643–54, at 645: "Competitive price discrimination is probably found most commonly in high-technology markets and other industries with low marginal cost, high fixed costs, and some product differentiation. In such markets, it may be necessary for sellers to charge at least some customers prices in excess of marginal cost in order to make it profitable for firms to enter the market (by covering fixed costs) or stay there (to the extent the fixed costs are not sunk). Marginal cost pricing, the usual competitive bench-mark, may thus be infeasible."

91. William J. Baumol and Daniel G. Swanson, "The New Economy and Ubiquitous Competitive Price Discrimination: Identifying Defensible Criteria of Market Power," *Antitrust Law Journal* 70, no. 3 (2003): 661–85, at 665. See also Baumol, "Regulation Misled," 3: "[I]n equilibrium, these discriminatory prices are not haphazard in their welfare properties but will generally constitute a Ramsey optimum—satisfying the second-best welfare attributes of revenue-constrained economic welfare." See also Einer Elhauge, "Why Above-Cost Price Cuts to Drive Out Entrants are Not Predatory—and the Implications for Defining Costs and Market Power," *Yale Law Journal* 112 (January 2003): 681–827, at 687: "Competition or low entry barriers will ensure that overall revenue from this output-maximizing price-discrimination schedule does not exceed economic costs."

92. See, e.g., Carl Shapiro and Hal R. Varian, *Information Rules* (Cambridge, MA: Harvard Business School Press, 1999), 26–27.

93. See Wallsten and Mallahan, "Residential Broadband Competition," 3: "In principle, [price discrimination] means charging high prices to consumers willing to pay a lot for broadband and low prices to consumers who are not willing to pay much for it. In reality, it is generally not possible to identify a particular consumer's preferences, so instead providers create different products that appeal to different groups, even though the marginal cost of serving each group may be similar."

94. See Fifteenth Report, ¶138: "In addition to network quality and advertising, a third component of non-price rivalry among mobile wireless service providers is the differentiation of the downstream products that they offer or

that rely on their networks, including handsets/devices, operating systems, and mobile applications."

95. This assumes, of course, that consumers' varying elasticities of demand cannot be observed directly.

96. *Ex Parte Submission of the United States Department of Justice*, 4. Emphasis added.

97. See e.g., Bresnahan, "New Modes of Competition," 159: "A platform is a shared, stable set of hardware, software, and networking technologies on which users build and run computer applications." See also Farrell and Weiser, "Modularity, Vertical Integration, and Open Access Policies," 95: "Modularity means organizing complements (products that work with one another) to interoperate through public, nondiscriminatory, and well-understood interfaces"; and Jeffrey Church and Neil Gandal, "Platform Competition in Telecommunications," in *Handbook of Telecommunications Economics*, Vol. 2, ed. S. K. Majumdar, I. Vogelsang and M. E. Cave (Amsterdam: Elsevier, 2005), 117–53, at 120: "The defining feature of network industries is that products consumed are systems of components: the ultimate 'good' demanded is comprised of a group of complementary products that provide value when they are consumed together. . . . For the complements to work together requires standards to insure compatibility. In this context, a 'standard' refers to a set of technical specifications that enable compatibility between products." For more detailed discussion, see Carliss Y. Baldwin and C. Jason Woodard, "The Architecture of Platforms: A Unified View" (working paper, 2009), www.people.bbs.edu /cbaldwin/DR2/BWPlatformArchitectureWorkingPaper.pdf (accessed October 1, 2012). Subsequent version was published in Annabelle Gawer (ed.), *Platforms, Markets and Innovation* (Cheltenham, UK: Edward Elgar, 2009), 19–44.

98. The number and diversity of modules and platforms in the Internet ecosystem is perhaps best evoked by simply naming a small subset of the firms that provide them, such as Adobe, Amazon, Apple, Clearwire, Comcast/NBC, Disney, eBay, Electronic Arts, Facebook, Google, Hewlett-Packard, Microsoft, Motorola Mobility, Netflix, Nintendo, Nokia, Pandora, RIM, Rovio, Sony, Twitter, and Verizon. Other platform participants, such as Akamai, Alcatel-Lucent, Broadcom, Cisco, Global Crossing, IBM, Intel, Level3, Micron, Oracle, Qualcomm, Rambus, and Symantec, may be less visible, but no less important.

99. See page 28 of Timothy F. Bresnahan and Shane Greenstein, "Technological Competition and the Structure of the Computer Industry," *Journal of Industrial Economics* 47, no. 1 (March 1999): 1–40.

100. See, e.g., Open Internet Order, ¶3.

101. Ibid., ¶1.

102. Ibid., ¶50 and n. 160.

103. This analysis also implicates the FCC's description of wireless markets in the Fifteenth Report. While the commission acknowledges the existence of a "mobile wireless ecosystem" and finds that "each of the segments in the mobile wireless ecosystem has the potential to affect competitive and consumer outcomes in the mobile wireless services segment," it embraces a traditional value chain model that portrays "mobile wireless services" as occupying a "middle part" of the mobile wireless ecosystem between "input/upstream segments" such as spectrum and network equipment and "edge/downstream" segments such as apps, content, and mobile commerce. See Fifteenth Report, ¶5–6 and figure 1. See also Fourteenth Report, ¶9–10 and figure 1.

104. See Bresnahan and Greenstein, "Technological Competition," 23. A great deal of academic attention has focused on the special case of a platform monopolist—a platform operator that faces neither intra- nor interplatform competition, and on the question of whether such a firm will make efficient choices regarding interoperability. See, e.g., Farrell and Weiser ("Modularity, Vertical Integration, and Open Access Policies"), who conclude that under limited circumstances a platform monopolist might inefficiently foreclose interconnection. For a concise critique (arguing inefficient foreclosure is highly unlikely), see Thomas M. Lenard and David T. Scheffman, "Distribution, Vertical Integration and the Net Neutrality Debate," in *Net Neutrality or Net Neutering*, ed. Lenard and May, 20–23.

105. See, e.g., Rysman, "The Economics of Two-Sided Markets," 32–33, as discussed in note 68. See also Kevin Boudreau, "Open Platform Strategies and Innovation: Granting Access vs. Devolving Control," *Management Science* 56, no. 10 (October 2010): 1849–72.

106. See Carliss Y. Baldwin, "Where Do Transactions Come From? Modularity, Transactions and the Boundaries of Firms," *Industrial and Corporate Change* 17, no. 1 (2007): 155–95, at 187: "*Modularizations, whatever their stated*

purpose, create new module boundaries with (relatively) low transaction costs. Modularizations thus make transactions feasible where they were previously impossible or very costly" (emphasis in original). See also Thomas W. Hazlett, "Modular Confines of Mobile Networks: Are iPhones iPhony?" (May 2009), http://ssrn.com/abstract=1533441 (accessed October 1, 2012), 13–14: "Modularity simultaneously yields gains from both economies of scale and specialization. When workable interfaces are achievable at low cost, competitive forces are unleashed to create complementary components of a value chain. Modularity eases entry by innovators able to contribute specific inputs in which they exhibit comparative advantage, even when such firms exhibit little or no competence as integrated providers of a larger suite of industry outputs."

107. See, e.g., Jeffrey H. Rohlfs, *Bandwagon Effects in High-Technology Industries* (Cambridge, MA: MIT Press, 2003), 35: "Nevertheless, interlinking [i.e., modularity] also involves costs, which depend on the type of interlinking involved. In some cases, interlinking is not cost-effective. Indeed, it may not even be feasible at reasonable cost."

108. Boudreau provides empirical evidence that limiting the number of providers of complementary inputs leads to more rapid innovation. See Kevin J. Boudreau, "Let a Thousand Flowers Bloom? An Early Look at Large Numbers of Software 'Apps' Developers and Patterns of Innovation," *Organization Science* (September 2011), 11: "Adding producers in the same genre to a platform slowed development in that genre. This is consistent with the presence of intensifying competition and crowding out of incentives among similar offerings."

109. For a general discussion, see e.g., Farrell and Weiser, "Modularity, Vertical Integration, and Open Access Policies," 97–100. See also Rohlfs, *Bandwagon Effects*, 42–43, and Ehrlich et al., "The Impact of Regulation on Innovation," 38–48.

110. See Baldwin and Woodard, "The Architecture of Platforms," 20: "At first glance, it might appear that the architect should retain control of the core of the system, but this conclusion is not always correct. In man-made systems, the core components of the platform can evolve over time, hence may be subject to competitive pressures." In the case of Android, development of the open-source operating system is governed by the Open Handset Alliance. For insight

into the governance challenges associated with such an endeavor, see Leslie Grandy, "Why Google's Open Handset Alliance Has Been a Disapointment," MocoNews.net, May 3, 2010, http://moconews.net/article/419-the-reasons-why-googles-open-handset-alliance-has-been-a-disappointment/ (accessed October 1, 2012).

111. A particularly colorful and litigious example of intraplatform competition involved the fight between Rambus and a host of other firms to affect the direction of the market for DRAM technology, where Rambus controls key patents. See, e.g., Federal Trade Commission, *In the Matter of Rambus, Inc.* Docket No. 9302, *Initial Decision* (February 23, 2004), www.ftc.gov/os/adjpro/d9302/040223initialdecision.pdf (accessed October 1, 2012).

112. See Bresnahan and Greenstein, "Technological Competition," 3.

113. ee Bresnahan, "New Modes of Competition," 166.

114. See Bresnahan and Greenstein, "Technological Competition," 3 and 31.

115. For example, mobile wireless carriers have tried, but mostly failed, to lead in the development of "app stores" for mobile broadband devices, the most successful of which are operated by device makers.

116. See Bresnahan, "New Modes of Competition," 166.

117. See Sallet, *The Creation of Value*, 15.

118. Jason Dedrick, Kenneth L. Kraemer, and Greg Linden, "The Distribution of Value in the Mobile Phone Supply Chain," *Telecommunications Policy* 35, no. 6 (2011): 505–21, at 515. See also Joel West and Michael Mace, "Browsing as the Killer App: Explaining the Rapid Success of Apple's iPhone," *Telecommunications Policy* 34, nos. 5–6 (2010): 270–86, at 283: "While firms in the mobile telecommunications industry worked together to create enough value to spur adoption of mobile data services, in response to increasing industry commoditization, they also engaged in zero-sum competition to capture the returns from this adoption. Such competition for profits occurred not only between traditional rivals among vendors, operators and content suppliers, but also between these complementary roles within the value network."

119. See Dedrick et al., "The Distribution of Value," 516: "The handset makers look far better than the carriers in terms of ROA, which reflects the difference between the huge capital investments by the carriers to build and

upgrade their cellular networks and the asset-light business models of these handset makers, who outsource much of their manufacturing."

120. Ibid., 517.

121. Fifteenth Report, ¶138, 143.

122. For an important early contribution to the literature on platform competition, see Feng Li and Jason Whalley, "Deconstruction of the Telecommunications Industry: From Value Chains to Value Networks," *Telecommunications Policy* 26, nos. 9–10 (2002): 451–72.

123. One way firms compete in this way is through a form of "sponsored entry." For example, in April 2012, Verizon CFO Frances Shammo indicated in a conference call with analysts that Verizon planned to push phones using Microsoft's Windows operating system as an antidote to the high costs of the iPhone: "It is important that there is a third ecosystem that's brought into the mix here, and we are fully supportive of that with Microsoft." See Greg Bensinger, "Verizon's Answer to iPhone: Windows," *Wall Street Journal* (April 20, 2012).

124. For a detailed discussion of the role of IP in the competitive dynamics of the Internet, see European Commission, Case No COMP/M.6381—*Google/Motorola Mobility Commission Decision Pursuant to Article 6(1)(b) of Council Regulation No. 139/2004*, http://ec.europa.eu/competition/mergers/cases/decisions/m6381_20120213_20310_2277480_EN.pdf (accessed October 1, 2012).

125. The right to control the customer experience played a key role in Apple's negotiations with wireless ISPs over the iPhone, which included a threat by Apple to start its own Mobile Virtual Network Operator and thus completely eliminate the carriers from the customer experience. See West and Mace, "Browsing as the Killer App," 276.

126. Sallet proposes replacing the notion of the "broadband value chain" with a "broadband value circle," with the consumer (rather than broadband ISPs or some other industry sector) at the center. Sallet's framework explains "the ability of firms anywhere along the value change to approach customers directly and attempt to catalyze a new form of consumer surplus, which is not limited to their products alone." See Sallet, *The Creation of Value*, 12.

127. Ibid., 42.

128. Chris Ziegler, "Nokia CEO Stephen Elop Rallies Troops in Brutally Honest 'Burning Platform' Memo?"

Engadget, February 8, 2011, www.engadget.com/2011/02/08/nokia-ceo-stephen-elop-rallies-troops-in-brutallyhonest-burnin/ (accessed October 1, 2012).

129. The launch of the Microsoft-Nokia collaboration was marred by rumors that Rovio—maker of popular smartphone game Angry Birds—might not adapt its content to run on the Windows Phone 7 operating system, which one analyst called a "worrying development" that "may cause some to think twice about the likelihood of Nokia's recovery." See Ingrid Lunden, "Update: Analyst: No Angry Birds Space on WP7 Affects Nokia Recovery," Techcrunch, March 23, 2012, http://techcrunch.com/2012/03/23/analyst-no-angry-birds-space-on-windows-phone-will-cause-others-to-think-twice-about-nokias-recovery/ (accessed October 1, 2012).

130. See Anthony Agnello, "Nokia, MSFT Bet Big on Lumia 900, But . . ." InvestorPlace, April 2, 2012, www.investorplace.com/2012/04/nokia-msft-bet-big-on-lumia-900-but-att-exclusivity-may-hurt-more-than-it-helps-t-nok-aapl-goog/ (accessed October 1, 2012).

131. Markets involving network effects and multisidedness are often referred to as "platforms" (e.g., television broadcasting as a "platform" that brings together advertisers with viewers), but the concept is subtly different from the modularity-defined IT platforms I described in Section 2. Modularity-defined platforms exhibit supply-side complementarities, but do not necessarily involve demand-side economies of scale or scope. Similarly, the "interoperability" between viewers and advertisers provided by a television station does not necessarily involve the realization of supply-side complementarities between inputs. See Baldwin and Woodard, "The Architecture of Platforms," 9–11.

132. See, e.g., Rysman, "The Economics of Two-Sided Markets," 125: "Broadly speaking, a two-sided market is one in which 1) two sets of agents interact through an intermediary or platform, and 2) the decisions of each set of agents affects the outcomes of the other set of agents, typically through an externality."

133. Telecommunications networks were subject to network effects long before there was an Internet. What has changed, as I discuss, is the interaction between the network and complementary goods—the emergence of platforms of which broadband networks are a part.

134. See Michael L. Katz and Carl Shapiro, "Antitrust in Software Markets," in *Competition, Innovation and the Microsoft Monopoly*, Eisenach and Lenard, eds., 29–82, at 30. See also Church and Gandal, "Platform Competition in Telecommunications," 134–6.

135. See generally Rohlfs, *Bandwagon Effects*.

136. As discussed below, there are potential exceptions, including the so-called "terminating monopoly" problem.

137. Philip J. Weiser, "The Internet, Innovation, and Intellectual Property Policy," *Columbia Law Review* 103, no. 3 (2003): 534–613, at 574–5. Similarly, Jeffrey Rohlfs notes that network effects (which he refers to as "bandwagon effects") are limited by the existence of "communities of interest" (subsets of relatively homogeneous consumers). See Rohlfs, *Bandwagon Effects*, 21. See also Michael L. Katz and Carl Shapiro, "Systems Competition and Network Effects," *Journal of Economic Perspectives* 8, no. 2 (Spring 1994): 93–115, at 106: "Consumer heterogeneity and product differentiation tend to limit tipping and sustain multiple networks. If the rival systems have distinct features sought by certain consumers, two or more systems may be able to survive by catering to consumers who care more about product attributes than network size. Here, market equilibrium with multiple incompatible products reflects the social value of variety. In some cases—Apple vs. IBM computers, perhaps—important variety benefits might be lost through standardization."; Rysman, "The Economics of Two-Sided Markets," 134–5; and Peter F. Cowhey and Jonathan D. Aronson, *Transforming Global Information and Communications Markets: The Political Economy of Innovation* (Cambridge, MA: MIT Press, 2009), ch. 3.

138. See Nicholas Economides, "The Economics of the Internet Backbone," in *Handbook of Telecommunications Economics*, ed. Majumdar et al., 373–412, at 401. While Internet peering has become more complex in recent years, ubiquitous interconnection remains the rule. See also Peyman Faratin et al., "The Growing Complexity of Internet Interconnection," *Communications & Strategies* 72 (4th quarter 2008), 51–71, at 67: "In response to [the growth of asymmetric traffic flows] and resultant changes in the Internet industry landscape, the range of interconnection contracts have expanded to include greater reliance on paid peering and partial transit, reflecting a filling in of the contracting space. . . . There is little evidence, aside from a

few highly visible events such as de-peering actions, that the range of negotiated contracts, whether discriminatory or not, has harmed the overall connectivity of the Internet."); and Christopher S. Yoo, "Innovations in the Internet's Architecture that Challenge the Status Quo," *Journal on Telecommunications and High Technology Law* 8 (2010): 79–99.

139. See, e.g., Rysman, "The Economics of Two-Sided Markets," 127: "[A] a good exhibits an indirect network effect if demand for the good depends on the provision of a complementary good, which in turn depends on demand for the original good."

140. Ibid.

141. Weiser, "The Internet, Innovation," 589.

142. In the United States, which unlike Europe chose not to mandate a single technology for 2G and 3G wireless technology, interplatform competition between CDMA and GSM standards is credited with generating significant benefits for consumers. See Fifteenth Report, ¶¶106–7: "Competition among mobile wireless providers using incompatible wireless network technologies has other advantages that can benefit consumers, including increased product variety and differentiation of services, more technological competition, and tougher price competition."

143. Weiser, "The Internet, Innovation," 586–7.

144. See Li and Whalley, Deconstruction of the Telecommunications Industry," 465: "Within the value network a multitude of market entry points exist, where a diverse range of companies can conceivably enter the market through different routes. Hence, many powerful new players from other industries are drawn into the previously neatly defined telecommunications market."

145. Indeed, Intel's investment in Clearwire was initially conditioned on Clearwire's agreement to rely exclusively on WiMAX, a condition which was subsequently renegotiated. See Stephen Lawson, "Clearwire Free to Use LTE under Changed Intel Deal," May 5, 2012, www.pcworld.com/article/195699/article.html (accessed October 1, 2012). Intel was, of course, not the only early investor in Clearwire. Others included Google and a coalition of cable companies, each of whom had interests—some "vertical," some "horizontal"—to sponsor a new entrant in the wireless broadband space.

146. See e.g., Abbey Klaassen, "Can Google's G1Smart Phone Be More Than an Apple Knockoff?" AdAgeDigital,

September 23, 2008, http://adage.com/article/digital/google-s-g1-smart-phone-apple-knockoff/131212/ (accessed October 1, 2012): "Of course, the focus for Google is not just the G1 but the many other Android phones that Google hopes will come after it."

147. See, generally, Jean-Charles Rochet and Jean Tirole, "Platform Competition in Two-Sided Markets," *Journal of the European Economic Association*, 1, no. 4 (June 2003): 990–1029.

148. See, e.g., E. Glen Weyl, "A Price Theory of Multi-Sided Platforms," *American Economic Review* 100, no. 4 (September 2010): 1642–72, especially 1667; see also Rysman, "The Economics of Two-Sided Markets," 125–143, at 131: "Another important issue in a two-sided framework is price discrimination. In a situation of demand heterogeneity, standard price discrimination—for instance, by manipulating the prices for participation and usage—allows a platform to capture more of the surplus on the side with discrimination. Thus, discrimination increases the value extracted on one side, which leads to lower prices on the other side which has now become more valuable."

149. The terminating monopoly concept appears to be central to the FCC's rationale in the Open Internet Order. See ¶24, n. 66.

150. See, e.g., Rysman, "The Economics of Two-Sided Markets," 131.

151. See Mark Armstrong, "Competition in Two-Sided Markets," *RAND Journal of Economics* 37, no. 3 (Autumn 2006): 668–91, at 670, n. 2: "This tendency toward high prices for the multi-homing side is tempered when the single-homing side benefits from having many agents from the other side on their platform. Then high prices to the multi-homing side will drive away that side and disadvantage the platform when it tries to attract the single-homing side."

152. See Brito et al., *Net Neutrality Regulation*, 10–19; see also Kevin W. Caves, "Modeling the Welfare Effects of Net Neutrality Regulation: A Comment on Economides and Tåg" (April 2010), http://papers.ssrn.com/sol3/papers.cfm?abstract_id=1585254 (accessed October 1, 2012).

153. Broadband ISPs do not appear to be any less prone to interconnection than other IT firms. For example, horizontal interlinking among broadband ISPs (i.e., peering and transit) is both voluntary and universal (see note 138 and accompanying text). On the other hand, platform leaders in other IT markets (e.g., game platforms) sometimes choose not to interconnect with competing platforms at all.

154. As noted above, entry has occurred and is occurring in the broadband ISP market. Casual observation suggests the frequency of successful entry in broadband ISP markets is not significantly lower than, and may be higher than, the frequency of successful entry in the markets for (for example) social networking platforms, search engines, and computer operating systems.

155. See, e.g., Manne and Wright, "Innovation and the Limits of Antitrust."

156. See, e.g., *Northern Pac. Ry. Co. v. United States*, 356 U.S. 1, 4 (1958): "The Sherman Act was designed to be a comprehensive charter of economic liberty aimed at preserving free and unfettered competition as the rule of trade. It rests on the premise that the unrestrained interaction of competitive forces will yield the best allocation of our economic resources, the lowest prices, the highest quality and the greatest material progress, while at the same time providing an environment conductive to the preservation of our democratic political and social institutions."

157. See e.g., Powell, "The Great Digital Broadband Migration."

158. See Open Internet Order, ¶116. Perhaps tellingly, the *National Broadband Plan* speaks not of an "Internet ecosystem" but rather a "broadband ecosystem," within which it subsumes applications and content. See NBP Report, 15: "The broadband ecosystem includes applications and content: e-mail, search, news, maps, sales and marketing applications used by businesses, user-generated video and hundreds of thousands of more specialized uses."

159. As noted above, the FCC's recent data roaming and universal service orders explicitly implicate broadband services.

160. Communications services remain subject to traditional antitrust principles, though the Supreme Court has found that the existence of ex ante regulation makes it unlikely that the antitrust laws "contemplate . . . additional scrutiny." *Verizon Communications Inc. v. Law Offices of Curtis V. Trinko, LLP* (02-682) 540 U.S. 398 (2004).

161. See Farrell and Weiser, "Modularity, Vertical Integration, and Open Access Policies," 86.

162. Antitrust Modernization Commission, *Report and Recommendations*, 3.

163. For example, Section 706 of the Communications Act directs the FCC to "encourage the deployment on a reasonable and timely basis of advanced telecommunications capability to all Americans." See 47 U.S.C. § 1302(a). The commission bases its authority to issue net neutrality regulations—i.e., to regulate broadband—largely on this provision, which opponents argue does not constitute a separate grant of regulatory authority.

164. The notion that the commission's role properly includes "promoting" the industries it oversees is not limited to one party or ideology. See, e.g., Statement of Chairman Kevin Martin, En Banc Hearing of the Federal Communications Commission, Cambridge, Massachusetts (February 25, 2009) ("The intent [of the FCC's 'four net neutrality principles'] was ... to *foster the creation, adoption and use of Internet broadband content, applications, and services.*") (emphasis added). See also Farrell and Weiser, "Modularity, Vertical Integration, and Open Access Policies," 134: "In particular, regulation sometimes adopts measures rationalized as infant industry protection that seek to produce certain innovative benefits—at the risk of falling victim to the perilous exercise of predicting winners and losers."

165. For a contrary view, see Jonathan B. Baker, "Sector-Specific Competition Enforcement at the FCC," *New York University Annual Survey of American Law* 66 (2011): 413–18, at 418: "The sector-specific agency has the expertise and ability to take a longer view of how the industry should evolve, allowing it to identify and address competitive issues that go beyond the practical ambit of antitrust enforcement. By drawing on the strengths of the sector-specific agency and the competition agency, concurrent review can thus enhance competition enforcement as a whole." The issue of jurisdiction—which agency or agencies should enforce competition policy in the broadband sector—is at least theoretically separate from the substantive issues addressed here.

166. See Andrea Renda, "Neutrality and Diversity in the Internet Ecosystem" (August 19, 2010), 32–33, http://papers.ssrn.com/sol3/papers.cfm?abstract_id=1680446 (accessed October 1, 2012).

167. The notion of "promoting" competition in telecommunications markets grew at least in part out of the 1996 Telecommunications Act, which was designed to transform the industry from its legacy-regulated monopoly structure to a more competitive structure as expeditiously as possible. In that context, "promoting competition" meant, in part, removing government barriers to entry (the statutory monopolies enjoyed by local telephone companies). To the extent government continues to erect barriers to entry (e.g., as, until recently, in local cable franchising regulations or by creating false scarcity in the market for spectrum), it is entirely appropriate for competition authorities to seek to lower them.

168. See, e.g., Jonathan Sallet, "The Internet Ecosystem and Legal Regimes: Economic Regulation Supporting Innovation Dynamism" (November 2011), http://papers.ssrn.com/sol3/papers.cfm?abstract_id=1957715 (accessed October 1, 2012), 3: "Because rulemaking is necessarily based on a current state of understanding about the market, it is ill-equipped to deal flexibly with the rapidly changing and ever-evolving nature of competition in the Internet marketplace."

169. NBP Report, 41.

170. See, e.g., Julius Genachowski, Hearing on "Ensuring Competition on the Internet: Network Neutrality and Antitrust Law," Statement before the Subcommittee on Intellectual Property, Competition, and the Internet Committee on the Judiciary, US House of Representatives (May 5, 2011), 4: "As we heard during our FCC proceeding, antitrust enforcement is expensive to pursue, takes a long time, and kicks in only after damage is done. Especially for start-ups in a fast-moving area like the Internet, that's not a practical solution."

171. Renda, "Neutrality and Diversity," 51–52: "One may wonder the difficulty of an antitrust authority in having to deal with competition between layers. The Internet ecosystem is indeed evolving towards a competitive arena in which some big players, having reached a strong position in the provision of a key gateway service, try to extend their control over the value chain to secure a bigger share of the value that is created by the whole system architecture. This is how powerful search engines, OS vendors, mainframe champions, mobile operators, fixed-line broadband providers, microprocessor manufacturers and conglomerate producers of proprietary goods ended up challenging themselves on countless battlefields and with a mix of open, semi-open and proprietary standards. Plus, all this is happening in a constantly changing environment, and—

even if one should resist the temptation to predict the future based exclusively on past experience—there is clear evidence that markets have been able to fix in the medium term most of the short-term concerns voiced by industry stakeholders. And there is also sufficient evidence that market developments have been quicker and more effective than antitrust decisions—let alone sectoral regulation—in fixing those problems."

172. See, e.g., Shapiro and Varian, *Information Rules*, 310.

173. Some regulatory regimes seem to attract sufficient constituencies as to be practically impossihle to reform. The FCC's efforts to reform its rules for intercarrier compensation, for example, have been ongoing for more than fifteen years since passage of the 1996 Telecommunications Act. By contrast, remedies associated with traditional antitrust enforcement are typically time-limited, and thus subject to automatic "sunset."

174. See Brito et al., *Net Neutrality Regulation*, 2. See also Jonathan B. Baker, "Promoting Innovation Competition through the Aspen/Kodak Rule," *George Mason Law Review* 7 (Spring 1999): 495–521, at 521 ("[W]hen the goal is to promote innovation, it is difficult to devise a general [monopolization] rule appropriate to the circumstances of all industries.")

175. Farrell and Weiser conclude that the lack of an adequate analytical framework to support its regulations has led to policy "vacillation" at the FCC. See Farrell and Weiser, "Modularity, Vertical Integration, and Open Access Policies," 132–33: "We see little evidence of subtle balancing to suggest that changes in circumstances explain the changes in policy, so it is tempting instead to describe the variation as 'vacillating' in an inadequate analytical framework."

176. See Shapiro and Varian, *Information Rules*, 311. The propensity of regulatory agencies to engage in such cross-subsidization is well-documented. See, e.g., Ronald H. Coase, "The Federal Communications Commission," *Journal of Law and Economics* 2 (1959): 1–40, and Richard A. Posner, "Taxation by Regulation," *Bell Journal of Economics and Management Science* 3, no. 1 (Spring 1972): 98–129.

177. See, e.g., Robin S. Lee and Tim Wu, "Subsidizing Creativity through Network Design: Zero-Pricing and Net Neutrality," *Journal of Economic Perspectives* 23, no. 3 (Summer 2009): 61–76, at 67: "Of course, for a given price level,

subsidizing content comes at the expense of not subsidizing users, and subsidizing users could also lead to greater consumer adoption of broadband. It is an open question whether, in subsidizing content, the welfare gains from the invention of the next killer app or the addition of new content offset the price reductions consumers might otherwise enjoy or the benefit of expanding service to new users."

178. For a discussion of difficulties of identifying predatory pricing in network markets, even on a case-by-case basis, see Joseph Farrell and Michael L. Katz, "Competition or Predation? Consumer Coordination, Strategic Pricing and Price Floors in Network Markets," *Journal of Industrial Economics* 53, no. 2 (June 2005): 203–31.

179. See Carl Shapiro, "Exclusivity in Network Industries," *George Mason Law Review* 7 (Spring 1999): 673–82, at 678.

180. Baker, "Competitive Price Discrimination," 649.

181. Renda, "Neutrality and Diversity," 47.

182. Ibid., 51. See also Rysman, "The Economics of Two-Sided Markets," 132: "Perhaps it is more natural to observe firms begin with a one-sided model and switch to a two-sided model as they become more established. Doing so allows potential platforms to overcome the 'chicken-and-egg' problem by first providing complementary goods themselves (sometimes requiring daunting capital expenditures). For example, Amazon first established itself as a fairly standard on-line book retailer before introducing its 'marketplace' options where sellers set prices and interact with consumers."

183. For a "new-economy" based critique of the Open Internet Order, see Bruce W. Owen, "Antitrust and Vertical Integration in 'New Economy' Industries with Application to Broadband Access," *Review of Industrial Organization* 38, no. 4 (2011): 363–86.

184. See Federal Communications Commission, *Video Device Competition, Implementation of Section 304 of the Telecommunications Act of 1996, Commercial Availability of Navigation Devices, Compatibility Between Cable Systems and Consumer Electronics Equipment, Notice of Inquiry*, MB Docket No. 10-91, CS Docket No. 97-80, PP Docket No. 00-67, FCC 10-60 (April 21, 2010).

185. On handset exclusivity, see Jeffrey Paul Jarosch, "Reassessing Tying Arrangements at the End of AT&T's iPhone Exclusivity," *Columbia Business Law Review* 2, no. 2 (2011): 296–362, at 361: "iPhone exclusivity has had

meaningfully pro-competitive effects in fostering innovation and differentiation among wireless networks."

186. See, e.g., Ehrlich et al., "The Impact of Regulation on Innovation," 22–23.

187. Weiser, "The Internet, Innovation," 585.

188. Ibid., 590–91. See also *Berkey Photo, Inc. v. Eastman Kodak Co.*, 603 F.2d 263 (2d Cir. 1979), 281: "It is the possibility of success in the marketplace, attributable to superior performance, that provides the incentives on which the proper functioning of our competitive economy rests. If a firm that has engaged in the risks and expenses of research and development were required in all circumstances to share with its rivals the benefits of those endeavors, this incentive would very likely be vitiated."

189. See, e.g., *United States v. Google Inc. and ITA Software, Inc, Competitive Impact Statement* (April 8, 2011), www.justice.gov/atr/cases/f269600/269620.pdf (accessed October 1, 2012), 3: "The proposed Final Judgment therefore strikes an appropriate balance between competing interests by preserving the potential significant efficiencies from the combination of Google's and ITA's complementary expertise while redressing the potential for anticompetitive foreclosure that could result from the acquisition."

190. See Herbert Hovenkamp, "Antitrust and Innovation: Where We Are and Where We Should Be Going," *Antitrust Law Journal* 77, no. 3 (2011): 749–56, at 754. For a dynamic competition-focused critique of mandatory unbundling policies, see Glen O. Robinson and Dennis L. Weisman, "Designing Competition Policy for Telecommunications," *Review of Network Economics* 7, no. 4 (December 2008): 509–46. See also Crandall et al., *The Long-Run Effects of Copper Unbundling*.

191. Renda, "Neutrality and Diversity," 54.

192. For a discussion of proposals for fiber unbundling, for example, see e.g. Crandall et al., *The Long-Run Effects of Copper Unbundling*.

193. On the wisdom of adopting rules for "IP interconnection," see Faratin et al., "The Growing Complexity of Internet Interconnection," 64: "We also have a cautionary conclusion: if one should be motivated (for whatever reason) to contemplate some regulatory rule to manage interconnection, the design of such a rule will be both complex and informationally demanding. Partial transit and paid peering may be seen as efficiency-enhancing responses to changing market conditions. While there may be opportunities for abuse by providers with excessive bargaining power, the complexity of what is in place today, and what seems to be working today, would argue that the best way to address any potential concern would be to focus on the sources of bargaining power and identify anti-competitive opportunism, rather than to impose *ex ante* restrictions on the range of bilateral contracts." See also Analysys Mason, *Overview of Recent Changes in the IP Interconnection Ecosystem* (May 2011), 32: "The commercially-driven evolution of Internet interconnection stands in contrast to the regulation that governs interconnection of telecommunications services, which may share the same network infrastructure with the Internet, and involve many of the same players. For example, in the past decade, during which the evolution in the Internet described above took place, the FCC has made countless attempts to modify the inter-carrier compensation system in response to changes in telecommunications—a process that is still ongoing. In contrast, since the commercialization of the Internet backbone, the Internet ecosystem has long proven itself to be able to develop and sustain interconnection in the absence of sector-specific regulation—and it now has shown itself to also be able to adapt well to rapid and profound market changes without regulatory intervention."

194. See US DOJ and FTC, *Horizontal Merger Guidelines*, 21–22.

195. See e.g., David S. Evans and Michael D. Noel, "The Analysis of Mergers that Involve Multisided Platform Businesses," *Journal of Competition Law and Economics* 4, no. 3 (2008): 663–95, and Lapo Filistrucchi, Tobias J. Klein, and Thomans Michielsen, "Assessing Unilateral Merger Effects in a Two-Sided Market: An Application to the Dutch Daily Newspaper Market" (Tilberg Law and Economics Center, October 2011), http://ssrn.com/abstract=1946163 (accessed October 1, 2012).

About the Author

Jeffrey Eisenach has served in senior positions at the Federal Trade Commission and the Office of Management and Budget. As a visiting scholar at AEI, he focuses on policies affecting the information technology sector, innovation, and entrepreneurship. Eisenach is also a managing director and a principal at Navigant Economics and an adjunct professor at the George Mason University School of Law, where he teaches Regulated Industries. He writes on a wide range of issues, including industrial organization, communications policy and the Internet, government regulations, labor economics, and public finance. He has also taught at Harvard University's Kennedy School of Government and at the Virginia Polytechnic Institute.

159

In Search of a Competition Doctrine for Information Technology Markets: Recent Antitrust Developments in the Online Sector

Jeffrey A. Eisenach and Ilene Knable Gotts†

Recent antitrust developments in the online sector – sometimes described as the "Internet Ecosystem" – demonstrate that the search for a coherent and reliable doctrine for evaluating competition issues in high-tech markets remains incomplete. While acknowledging that traditional approaches are often inapposite for assessing the competitive dynamics of high-tech markets, enforcers continue to struggle to devise a coherent alternative framework. We review some recent cases that illustrate the challenges of enforcing competition law in information technology markets.

I. INTRODUCTION

Information technology ("IT") markets have been raising difficult issues for competition authorities for over a century. Indeed, December 2013 marked the 100th anniversary of AT&T's controversial "Kingsbury Commitment"[1] in which AT&T agreed to interconnect its long-lines networks with local telephone companies in return for a legal monopoly over long distance service—a deal that ultimately led to decades of litigation and perhaps the most famous consent decree in antitrust history, the 1982 "Modified Final Judgment."[2] Competition authorities have struggled to devise solutions to real or theoretical antitrust concerns in virtually every major IT market, from mainframe computers (IBM)

---

† Forthcoming in *Communications and Competition Law: Key Issues in the Telecoms, Media and Technology Sectors* (Alphen aan den Rijn, The Netherlands: Kluwer Law International/International Bar Association series). Jeffrey A. Eisenach is a Senior Vice President at NERA Economic Consulting. Ilene Knable Gotts is a partner at Wachtell, Lipton, Rosen & Katz in New York. The views expressed in this paper are the authors' and should not be attributed to their firms, clients or other institutions with which they are affiliated.
[1] http://vcxc.org/documents/KC1.pdf.
[2] United States v. AT&T, 552 F. Supp. 131 (D.D.C. 1982), *aff'd sub nom.* Maryland v. United States, 460 U.S. 1001 (1983).

to operating systems (Microsoft), from "enterprise management software" (Oracle-PeopleSoft) to search engines (Google).

IT markets pose a variety of analytical challenges. They are characterized by both supply- and demand-side economies of scale and scope, typically implying high market share and/or high levels of concentration (*e.g.*, HHI). Although such dynamics could result in market power to the extent that the assets are "essential" to compete, traditional concentration measures are meaningless for determining such potentialities given their limited and static nature. Indeed, rapid innovation and the potential for disruptive entry imply such market power may be ephemeral, even illusory. Strong complementarities (*e.g.*, between smart phones and networks, or operating systems and microchips) place interoperability and interconnection issues at center stage. Particular business practices (*e.g.*, a decision to standardize around one technology but deny interoperability to others) may be efficiency-enhancing and competition-inhibiting at the same time. Consolidation may harm competition in a static sense, yet generate real but sometimes difficult-to-assess benefits for innovation, or demand-side externalities from network effects. Products tend to be highly differentiated (*e.g.*, smartphones with different operating systems and features), leading to prices above marginal cost, and, in many cases, prices and terms are set through bilateral bargaining over actual or anticipated quasi-rents.

Our goal in this article is certainly not to resolve these issues, but rather to describe them in a way that illuminates the analytical challenges, provide some recent examples of antitrust reviews involving IT markets, and offer some thoughts on how these issues are likely to present themselves in the future. We also note that while economists continue to make progress towards a better understanding of the competitive dynamics of IT markets, much of that understanding is not yet fully or consistently reflected in practice. We are not suggesting, however, that IT markets get a "free pass" and not be subject to antitrust law principles, or even worse, that there is a need for regulation to supplant free market behavior. To the contrary: antitrust law enforcement is usually the correct place for addressing both IT market behavior and transactions.

The remainder of this paper is organized as follows. Section II presents a taxonomy of the economic characteristics that distinguish IT markets from more traditional markets, grouping them into three categories—*dynamism*; *modularity*; and *demand-side effects*—and provides some examples of the implications of these characteristics for competition analysis. Section III discusses several recent situations in which competition authorities have wrestled with such issues in practice. Section IV offers some thoughts on how these issues are likely to present themselves in the immediate future. Section V presents a brief conclusion.

II. THE IT CHALLENGE TO TRADITIONAL ANTITRUST DOCTRINE

Effective antitrust policy is premised on the ability to recognize monopoly power; assess its effects on prices and quality; identify the anticompetitive conduct it sometimes enables (*e.g.*, by raising rivals' costs); and, ultimately, determine its effects on consumer welfare—which, half a century after the Chicago revolution, continues to be acknowledged as the central objective of antitrust. Towards these ends, academics and practitioners have developed various analytical tools, empirical proxies, and rules of thumb (*e.g.*, high market shares and/or high concentration ratios create a presumption of monopoly power or high likelihood of collusion) that together constitute traditional antitrust doctrine.[3] IT markets have characteristics that limit the usefulness of these traditional approaches, often in ways that are not yet well understood. We begin by describing the characteristics that distinguish IT markets from more traditional ones, and then discuss some of the challenges these characteristics pose for traditional antitrust doctrine.

A. *The IT Trifecta: Dynamism, Modularity, Demand-Side Effects*

IT markets exhibit at least three meaningful distinguishing characteristics: *dynamism, modularity*, and *demand-side effects.*[4]

Dynamism refers to the significance of innovation as a measure of market performance: In dynamic markets, the ability of a firm to offer new and improved products plays at least as significant a role in its success (*i.e.*, its profitability) as the ability to produce and sell existing products at lower prices.[5]

In such markets, firms incur significant sunk cost investments to create new products, causing average costs to exceed marginal costs over the relevant range of output, but resulting in product differentiation (innovation being simply product differentiation over time) that allows sellers to recoup their investments by earning high margins (relative to marginal cost). Under current doctrine, high margins are easily mistaken for traditional monopoly power, but assuming low entry barriers, they are not only consistent with, but necessary for, maximization of consumer welfare: They not only allow firms to recoup sunk cost investments, but also provide the incentive to take the risks inherent in innovation.

The assumption of low entry barriers is not a trivial one, and other characteristics of IT markets—*e.g.*, demand-side network effects—may call it into question. But it is nevertheless true that the sort of market power that is so commonplace in IT markets frequently contains the seeds of its own destruction, as today's hot product can easily become tomorrow's obsolete clunker (*see, e.g.*, "Apple Newton" and "Palm Pilot").

A second characteristic that distinguishes IT markets is modularity, or what is sometimes referred to as "platform competition." From an economic perspective, modularity is associated with strong complementarities in production or consumption: Operating systems are strong complements with personal computers; online music stores are strong complements with smart phones; smart phones are strong complements with communications networks, etc. Modularity also creates demand for compatibility or "interconnection." Firms that produce complementary products (*e.g.*, Microsoft and Nokia; Google and Samsung) may team up to create platforms (sets of compatible

---

[3] By "traditional antitrust doctrine," we mean "modern doctrine as applied to traditional markets."

[4] For a more extensive discussion of these phenomena and their implications for competition analysis, *see* JEFFREY A. EISENACH, BROADBAND COMPETITION IN THE INTERNET ECOSYSTEM (American Enterprise Institute, 2012); *see also* OZ SHY, THE ECONOMICS OF NETWORK INDUSTRIES (Cambridge University Press, 2001).

[5] WILLIAM J. BAUMOL, THE FREE MARKET INNOVATION MACHINE: ANALYZING THE GROWTH MIRACLE OF CAPITALISM (Princeton University Press, 2002), at 4 ("Innovation has replaced price as the name of the game in a number of important industries. The computer industry is only the most obvious example, whose new and improved models appear constantly, each manufacturer battling to stay ahead of its rivals."); *see also* JOSEPH SCHUMPETER, CAPITALISM, SOCIALISM AND DEMOCRACY (1942).

complements); in other cases (*e.g.*, Apple, Blackberry) firms choose to achieve compatibility through vertical integration.

Competition in such markets takes place both within platforms (*e.g.*, between HTC and Samsung for leadership on the Android platform) and among them (*e.g.*, between Android and iOS). Disputes over interconnection terms—in which firms seek to create and exercise bargaining power and so maximize their shares of the economic profits created by a successful platform—are commonplace.

Finally, IT markets are also characterized by significant demand-side effects, including economies of both scale and scope. Demand-side economies of scale, also known as network effects, imply that a product is more valuable to consumers as the number of users increases: The prototypical, if now somewhat dated, example is the fax machine. Demand-side economies of scope, by contrast, imply that a product's value increases with the diversity (as opposed to simply the number) of users: The value of a newspaper to both advertisers and users depends on the presence of the other *type* of consumer (though for some consumers, the presence of advertisers may detract from the value rather than add to it).

The relationship between competition and consumer welfare in markets with demand-side effects is more complicated than in more traditional markets in several ways. For example, it is well established that a monopolist in a two-sided market has strong incentives to set efficient relative prices (*i.e.*, to engage in efficient price discrimination).[6] In markets with strong network effects, the efficiency benefits of monopoly may exceed the costs in terms of foregone competition.[7]

B. *Implications for Enforcement*

These characteristics of IT markets have important implications for competition policy and antitrust enforcement, challenging accepted rules of thumb, complicating application of time-tested techniques, and forcing regulators to take account of factors that do not play a significant role in more traditional markets.

Perhaps most obviously, the dynamic nature of IT markets—the fact that they are characterized by rapid technological change—forces competition authorities to pay greater heed to forecasts of future events than is often the case in more traditional markets, even up to the point of forecasting the impact of mergers and potentially anticompetitive conduct on the development of markets for products that do not yet exist. No combination of economists, lawyers and technologists has thus far demonstrated much competence in performing this task,[8] and for good reason. As Professor Hovenkamp points out:

---

[6] *See, e.g.*, Julian Wright, *One-Sided Logic in Two-Sided Markets*, 3(1) REVIEW OF NETWORK ECONOMICS 44 (2004).

[7] *See* Michael L. Katz & Carl Shapiro, *Systems Competition and Network Effects*, 8 THE JOURNAL OF ECONOMIC PERSPECTIVES 93 (Spring 1994).

[8] *See generally* Ilene Knable Gotts and Richard T. Rapp, *Antitrust Treatment of Mergers Involving Future Goods*, ANTITRUST 178 (2004). Inaccurate predictions of future events can prove embarrassing. The Federal Trade Commission ("FTC"), for example, justified the imposition of conditions in the 2000 AOL-Time Warner merger on the basis of its finding that AOL, as the "leading provider of narrowband internet access," was "likely to become the leading provider of broadband internet access as well." *See* U.S. Federal Trade Commission, In the Matter of America Online, Inc. and Time Warner Inc., Docket

163

[I]nnovation often produces very sudden and quite unpredictable results. It can completely kill an industry in a few years, as electronic calculators did to slide rules in the 1960s. In the process, it can bring an entirely new industry into existence in an equally short time. It can produce results far different than researchers expected, such as the blockbuster drug Viagra, which was the culmination of a research project seeking a treatment for angina, not for erectile dysfunction. Innovation can produce sudden and dramatic shifts in prices or output and almost instantly expand the range of consumer choices. As a result, predicting and managing competitive processes in highly innovative industries is much more difficult than in markets where technology is very largely constant and most movements affect only the output and price of a set of unchanging products.[9]

It is well understood that dynamism implies that existing monopoly power may be ephemeral,[10] but its implications for antitrust regulation are in fact far more complex and multifaceted than that simple thesis suggests. For example, a merger might be defended on the grounds that the combination is necessary to advance development of a new product—but only if regulators can be persuaded the new product will be successful (and so enhance consumer welfare).

A second implication of dynamism is its inextricable relationship with the economics of innovation—the cycle of investment, product differentiation, and pricing power (the return on risk and entrepreneurship) that incentivizes innovation in the first place. Dynamic industries display strong economies of scale, tend to have high levels of concentration at any point in time, and are characterized by high profit margins. The implications are profound, calling into question the predictive power of the two most commonly used proxies for

No. C-2989 (Complaint) (Dec. 14, 2000) at 3. As it turned out, AOL never became a significant, let alone leading, broadband Internet Service Provider ("ISP"). Similarly, in the AT&T-MediaOne transaction, the Antitrust Division of the U.S. Department of Justice ("DOJ"), expressed concern with the indirect ownership interests that AT&T would have had in both Excite@Home and RoadRunner, two broadband Internet companies, and required AT&T to divest its RoadRunner interest. *See* Press Release, U.S. Dep't of Justice, Justice Department Requires AT&T to Divest MediaOne's Interest in RoadRunner Broadband Internet Access Service (May 25, 2000), *available at* http://www.justice.gov/atr/public/press_releases/2000/4829.pdf. At the time of the acquisition, Excite@Home and RoadRunner together served the vast majority of subscribers who received broadband Internet service over cable facilities. The DOJ was concerned that AT&T would be able, post-closing, to facilitate collusion and coordination between Excite@Home and RoadRunner in ways that would result in a substantial lessening of competition in the market for aggregation, promotion, and distribution of residential broadband content. Instead, in 2001, Excite@Home declared bankruptcy.

[9] *See* Herbert Hovenkamp, *Antitrust and the Movement of Technology*, 19 GEO. MASON L. REV. 1119, 1120-1121 (2012).

[10] *See, e.g.*, Douglas H. Ginsburg and Joshua D. Wright, *Dynamic Analysis and the Limits of Antitrust Institutions*, 78 ANTITRUST LAW JOURNAL 1, 22 (2012).

actionable market power, market concentration[11] and profit margins.[12] Moreover, the costs associated with Type II error (imposition of remedies on the basis of falsely identified monopoly power) are especially high, as such remedies—often in the form of "sharing" requirements or barriers to consolidation—not only deprive existing firms of the returns on innovation, but signal to future entrepreneurs that the payoff for successful innovation is subject to regulatory truncation.[13]

Since the Fifth Century BC, medical doctors have sworn to a Hipprocratic Oath that recognizes before all else, that they are "to do no harm." It would be admirable if antitrust enforcers could adopt the same approach—and recognize that enforcement should seek to do more good than harm and that harm will result if they unnecessarily deter innovation or synergies by stopping or conditioning a transaction or conduct that, left alone, would not have been anticompetitive. FTC Commissioner Maureen Ohlhausen has consistently in her public pronouncements advocated for "regulatory humility." As recently described in a speech before the Free State Foundation:

> It is exceedingly difficult to predict the path of technology and its effects on society. The massive benefits of the Internet in large part have been a result of entrepreneurs' freedom to experiment with different business models. The best of these experiments have survived and thrived, even in the face of initial unfamiliarity and unease about the impact on consumers and competitors . . . Early skepticism does not predict potential consumer harm. Conversely, as the failures of

[11] Dissenting Statement of Commissioner Joshua D. Wright, In re Fidelity Nat'l Financial, Inc. (F.T.C. File No. 131-0159 (Dec. 23, 2013), *available at* http://www.ftc.gov/sites/default/files/documents/public_statements/dissenting-statement-commissioner-joshua-d.wright-matter-fidelity-national-financial-inc.lender-processing-services-inc.december-2013/131224fidelitywrightstatement.pdf; American Bar Association, Section of Antitrust Law, MARKET POWER HANDBOOK: COMPETITION LAW AND ECONOMIC FOUNDATIONS (2d ed.) (2012); Ilene Knable Gotts, *Market Definitions in the Merger Context: Hard Work Pays Off in the Long Run*, FORDHAM COMPETITION LAW INSTITUTE, ANNUAL PROCEEDINGS, INTERNATIONAL ANTITRUST LAW & POLICY, Ch. 16 (B.E. Hawk ed., 2013).

[12] *See* Kenneth G. Elzinga and David E. Mills, *"The Lerner Index of Monopoly Power: Origins and Uses,"* AMERICAN ECONOMIC REVIEW: PAPERS & PROCEEDINGS 101, 3 (2011); American Bar Association, *supra* note 11.

[13] *See* Franklin W. Fisher, *Diagnosing Monopoly*, in INDUSTRIAL ORGANIZATION, ECONOMICS AND THE LAW: COLLECTED PAPERS OF FRANKLIN M. FISHER (MIT Press, 1991) 3-32. *See also* Novell, Inc. v. Microsoft Corp., 731 F.3d 1064, 1073 (10th Cir. 2013) ("If the law were to make a habit of forcing monopolists to help competitors by keeping prices high, sharing their property, or declining to expand their own operations, courts would paradoxically risk encouraging collusion between rivals and dampened price competition—themselves paradigmatic antitrust wrongs, injuries to help one another would also risk reducing the incentive both sides have to innovate, invest, and expand—again results inconsistent with the goals of antitrust. The monopolist might be deterred from investing, innovating, or expanding (or even entering a market in the first place) with the knowledge anything it creates it could be forced to share; the smaller company might be deterred, too, knowing it could just demand the right to piggyback on its larger rival.").

thousands of dotcoms show, early enthusiasm does not predict consumer benefit.

Because it is so difficult to predict the future of technology, government officials, like myself, must approach new technologies and new business models with a significant dose of regulatory humility. . . . We must identify benefits and any likely harm. If harms do arise, we must ask if existing laws and regulations are sufficient to address them, rather than assuming that new rules are required.

And we must remain conscious of our limits . . . Even worse, data-driven decisions can seem right while being wrong. Political polling expert Nate Silver notes that "[o]ne of the pervasive risks that we face in the information age . . . is that even if the amount of knowledge in the world is increasing, the gap between what we know and what we think we know may be widening." Regulatory humility can help narrow that gap.[14]

It is important for the U.S. economy that the appropriate balance is achieved.

The presence of strong complements in production—modularity—poses a related but distinct set of challenges, forcing regulators to judge the competitive and consumer welfare implications of interoperable (or interconnected) technologies relative to proprietary or "closed garden" approaches. Refusals to interconnect or to facilitate interoperability (*e.g.*, Microsoft's refusals to reveal APIs to Netscape or, to take an even earlier example, AT&T's attempts to prohibit attachment of foreign devices such as the "Hush-A-Phone" to its network) may evidence an intent to foreclose competition and raise rivals' costs or, alternatively, a welfare-maximizing choice by the platform operator to optimize system functionality[15] (as Comcast argued in its defense of its throttling of *BitTorrent* in the first litigated net neutrality case).[16] Where achieving interoperability involves incurring sunk costs (as in the case of standard essential patents ("SEPs")), the potential arises for opportunistic behavior, though courts have been reluctant to conclude such behavior violates the antitrust laws.[17]

Lastly, demand-side effects present a multitude of challenges. Most obviously, markets in which demand-side economies of scale (*i.e.*, "network effects") are significant are subject to "tipping" and may create barriers to entry. Conversely, the very same network effects responsible for these results create real benefits for consumers, who *really are* better off when, for instance, everyone can learn to use the same (QWERTY) keyboard.[18] Multisided markets (demand-side economies of scope) pose their own special concerns, forcing

---

[14] Remarks of Maureen K. Ohlhausen, Commissioner, U.S. Federal Trade Commission, *The Procrustean Problem with Prescriptive Regulation, Sixth Annual Telecom Policy Conference, Free State Foundation* (Washington, D.C. Mar. 18, 2014), *available at* http://www.ftc.gov/system/files/documents/public_statements/291361/140318fsf.pdf.

[15] *See generally* Kevin Boudreau, *Open Platform Strategies and Innovation: Granting Access vs. Devolving Control*, 56 MANAGEMENT SCIENCE 1849 (Oct. 2010).

[16] *See* Comcast Corp. v. FCC, 600 F.3d 642 (D.C. Cir. 2010).

[17] *See, e.g.*, Susan Decker, *Rambus Antitrust Case on Royalties Dropped by FTC*, BLOOMBERG (May 14, 2009), *available at* http://www.bloomberg.com/apps/news?pid=newsarchive&refer=home&sid=at5P6AmiOMsQ; *see also* http://www.ftc.gov/enforcement/cases-proceedings/011-0017/rambus-inc-matter.

[18] *See, e.g.*, Katz & Shapiro, *supra* note 7.

regulators to consider the effects of mergers, for example, on both downstream "consumers" and upstream "suppliers."[19] Economists have only recently begun to develop the tools necessary to assess such effects. Thus, as Ballon and Van Heesvelde conclude:

> [C]urrently no clear, general principle exists about how to regulate platforms, and regulators have no operational frameworks that can easily accommodate the particular characteristics of platform markets—such as the existence of externalities across different sides of the platform, and the complex effects of multi-homing of service providers and/or end users.[20]

The depth of the IT challenge to traditional antitrust doctrine is evidenced by the fact that even the Holy Grail of antitrust enforcement—stable or lower prices—can no longer be taken for granted. In IT markets, price effects in one market have to be weighed against (possibly countervailing) effects in others, as well as against changes in quality, not only contemporaneously but over time: A price increase which leads to higher returns to suppliers may lead to static losses (from lower consumption), but higher rates of innovation and ultimately higher consumer welfare.

III. FROM THEORY TO PRACTICE: RECENT ENFORCEMENT REVIEW INVOLVING IT (AND RELATED) MARKETS

The challenges to traditional antitrust doctrine described above are on vivid display almost daily as competition authorities struggle to identify actionable conduct and assess the competitive effects of proposed transactions throughout the IT sector. In this section, we discuss several recent cases, including transactions involving content providers, database software, hardware, devices and networks, as well as cases involving potential competition and future markets. The cases discussed highlight the issues agencies face across a diverse, complex and rapidly changing set of markets in identifying market power and fashioning appropriate remedies.

A. Transactions Involving Content Providers

In recent years, both the FTC and the DOJ have reviewed acquisitions involving firms that compete in providing data or content to others. These transactions often held the potential of increasing the rate of innovation, enhancing modularity, and providing demand-side scale and scope efficiencies. Such effects could drive down costs, particularly in nascent sectors. On the other hand, these developments could increase entry barriers or eliminate competition through foreclosure, thereby raising rivals' costs. The agencies' response has

---

[19] *See, e.g.*, David S. Evans & Richard Schmalensee, *The Antitrust Analysis of Multi-Sided Platform Businesses*, in OXFORD HANDBOOK ON INTERNATIONAL ANTITRUST ECONOMICS at 19-21, Roger Blair & Daniel Sokol, eds. (forthcoming), *available at* http://papers.ssrn.com/sol3/papers.cfm?abstract_id=2185373 (warning against "basing judgments about market power on analysis of only a single side of a multi-sided platform").

[20] Pieter Ballon & Eric Van Heesvelde, *ICT Platforms and Regulatory Concerns in Europe*, 35 TELECOMMUNICATIONS POLICY, 702, 707 (2011).

often been to impose some form of licensing or open access requirements designed to create a "level playing field" for competitors.

(1) Horizontal Theories

A number of recent transactions have involved the combination of firms with databases, in which the agency required that competition be maintained by providing to a third party the rights to one of the databases.

Most recently, on March 24, 2014, the FTC conditioned its approval of CoreLogic, Inc.'s acquisition of DataQuick Information Systems, Inc.[21] The FTC's complaint alleges that CoreLogic and DataQuick are two of three providers of national accessor and recorder bulk data, and that their combination would have increased the risk of both coordinated and unilateral effects. CoreLogic, which offers a variety of products tailored to lending, investment, and real estate industries, collects and maintains data and is the largest provider of data in the United States. DataQuick offered licenses for such data and had a unique license with CoreLogic that allowed it to relicense data in bulk. The data at issue include current and historical public record data in a standardized bulk format for the vast majority of real estate properties in the U.S. Customers use these data as inputs into proprietary programs and systems for internal analyses. The database includes over a decade of information.

It appears likely that the transaction parties argued that combining operations would lower costs of maintaining the database and broaden the userset. To the extent there was competition between the merging firms, that competition would be eliminated. Moreover, the FTC alleged that new competitors were not likely to emerge in this market because of the high cost of obtaining the necessary data (especially historical information). Accordingly, the FTC's remedy aims to replace DataQuick as a competitive force. The consent requires CoreLogic to license to Renwood RealtyTrac ("RealtyTrac") historical data and to deliver going-forward data for up to seven years as well as to provide RealtyTrac access to several ancillary data sets that DataQuick provides to its customers. The consent also provides RealtyTrac with access to information regarding customers and data management, requires CoreLogic to provide it with access to technical support for 18 months, and requires CoreLogic to provide certain DataQuick customers with the opportunity to terminate their contracts early and switch to RealtyTrac without penalty. RealtyTrac currently operates an online marketplace of foreclosure real property listings and provides national foreclosure data services to real estate consumers, investors, and professionals, and with this license, will be a new entrant into the business.

In 2012, the FTC similarly conditioned its approval of CoStar's acquisition of LoopNet on the sale of LoopNet's ownership interest in Xceligent to DMG Information, Inc. and other behavioral relief. CoStar, LoopNet, and Xceligent offered listing databases and information services used by brokers, investors, appraisers, developers, and others in the commercial real estate industry. CoStar actively tracks and aggregates commercial real estate listings and property-specific information nationwide and provides subscription-based access to its

---

[21] Press Release, Fed. Trade Comm'n, FTC Puts Conditions on CoreLogic, Inc.'s Proposed Acquisition of DataQuick Information Systems (Mar. 24, 2014), *available at* http://www.ftc.gov/news-evehttp://www.ftc.gov/news-events/press-releases/2014/03/ftc-puts-conditions-corelogic-incs-proposed-acquisition-dataquick.

comprehensive database. LoopNet operated the most heavily trafficked commercial real estate listings database in the United States and offered some commercial real estate information services. Xceligent also actively tracked and aggregated commercial real estate listings and property-specific information and maintained a detailed and comprehensive database.

The FTC's complaint alleges that the proposed acquisition would reduce competition in the markets for these listing databases and information services, and that CoStar and LoopNet are the only two providers with nationwide coverage. The complaint also alleges that Xceligent is the "most similar competitor for information services" to CoStar, and, therefore, the combination would eliminate the direct and substantial competition between the two companies, due to LoopNet's ownership stake in Xceligent.[22] The consent requires that the combined Co-Star-LoopNet take certain steps to ensure that Xceligent is able to compete and expand aggressively in the U.S. market for commercial real estate listings databases and information services. Specifically, the consent "imposes certain conduct requirements to assure the continued viability of Xceligent as a competitor to the merged firm and to reduce barriers to competitive entry and expansion. These additional provisions will facilitate Xceligent's geographic expansion and prevent foreclosure of [the parties'] established customer base."[23] The consent requires, among other things, CoStar and LoopNet to continue to offer their customers core products on a stand-alone basis for three years.[24] A related provision prohibits the parties from limiting use of the REApplications product, a software tool for managing market research in connection with customers' purchase, lease, or license of CRE database services from competitors. Also, in 2013, the FTC required Fidelity to sell a copy of LPS's title plants (databases used to determine title status of real property) in six Oregon counties.[25]

(2) Vertical Theories

Some of the most interesting transactions involving content providers were not horizontal, but "vertical" in nature. The DOJ's Guide for Merger Remedies indicates that vertical mergers "can create changed incentives and enhance the ability of the merged firm to impair the competitive process. In such situations, a remedy that counteracts these changed incentives or eliminates the merged firm's

---

[22] *Analysis of Agreement Containing Consent Order to Aid Public Comment, CoStar Grp, Inc., Lonestar Acquisition Sub, Inc., and LoopNet, Inc.*, File No. 111-0172 (F.T.C. May 2, 2012), *available at* http://www.ftc.gov/sites/default/files/documents/cases/2012/04/120426costaranal.pdf.

[23] *Id.*

[24] The "anti-bundling" provisions are aimed to protect Xceligent for a limited period while it expands the breadth and geographic scope of its services.

[25] Press Release, Fed. Trade Comm'n, FTC Puts Conditions on Fidelity National Financial's Acquisition of Lender Processing Services (Dec. 24, 2013), *available at* http://www.ftc.gov/news-press-releases/2013/12/ftc-put-conditions-fidelity-national-financials-acquisition. This matter is also noteworthy in the debate that Commissioner Wright started where he challenged in his dissent the presumption that a decrease in the number of competitors from four to three, or even three to two, will necessarily harm competition even in highly concentrated markets where entry is unlikely.

ability to act on them may be appropriate."[26] The Guide recognizes that "there is a panoply of conduct remedies that may be effective in preserving competition. No matter what type of conduct remedy is considered, however, a remedy is not effective if it cannot be enforced... The most common forms of conduct relief are firewall, non-discrimination, mandatory licensing, transparency, and anti-retaliation provisions, as well as prohibitions on certain contracting practices."[27]

In 2009, Comcast proposed acquiring NBC Universal ("NBCU"). Comcast argued that the transaction would bolster its role as a creator and distributor of content, by offering "multiplatform anytime, anywhere" media. Thus, the transaction offered potential gains in terms of dynamism, modularity, and demand-side scale and scope. Although the transaction had certain horizontal aspects since it included NBCU's cable networks and Comcast already had some content, the DOJ's focus was vertical in nature: the merger as proposed would allegedly have enabled Comcast to harm competition by either withholding or raising the price of NBCU content for firms that competed with Comcast's cable operations. In addition to traditional competitors, such as cable overbuilders, satellite services, and telephone companies, the DOJ noted the emerging online competition from online video distributors ("OVDs").

The DOJ indicates that the settlement ensures that the transaction will not chill the nascent competition posed by online competitors that have the potential to reshape the marketplace by offering innovative online services. Under the terms of the consent, the joint venture agreed to license its programming to OVDs on similar, or better, terms than (1) those that have obtained under distribution agreements with one of NBCU's peers[28] or (2) NBCU offers to traditional video programming distributors. The consent also prohibits Comcast from imposing upon content owners contractual terms that unduly limit a content owner's ability to negotiate freely creative arrangements with Comcast competitors. The settlement prohibits the joint venture from retaliating against (1) any broadcast network, affiliate, cable programmer, production studio or content provider for licensing content to Comcast competitors or (2) any firm that raised concerns with the DOJ or the FCC about the transaction. The consent also requires NBCU to adhere to the FCC's Open Internet provisions regardless of whether they are overturned.[29]

B. Transactions Involving Database Software

As with cases involving data bases, the agencies' views of acquisitions involving database software often seem to turn on predictions regarding the

---

[26] U.S. Dep't of Justice, Antitrust Div., Antitrust Division Policy Guide to Merger Remedies (June 2011), *available at* www.justice.gov/atr/public/guidelines/272350.pdf.

[27] *Id.*

[28] United States v. Comcast Corp., No. 1:11-CV-00106-RJL (proposed judgment, D.D.C. June 29, 2011) Definition V, *available at* http://www.justice.gov/atr/cases/f272600/272610.pdf. Peers include broadcast competitors ABC, CBS, and Fox, cable programmers News Corp., Time Warner, Viacom, and The Walt Disney Co., and video production studios News Corp., Sony, Time Warner, Viacom, and Walt Disney.

[29] *Id.* Specifically, Comcast cannot unreasonably discriminate in the transmission of OVD's lawful network traffic to a Comcast broadcast customer and is required to give other firms' content equal treatment under any of its broadcast offerings that involve caps, tiers, metering for consumption or other usage-based pricing.

competitiveness and conduct of alternative providers and the changes in the incentives of the merged firm following the transaction.

The 2009 Oracle/Sun transaction illustrates these themes. Oracle acquired Sun Microsystems, Inc. for two primary reasons: (1) to gain control over Java; and (2) to integrate vertically its stack of offerings to compete with firms such as IBM and EMC/VMware.[30] Oracle makes databases and other software for large corporations. Sun Microsystems, Inc., made computer servers and owned the widely used Java platform, which is one of the key software building blocks used in Internet programs, and MySQL, an open source database program, that critics of the transaction said could someday evolve into a competitor of Oracle and/or Microsoft. Nevertheless, as proposed, the transaction held the potential of jump-starting innovation among rivals IBM and EMC, increasing modularity, and expanding demand-side efficiencies of scale and scope.

The DOJ issued a second request, but ultimately closed the investigation on the basis that, according to the DOJ, (1) there were many (perhaps eight or more) open and proprietary database competitors so customers would continue to have choices, and (2) there is a large community of developers and users of Sun's open source database with significant expertise in maintaining and improving the software and who could support a derivative version of it.[31] Thus, the transaction would neither affect the viability of alternative providers nor change Oracle/Sun's incentives to engage in anticompetitive conduct.

The FTC reached the opposite conclusion in a 2013 consent in which it required that Solera, which had acquired Actual Systems (and two related companies) on May 29, 2012, sell one of the U.S. and Canadian yard management systems ("YMS") and provide a 10-year license to a key database to ASA Holdings, a company started by former employees of Actual Systems. At the time of the 2012 acquisition, both Solera and Actual Systems developed and sold YMS used by automotive recycling yards. Presumably, the combination would produce cost savings. According to the FTC, however, the market for YMS software was already highly concentrated at that time and the elimination of the competition between the two companies had reduced innovation for software and caused higher prices for automotive recycling industry customers. In the relevant geographic market of the United States and Canada, Solera and Actual Systems were allegedly two of only three providers of YMS. In this case, the FTC's prediction was that alternative providers would not emerge, and that (absent relief) incentives for anticompetitive conduct would be increased.

The potential for such vertical theories to lead to complex conduct remedies is illustrated by the DOJ's 2011 examination of Google's acquisition of ITA Software, which it saw primarily as a vertical merger.

ITA had developed the leading independent airfare pricing and shopping system "QPX." QPX collects and organizes airline flight schedules, pricing and seat availability for travel services companies. It is used by online travel agents

---

[30] *See* John Furrier and Dave Vellante's Analysis: *Is Oracle Better Off After Sun Acquisition?*, FORBES (July 9, 2013), *available at* http://www.forbes.com/sites/siliconangle/2013/07/09/analysis-is-oracle-better-off-after-sun-acquisition/.

[31] Press Release, U.S. Dep't of Justice, *Department of Justice Antitrust Division Issues Statement on the European Commission's Decision Regarding the Proposed Transaction Between Oracle and Sun* (Nov. 9, 2009), *available at* http://www.justice.gov/atr/public/press_releases/2009/251782.htm.

(*e.g.*, Orbitz) and other flight search services.[32] Google, the largest Internet search provider, planned to launch an Internet travel site to offer comparative flight search services. Google indicated at the time that it was "buying ITA Software to create a new, easier way for users to find better flight information online. By combining ITA Software's expertise with Google's technology, [Google would] . . . be able to bring new flight search tools for users that [would] . . . make it easier for them to search for flights, compare flight options and prices, and get them quickly to sites where they can buy their tickets."[33] Moreover, according to Google, the combination would permit it to make more significant innovations and bigger breakthroughs than possible if Google had simply licensed ITA Software's data service.[34] Thus, Google presented the transaction as one that fostered dynamism and demand-side benefits.

The DOJ did not conclude that Google would use its positioning in general search to gain unfair advantage in travel search. Rather, the DOJ alleged that, after acquiring ITA, Google could deny QPX to other flight search companies or disadvantage their access to it, to gain an advantage for Google's new flight search services. These foreclosure concerns arose because the DOJ believed that the remaining options to QPX were not suitable alternatives.

To address these concerns the DOJ required Google/ITA (1) to continue to license QPX to other flight search companies on fair, reasonable and nondiscriminatory ("FRAND") licensing terms; (2) to make available to other flight search services any QPX upgrades it makes available to other customers; and (3) not to enter into agreements with airlines that would "inappropriately" restrict the airlines' right to share seat and booking class information with Google's competitors. In addition, Google committed to continue to fund for two years research and development of QPX at least at similar levels to what ITA had invested in recent years and to develop and offer to travel websites ITA's next generation "Instasearch" product. The consent provides for mandatory arbitration under certain specified circumstances and establishes internal firewalls to prevent unauthorized use of competitively sensitive information and data gathered from ITA's customers. The consent also prevents Google's tying of the system to other products. The duration of the consent is five years (shorter than the typical 10 years found in most consent decrees).

Google's acquisition of ITA also exemplifies the difficulties in analyzing high-technology transactions and in fashioning remedies. Google's acquisition held the potential of benefiting consumers by, among other things, resulting in better ways to access ITA's data and improving overall travel-related searches. For example, Google might facilitate expansion of ITA's search offerings beyond travel to include hotels. To the extent that Google made fare offerings more transparent, consumers could benefit. Given that Google did not plan to sell tickets, but would instead simply direct consumers to airline or online travel sites to make a purchase, Google's entry could also benefit consumers by increasing competition to meta-search companies.

As mentioned above, the DOJ thought that Google, which apparently had planned to enter into the flight search service, would use its control over what the

---

[32] United States v. Google Inc. and ITA Software, Inc., No. 1:11-cv-00688-RLW (proposed judgment, D.D.C. Oct. 5, 2011).
[33] Google, *Facts about Google's acquisition of ITA Software, available at* http://www.google.com/press/ita/faq.html.
[34] *Id.*

DOJ identified as a "critical input" to disadvantage its competitors post-merger. Implicitly recognizing the potential consumer benefits from Google's acquisition of ITA, the DOJ focused on behavioral conditions that would ensure that the change of ownership of ITA's business would not result in a change in the access terms to QPX and its improvements or ITA's internal decisions regarding R&D. The behavioral conditions imposed, however, are highly complex and interventionist in nature. Given the speed at which high technology marketplaces evolve as well as the potential that such restrictions could actually hinder competition if left in place too long, it is not surprising to see the DOJ limit the consent duration to five years, rather than the 10-year terms typically seen in consents.

C. *Transactions Involving Hardware, Platforms, or Networks*

As with other IT markets, acquisitions involving hardware, platforms or networks are often scrutinized to determine whether or not they will create or enhance entry barriers by becoming a bottleneck for rivals to compete. These transactions often involve nascent or quickly evolving marketplaces, with agency decisions premised on imprecise facts regarding the actions and ability of third parties to develop competing products or platforms.

In 2010, the FTC closed its investigation of Google's acquisition of AdMob, a mobile advertising network.[35] AdMob had been one of the first mobile advertising networks to focus on the iPhone when the Apple App Store opened in June 2009. At the time that Google announced its proposed acquisition of AdMob, Google had a beta advertising network for mobile applications that also operated on some iPhone apps. The parties indicated that the transaction would (1) accelerate the pace of innovation and engaging ad units across platforms, (2) build more powerful relevance and optimization capabilities, and more powerful technology and tools to monetize mobile traffic, and (3) leverage Google's sales team, infrastructure and relationships to increase the effectiveness of display advertising.[36] In other words, to use our paradigm, the transaction would foster dynamism, modularity and demand-side benefits.

The FTC's closing statement indicated that the decision not to challenge the transaction "was a difficult one because the parties currently are the two leading mobile advertising networks . . . [and] each of the merging parties viewed the other as its primary competitor. . . ." The FTC decided not to challenge the transaction because Apple announced in April 2010 that it had acquired Quattro Wireless and had transformed Quattro into a new mobile advertising platform called "iAd" that would be released in June 2010. The FTC concluded that Apple had both the ability and the incentive to ensure that advertising networks would not raise prices or reduce the percentage of advertising revenue that they share with app developers.[37]

---

[35] Press Release, Fed. Trade Comm'n, FTC Closes Its Investigation of Google AdMob Deal (May 21, 2010), *available at* http://www.ftc.gov/news-events/press-releases/2010/05/ftc-closes-its-investigation-google-admob-deal.

[36] *See generally* Google Official Blog *We've officially acquired AdMob!*, *available at* http://googleblog.blogspot.com/2010/os/weve-offically-acquired-admob.html.

[37] Perhaps ironically, in April 2014, Apple faced accusations of denying access to its iAd service to an online radio competitor, Bloom.fm, for anticompetitive purposes. *See* Stuart Dredge, *Apple bans music app Bloom.fm from running ads on its iAd network*, THE GUARDIAN (Apr. 11, 2014), *available at*

Also, on December 2, 2011, the DOJ issued a statement indicating that it was closing its investigation of Google's proposed acquisition of Admeld Inc. ("Admeld"), an online display advertising service provider.[38] In a blog post on the day of announcement, Google indicated that "[b]y combining Admeld's services, expertise, and technology with Google's offerings, [it was] . . . investing in what [it hoped would] be an improved era of flexible ad management tools for major publishers.[39] In addition, Google promised to continue to support other ad networks, demand-side platforms, exchanges and adservers. The DOJ statement indicates that the DOJ focused on the potential effect of the transactions on competition in the digital advertising industry. Both companies provide services and technology to web publishers that facilitate the sale of those publishers' display advertising space. Admeld operated a supply-side platform that helps publishers optimize the yield from their display advertising. The investigation found that web publishers often rely on multiple display advertising platforms and can move business among them in response to changes in price or the quality of ad placements. As a result, the risk that the market will tip to a single dominant platform is lessened. In addition, there had been recent entrants. The DOJ also evaluated whether the acquisition would enable Google to extend its market power in the Internet search industry to online display advertising through anticompetitive means, and concluded the acquisition is not likely to substantially lessen competition in the sale of display advertising.

On the other hand, the DOJ also successfully challenged Bazaarvoice, Inc.'s ("Bazaarvoice") July 2012 acquisition of PowerReviews, Inc. ("PowerReviews").[40] In that case, the DOJ alleged as the relevant market "rating and review platforms ("R&R platforms") used to collect and display consumer-generated product ratings and reviewing online."[41] The DOJ asserted that Bazaarvoice was the leading commercial supplier of R&R platforms and PowerReviews was its closest competitor by a wide margin; further, it argued, although some retailers used in-house R&R platforms, for many retailers such in-house solutions are not a substitute and therefore do not provide a meaningful constraint on the company's pricing.

The DOJ alleged that PowerReviews had been positioned as the low-price alternative to Bazaarvoice and that the fierce competition between the two companies had led to innovation and new platform features. The complaint quotes several internal company "hot" documents indicating the transaction eliminated Bazaarvoice's "only competitor" who had "suppressed prices." In addition, internal documents, among other things, stated that the combination

http://www.theguardian.com/technology/2014/apr/11/apple-bloom-fm-music-app-iads. It is unclear whether competitive authorities plan to investigate.

[38] Press Release, U.S. Dep't of Justice, Statement of the Department of Justice's Antitrust Division on its Decision to Close its Investigation of Google Inc.'s Acquisition of Admeld Inc. (Dec. 2, 2011), *available at* http://www.justice.gov/atr/public/press_releases/2011/277935.htm.

[39] Google Official Blog, *Helping publishers get the most from display advertising with Admeld* (June 13, 2011), *available at* http://googleblog.blogspot.com/2011/06/helping-publishers-get-most-from.html.

[40] United States v. Bazaarvoice, Inc., No. C-13-0133JSC (opinion, N.D. Cal. Jan. 1, 2014).

[41] *Id.* at ¶ 1.

would "avoid margin erosion," "eliminate feature driven one-upmanship and tactical competition," and "create significant barrier to entry."[42]

The key allegation of the complaint is that "PowerReviews was routinely the only significant threat that Bazaarvoice faced for U.S.-based sales opportunities." The complaint is also unusual in its failure to allege any ongoing competitive harm, such as higher prices, poorer service, or less innovation—claims typically made in cases challenging a consummated merger. Rather, the complaint simply states that as "a result of the transaction, Bazaarvoice will be able to profitably impose price increases on retailers and manufacturers based in the United States."

In its defense, Bazaarvoice asserted that the alleged product market was too narrow given that ratings and reviews are one of many tools that brands and retailers use to engage with customers. PowerReviews, it argued, was a small company and generally unprofitable, and was acquired by Bazaarvoice because its operations provided a base for Bazaarvoice's expansion. According to Bazaarvoice, since the acquisition, there had been substantial competitor repositioning and entry and intense competition on price and innovation. For example, immediately after the merger, Reevoo, a U.K.-based competitor, opened a U.S. office and won customers from Bazaarvoice. In addition, the company argued that the complaint was based on dated, superseded and excerpted documents and predictions that bear no resemblance to marketplace realities and that the DOJ had ignored what the totality of the ordinary course documents and economic evidence show. The merger parties argued that there had been no harm to customers.

The bench trial occurred from September 23, 2013 to October 15, 2013. The DOJ's opening statements and briefs heavily relied on Bazaarvoice's internal documents and contended that the reason there was no evidence of higher prices post-merger was the existence of the ongoing DOJ investigation and challenge. Bazaarvoice argued there had been no harm to customers and that most customers were not worried about the merger; the reason that rival reviews and ratings software companies had not grown is because the market changed following the transaction, with Google and Amazon offering their own ratings systems and other software companies facilitating retailers and brands to undertake such systems in-house.

On January 8, 2014, the court ruled for the DOJ, finding that Bazaarvoice was unable to rebut the government's prima facie case. According to the court, "the purchase of PowerReview's provides 'breathing space' for Bazaarvoice in R&R while it prepares to compete in the broader market. . . . It is unlikely that PowerReviews will be replaced by the existing R&R competitors in the next two years, the time frame in which the Court evaluates the likely effects of the merger."

Specifically, the court rejected the fact that none of the 104 customers whose depositions were taken complained that the merger had hurt them, indicating that it would be a mistake to rely on customer testimony about effects for several reasons: (1) Bazaarvoice's business conduct was likely tempered by the government's immediate investigation; (2) the customers were not privy to the evidence, including the economic experts' opinions; (3) many customers had paid little or no attention to the merger and had different levels of knowledge, sophistication and experience; and (4) with the pricing policies utilized, it is

---

[42] *Id.* at ¶¶ 4, 5, 9.

difficult for customers to discern what is actually happening in the market. In addition, the Court indicated that "the potential for witness bias was greater in this case than most. . . . Third-party customers had to testify about their market strategy in front of a vendor that would be negotiating with within a short time."

Although Judge Orrick notes that "intent is not an element of a Section 7 violation," a significant portion of the decision discusses the strong documentary evidence that establishes PowerReview as Bazaarvoice's fiercest (and perhaps only significant) competitor. The court further indicates that Bazaarvoice's defenses against the government's arguments were often "undermined by the pre-acquisition statements of its and PowerReview's executives. Indeed, the court finds that "anticompetitive rationales infused virtually every pre-acquisition document describing the benefits of purchasing PowerReviews."[43] Another, long-term purpose of the transaction, however, was to grow the business beyond basic R&R. While acknowledging this objective as well, the court indicates that "Bazaarvoice's efforts at trial to walk away from its central rationale leading up to the merger—that acquiring PowerReviews would significantly diminish price competition for R&R platforms—was, at best, unconvincing."[44]

The economic testimony appears to have also played a role in the court's decision to define the market narrowly—and to reject the inclusion in the market firms that defendants argued could enter rapidly. According to the court, the analysis of DOJ's expert (Dr. Carl Shapiro) confirmed what the Judge believed was apparent from the non-expert testimony: "other social commerce tools, including social networking sites, Q&As, and forums, either serve a different purpose than R&R or are insufficient substitutes such that customers would not switch from R&R to a social commerce tool in the face of a SSNIP."[45]

The court expressly addresses whether its conclusions regarding the merger's anticompetitive effects should be impacted by the fact that it involves dynamic high technology market. While noting that it is debatable whether the antitrust laws are well suited for dynamic markets or if they potentially undermine innovation or are needed because market power is transitory when technology changes too fast for companies to become entrenched, the court indicates that "it is not the court's role to weigh in on this debate" but instead "the court's mission is to assess the alleged antitrust violations presented, irrespective of the dynamism of the market at issue."[46] The court concludes that 'while Bazaarvoice indisputably operates in a dynamic and evolving field, it did not present evidence that the evolving nature of the market itself precludes the merger's likely anticompetitive effects."[47]

Finally, although most of the focus of Verizon's 2011 agreements with SpectrumCo and Cox to purchase broadband wireless spectrum was on the impact on competition in the wireless broadband sector, these agreements also raised some interesting issues with respect to their potential to impact the development of a proprietary set-top box.[48] As proposed, the deal included the

---

[43] *Id.* at ¶ 35.

[44] *Id.* at ¶ 89.

[45] *Id.* at ¶ 147.

[46] *Id.* at ¶ 141.

[47] *Id.* at ¶ 141.

[48] Press Release, Verizon, Inc., Comcast, Time Warner Cable, and Bright House Networks Sell Advanced Wireless Spectrum to Verizon Wireless for $3.6 Billion (Dec. 2, 2011), *available at* http://www.comcast.com/About/PressRelease/PressRelease

creation of a new joint venture (referred to as the "Joint Operating Entity" or the "JOE") in which the parties would collaborate to develop innovative technology and intellectual property that would integrate wired video, voice, and high-speed Internet with wireless technologies. In other words, the agreement would potentially result in increased dynamism, modularity, and demand-side benefits.

As originally proposed, however, the JOE would function as the exclusive vehicle for R&D for these companies within the JV's exclusive field for a potentially unlimited duration. The exclusive sales partnerships and research and development collaborations among these rivals, particularly with no end date, could blunt the long-term incentives of the parties to compete against each other, and others, as the industry evolves. Implicit in the concern is that such long-term exclusivity was unnecessary to achieve the potential benefits.

Therefore, the DOJ consent announced on August 16, 2012,[49] among other things, required that the JOE Agreement be amended to allow Time Warner Cable and Bright House Networks to develop independently any technology that they have presented to the JOE for potential development but that the joint venture declines or ceases to pursue. The DOJ consent is somewhat unusual in that it contains certain restrictions that, unless the DOJ later modifies the consent, become effective on December 2, 2016 (five years after the commercial agreements were entered into) that: require the parties to withdraw from JOE by that date, and require the JOE to (a) license the exiting party with an immediate, irrevocable, perpetual, royalty-free fully paid-up non-exclusive license with immediate rights to sublicense, exploit, and commercialize any IP then owned by the JOE and (b) permit the cable companies to license JOE-developed technology to other wireless carriers if they choose to do so upon leaving the JOE.

D. *Transactions Involving Potential Competition and Future Markets*

As discussed above, the "regulatory humility" advocated by Commissioner Ohlhausen should be the governing principle when dealing with less certain terrain. The trend, however, has been in the reverse. In *Google/AdMob*, the Commission expressly dismissed the proposition that it should be careful not to intervene when the market is nascent, every current competitor is a recent entrant, entry barriers are unclear, and there are little historical data. Instead, in that merger the Commission indicated that it "must subject mergers in nascent markets to the same level of antitrust scrutiny as mergers in other markets." Similarly, the judge in *Bazaarvoice* discusses (and even debates) whether applying the antitrust laws might *impede* competition in a dynamic market, but ultimately concludes that the defendant did not establish that the evolving nature of the market itself precludes the merger's likely anticompetitive effects. In *Verizon/SpectrumCo*, the DOJ includes a "springing" provision that becomes effective only five years after the transactions closed and seeks to create competition in the future in innovation of wireless devices.

Detail.ashx?PRID=1134&SCRedirect=true. SpectrumCo, a joint venture originally consisting of Comcast, Time Warner, Cox (which later withdrew), Bright House Networks, and Sprint (which later withdrew), was the successful bidder for 137 wireless spectrum licenses in the AWS auction that concluded in September 2006.

[49] Press Release, U.S. Dep't of Justice, Justice Department Requires Changes to Verizon-Cable Company Transactions to Protect Consumers, Allows Procompetitive Spectrum Acquisitions to Go Forward (Aug. 16, 2012), *available at* http://www.justice.gov/atr/public/press_releases/2012/286098.htm.

In *Nielsen/Arbitron*, the FTC goes even further, however, seeking to protect a *future* market for audience measurement services.[50] Nielsen had announced plans to acquire Arbitron on December 17, 2013. The two companies were the leading media ratings businesses, although their operations prior to combining—Nielsen in TV and Arbitron in radio—do not overlap. Both were developing, however, syndicated cross-platform audience measurement services, which would measure the audience for a program through traditional platforms (TV or terrestrial radio) and the Internet, satellite, or other means. According to the FTC, the elimination of future competition between Nielsen and Arbitron would likely cause advertisers, ad agencies, and programmers to pay more for national cross-platform audience measurement services. As a result, FTC Chairman Edith Ramirez and Commissioner Julie Brill voted to condition the transaction's approval on Nielsen's obligation to (1) continue its cross-platform project with ESPN Inc. and Comscore Inc. and (2) license Arbitron's portable people meter and related data, as well as software and technology being used in the ESPN project, to an FTC-approved third party for up to eight years.[51] Commissioner Wright dissented from the decision on the basis that there was insufficient evidence to believe the merger will substantially lessen competition in the future market for the audience measurement services.[52] Commissioner Wright argues that the intervention is premised on "a novel theory—that is, that the merger will substantially lessen competition in a market that does not today exist."[53] Commissioner Wright would impose a higher standard of evidence regarding likely competitive effects in a matter involving future markets.

IV. LOOKING AHEAD: SOME ISSUES FOR THE FUTURE

As the cases discussed above demonstrate, IT markets are generating an abundant volume of thorny issues, and there is no reason to expect a slowdown anytime soon. Much of what lies ahead for regulators is by nature as unpredictable as innovation itself. Two sets of issues seem certain to play important roles: net neutrality and "big data."

A. *Net Neutrality: When (if Ever) is* Ex Ante *Regulation Appropriate?*

The concept of net neutrality means different things to different people, but from a competition-law perspective the central question is the extent to which refusals to interconnect (or imposition of "discriminatory" interconnection fees) by firms with market power are sufficiently likely to be harmful that they should be *per se* illegal. Specifically, advocates of net neutrality regulation argue that broadband ISPs have incentives to refuse interconnection with (or discriminate against) "edge" providers of content and applications. They argue further that

---

[50] Press Release, Fed. Trade Comm'n, FTC Puts Conditions on Nielsen's Proposed $1.26 Billion Acquisition of Arbitron (Sept. 20, 2013), *available at* http://www.ftc.gov/opa/2013/09/nielsen.shtm.

[51] *See* Statement of the Fed. Trade Comm'n, *In the Matter of Nielsen Holdings N.V. and Arbitron Inc.*, FTC File No. 131-0058 (Sept. 20, 2013), *available at* http://www.ftc.gov/os/caselist/1310058/130920nielsenarbitroncommstmt.pdf.

[52] *See* Dissenting Statement of Commissioner Joshua D. Wright, *In the Matter of Nielsen Holdings N.V. and Arbitron Inc.*, FTC File No. 131-0058 (Sept. 20, 2013), *available at* http://www.ftc.gov/os/caselist/1310058/130920nielsenarbitron-jdwstmt.pdf.

[53] *Id.* at 1.

traditional antitrust standards—which would in general proscribe only conduct that results in the foreclosure of equally efficient competitors—are inapposite in the context of the Internet Ecosystem, since traditional antitrust standards fail to account for the beneficial effects of "openness" (*i.e.*, free interconnection) on innovation by edge providers.[54]

The FCC's 2010 Open Internet Order embraced this expansive view of the need for net neutrality regulation, and on that basis imposed an open access mandate on ISPs, prohibiting them from refusing interconnection with edge providers ("blocking") or charging them for delivering traffic ("discriminating").[55] Four years later, in January 2014, the D.C. Circuit Court of Appeals overturned the Order on jurisdictional grounds, while at the same time embracing the Commission's underlying economic rationale and describing an alternative legal theory, under Section 706 of the Communications Act, upon which the Commission might formulate a new set of rules.[56] The Commission is currently drafting a Notice of Proposed Rulemaking under which it is expected to propose reinstituting the rules (in some as-yet undetermined form). In the meantime, in April 2014, the European Parliament voted to adopt strict net neutrality rules, which essentially ban all payments from content and application providers to broadband ISPs, though at the time this is written final adoption of the rules depends on a second vote likely to occur later in the year.[57]

It is impossible to predict how continuing efforts to impose such rules will play out politically and in the courts. What is certain, however, is that the debate will continue over whether certain platforms—in this case broadband ISPs—have both sufficient market power and sufficiently perverse incentives to justify *ex ante* bans on a broad class of two-sided business models. The political forces favoring such regulation—driven by a combination of misplaced concerns over censorship by ISPs and self-interested efforts by edge providers to avoid bearing the full costs of their services—are powerful, but and it is our sense that the debate will continue to evidence a lack of both theoretical and empirical support for such sweeping ex ante interventions, leading in the end towards adoption of a case-by-case enforcement regime for all platform providers markets, including broadband ISPs.[58]

---

[54] *See, e.g.*, Robin S. Lee & Tim Wu, *Subsidizing Creativity through Network Design: Zero Pricing and Net Neutrality*, 23 J. ECON. PERSPECTIVES, 61–76 (2009).

[55] *In re Preserving the Open Internet*, 25 F.C.C.R. 17905 (2010).

[56] *See* Verizon v. FCC, 740 F.3d 623 (2014).

[57] *See, e.g.*, Mark Scott and James Kanter, *E.U. Lawmakers Approve Tough 'Net Neutrality' Rules*, NEW YORK TIMES (Apr. 3, 2014), *available at* http://www.nytimes.com/2014/04/04/business/international/eu-lawmakers-approve-tough-net-neutrality-rules.html?_r=0.

[58] *See generally* Jonathan Sallet, *The Internet Ecosystem and Legal Regimes: Economic Regulation Supporting Innovation Dynamism* (Nov. 11, 2011), *available at* http://papers.ssrn.com/sol3/papers.cfm?abstract_id=1957715. For a discussion of how such a regime might operate in relation to the antitrust laws, *see* Comcast Cable Communications LLC v. Fed. Communications Comm'n, 71 F.3d 982 (D.C. Cir. 2013), *cert. denied*, 134 S. Ct. 1287 (2014).

B. Big Data and the Internet of Things

The FTC held a workshop in November 2013 on the "Internet of Things."[59] As described by Commissioner Ohlhausen, the one-way conversations at the outset of the Internet where websites provided information to users evolved into the rise of social media, where users responded to websites and created conservations to themselves, to now, the Internet of Things, where our phones, appliances, cars and other items are able to carry on conversations without human intervention, and just inform humans as necessary.[60] The Internet of Things is one of the factors (perhaps the most significant factor) driving the related phenomena commonly referred to as "big data": the capacity to collect, synthesize and analyze previously incomprehensible amounts of data. *Science Daily* reported in 2013 that ninety percent of the world's data has been generated over the past two years.[61]

While much of the focus on "big data" has involved its implications for data security, privacy, and other consumer protection issues, it is also true that access to database information is becoming increasingly important from a competition perspective. Indeed, the central theme of cases like Bazaarvoice, Nielson/Arbitron and the Google "search neutrality" investigations is the capacity for market leaders to capitalize on economies of scale and scope in the collection and analysis of "big data."

For reasons that should be apparent, we will not try to predict the precise course technology will follow in coming years, let alone the exact implications for competition policy. It seems self-evident, however, that the capacity to collect and assess ever larger amounts of data will continue to expand both technologically and in terms of economic significance; further, that the fundamental economic characteristics of information markets will continue to lead to concerns about market power and anticompetitive conduct in such markets; and, finally, that competition authorities will continue to wrestle with the challenge of determining when intervention is appropriate, and in what form.

VI. CONCLUSIONS

Policing competition in information technology markets presents profound challenges. The defining characteristics of such markets lead naturally to high market shares, apparent barriers to entry, and potential market power. On the other hand, their dynamic nature and the potential for high returns for successful innovation challenge the longevity of even the most entrenched monopolists.

The cases discussed above highlight the tensions regulators will continue to face in the years ahead, as well as the challenges facing academics and practitioners in terms of developing more useful frameworks and analytical tools. In particular, regulators need better approaches for assessing the extent to which market power in IT markets is likely to be sustainable as opposed to transitory, for balancing efficiency benefits of both consolidation and conduct against the

---

[59] *See* http://www.ftc.gov/news-events/events-calendar/2013/11/internet-things-privacy-security-connected-world.

[60] *See* Ohlhausen speech, *supra* note 14.

[61] *Big Data for Better or Worse: 90% of World's Data Generated over Last Two Years*, SCIENCE DAILY (May 22, 2013), *available at* http://www.sciencedaily.com/releases/2013/05/130522085217.htm.

competitive costs, and for assessing the efficiency tradeoffs, over time, of various forms of remedies.

BEFORE THE
FEDERAL COMMUNICATIONS COMMISSION
WASHINGTON, DC 20554

In the Matter of	)	
	)	
Framework for Broadband Internet Service	))	GN Docket No. 10-127
	)	
Open Internet Rulemaking	)	GN Docket No. 14-28

REPLY COMMENTS OF SYNTONIC WIRELESS, INC.

Gary S. Greenbaum
CEO, Syntonic Wireless, Inc.
119 First Avenue South, Suite 100
Seattle, WA 98104

September 3, 2014

BEFORE THE
FEDERAL COMMUNICATIONS COMMISSION
WASHINGTON, DC 20554

In the Matter of	)	
	)	
Framework for Broadband Internet	)	GN Docket No. 10-127
Service	)	
	)	
Open Internet Rulemaking	)	GN Docket No. 14-28
	)	

REPLY COMMENTS OF SYNTONIC WIRELESS, INC.

Introduction

The Commission is unquestionably correct that the Internet is "America's most important platform for economic growth, innovation, competition, [and] free expression."[1] From its inception, the Commission's effort to preserve the Open Internet has stressed the need to promote dynamic competition and innovation. The Commission has also long recognized that consumer welfare should be the touchstone of these efforts: the original 2005 Internet Policy Statement emphasized that "*consumers* are entitled to access the lawful Internet content of their choice...run applications and use services of their choice...[and] connect their choice of legal device" to the network.[2] The goal of the Open Internet proceeding should be to protect consumers by promoting innovation that enhances

---

[1] Protecting and Promoting the Open Internet, Notice of Proposed Rulemaking, GN Docket No. 14-28, FCC 14-61, ¶ 1 (May 15, 2014) (hereafter "NPRM").
[2] Appropriate Framework for Broadband Access to the Internet over Wireline Facilities, CC Docket No. 02-33, FCC 05-151, ¶ 4 (Sept. 23, 2005) (emphasis added).

consumers' ability to access the content and services they desire, regardless of where that innovation occurs within the Internet ecosystem.

Unfortunately, the most recent Notice of Proposed Rulemaking, and numerous filed comments, threaten to retard the consumer-beneficial competition that the Commission hopes to promote. The NPRM focuses primarily upon the largely hypothetical concern that broadband providers will interfere anticompetitively in upstream markets for Internet content and applications. But to protect competition in these upstream markets, several commenters advocate sweeping prophylactic policies that would *reduce* the ability to innovate in the broadband market. Just as consumer welfare can benefit from new Internet content and applications, consumers can also benefit from innovative new broadband offerings and partnerships between broadband and content providers.

Syntonic Wireless has built its business model upon finding innovative new ways to deliver to consumers the Internet-based content and applications that they demand. By exploring alternatives to traditional mobile broadband delivery, Syntonic helps content providers reach new customers that cannot afford or do not want traditional mobile broadband data plans. Syntonic also seeks to open new channels for dissemination of Internet-based content, such as connected automobiles and "wearables," remote healthcare monitoring, and improved educational opportunities for our nation's students. And by experimenting with different ways to deliver and track mobile data, Syntonic helps companies promote employee connectivity in innovative and more efficient ways. Ultimately, our efforts are helping to challenge existing business models, create new markets for Internet-based content, and narrow the digital divide by reducing the consumer's cost of accessing Internet-based services.

The Commission's proposed rules, and especially the more stringent alternatives pressed by many commenters, threaten these consumer-friendly initiatives and similar efforts currently underway at other companies. The essence of common carriage is to provide the same service to all customers, which homogenizes the broadband product and eliminates a plane of dynamic competition. The philosophy underlying these recommendations is that broadband providers must provide access to all Internet content or none at all, and must treat all Internet traffic identically. But while such undifferentiated common carriage principles worked for telephone providers using one dominant and relatively static model, the technology-driven and rapidly evolving broadband market is not similarly situated and should not be treated the same. This one-size-fits-all approach to broadband delivery is increasingly at odds with a diverse population that relies on the Internet for a wide range of disparate tasks through a variety of technologies and devices.

Syntonic Wireless urges the Commission to avoid prophylactic rules that would prohibit the creation of new, potentially consumer-friendly products and services. We recognize that some broadband providers have incentives to use their market position in anticompetitive ways, and therefore some regulation may be necessary to protect the Open Internet. But the Commission should reject the call to reclassify broadband as a Title II telecommunications service subject to common carriage obligations. The flexibility and individualized negotiations that the D.C. Circuit required in the *Verizon* decision[3] are not limits on the Open Internet regime; they are, rather, essential prerequisites to preserve dynamic competition and innovation in the delivery segment of an Open Internet ecosystem. Whatever rules the Commission ultimately adopts should leave room for

---

[3] Verizon v. FCC, 740 F.3d 623 (DC Cir. 2014).

differentiated product offerings and innovations within the broadband market, and for pro-consumer collaborations between broadband providers and upstream providers. Finally, the Commission should continue to apply a "light touch" to mobile broadband service, as the unique technical demands of wireless communication demand increased flexibility for providers to deliver content most efficiently to consumers.

I.   Overview of Syntonic Wireless

Syntonic Wireless is a technology platform provider enabling new commercial models for anytime, anywhere Internet connectivity on mobile devices. Our proprietary technology allows Internet content providers to provide application-specific bandwidth to mobile devices. Our company was founded in 2012 by a team of high-tech veterans with expertise in mobile computing, architecting large-scale multi-platform client-service solutions, and implementing innovative business-to-business and business-to-consumer commercial models.

The heart of the company is Syntonic's Connected Services Platform. This cloud-based system couples specific applications with 3G or 4G connectivity over the nation's wireless broadband networks and is designed to work with any mobile application, on-line service, or content. Through the Connected Services Platform, content providers can reach any customer with a mobile device regardless of whether the consumer has a data plan. Simply put, it allows consumers to access content without incurring hefty data plans or overage charges that they neither want nor can afford. As discussed in greater detail below, the Connected Services Platform is an invaluable tool for content providers to reach new customers on traditional mobile devices, but also offers opportunities to expand mobile content delivery into innovative new markets such as automobiles, "wearables", healthcare, education, and enterprise services.

II. The Open Internet Proceeding Should Promote Consumer-Friendly Innovation Throughout the Internet Ecosystem

The Commission's long-standing commitment to an Open Internet originated in its commitment to consumer welfare. As the NPRM notes,[4] former Chairman Michael Powell first articulated the Commission's basic guiding principles at a 2004 Silicon Flatirons speech which focused on "empowering consumers."[5] He explained that "ensuring that consumers can obtain and use the content, applications, and devices they want[] is critical to unlocking the vast potential of the broadband Internet."[6] The following year, the Commission adopted the Internet Policy Statement, which similarly sounded in consumer welfare terms: "[t]o encourage broadband deployment and preserve and promote the open and interconnected nature of the public Internet, *consumers* are entitled to access the lawful Internet content of their choice…run applications and user services of their choice…[and] connect their choice of legal devices that do not harm the network."[7] From the beginning, maintaining an Open Internet has been inextricably intertwined with maximization of consumer choice and welfare.

The Commission also stressed the importance of innovation and competition. The Internet Policy Statement emphasized that in addition to the three freedoms listed above, "consumers are entitled to competition among network providers, application and service

---

[4] NPRM ¶ 12.

[5] Michael K. Powell, Chairman, Federal Communications Commission, Preserving Internet Freedom: Guiding Principles for the Industry 3, Remarks at the Silicon Flatirons Symposium (Feb. 8, 2004), available at https://apps.fcc.gov/edocs_public/attachmatch/DOC-243556A1.pdf.

[6] *Id.*

[7] Appropriate Framework for Broadband Access to the Internet over Wireline Facilities, CC Docket No. 02-33, FCC 05-151, ¶ 4 (Sept. 23, 2005) (emphasis added).

providers, and content providers."[8] The Commission saw promotion of dynamic competition—throughout the Internet ecosystem—as key to promoting broadband deployment as required by Section 706 of the Act and as a tool to maintain an open Internet.

But when codifying these principles, the Commission has shifted away from these broad goals and toward a more narrow effort to protect edge providers. The Commission's primary concern in the Open Internet proceedings has been the potential threat that broadband Internet providers would interfere anticompetitively in upstream markets for Internet-based content and applications. But to preserve competition in this part of the Internet ecosystem, the 2010 rules and, to a lesser extent, the current proposed rules have significantly reduced the opportunities for innovation in the broadband service market. Both proposals consist primarily of structural rules that limit broadband providers' ability to offer differentiated services and reduce opportunities for partnerships with upstream purveyors of Internet content and applications.

Embedded in these structural rules is an unjustified bias in favor of existing broadband service models. The 2010 rules made this quite explicit: "These rules are generally consistent with, and should not require significant changes to, broadband providers' current practices, and are also consistent with the common understanding of broadband Internet access service as a service that enables one to go where one wants on the Internet and communicate with anyone else online."[9] While the present NPRM makes some concessions toward the "development of new business arrangements in the market

---

[8] *Id.*

[9] *Preserving the Open Internet: Broadband Industry Practices*, GN Docket No. 09-191, WC Docket No. 07-52, Report and Order, 25 FCC Rcd. 17905 ¶ 43 (2010) (hereafter "2010 Rules").

between broadband providers and edge providers,"[10] the proposed rules still exhibit a bias in favor of existing broadband service practices.

But placing the Commission's imprimatur of approval on "current practices" at one moment in time is myopic, particularly given the evolution of consumer behavior online. Consumers are using the Internet in new and different ways, meaning that a one-size-fits-all access model is unlikely to serve consumers efficiently.[11] As the market becomes saturated, providers must innovate to deliver increasing value to this disparate array of consumers.[12] Companies often test new business models without a definitive understanding of the model's benefits. Instead they rely on a trial-and-error process to identify better methods of delivering value to consumers.[13] To protect consumer welfare in the Internet ecosystem, it is insufficient to promote innovation simply among edge providers; the Commission must recognize the value of innovation in broadband service markets as well.

Syntonic Wireless's business model is predicated upon developing novel ways to bring consumers the content and applications that they desire. We do so by bringing together content providers and wireless broadband network operators in ways that differ, sometimes significantly, from the traditional broadband model favored by the Open Internet rules. But our intent, and our results, unquestionably enhance consumer welfare. Our innovative practices can reduce consumers' cost of acquiring Internet-based content, expand the universe of available Internet-based services, and provide improved service to

---

[10] NPRM ¶ 38; *id.* ¶ 116 (proposing to allow "commercially reasonable" practices).
[11] Comments of Christopher S. Yoo, In re Preserving the Open Internet: Broadband Industry Practices, GN Docket No. 09-191, WC Docket No. 07-52, at 13.
[12] *Id.*
[13] *Id.* at 33.

niche players and those on the wrong side of the digital divide whose needs are not well served by traditional broadband access models.

Syntonic Wireless and similar companies are challenging the notion that broadband innovation should be limited and that cooperation between broadband providers and edge providers should inherently be suspect. Numerous scholars, regulators, and even the Commission's own Open Internet Advisory Committee[14] have recognized the potential value to consumers of experimenting with new and alternative broadband business models. Speaking about the 2010 rules, FTC Commissioner Joshua Wright explained that

> What the theoretical literature and empirical evidence demonstrates…is that vertical contracts, including those captured by the Neutrality Order, are not always anticompetitive and in most cases are procompetitive. This is a critical observation for answering the question: "what kind of regulatory regime and legal rules governing this behavior will best serve consumers?"[15]

Commissioner Wright's comments provide important guidance to this proceeding. The Commission's goal should not be the protection of edge providers. Instead, harkening back to the original 2005 Policy Statement, the goal should be to protect *consumers*, by promoting innovation that enhances consumers' ability to access the content and services they desire—no matter where in the Internet ecosystem this innovation occurs.

III. Today's Broadband Marketplace Exhibits Innovative, Consumer-Friendly Offerings that are Threatened by Open Internet Principles

---

[14] Open Internet Advisory Committee 2013 Annual Report 58, available at http://transition.fcc.gov/cgb/oiac/oiac-2013-annual-report.pdf (discussing the potential benefits to consumers of allowing two-sided markets to develop in mobile broadband).

[15] Joshua D. Wright, *Broadband Policy & Consumer Welfare: The Case for an Antitrust Approach to Net Neutrality Issues*, Remarks of Joshua D. Wright, Commissioner, Federal Trade Commission, at the Information Economy Project's Conference on US Broadband Markets, 12 (2013), available at http://www.ftc.gov/sites/default/files/documents/public_statements/broadband-policy-consumer-welfare-case-antitrust-approach-net-neutrality-issues/130423wright_nn_posting_final.pdf.

In the United States and around the world, numerous companies are working to deliver alternatives to traditional broadband consumption models. Syntonic Wireless is a leading pioneer in the effort to develop innovative new ways to bring Internet content and application to consumers—through consumer-friendly initiatives whose futures may be jeopardized by this proceeding.

A. Syntonic Wireless Product Offerings

1. Syntonic Sponsored Content Store and other Consumer Initiatives

In August 2014, Syntonic Wireless launched the Freeway™ application, a sponsored content store for AT&T mobile subscribers. Powered by the Syntonic Connected Services Platform, Freeway provides a one-stop shop for AT&T mobile customers to access free or premium mobile content without incurring data charges. The cost of connectivity is instead paid by the participating content provider as a way to facilitate the delivery of the content to consumers.

Freeway, and other sponsored data initiatives, benefits both consumers and content providers. For consumers, sponsored content increases the value of a wireless subscription, by offering additional content that the consumer may enjoy in addition to whatever data is consumed under the consumer's traditional monthly data plan. Consumers can also "sample" sponsored content without the risk that they are stuck paying for a suboptimal product or service. And technophobic consumers who are unsure whether to purchase a mobile broadband service can potentially access a broad array of sponsored content on a minimal data plan, to decide whether to upgrade to a more comprehensive service. For content providers, sponsored content is a way to differentiate one's product from the competition, and thus adds an additional plane of competition within edge provider markets.

Beyond Freeway, Syntonic Wireless offers content providers additional opportunities to reach consumers. The Connected Services Platform is designed to work with any content and any mobile device on any wireless network. This means that in the future, content providers will be able to pay to make their content available to consumers for free on any mobile-enabled device—including devices that are not currently attached to monthly data plans. In this way, Syntonic can help narrow the digital divide, by bringing connectivity to those who cannot afford, or otherwise choose not to purchase, a traditional monthly data plan that provides access to the full Internet.

2. Enterprise: Facilitating Mobile Employee Connectivity

As companies struggle to cut costs, many have replaced company-provided wireless devices with bring-your-own-device (BYOD) policies that allow employee-owned equipment to join the company network. But BYOD programs are often complicated by the difficulties of ensuring company software works with myriad different handheld devices and of billing for services that support both company and personal use.

The Connected Services Platform offers a turnkey solution to this problem. Through the platform, the company can make available a suite of firm-specific applications to employee devices at no cost to the employee. Because the platform works with all devices, it eliminates technical integration issues. And with segmented billing, the employer is billed for company-related activities through the company's apps, while the employee incurs all other charges under his or her traditional monthly data plan. The Platform could also support the distribution of employer-specific mobile devices to employees who lack a personal mobile device, with connectivity limited to the suite of employer-provided apps.

3. *Education: Bridging the Digital Access Divide*

Syntonic On-Ramp Education Services™ was launched in September, 2014 with the Highline School District in Washington State to bring improved connectivity to schools and to the community they serve. There are numerous school districts nationwide that lack quality Internet access, and even in broadband-equipped schools, many students lack affordable Internet access at home. Syntonic's On-Ramp services can help bridge this gap. A participating school district can distribute digital mobile devices to students that are dedicated exclusively to educational purposes. The school district can limit student access to curriculum-approved applications and content, which provides a cost-efficient alternative to traditional broadband access and allows the district to avoid the costs and security risks of unauthorized personal use of school-provided devices.

4. *New Markets: Automotive, Wearables, Healthcare Solutions*

Syntonic Wireless is also poised to help to pioneer new markets for mobile broadband content, by providing connectivity to limited-purpose devices that cannot support, or do not need, access to all content and applications available online. For example, Syntonic Wireless can help connect mobile-equipped automobiles with content and applications that would appeal to drivers, such as streaming audio that could rival traditional and satellite radio offerings, or turn-by-turn navigation applications. Car rental companies could use the service to provide in-car premium content to customers and to track fleets remotely and simplify vehicle pick-up and return. Similarly, health care providers can use the Connected Services Platform to create highly targeted, remote patient monitoring and diagnostic systems using app-specific mobile devices.

B. Other Innovative Product Offerings

Syntonic Wireless is not the only company experimenting with innovative new ways to deliver broadband content to consumers. For example, T-Mobile recently introduced a data plan that includes unlimited streaming from selected Internet-based streaming audio services such as Pandora and iHeartRadio.[16] Similarly, Sprint has announced that it will soon test-market wireless plans that will offer customers unlimited talk and text, plus access to a limited suite of mobile broadband services, such as Facebook, Twitter, Instagram, or Pinterest.[17]

While these new business models will bring increased choice to consumers, in some ways they are merely catching up to innovations that have long existed in international markets unencumbered by net neutrality rules. For example, French telecommunications provider Orange couples mobile data plans with a complementary subscription to the customer's choice of several content-based applications including Sky Sports TV or music service Deezer. And numerous wireless providers including Turkey's Turkcell, Claro of Latin America, and Ucell in Uzbekistan have long offered social media plans that provide access to Facebook or Twitter at a fraction of the cost of full Internet access.[18]

C. Opposition from Open Internet Proponents

---

[16] Thomas Gryta, T-Mobile Will Waive Data Fees for Music Services, Wall Street Journal Blog, June 18, 2014, available at http://online.wsj.com/articles/t-mobile-will-waive-data-fees-for-music-service-1403142678.

[17] Ryan Knutson, *Sprint Will Sell a $12 Wireless Plan that Only Connects to Facebook or Twitter*, WALL STREET JOURNAL BLOG, July 30, 2014, available at http://blogs.wsj.com/digits/2014/07/30/sprint-tries-a-facebook-only-wireless-plan/.

[18] See Daniel A. Lyons, *Innovations in Mobile Broadband Pricing*, Mercatus Working Paper No. 14-08 (March 2014) at 17-18, available at http://papers.ssrn.com/sol3/papers.cfm?abstract_id=2418563.

Like the Freeway application, these innovative new wireless services benefit consumers. T-Mobile's streaming music plan targets music-savvy consumers whose demands are not adequately met by traditional data plans. For those customers, the Simple Choice Plan is a superior alternative to paying to stream data, or choosing not to consume music because the price is too high. Sprint's social media plan appeals to cost-conscious customers who are interested in having mobile access to Facebook but who are unable or unwilling to pay for more expensive all-inclusive Internet plans.

But despite the fact that these alternative business models increase consumer choice and help bring consumers the content they desire more efficiently, many net neutrality advocates—including numerous commenters calling on the Commission to adopt more stringent rules in this proceeding—have condemned these innovations. Shortly after Sprint announced its future plans, Free Press decried the fact that the alternative "helps lock in the existing choices and not let the new ones grow more organically. That's just not the way the Internet has worked." Similarly, Public Knowledge described T-Mobile's plan as "the latest example of ISPs using data caps to undermine net neutrality....This type of gatekeeping interference by ISPs is exactly what net neutrality rules should be designed to prevent." And both have condemned sponsored data as "a lose-lose for customers and app makers"[19] and a "tremendous loss for all of us."[20]

These opponents can use stringent net neutrality rules to impose homogeneity on broadband markets and destroy even the most consumer-friendly alternatives to the status

[19] Press Release, AT&T Sponsored Data Scheme is a Lose-Lose for Customers and App Makers, http://www.freepress.net/press-release/105490/att-sponsored-data-scheme-lose-lose-customers-and-app-makers.

[20] Michael Weinberg, AT&T's New Sponsored Data Scheme is a Tremendous Loss for All of Us, https://www.publicknowledge.org/news-blog/blogs/attas-new-asponsored-dataa-scheme-tremendous.

quo. For example, in 2010 these groups successfully pressured MetroPCS to withdraw an innovative plan that offered unlimited talk, text, web, and YouTube videos for $40/month because it allegedly violated the 2010 rules—despite the fact that those rules were not yet in force.[21] One sees a similar anti-consumer result in Chile, which earlier this year held that free social media plans similar to those Sprint is considering violated the nation's first-in-the-world net neutrality law. By allowing consumers to reach some online services but not others, these plans effectively "blocked" access to all services not included in the promotion, which violated the country's prohibition on blocking legal services over the Internet—despite the fact that the likely result of the decision was to increase the cost of Internet service and enhance Chile's digital divide by eliminating a low-cost option for mobile connectivity.[22]

These cases show the danger of structural rules designed to protect edge providers rather than consumers. The Commission is unquestionably correct that some broadband providers have incentives to use their position in the Internet ecosystem in an anticompetitive way. And that risk may be sufficiently grave to justify some regulation to reduce the risk of this harm. But when enacting any such regulation, the Commission must not lose focus on the consumer welfare that first prompted it to action—and any rules must leave room for pro-consumer innovation in broadband as well as edge markets.

IV.   The Commission Should Reject Calls to Reclassify Broadband Service Under Title II

Numerous commenters have called upon the Commission to reclassify broadband service as a Title II telecommunications service subject to common carriage obligations.

---

[21] Lyons, supra note 18, at 3-6.
[22] See Daniel A. Lyons, In Chile, Net Neutrality Widens the Digital Divide,
http://www.techpolicydaily.com/communications/chile-net-neutrality-widens-digital-divide/.

As the NPRM explained, the *Verizon* court held that the 2010 rules improperly imposed common carriage obligations on non-Title II services, and if the Commission intends to go forward with Open Internet rules under Section 706, it must assure that the rules leave "substantial room for individualized bargaining and discrimination in terms" between carriers and edge providers.[23] Because individualized bargaining is inconsistent with net neutrality advocates' view of a homogenized broadband service, they advocate reclassification as the preferred way for the Commission to avoid the *Verizon* court's mandate.

Syntonic Wireless would urge the Commission to view the *Verizon* decision not as a limit on the Open Internet initiative, but rather an essential element protecting it. Individualized bargaining and discrimination in terms preserve space for innovation in the broadband market. It is through individualized negotiations that Syntonic Wireless and other edge providers can partner with broadband providers to test potentially more efficient methods of delivering Internet services to consumers.

V. Any Blocking or Nondiscrimination Rules Should Allow Room for Pro-Consumer Innovation

Consistent with a focus on consumer welfare, any rules to enforce an Open Internet should take care not to restrict the potential for differentiation and innovation that benefit consumers. For example, the Commission may find it appropriate to enact a rule that prohibits broadband providers from blocking access to content included within a consumer's subscription. But this rule should not preclude broadband providers from offering differentiated services whose entire value proposition depends on accessing only a portion of the Internet—such as Syntonic's education initiative, which allows school

---

[23] Verizon v. FCC, 740 F.3d 623, 652 (DC Cir. 2014).

districts to deploy devices that can reach only curriculum-related, district-approved online resources, or Sprint's proposed social media plan.

These differentiated services are seemingly at odds with the no-blocking rule proposed in the NPRM. The Commission has proposed to re-enact verbatim the 2010 no-blocking rule. Although the NPRM offers little guidance as to how this rule should be enforced, the 2010 Open Internet rule explained that

> an Internet access service that provides access to a substantial subset of Internet endpoints based on end users preference to avoid certain content, applications, or services; Internet access services that allow some uses of the Internet (such as access to the World Wide Web) but not others (such as e-mail); or a "Best of the Web" Internet access service that provides access to 100 top websites could not be used to evade the open Internet rules applicable to "broadband Internet access service."[24]

But as noted above, such plans can benefit consumers who are interested in something less than full Internet access. As an increasing amount of our daily activities migrate online, different customers are likely to demand different services from their network providers. Moreover, proliferation of Internet-connected devices means consumers have multiple ways of reaching the Internet, and do not necessarily need every device to access every Internet endpoint at all times. Allowing broadband providers to tailor offerings to customers' particular preferences can be more efficient than forcing them into one-size-fits-all plans that are ill-suited to their needs.

Moreover, as the "Internet of Things" expands to include devices such as Syntonic's proposed remote healthcare monitoring solution, an increasing portion of network capacity will be dedicated to devices needing only limited connectivity. The Commission may explain that service to such devices falls outside its definition of

---

[24] 2010 rules ¶ 47.

"broadband Internet access service" and are therefore exempt from the rules. But as the spectrum of devices expands, the line between covered and non-covered services becomes difficult to discern. Consumer welfare is enhanced by allowing greater flexibility to offer less-than-full-Internet-access plans, subject perhaps to ex post review by the Commission in the event of demonstrated consumer harm.

Similarly, for reasons stated above, any nondiscrimination or commercial reasonableness standard must make provision for innovative, differentiated service offerings that benefit consumers. Numerous commenters have suggested that initiatives such as the Freeway application violate at least the spirit of net neutrality by treating content differently: sponsored content is exempt from a customer's monthly data cap while non-sponsored content is not. Certain edge providers may object to such an arrangement, but it should be without question that most sponsored data agreements are good for consumers. As consumer conduct online continues to grow and evolve, the law should allow broadband providers the flexibility to enter into new arrangements that better fit consumers' and edge providers' needs, again perhaps subject to Commission review to correct instances of demonstrable consumer harm.

VI.   The Commission Should Maintain a Light Touch When Regulating Mobile Services

Syntonic Wireless encourages the Commission to maintain its policy, first incorporated within the 2010 rules, of applying a lighter regulatory touch to mobile broadband. Our business model requires us to work closely with wireless broadband networks, and we recognize from first-hand experience that the unique challenges of managing a wireless broadband network strongly suggest the need for greater regulatory flexibility in this space.

As numerous other commenters have indicated, the mobile broadband environment is rapidly evolving. Sandvine estimates that median monthly data consumption over North American wireless networks has grown twenty percent in the last six months alone.[25] Mobile networks also face unique capacity constraints and less predictable traffic patterns, which makes management of network capacity more difficult. Syntonic routinely partners with mobile providers to navigate these capacity constraints to deliver growing amounts of Internet content wirelessly—a task that would prove much more difficult if wireless networks were treated identically to their wireline counterparts.

Conclusion

Consumer welfare has been, and should continue to be, the lodestar guiding the Commission's efforts to preserve the Open Internet. Syntonic Wireless has staked its company's future on its ability to provide novel new ways to deliver to consumers the content they demand. Any effort to promote the Open Internet must allow companies like ours to innovate in ways that promote consumer welfare, in broadband markets as well as upstream markets. In this fashion, the Commission can best assure that its rules enhance the ability of the Internet ecosystem to evolve to meet changing consumer demand.

Respectfully submitted,

---

[25] Sandvine, Global Internet Phenomena Report 1H2014, at 8, available at https://www.sandvine.com/downloads/general/global-internet-phenomena/2014/1h-2014-global-internet-phenomena-report.pdf.

September 3, 2014

Gary S. Greenbaum
CEO, Syntonic Wireless, Inc.
119 First Avenue South, Suite 100
Seattle, WA 98104

PREPARED STATEMENT OF NUALA O'CONNOR

TESTIMONY

Of

NUALA O'CONNOR

PRESIDENT & CEO

CENTER FOR DEMOCRACY & TECHNOLOGY

BEFORE

THE JUDICIARY COMMITTEE

of the

UNITED STATES SENATE

Wednesday, September 17, 2014

Chairman Leahy, Senator Grassley, distinguished members of the Committee, esteemed colleagues on the panel, thank you. I am honored to appear before you representing the Center for Democracy & Technology, one of the country's oldest Internet advocacy organizations. For over 20 years, CDT has worked to promote and sustain public policies that protect a free and open Internet. Above all, we are dedicated to the individual's interest in a digital world that allows free expression, free association, privacy, and growth. Both the Internet technology and policy architectures must support the individual's rights, while also fostering innovation and the free flow of information—not only within the United States, but globally.

We are also an organization that has long supported a light hand in the regulatory structures governing the Internet, both domestically and internationally. We believe that ensuring global access to the Internet requires deference to the decentralized technology architecture, to the unprecedented pace of technology innovation, and to the truly global, dynamic, and organic growth of the Internet community.

As we enter into the era of Internet 3.0, where the Internet is no longer something you sit down at a computer terminal to access, or even access via your phone or other mobile device, but rather, becomes embedded in every aspect of your daily life—your home, your car, your school or workplace, your very relationships, there has never been a more important time to work to protect, defend, and promote the rights of the individual in the digital world. As connected technologies become the interface between ourselves and our world, we must continue to be vigilant about the fundamental principles of free expression, personal privacy, and freedom of movement and association, among so many others. It is an important time to re-dedicate ourselves to these values and for the FCC and Congress to articulate clear guidance about the rights of the individual online.

However, the Internet, at just over two decades, is still in its infancy. And thus, while it is an appropriate time to evaluate our norms and strengthen our rules regarding the interaction between the individual and the digital world, we must be thoughtful about the consequences, while zealous in our creation of these new norms and rules. We must seek to protect an individual's profound need to fully engage in the digital world at reasonable costs and effective speeds, and must remain dedicated to growth and innovation—both in the commercial space and in the policy space.

Action is necessary at this time to clarify norms and reinstate prior rules

Thus, the Center for Democracy & Technology strongly supports the concept of net neutrality, as we believe that Internet access is an enabler of knowledge, of community, of economic advancement, and of democracy throughout the world. We applaud the FCC in taking decisive action to establish clear rules that create a level playing field for consumers. We seek rules undergirded by strong principles of fairness and Internet openness. We believe that all options should be on the table for the FCC to consider. We support the FCC's efforts to find a solution that advances the needs of individual consumers to have low-cost options to engage in digital life, while respecting the role that companies have played and will continue to play in fostering innovation and growth in the digital world.

Any action must be based in principles of openness and nondiscrimination

In our comments to the FCC, the Center for Democracy & Technology articulated several principles on which this regulatory decision should be based, and which should be reinforced through the agency's actions and enforcement choices. Any regulatory solution:

1. Must include an anti-blocking rule.

2. Must be based on a general expectation of nondiscrimination for Internet service.

3. Must allow for reasonable network management.

4. May include flexibility for different/additional data delivery models that don't degrade ordinary Internet access.

5. Must demonstrate clarity of scope.

All available options should be considered

We believe that all available regulatory options should be considered, including Title II reclassification, Section 706 authority, and a range of hybrid proposals. In our prior comments to the Federal Communications Commission, we examined the pros and cons of both Title II and Section 706. While both of these remain real options, we remain concerned about limitations inherent in the structure of either solution and in the likelihood of speedy implementation.

I.   Support for Title II.

We believe that public policy must support principles that promote access, free expression, and enable more individuals to fully engage in the digital world. Many in the advocacy community believe that Title II reclassification is the only option that satisfies these principles. The support for Title II has been well documented in the majority of comments submitted, and demonstrates the public's overwhelming interest in Internet life. Title II also provides a clear path forward for FCC action. Title II does, however, present significant hurdles, both procedurally and substantively, in adoption, implementation, forbearance, and, yes, potential litigation.

Reclassifying broadband Internet access as a telecommunications service subject to Title II of the Communications Act would be the most direct and simplest course to eliminate the specific legal obstacle that caused the court to strike down the Commission's 2010 Open Internet rules. A reclassification action would create the durable legal basis for the Commission to craft rules in support of an open Internet. There is a strong argument that Internet access is a "telecommunications service" within the definitions of the act. However, significant portions of Title II would require forbearance, as they are a poor fit for the current Internet access marketplace. Price regulation and construction approval are just two of the myriad of provisions that even many in the advocacy community recognize might require forbearance. Still, Title II remains a significant option for the FCC to consider as it creates an environment of Internet openness.

As I have worked now for almost 20 years in the legal and policy space related to the Internet and emerging technologies, I am most curious about the proposals that represent real policy innovation. Thus, I would like to discuss several proposals that draw upon, or are hybrids of, Title II and Section 706, and several implementation issues applicable to any approach.

II.   Section 706 and A New Alternative to "Commercially Reasonable."

There are certainly valid concerns about Section 706 and its implementation and enforcement. None more salient, however, than whether a commercially reasonable standard is the appropriate one for determining whether business practices support the concept of Internet openness. As we discussed at length in our comments to the FCC on this issue, a "commercially reasonable" standard is simply inappropriate for open Internet rules, and the Commission should consider alternative formulations. Modifying the Commission's proposed legal standard could strengthen protections for the Internet user and clarify the intent and norms the Commission seeks to reinforce. CDT agrees with the Commission's observation that "[s]ound public policy requires that Internet openness be the touchstone of a new legal standard."[1]

An alternative policy approach would be to articulate a new standard that is tailored to the particular aims of this proceeding and that is based upon the compelling public policy and societal need underpinning an open Internet. Choosing the appropriate shorthand for such a standard is less important than articulating its content, but CDT would suggest that a

---

[1] *Protecting and Promoting the Open Internet*, GN Docket No. 14-28, Notice of Proposed Rulemaking, FCC 14-61 (rel. May 15, 2014) (hereinafter "NPRM"), ¶ 116.

standard might require practices to be "consistent with Internet openness" or prohibit practices that would tend to "undermine Internet openness."

A standard could further be articulated that would determine whether a practice is in violation of this standard if substantial adoption of the practice would tend to undermine:

(i) the ability of broadband Internet access subscribers to access and use the lawful Internet content, applications, services, and devices of their choice without interference from their provider of broadband services; or

(ii) the ability of developers of independent online content, applications, services, or devices to make those offerings available to interested Internet users everywhere without having to negotiate for or obtain any kind of permission or agreement from those users' providers of Internet service.

Alternative formulations are possible, but the legal standard should reflect the public's interest in an Internet that fosters free expression, accumulation of knowledge, freedom of association and movement, and a policy architecture that maximizes public engagement in digital life and online communities, discourse, and commerce.

III.   A Title II/Section 706 Hybrid Approach.

The Commission might also consider a hybrid approach that builds upon the recent D.C. Circuit decision and some of the strengths of Title II and Section 706. Section 706 authority could be utilized to adopt rules regarding broadband Internet access service, augmented with new policies focused on the second side of broadband providers service, following the D.C. Circuit's finding that network operators effectively provide a service to all the websites and Internet content providers the operators' subscribers choose to access.

The D.C. Circuit's holding that broadband providers "furnish a service to edge providers"[2] presents an opportunity to consider open Internet policy from a new angle. A new policy expressly addressing this edge-facing service that carriers provide could augment the Commission's proposed rules.

The Commission's proposed rules, like the 2010 rules, apply to "broadband Internet access service," defined in relevant part as the "capability to transmit data to and receive data from all or substantially all Internet endpoints." This is a reasonable description of the functionality broadband providers provide to subscribers: Subscribers get the ability to send and receive traffic to and from the entire Internet. That includes not only the carriage of traffic over the broadband provider's own network, but also the onward forwarding of traffic over other networks with which that broadband provider has arranged to interconnect.

The definition is not, however, an accurate description of the functionality broadband providers provide to edge providers (i.e., the websites and other providers of online content or services that Internet subscribers choose to access). What edge providers get from each broadband provider is more limited: not the ability to reach the entire Internet, but rather the ability to reach the subscribers of that particular broadband provider. Additionally, the service is limited to carriage across the broadband provider's own network. Edge providers make their own arrangements (via their own Internet access, transit providers, or content delivery networks) for the delivery of traffic to and from the edge of the broadband provider's network. The edge-facing service of the broadband

---

[2] *Verizon v. FCC* at 51.

provider is to carry that traffic between the interconnection point and the relevant subscribers across its own local network.

In short, what Internet carriers provide to edge services is different from what they provide to subscribers, and it does not meet the definition of broadband Internet access service. This disparity did not concern the Commission prior to *Verizon v. FCC*, because the Commission's position was that broadband providers only provided service to their subscribers. Edge providers were not considered to be customers or recipients of a service from broadband providers.

Now that the D.C. Circuit has rejected that position, it is appropriate for the Commission to consider this edge-facing service as a distinct offering warranting distinct analysis. The Commission has an opportunity to craft an appropriate definition of these services and develop an appropriate policy framework for them – a framework which may augment whatever open Internet rules the Commission adopts for "subscriber-side" services. There are at least two ways that a focus on edge-facing service, thus defined, could contribute to a policy framework to promote the open Internet.

1. *Possible Applicability of Title II to the Edge.*

One option is discussed in Mozilla's May 5 petition to the FCC.[3] As set forth in that petition, there is a strong argument that the edge-facing functionality that broadband carriers provide could qualify as a telecommunications service subject to Title II. The service that edge providers receive consists exclusively of the transmission of traffic across the

---

[3] Mozilla Petition to Recognize Remote Delivery Services in Terminating Access Networks and Classify Such Services as Telecommunications Services Under Title II of the Communications Act, May 5, 2014, https://blog.mozilla.org/netpolicy/files/2014/05/Mozilla-Petition.pdf.

broadband provider's network. On the Internet side, the transmission function does not come bundled with any of the other services (email, newsgroups, website hosting, etc.) that were key to the Commission's decision to classify subscriber side services as information services. The main question would be whether edge-facing service can be considered to be provided "for a fee," possibly on a theory that carriers receive valuable consideration for the exchange and carriage of edge provider traffic via interconnection agreements or subscriber revenues, or possibly if carriers start charging edge providers directly, as Verizon told the D.C. Circuit it intended to start doing.[4]

Classifying edge-facing services under Title II would not require the Commission to reverse prior classification decisions for the simple reason that the Commission has not previously recognized the existence of such a service and hence has had no occasion to consider its regulatory treatment. Now that the D.C. Circuit has ruled that broadband carriers do provide a service to edge providers, it would be perfectly reasonable for the Commission to consider how those services might be treated under the statute. And the fact that the Commission has judged the subscriber side of broadband (the only side it previously recognized) as information services is no bar to different treatment of the Internet side. The D.C. Circuit has observed that "one may be a common carrier with regard to some activities but not others."[5]

Applying Title II would not automatically create a complete policy framework. Rather, it would provide the Commission with a stable base of authority to craft appropriate

---

[4] See *Verizon v. FCC* at 37 (quoting Verizon's counsel from the oral argument transcript at 31: "but for [the Open Internet Order] rules we would be exploring those commercial arrangements.").

[5] *NARUC v. FCC*, 533 F.2d 601, 608 (D.C. Cir. 1976).

nondiscrimination rules for edge-facing service. Such rules could be based on provisions of Title II, on section 706, or both. Importantly, however, they would not be subject to the common-carrier prohibition that doomed the Commission's 2010 rules. They would also need to be coupled with extensive forbearance, as many provisions of Title II would not be sensible to apply to edge-facing services.

2. *Linking the Concepts of Individualized Negotiations and Specialized Services*

Alternatively, focusing on edge-facing service may provide a new avenue for an open Internet policy framework to avoid the common carrier prohibition, even without classifying edge-facing service under Title II. The idea would be to link the concepts of individualized negotiations on the Internet side with the offering of specialized services to subscribers, so that specialized services become the vehicle for creating the flexibility in terms that the D.C. Circuit has held the common carrier prohibition to require.

The 2010 rules allowed broadband providers to offer specialized services in addition to broadband Internet access service. Thus, there was always some potential for edge providers and broadband providers to negotiate special delivery arrangements. In litigating *Verizon v. FCC*, however, the Commission never pointed to the allowance for specialized services as a possible source of the "substantial room for individualized bargaining and discrimination in terms"[6] necessary to distinguish the Commission's rules from common carriage.

The challenge facing such an argument would have been that the Commission's approach treated broadband Internet access service and specialized services as distinct, and the case

---

[6] *Cellco Partnership v. FCC*, 700 F.3d at 548.

concerned the permissible regulatory treatment of the former standing alone. But even if

the two services are treated as distinct on the subscriber side, they need not be treated that

way on the Internet side. If the relevant edge-facing service is defined consistently with our

proposal above and with the D.C. Circuit's suggestion in Verizon v. FCC[7] – in effect, as the

provision of a capability to reach a broadband provider's subscribers, without regard to the

precise manner or quality of transmission – then the edge-facing service could include the

transmission of traffic to subscribers via both regular Internet service (standard

transmission) and specialized service (e.g. including quality-of-service guarantees). The

overall edge-facing service would be transmission, with different options constituting tiers

of service that "permit broadband providers to distinguish somewhat among edge

providers."[8]

In other words, the Commission could consider a regime under which, as per the D.C.

Circuit's suggestion, a broadband provider would be required to provide a baseline level of

service to all edge providers, while still retaining some flexibility to negotiate for special

treatment in individual cases. The Commission could require such special arrangements,

however, to be provided in a manner consistent with specialized services treatment on the

subscriber side. Under such a regime, there would be flexibility for special deals, but not

unlimited flexibility. The constraint would depend on the definition of specialized services.

The end result of this kind of approach could be a policy framework that in principle could

be similar to the 2010 rules. Edge providers would be entitled to a standard level of access

to broadband subscribers. They could also try to negotiate special arrangements with

---

[7] See *Verizon v. FCC* at 61 (suggesting that "the relevant 'carriage' broadband providers furnish [to edge providers] might be access to end users more generally," rather than access at any particular level of speed or service).

[8] *Verizon v. FCC* at 61.

broadband providers. To avoid violating the rules, though, such special arrangements would need to be carried as specialized services to and from subscribers, rather than being commingled with ordinary broadband Internet access traffic.

As the Commission noted in 2010, permitting special treatment via specialized services carries some policy risks. The Commission would need to carefully monitor the marketplace for signs that specialized services are "retarding the growth of or constricting capacity available for broadband Internet access service." But integrating specialized services into the analysis of how much leeway open Internet rules leave for individualized negotiations, and considering the issue through an edge-facing lens, may create a new opening to argue that rules quite similar to the 2010 rules could nonetheless be consistent with the approach the D.C. Circuit suggested might pass muster.

It is in the public's interest to adopt clear rules, now.

We believe that public policy must support principles that promote access, free expression, and enable more individuals to fully engage in the digital world. Whichever path the FCC chooses to take, it must act swiftly to create policy certainty that protects the individual and promotes future growth and innovation.

Thank you.

PREPARED STATEMENT OF CHAIRMAN PATRICK J. LEAHY

**Statement of Senator Patrick Leahy (D-Vt.),
Chairman, Senate Judiciary Committee,
Hearing on
"Why Net Neutrality Matters: Protecting Consumers and Competition Through
Meaningful Open Internet Rules"
September 17, 2014**

On Monday, the Federal Communications Commission (FCC) closed the public comment period on its proposed rules to protect an open Internet. An astounding 3.7 million Americans made their voices heard on an issue that is of critical importance to consumers and businesses. An overwhelming number of comments called on the FCC to enact meaningful rules that will protect consumers and preserve competition online. I agree, and the FCC should heed their call.

This is the second hearing the Judiciary Committee has convened on this issue. The first hearing, which I chaired in Vermont this summer, was an important opportunity to hear from voices outside of the Beltway. Vermont-based small businesses now have a reach they only dreamed of thanks to the transforming power of the Internet. For the Vermont Country Store, which has long operated two retail outlets and a mail order business, the Internet now accounts for a remarkable 40 percent of its business and one third of its employees. Logic Supply is based entirely online and sells industrial computers to customers around the world.

Their testimony was simple: keep the Internet an open playing field for small businesses so that they can launch and thrive. As Cabot Orton from the Vermont Country Store testified: "All the small business community asks is simply to preserve and protect Internet commerce as it exists today, which has served *all* businesses remarkably well." He couldn't be more right.

Martha Reid, the Vermont State Librarian, also testified about the important role that libraries play in communities throughout the country, particularly in underserved areas. She said: "All Americans, including the most disenfranchised citizens who would have no way to access the Internet without the library, need to be able to use Internet resources on an equal footing."

This testimony and the testimony we will hear today underscore the importance of why net neutrality matters. It matters for our economic growth and competitiveness. It matters because the Internet is an equalizer that can help break cycles of unemployment and poverty. It matters because the online world is the ultimate tool for free expression and democracy—a tool so powerful that it has helped topple totalitarian governments. Allowing the Internet to become a two-tiered system of "haves" and "have-nots," controlled by a small number of corporate gatekeepers, would destroy everything that has made it one of the greatest innovations in human history. The FCC must act in a meaningful way to protect its openness.

Meaningful rules would stop so-called "paid prioritization" deals that would allow large corporations to drown out smaller competitors. I introduced legislation with Congresswoman Doris Matsui of California that would require the FCC to develop rules to stop these deals. Regardless of whether our bill passes, the FCC should act to block this kind of behavior. Meaningful rules must go beyond the antitrust laws, which play an important role as a backstop but alone are not enough to promote and preserve free speech and innovation online.

The FCC's action will determine whether the Internet as we know it will stay open, vibrant, and competitive, or whether it will become a place where only the most powerful have a say. I know the outcome that this Vermonter wants to see.

I thank the witnesses for coming today and I look forward to hearing your testimony.

# # # # #

Statement of Senator Charles Grassley, Senate Judiciary Committee Hearing, "Why Net Neutrality Matters: Protecting Consumers and Competition through Meaningful Open Internet Rules", September 17, 2014

Good morning and welcome to all of the witnesses. Mr. Chairman, I appreciate your holding this hearing on net neutrality. This is a complex topic, and I'm glad that the Committee can hear from all sides of the debate. It's important for the Committee to consider the state of the Internet and whether new rules are necessary to ensure that it continues to thrive.

Mr. Chairman, I believe that many, if not all, of us share similar goals with respect to the Internet. We all want the Internet to grow and prosper. We all want faster and cheaper Internet access. We all want more deployment of broadband technologies, particularly to areas that remain without access. We all want more innovations and new avenues by which to access information. We all want consumers to have more choice and options.

The FCC is in the process of considering whether to adopt rules that would regulate the Internet. Chairman Wheeler has taken the position that there is not enough competition in the high-speed broadband marketplace, and because of this, the agency should advance net neutrality rules.

Many would dispute the FCC's assessment of the Internet. Rather, they would take the position that we have a competitive, dynamic Internet <u>right now</u>, and the push for new rules and regulations is a "solution in search of a problem." Is the Internet really broken? Broadband and Internet technologies are advancing every day. New products are constantly entering the market, and consumers can choose when, where, and how to access their information and entertainment.

Overall broadband deployment and speeds –both wired and wireless – are estimated to reach 98% of American households with broadband speeds of 10 megabytes or faster. 82% of American households have access to broadband speeds of 50 megabytes or faster. The overall broadband industry – cable, telco, satellite, wired and wireless – has invested over $1.2 trillion in infrastructure, $60 billion a year recently. Further, it's estimated that broadband speeds double every 2 to 3 years.

So, many would contend that the Internet is highly competitive and responsive to consumer demands and that the FCC and others are just speculating about future harms. They'd say there is no need to deviate from the current policies that have allowed the Internet's phenomenal growth.

Moreover, many – including myself – are highly skeptical about the prospect of expansive FCC regulation over every aspect of the Internet. The Internet has been so successful precisely because of a hands-off approach. I'd note that this policy was first implemented under the Clinton Administration. The lack of government intervention and regulation has allowed competition to flourish beyond our wildest imagination. Businesses of all sizes have benefitted from a regime that hasn't been bogged down by prescriptive or onerous regulations. We all want more deployment of technologies and infrastructure. In fact, I'd like to see more broadband growth and options take place in rural America. However, it's more likely we'll see improvements in this area as a result of innovation and investment, than as a result of more regulation.

Internet technology is advancing at a rapid pace. New products are changing the Internet's infrastructure by delivering faster access through fiber optic cables. New technologies are allowing people to "cut the cord" and access their media content through the Internet and handheld devices rather than on traditional television sets. Investments in next-generation broadband technologies and infrastructure are booming.

Because of the fast changing Internet market, we need to be particularly careful when looking to impose rules and regulations. They could just end up impeding the development and adoption of new technologies and services. They could threaten investment in network upgrades, generate legal and marketplace uncertainty, and ultimately cost jobs and harm the economy.

It's doubtful that creating an expansive regulatory regime will increase broadband deployment, spur innovation, or ensure better quality services and consumer satisfaction. Net neutrality rules radically would change the hands-off approach that has allowed the Internet to work so well thus far. Supporters of net neutrality contend that new regulations will restore Internet protections and ensure the vitality of the Internet. If anything, I'm concerned that that the imposition of new regulations – and in particular expansion of 80 year-old rules designed to regulate old telephone monopolies under Title II – will have the exact opposite effect on the Internet. More regulation normally isn't seen as something that incentivizes businesses to advance and grow, so it seems counterintuitive in this case as well.

Nonetheless, there are legitimate concerns about making sure Internet competition and consumers are protected from corporate bad actors. I don't support monopolistic, anti-competitive or predatory practices in the Internet marketplace.

But rather than allow the FCC to impose regulations on an industry that has been so successful under a hands-off regime, antitrust and consumer protection laws may provide a better option to ensure consumers and businesses are not harmed by anti-competitive conduct in the modern Internet ecosphere. Antitrust and consumer protection laws are already on the books to guard against anti-competitive activity and to prevent companies from engaging in deceptive and unfair behavior. I've been a strong supporter of vigorous enforcement of the antitrust laws by the Justice Department and the Federal Trade Commission to ensure a fair playing field in many sectors of our economy. I hope that they'd be paying close attention to this critical market as well.

In conclusion, because the Internet is so important to consumers and to our economy, we should proceed with caution. No one wants to undermine the Internet's competitive vibrancy. This is a complex policy debate, so I look forward to hearing the testimony of the witnesses.

Senate Judiciary Committee Hearing On
Why Net Neutrality Matters: Protecting Consumers and Competition Through Meaningful Open
Internet Rules
September 17, 2014
Questions for the Record from Senator Patrick Leahy

Question for Brad Burnham

1. Some witnesses at the hearing challenged whether, in a paid prioritization world, broadband providers would have an incentive to discriminate against particular content providers or websites. Do you share this view, particularly with respect to vertically integrated broadband providers?

Senate Judiciary Committee Hearing On
Why Net Neutrality Matters: Protecting Consumers and Competition Through Meaningful Open
Internet Rules
September 17, 2014
Qnestions for the Record from Senator Patrick Leahy

Question for Ruth Livier

1. Opponents of FCC action to create new rules that protect consumers and promote an open
   Internet argue that the antitrust laws are sufficient to achieve these goals. As an independent
   producer and writer, do you agree that antitrust laws would adequately protect your content
   online? Would you be able to afford to bring a claim under these laws if you felt you had been
   harmed by a broadband provider?

Senate Judiciary Committee Hearing On
Why Net Neutrality Matters: Protecting Consumers and Competition Through Meaningful Open
Internet Rules
September 17, 2014
Questions for the Record from Senator Patrick Leahy

Question for Robert McDowell

1. You testified at the hearing that consumers could rely on contractual commitments in their service agreements, in which you claim that most major broadband providers pledge to protect Internet openness and freedom. You noted that such contracts are enforceable by state and federal law. What specific contractual requirements do these pledges create for broadband providers? How common is it for contracts between consumers and broadband providers to be subject to mandatory arbitration? What would protect consumers in the event that broadband providers altered the terms of their contracts to no longer cover open Internet principles?

Senate Judiciary Committee Hearing On
Why Net Neutrality Matters: Protecting Consumers and Competition Through Meaningful Open
Internet Rules
September 17, 2014
Questions for the Record from Senator Patrick Leahy

<u>Question for Jeffrey Eisenach</u>

1. You testified that in a paid prioritization world, broadband providers would have an incentive to give startups the lowest cost access. Doesn't that argument ignore the fact that many startups offer products or services that compete with products or services offered by broadband providers?

Senate Judiciary Committee Hearing On
Why Net Neutrality Matters: Protecting Consumers and Competition Through Meaningful Open
Internet Rules
September 17, 2014
Questions for the Record from Senator Patrick Leahy

<u>Question for Nuala O'Connor</u>

1. Some have said that if the FCC adopts strong rules to promote net neutrality, it could undermine our Nation's message to oppressive regimes that restrict free expression online and otherwise control the Internet. Isn't there a fundamental difference between rules to ensure that the Internet remains free, open and competitive, and regulating the Internet to oppress?

Senator Grassley's Written Questions for Senate Judiciary Committee Hearing, "Why Net Neutrality Matters: Protecting Consumers and Competition through Meaningful Open Internet Rules" – September 17, 2014

Questions for Commissioner McDowell

1. Proponents of net neutrality claim that if we want broadband Internet access to operate in a manner that preserves the Internet's open character, then the best approach is to establish that expectation in advance through regulation.
    a. Do you agree with this approach? Will regulation-before-the-fact preserve and promote the Internet's openness better than, let's say, targeting an actual market failure or anti-competitive behavior that has occurred?
    b. In a dynamic, ever-changing environment such as the Internet, is there a greater justification for ex ante regulation as compared to ex post enforcement?

2. I asked this question at the hearing, but would like you to give a more detailed response in writing. It has been argued that antitrust analysis is purely a numbers game that doesn't take into account important non-economic values.
    a. Do you agree? Does an antitrust analysis only consider financial and economic values, or can it, in fact, constitute a broader consumer welfare-based analysis that looks at other consumer values?

3. Some proponents of net neutrality argue that antitrust law is "too slow" to adequately deter and remedy anti-competitive behavior, particularly those behaviors that hurt small startup companies. Do you agree with this? Is a regulatory framework necessary to protect the rapid and dynamic nature of the Internet startup marketplace?

4. It has been claimed that we have had a *de facto* net neutrality policy regime for the past 20 years. Do you agree with this observation? Why or why not?

5. It has been claimed that the Internet needs "basic rules of the road to ensure that it remains open." Do you agree with this sentiment? Would adopting clear rules provide marketplace certainty and promote investment? If so, what rules specifically should we adopt?

6. How do you respond to the claim that in the absence of net neutrality regulations, freedom of speech and expression, freedom of association, and the First Amendment

itself, will be threatened? How do you respond to the claim that if the FCC does not adopt net neutrality rules, we'll create an Internet of have and have-nots and certain groups will be left behind?

7. Some net neutrality proponents argue that without government regulation, certain content providers may be prohibited from getting their content online. Do you agree or disagree with this statement and why?

8. It has been said that there is a "strong argument that Internet access is a 'telecommunications service'" within the definitions of the Communications Act.
    a. Do you agree with this assertion? Why or why not?
    b. How would classifying Internet access as a Title II "telecommunications service" result in the regulation of the larger Internet ecosystem? Are you concerned that it could possibly ensnare other things like content, applications or edge providers? How could that impact the Internet?

Senator Grassley's Written Questions for Senate Judiciary Committee Hearing, "Why Net Neutrality Matters: Protecting Consumers and Competition through Meaningful Open Internet Rules" – September 17, 2014

Questions for Dr. Eisenach

1. Proponents of net neutrality claim that if we want broadband Internet access to operate in a manner that preserves the Internet's open character, then the best approach is to establish that expectation in advance through regulation.
    a. Do you agree with this approach? Will regulation-before-the-fact preserve and promote the Internet's openness better than, let's say, targeting an actual market failure or anti-competitive behavior that has occurred?
    b. In a dynamic, ever-changing environment such as the Internet, is there a greater justification for ex ante regulation as compared to ex post enforcement?

2. I asked this question at the hearing, but would like you to give a more detailed response in writing. It has been argued that antitrust analysis is purely a numbers game that doesn't take into account important non-economic values.
    a. Do you agree? Does an antitrust analysis only consider financial and economic values, or can it, in fact, constitute a broader consumer welfare-based analysis that looks at other consumer values?

3. It has been claimed that we have had a *de facto* net neutrality policy regime for the past 20 years. Do you agree with this observation? Why or why not?

4. It has been claimed that the Internet needs "basic rules of the road to ensure that it remains open." Do you agree with this sentiment? Would adopting clear rules provide marketplace certainty and promote investment? If so, what rules specifically should we adopt?

5. Some net neutrality proponents argue that without government regulation, certain content providers may be prohibited from getting their content online. Do you agree or disagree with this statement and why?

6. You testified that free market principles should guide the interactions of a dynamic internet ecosystem. However, another witness testified that there should be an internet market "open to all." Are these two principles compatible under economic theory?

7. It has been said that there is a "strong argument that Internet access is a 'telecommunications service'" within the definitions of the Communications Act.
    a. Do you agree with this assertion? Why or why not?
    b. How would classifying Internet access as a Title II "telecommunications service" result in the regulation of the larger Internet ecosystem? Are you concerned that it could possibly ensnare other things like content, applications or edge providers? How could that impact the Internet?

8. I've heard concerns that vertical contracts between ISPs and content providers – such as "paid prioritization" agreements and differentiated pricing structures – will only harm consumers and the Internet marketplace overall. It has been claimed that the proposed FCC regulations are necessary to "preserve" the freedom and openness that has until now been a central characteristic of the Internet.
    a. Are these concerns warranted?
    b. Are there any benefits or efficiencies that consumers will gain from such arrangements?

Questions for the Record
Sept. 17, 2014 Judiciary Committee Hearing
Senator Lee

For Mr. McDowell:

1. At the Committee's hearing, you suggested that industry groups advocating net-neutrality regulation should be careful what they wish for. Could you give a concrete example of what you mean?

2. Do you agree with Dr. Eisenach's testimony that FCC net-neutrality regulations may encourage rent-seeking behavior?

3. Apart from the net-neutrality regulations discussed at the hearing, I would like to ask you about a related subject concerning the future of the Internet: the transition of oversight of the domain name system from the U.S. National Telecommunications and Information Administration to the independent Internet Corporation for Assigned Names and Numbers (ICANN).

   a. A number of groups and individuals have expressed concerns with the Administration's vague announcement that it would not renew its contract with ICANN—and that ICANN must implement a new mechanism, built on a multi-stakeholder model, that maintains the openness of the Internet. Some of these groups have proposed a minimum set of protections that should be in place before the United States agrees to relinquish its oversight. What protections do you believe ICANN should implement before the United States relinquishes its oversight, and why are such protections necessary?

   b. If the transition is not completed in a thoughtful way, is there any potential for other governments or intergovernmental organizations to hijack the Internet and threaten its openness?

   c. In your opinion, assuming adequate protections are in place, will the proposed transition create a more open and freedom-enhancing Internet?

QUESTIONS SUBMITTED TO JEFFREY A. EISENACH, PH.D., BY SENATOR LEE

Questions for the Record

Sept. 17, 2014 Judiciary Committee Hearing

Senator Lee

For Dr. Eisenach:

1. At the Committee's hearing, you expressed concern that FCC net neutrality regulations might encourage rent-seeking behavior. In particular, you mentioned that the FCC has had a regrettable history of encouraging rent seeking by special interests.

    a. Please elaborate on the FCC's past experience with rent-seeking behavior by regulated parties.

    b. Do you believe the proposed net-neutrality regulations could lead to similar problems?

2. Apart from the net-neutrality regulations discussed at the hearing, I would like to ask you about a related subject concerning the future of the Internet: the transition of oversight of the domain name system from the U.S. National Telecommunications and Information Administration to the independent Internet Corporation for Assigned Names and Numbers (ICANN).

    a. A number of groups and individuals have expressed concerns with the Administration's vague announcement that it would not renew its contract with ICANN—and that ICANN must implement a new mechanism, built on a multi-stakeholder model, that maintains the openness of the Internet. Some of these groups have proposed a minimum set of protections that should be in place before the United States agrees to relinquish its oversight. What protections do you believe ICANN should implement before the United States relinquishes its oversight, and why are such protections necessary?

    b. If the transition is not completed in a thoughtful way, is there any potential for other governments or intergovernmental organizations to hijack the Internet and threaten its openness?

    c. In your opinion, assuming adequate protections are in place, will the proposed transition create a more open and freedom-enhancing Internet?

Questions for the Record
Sept. 17, 2014 Judiciary Committee Hearing
Senator Lee

For Ms. O'Connor:

1. Apart from the net-neutrality regulations discussed at the hearing, I would like to ask you about a related subject concerning the future of the Internet: the transition of oversight of the domain name system from the U.S. National Telecommunications and Information Administration to the independent Internet Corporation for Assigned Names and Numbers (ICANN).

    a. A number of groups and individuals have expressed concerns with the Administration's vague announcement that it would not renew its contract with ICANN—and that ICANN must implement a new mechanism, built on a multi-stakeholder model, that maintains the openness of the Internet. Some of these groups have proposed a minimum set of protections that should be in place before the United States agrees to relinquish its oversight. What protections do you believe ICANN should implement before the United States relinquishes its oversight, and why are such protections necessary?

    b. If the transition is not completed in a thoughtful way, is there any potential for other governments or intergovernmental organizations to hijack the Internet and threaten its openness?

    c. In your opinion, assuming adequate protections are in place, will the proposed transition create a more open and freedom-enhancing Internet?

Senate Judiciary Committee Hearing On
Why Net Neutrality Matters: Protecting Consumers and Competition Through Meaningful Open
Internet Rules
September 17, 2014
Questions for the Record from Senator Patrick Leahy

Question for Brad Burnham

1. Some witnesses at the hearing challenged whether, in a paid prioritization world, broadband
    providers would have an incentive to discriminate against particular content providers or
    websites. Do you share this view, particularly with respect to vertically integrated broadband
    providers?

Broadband providers are for profit corporations with a duty to maximize profits on behalf of
shareholders. The profit maximizing move is to leverage their powerful market position to
collect fast lane tolls and access fees from applications providers, while at the same time
discriminating against competitive consumer services to privilege their own offerings. So,
even in a paid prioritization world broadband access providers have an incentive to
discriminate against competitive content or applications.

If the witnesses are arguing broadband access providers have no incentive to discriminate
against competitive content and applications because they can make more money charging
fast lane tolls and access fees, this is only true because there is so little competition for their
network services they they can charge what they like for the fast lane and for access to their
subscribers.

In a competitive market, it would be disastrous for a broadband provider to focus on fast
lane tolls and access fees. There is little innovation or differentiation in those services. That
business would quickly be commoditized and afford only the thinnest margins.

So the witnesses making the argument that broadband providers would have no incentive to
discriminate in a world where they can collect fast lane tolls and access fees cannot have it
both ways. If broadband access providers face real competition for their network services,
they absolutely have an incentive to vertically integrate into consumer services and to favor
their services over those of their competitors. If they have a natural monopoly in their
network, then yes, they can make more money if they drop their consumer services and just
collect monopoly rents for use of the fast lane and access to subscribers. But to make that
argument is to admit that broadband access providers have monopoly power in their
network.

So no, I do not agree with the witnesses who argue that in a paid prioritization world
broadband access providers have no incentive to discriminate against content or
applications. To the contrary, the profit maximizing move is to charge high fast lane tolls and
access fees **and** to discriminate against competitive applications and content.

Senate Judiciary Committee Hearing On
Why Net Neutrality Matters: Protecting Consumers and Competition Through Meaningful Open
Internet Rules
September 17, 2014
Questions for the Record from Senator Patrick Leahy

Question for Ruth Livier

1. Opponents of FCC action to create new rules that protect consumers and promote an open Internet argue that the antitrust laws are sufficient to achieve these goals. As an independent producer and writer, do you agree that antitrust laws would adequately protect your content online? Would you be able to afford to bring a claim under these laws if you felt you had been harmed by a broadband provider?

As an independent artist, antitrust laws would not be sufficient since, should I need to protect myself, I would lack the resources to do so. As a writer/producer/actress and student, I have to juggle different roles to make ends meet so I would not be able to either afford to bring a claim under these laws, if I felt I was being harmed by a broadband provider, nor would I have the time to focus on even preparing for the claim while at the same time continuing to create content and trying to make a living wage.

Further, antitrust law is narrowly focused and would provide uncertain outcomes. Antitrust law is focused narrowly on competition and requires a broad understanding of complex economic issues and antitrust law. It is, at once, too narrow to confront all harms that I could potentially face at the hands of Internet service providers, and too complex to offer any certainty or realistic hope of redress to individuals in my field.

The only way to protect and encourage the creation of diverse, independent content online, and to ensure that artists can make a living creating such content, is for the FCC to create strong rules that prohibit practices like blocking, unreasonable discrimination, and paid prioritization online. These types of harmful practices would jeopardize my opportunity for artistic expression and my livelihood. The FCC can only create these types of rules if it classifies Internet access services as a Title II common carrier service.

RESPONSES OF HON. ROBERT M. MCDOWELL TO QUESTIONS SUBMITTED
BY SENATORS GRASSLEY, LEAHY, AND LEE

THE HON. ROBERT M. MCDOWELL
Questions for the Record from the Sept. 17, 2014 Judiciary Committee Hearing: "Why Net Neutrality Matters"
—*The views expressed in these responses are my own and do not necessarily represent the views of Wiley Rein or
any of its clients*—

ATTACHMENT 1—MEMBER REQUESTS FOR THE RECORD

The Honorable Patrick Leahy

1. You testified at the hearing that consumers could rely on contractual commitments in their
   service agreements, in which you claim that most major broadband providers pledge to protect
   Internet openness and freedom. You noted that such contracts are enforceable by state and
   federal law. What specific contractual requirements do these pledges create for broadband
   providers? How common is it for contracts between consumers and broadband providers to be
   subject to mandatory arbitration? What would protect consumers in the event that broadband
   providers altered the terms of their contracts to no longer cover open Internet principles?

   Thank you for the opportunity to expand upon my view that broadband providers have made
   enforceable commitments to Internet openness and freedom. Major broadband providers have
   made specific commitments to their customers to protect Internet openness and freedom. For
   example, Verizon promises users that they "can access and use the legal content, applications,
   and services of your choice, regardless of their source" on "any of our Internet access services,
   wireline or wireless," "so long as they are legal and do not harm our networks or the provision of
   Internet access service, facilitate theft of service, or harm other users of the service."[1] Similarly,
   Comcast commits to providing its customers with "full access to all the lawful content, services,
   and applications that the Internet has to offer."[2] AT&T assures customers that it "does not favor
   certain Internet applications by blocking, throttling or modifying particular protocols, protocol
   ports, or protocol fields in ways not prescribed by the protocol standards."[3]

   Consumers may rely on these commitments. Current legal regimes, including the Federal
   Communications Commission's transparency rule and generally applicable antitrust and
   consumer protection laws can fully address any issues that might emerge. Indeed, the Federal
   Trade Commission has built expertise over many years protecting consumers in the Internet and
   broadband space. This oversight, coupled with market accountability, protects consumers.

   You inquire about arbitration clauses, which are often included in agreements between
   broadband providers and their customers.[4] The presence of arbitration clauses does not
   undermine consumer protections in the area of Internet openness. Agreements to arbitrate

---

[1] *See Verizon's Commitment to Our Broadband Internet Access Customers*, Verizon,
http://www.verizon.com/about/sites/default/files/Verizon_Broadband_Commitment.pdf (last visited Oct. 1,
2014).

[2] *See Frequently Asked Questions About Network Management*, Comcast,
https://customer.comcast.com/Pages/FAQViewer.aspx?seoid=Frequently-Asked-Questions-about-Network-
Management#manage, (last visited Oct. 1, 2014).

[3] *See Broadband Information*, AT&T, http://www.att.com/gen/public-affairs?pid=20879, (last visited Oct. 1, 2014).

[4] *See, e.g., Comcast Agreement for Residential Services*, Comcast, at ¶ 13, http://cdn.comcast.com/~/Media/Files/
Legal/Subscriber%20 Agreement/CustomerAgreement_ENG.pdf?vs=7 (last visited Oct. 1, 2014); *Verizon Online
Terms of Service*, Verizon, at ¶ 18, https://my.verizon.com/central/vzc.portal?_nfpb=true&_pageLabel=vzc_help
_policies&id=TOS (last visited Oct. 1, 2014); *Terms and Conditions*, Windstream, at ¶ 10, http://www.windstream.
com/Terms-and-Conditions/ (last visited Oct. 1, 2014).

THE HON. ROBERT M. MCDOWELL
Questions for the Record from the Sept. 17, 2014 Judiciary Committee Hearing: "Why Net Neutrality Matters"
—*The views expressed in these responses are my own and do not necessarily represent the views of Wiley Rein or any of its clients*—

provide an efficient and effective venue for resolving disputes; they do not extinguish substantive rights and would not vitiate providers' commitments.

Providers' commitments, market pressure, and regulatory oversight provide powerful incentives to ensure that customers continue to enjoy full access to the open Internet.

THE HON. ROBERT M. MCDOWELL

Questions for the Record from the Sept. 17, 2014 Judiciary Committee Hearing: "Why Net Neutrality Matters"

—The views expressed in these responses are my own and do not necessarily represent the views of Wiley Rein or any of its clients—

The Honorable Mike Lee

1. At the Committee's hearing, you suggested that industry groups advocating net-neutrality regulation should be careful what they wish for. Could you give a concrete example of what you mean?

   Thank you, Senator, for the opportunity to elaborate. Creating a new body of law in the Internet ecosphere may fit the short-term business goals of some companies that want to gain a competitive advantage or offload costs to others by regulating their rivals, but history teaches us new rules will likely result in only more expansive regulation. Indeed, it is not difficult to imagine a continued expansion of regulatory powers to encompass the entire Internet ecosystem, including not only broadband networks, but content and applications as well. In short, as Professor Adam Thierer has observed many times, "regulation only grows."

   Proposed net neutrality rules may very well eventually ensnare all aspects of the Internet marketplace. The reason for this is simple: innovation and consumer demand are blurring the lines between what used to be clearly defined legal and regulatory silos between network operators (such as phone, cable and wireless companies) and "tech" companies, both of which offer "information services"—such as computer processing and storage processing—as well as content and applications. Market analysts call this phenomenon "convergence."

   Many companies that may look like pure network operators, such as cable, phone and wireless operators, offer a combination of transmission as well as information services, including content, applications and other value-added services. At the same time, companies that may look like pure content and application providers have state-of-the-art delivery networks that provide substantially similar types of transmission—or delivery—functions as those offered by network operators. In short, the distinction between information service providers and "telecommunications" service providers has all but disappeared in the ever-evolving all-IP world.

   Examples of this convergence are "tech" companies that offer e-readers, resold content (such as books) to consume on e-readers and resold wireless connectivity to deliver the content to the e-reader. Proposed net neutrality rules could easily be interpreted to give the FCC the power to regulate all of the above as it becomes increasingly difficult for bureaucrats to parse with surgical precision the differences between transmission and information services. Accordingly, the entire package of products and services could end up being regulated.

   Being in this position is partly due to the fact that he Communications Act of 1934 is now more than 80 years old. The New Deal Congress that wrote it did not envision the amazing innovations we have today or how they would scramble and blur the neat little silos of yesterday's technologies. From a consumer's perspective, is a "tech" company offering transmission services like a telecom company? Yes. Is a telecom company offering content and applications like a "tech" company? Yes. The logic flowing from these realities provides the basis for treating *all* such companies the same under proposed net neutrality rules. As companies start to "look" more alike, decisions to regulate one company, but not another, may start to be made more on political grounds than the facts and law. Uncertainty will abound as a result, and the entire Internet ecosphere will become more regulated. As I mention in my filed testimony, for a glimpse into this possible future here in America, look to recent actions by regulators and

THE HON. ROBERT M. MCDOWELL
Questions for the Record from the Sept. 17, 2014 Judiciary Committee Hearing: "Why Net Neutrality Matters"
—The views expressed in these responses are my own and do not necessarily represent the views of Wiley Rein or any of its clients—

courts in Europe which view "Internet companies" as one category to be regulated more heavily by the day.

Rather than creating a new breed of uber regulations for the Internet, Congress should re-write and modernize our laws to focus on preventing consumer harm rather than deciding whether or not to regulate based on antiquated early-20th Century notions.

2. Do you agree with Dr. Eisenach's testimony that FCC net-neutrality regulations may encourage rent-seeking behavior?

Yes.

3. Apart from the net-neutrality regulations discussed at the hearing, I would like to ask you about a related subject concerning the future of the Internet: the transition of oversight of the domain name system from the U.S. National Telecommunications and Information Administration to the independent Internet Corporation for Assigned Names and Numbers (ICANN).

    a. A number of groups and individuals have expressed concerns with the Administration's vague announcement that it would not renew its contract with ICANN—and that ICANN must implement a new mechanism, built on a multi-stakeholder model, that maintains the openness of the Internet. Some of these groups have proposed a minimum set of protections that should be in place before the United States agrees to relinquish its oversight. What protections do you believe ICANN should implement before the United States relinquishes its oversight, and why are such protections necessary?

    b. If the transition is not completed in a thoughtful way, is there any potential for other governments or intergovernmental organizations to hijack the Internet and threaten its openness?

    c. In your opinion, assuming adequate protections are in place, will the proposed transition create a more open and freedom-enhancing Internet?

Thank you for the opportunity to answer this question. By way of background, the IANA functions contract that was renewed with ICANN in April of 2013 is in place to ensure the technical functionality of any domain name address that is entered into the root zone. The purpose is a simple function of cross checking that the technical information is accurate and will not harm any other information by being placed onto the A root file with a third party validation. It's meant to be a technical security check and nothing else.

Over the years, the U.S. Department of Commerce has done an excellent job of keeping this function purely technical. Throughout both Republican and Democratic administrations, the U.S. Department of Commerce has ensured that the IANA function remain purely a technical - and not a political - function.

Additionally, as a general matter, further privatization of Internet governance functions is also a principle that has been embraced by Republican and Democratic administrations over the years. In that spirit, the key to the long-term success of this proposal is whether ICANN can be kept free from governmental and multilateral manipulation and continue in the *non-governmental* "multi-stakeholder" tradition that has served the Internet so well since it was privatized in the early 1990's. The plan that is put in place as the replacement to the current IANA function

THE HON. ROBERT M. MCDOWELL
Questions for the Record from the Sept. 17, 2014 Judiciary Committee Hearing: "Why Net Neutrality Matters"
--*The views expressed in these responses are my own and do not necessarily represent the views of Wiley Rein or any of its clients*--

should have the same rigorous technical standard applied to all applications for A root entry. The IANA function should always be insulated from political agendas whether they are domestic or foreign. Furthermore, ICANN must have a viable and long-term accountability plan and effective structure in place to prevent direct and indirect influence from governments or manipulation by some "civil society" groups that may, in reality, be working on behalf of governments and/or multilateral or intergovernmental organizations. The Department of Commerce and the Department of State have said repeatedly that they share these goals. Nonetheless, the details of executing the proposed transition will determine whether it is a long term success or failure.

THE HON. ROBERT M. MCDOWELL
Questions for the Record from the Sept. 17, 2014 Judiciary Committee Hearing: "Why Net Neutrality Matters"
—*The views expressed in these responses are my own and do not necessarily represent the views of Wiley Rein or any of its clients*—

The Honorable Chuck Grassley

1. Proponents of net neutrality claim that if we want broadband Internet access to operate in a manner that preserves the Internet's open character, then the best approach is to establish that expectation in advance through regulation.

    a. Do you agree with this approach? Will regulation-before-the-fact preserve and promote the Internet's openness better than, let's say, targeting an actual market failure or anti-competitive behavior that has occurred?

    Thank you, Senator, for the opportunity to discuss this issue further. At the outset of this debate, it is important to note that today's Internet is the greatest deregulatory success story of all time. The Net has proliferated beautifully precisely *because* government largely kept its hands off of it. It grew and evolved in the absence of economic regulation, including net neutrality rules. At the same time, nimble and long-standing consumer protection and antitrust laws were in place to deter, or cure, anticompetitive behavior that may harm consumers. To date, there has never been evidence of any systemic market failure in the Internet access market. This inconvenient fact is perhaps why net neutrality regulation proponents have resisted conducting a *bona fide*, peer-reviewed market study of the Internet access market. Such a study would likely show that there is no market failure that requires a government "cure." In short, nothing is broken that needs fixing.

    Creating a new and unnecessary body of law in the form of *ex ante*, or before-the-fact, regulations would create tremendous uncertainty as engineering and business decisions became politicized by unelected bureaucrats at the FCC. This scenario would create a "mother-may-I" regulatory regime where innovators are forced to seek government permission before developing new products and services. The lightning-fast pace of innovation in the Internet sphere would slow to a crawl. The end result would be less investment and innovation and fewer choices for consumers.

    Targeting actual market failure and consumer harms through existing laws is a far better approach and has worked tremendously well thus far in the Internet ecosystem. Let's let history be our guide and stick with what has worked rather than creating a risky new government scheme.

    b. In a dynamic, ever-changing environment such as the Internet, is there a greater justification for ex ante regulation as compared to ex post enforcement?

    No. As I state above and in my written and spoken testimony, trying to predict how the constantly changing Internet economy will evolve is impossible. This is true for entrepreneurs, and even more so for regulators. Rather than trying to guess where markets are headed through *ex ante* or "mother-may-I" industrial policy-style regulation, the public policy approach should be to examine whether concentrations of market power exist, whether that power is being abused and whether consumers are being harmed as a result. Conducting periodic peer-reviewed market studies, and putting them out for public comment, would better inform policy makers to determine whether they should act

THE HON. ROBERT M. MCDOWELL
Questions for the Record from the Sept. 17, 2014 Judiciary Committee Hearing: "Why Net Neutrality Matters"
—*The views expressed in these responses are my own and do not necessarily represent the views of Wiley Rein or any of its clients—*

in the first place. In the meantime, policymakers and consumer protection agencies should take an inventory of the myriad laws that exist at both the state and federal levels to combat potential anticompetitive behavior in the Internet sphere. Sticking with what has worked so well in the complex Internet marketplace (a hands-off approach by governments, relatively unfettered opportunities to innovate, invest and experiment plus a reliance on the certainty of *existing* consumer protection and antitrust laws) has allowed for a nimble, positive and constructive approach to making sure nothing "breaks" in this space.

2. I asked this question at the hearing, but would like you to give a more detailed response in writing. It has been argued that antitrust analysis is purely a numbers game that doesn't take into account important non-economic values.

    a. Do you agree? Does an antitrust analysis only consider financial and economic values, or can it, in fact, constitute a broader consumer welfare-based analysis that looks at other consumer values?

    Competitive markets unfettered by unnecessary government regulation are the best producers of positive and constructive consumer welfare and societal benefits. Allowing for investment, innovation and experimentation is what best serves consumers. As a result, especially in the larger Internet marketplace, it has never been a better time to be a consumer than today. Consumers, even in the poorest countries, have more access to more information that at any other time in human history. Consumer welfare has skyrocketed as a result.

    Dramatic increases in global consumer welfare are especially obvious when we look at how the mobile Internet is affecting the basic needs of people across the globe. Farmers are able to find buyers for their products without taking the risk of hauling them to markets in search of buyers who may never materialize. Parents are able to find potable water for their families. Millions are able to open mobile online bank accounts for the first time in the history of their families. Teachers are able to access the best information, online courses and teaching methods online to the benefit of their students. And people suffering under repressive regimes are able to access information to better learn about ideas that promote freedom and democracy. These are just a few examples of the social benefits produced by free markets. The mobile Internet in particular has enjoyed such tremendous success precisely because entrepreneurs have had the freedom to take risks without having to ask the government for permission. Laws cannot mandate innovation, nor can industrial policy. Only unfettered markets can produce the wonderful explosion of entrepreneurial brilliance, consumer welfare and societal benefits we have enjoyed in the Internet marketplace.

    In short, if markets are allowed to flourish in the absence of unnecessary, cumbersome and confusing government rules, consumers will have access to more products and services at lower prices. This virtuous cycle produces far more consumer value and societal benefits than any industrial policy or law could ever envision. Use of antitrust

THE HON. ROBERT M. MCDOWELL
Questions for the Record from the Sept. 17, 2014 Judiciary Committee Hearing: "Why Net Neutrality Matters"
—The views expressed in these responses are my own and do not necessarily represent the views of Wiley Rein or any of its clients—

and consumer protection laws keep markets competitive thus helping to promote consumer welfare and other societal values.

3. Some proponents of net neutrality argue that antitrust law is "too slow" to adequately deter and remedy anti-competitive behavior, particularly those behaviors that hurt small startup companies. Do you agree with this? Is a regulatory framework necessary to protect the rapid and dynamic nature of the Internet startup marketplace?

As a threshold matter, it is important to note that, since its inception, the Internet ecosphere has operated—and flourished—under *existing* laws that did not include net neutrality regulations. The barriers to entry to be a start-up in the Internet marketplace are extremely low. As a result, thousands of Internet-related start-ups sprout each year. At the same time, proponents of net neutrality regulations have spent the past decade trying to get the FCC to issue rules that have been largely struck down by the appellate courts twice. During this time, several antitrust cases could have been brought, and resolved, if there were any evidence of market failure (which there is not). Accordingly, it would appear that following the antitrust and consumer protection law path would be speedier and more effective than untested *ex ante* regulation/industrial policy.

On that note, the Federal Trade Commission (FTC), which has statutory powers in both the antitrust and consumer protection realms, can act at the same pace as the FCC. So can state attorneys general, consumer advocates and trial lawyers—all of whom are poised to act if Internet service providers were to act in an anticompetitive manner.

Not only is a new regulatory regime not needed, but as I testified, new rules could cause unintended consequences and uncertainty that actually *harm* start-ups. Let's stick with what has worked so well for start-ups: existing law.

4. It has been claimed that we have had a *de facto* net neutrality policy regime for the past 20 years. Do you agree with this observation? Why or why not?

Such novel claims are clever, but they are not factually true on their face. A complete answer would hinge on how one is defining "net neutrality," a term that is about a decade old. The definition of "net neutrality" seems to morph daily depending on whose interests are served by a new definition. In short, net neutrality rules did not exist at the time the FCC first attempted to enforce an unenforceable policy statement in 2008, over my dissent. That attempt was overturned by the DC Circuit. Prior to 2010, the Internet blossomed under pre-net neutrality law.

If that claim is supposed to mean that laws have been in place to prevent Internet service providers from acting in anticompetitive ways that could harm consumers or rivals, such as antitrust and consumer protection laws, then yes, public policy has been in place to protect an open Internet.

If that claim is supposed to mean there has never been evidence of systemic failure in the Internet access market due to existing laws then yes, an open Internet has existed since it was privatized in the mid-1990s *due to market forces and laws that pre-date net neutrality rules.*

THE HON. ROBERT M. MCDOWELL
Questions for the Record from the Sept. 17, 2014 Judiciary Committee Hearing: "Why Net Neutrality Matters"
—The views expressed in these responses are my own and do not necessarily represent the views of Wiley Rein or any of its clients—

What is not true is the myth that once upon a time Internet access services were regulated as common carriage under Title II of the Communications Act of 1934. In my prepared testimony I included a letter to then-House Energy and Commerce Committee Chairman Henry Waxman from May of 2010 that outlines the history of the classification of Internet access services in detail.

5. It has been claimed that the Internet needs "basic rules of the road to ensure that it remains open." Do you agree with this sentiment? Would adopting clear rules provide marketplace certainty and promote investment? If so, what rules specifically should we adopt?

As outlined in my prepared and spoken testimony, I disagree with this assertion. In short, existing antitrust and consumer protection laws are in place to provide more than adequate and nimble "rules of the road" for the complex and dynamic Internet marketplace. Proof of my assertion can be found in the history of growth in the Internet economy—unprecedented growth that has occurred in the absence of prescriptive "rules of the road."

6. How do you respond to the claim that in the absence of net neutrality regulations, freedom of speech and expression, freedom of association, and the First Amendment itself, will be threatened? How do you respond to the claim that if the FCC does not adopt net neutrality rules, we'll create an Internet of have and have-nots and certain groups will be left behind?

As discussed in detail in my December 21, 2010, dissent against the FCC's "Open Internet" Order, which is included as an attachment to my filed testimony, freedom of speech and investment abound in the Internet space without new rules. Broadband build out and adoption proliferated wonderfully without industrial policy from the government or net neutrality rules. In fact, Internet access is the fastest penetrating technology created by humans in modern times. Market forces are responsible for this success, not government mandates.

As a separate matter, also as discussed in my 2010 dissent and other attachments in my written testimony, as a matter of constitutional law "censorship" involves the government muting, amplifying or "balancing" speech on private platforms, even if it is done in the name of "free speech."[5] The act of private parties shouting each other down is not censorship because no government action is involved.[6] In that constitutional context, the market-created open Internet has done more to lower barriers to entry for speakers, and promote the freedom of expression, than any invention since Gutenberg's 15th Century printing press. On the American Internet, free speech is abundant and thriving. Furthermore, having more speech on the Net is good for the businesses of ISPs as well as app and content providers. More traffic on the Internet translates into more revenue for Internet-related companies. In the meantime, existing laws protect the free flow of information on the Net sparking a virtuous cycle.

7. Some net neutrality proponents argue that without government regulation, certain content providers may be prohibited from getting their content online. Do you agree or disagree with this statement and why?

---

[5] *United Bhd. of Carpenters, Local 610 v. Scott,* 463 U.S. 825, 832 (1983).

[6] *Id.*

THE HON. ROBERT M. MCDOWELL
Questions for the Record from the Sept. 17, 2014 Judiciary Committee Hearing: "Why Net Neutrality Matters"
—*The views expressed in these responses are my own and do not necessarily represent the views of Wiley Rein or any of its clients—*

I disagree. First, no evidence exists that shows that lawful content is prohibited from being placed online in a systemic or anticompetitive way. If that were to happen, competition, consumer protection and antitrust laws, not to mention tortious interference with contract, fraud, Section 5 of the Federal Trade Commission Act and many common law causes of action could be brought against ISPs if they were to exclude or block content under most circumstances. If net neutrality proponents believe content providers are being harmed, then they should support the concept of the Commission conducting a *bona fide*, peer-reviewed market study; yet they don't.

8. It has been said that there is a "strong argument that Internet access is a 'telecommunications service'" within the definitions of the Communications Act.

   a. Do you agree with this assertion? Why or why not?

      I strongly disagree with that statement. As stated above, please refer to my May, 2010 letter to Rep. Henry Waxman outlining why Internet access is, and always has been, an "information service."

   b. How would classifying Internet access as a Title II "telecommunications service" result in the regulation of the larger Internet ecosystem? Are you concerned that it could possibly ensnare other things like content, applications or edge providers? How could that impact the Internet?

      Thank you, Senator, for the opportunity to elaborate. Creating a new body of law in the Internet ecosphere may fit the short-term business goals of some companies that want to gain a competitive advantage or offload costs to others by regulating their rivals, but history teaches us new rules will likely result in a continued expansion of regulatory powers to encompass the entire Internet ecosystem, including not only broadband networks, but content and applications as well. In short, as Professor Adam Thierer has observed many times, "regulation only grows."

      Proposed net neutrality rules may very well eventually ensnare all aspects of the Internet marketplace. The reason for this is simple: innovation and consumer demand are blurring the lines between what used to be clearly defined legal and regulatory silos between network operators (such as phone, cable and wireless companies) and "tech" companies that offer "information services"—such as computer processing and storage processing— as well as content and applications. Market analysts call this phenomenon "convergence."

      Companies that used to look like pure network operators, such as cable, phone and wireless operators, now offer a combination of enhanced and transmission services as well as content, applications and other value-added services. At the same time, companies that used to look like pure content and application providers now have state-of-the-art delivery networks that provide substantially similar types of transmission—or delivery—functions as those offered by network operators. In short, the distinction between "enhanced" service providers and "telecommunications" service providers has all but disappeared in the ever-evolving all-IP world.

THE HON. ROBERT M. MCDOWELL
Questions for the Record from the Sept. 17, 2014 Judiciary Committee Hearing: "Why Net Neutrality Matters"
—*The views expressed in these responses are my own and do not necessarily represent the views of Wiley Rein or any of its clients—*

Examples of this convergence are "tech" companies that offer e-readers, resold content (such as books) to consume on e-readers and resold wireless connectivity to deliver the content to the e-reader. Proposed net neutrality rules could easily be interpreted to give the FCC the power to regulate all of the above as it becomes increasingly difficult for bureaucrats to parse with surgical precision the differences between transmission and information services. Accordingly, the entire package of products and services could end up being regulated.

Being in this position is partly due to the fact that he Communications Act of 1934 is now more than 80 years old. The New Deal Congress that wrote it did not envision the amazing innovations we have today or how they would scramble and blur the neat little silos of yesterday's technologies. From a consumer's perspective, is a "tech" company offering transmission services like a telecom company? Yes. Is a telecom company offering content and applications like a "tech" company? Yes. The logic flowing from these realities provides the basis for treating all such companies the same under proposed net neutrality rules. As companies start to "look" more alike, decisions to regulate one company, but not another, may start to be made more on political grounds than the facts and law. Uncertainty will abound as a result and the entire Internet ecosphere will become more regulated. As I mention in my filed testimony, for a glimpse into this possible future here in America, look to recent actions by regulators and courts in Europe which view "Internet companies" as one category to be regulated more heavily by the day.

Rather than creating a new breed of uber regulations for the Internet, Congress should re-write and modernize our laws to focus on preventing consumer harm rather than deciding whether or not to regulate based on antiquated early-20th Century notions.

RESPONSES OF JEFFREY A. EISENACH, PH.D., TO QUESTIONS SUBMITTED
BY SENATORS GRASSLEY, LEAHY, AND LEE

Senate Judiciary Committee Hearing On
Why Net Neutrality Matters: Protecting Consumers and Competition Through Meaningful Open
Internet Rules
September 17, 2014
Questions for the Record from Senator Patrick Leahy

<u>Question for Jeffrey Eisenach</u>

1. You testified that in a paid prioritization world, broadband providers would have an incentive to give startups the lowest cost access. Doesn't that argument ignore the fact that many startups offer products or services that compete with products or services offered by broadband providers?

Answer: No. First, edge providers do not, by definition, offer Internet access services. However, to the extent Internet access providers may offer services that compete with those offered by new entrants, the entrants' rights to compete fairly are protected by the antitrust laws. Net neutrality regulation goes much further, by forcing Internet access providers to provide free services to all edge providers, regardless of whether there is any chance of competition. Second, Internet access providers benefit from the innovative services generated by edge providers of all kinds, including new entrants, while entrants are far more likely to pose a competitive threat to existing edge providers than to the ISPs.

Senator Grassley's Written Questions for Senate Judiciary Committee Hearing, "Why Net Neutrality Matters: Protecting Consumers and Competition through Meaningful Open Internet Rules" – September 17, 2014

Questions for Dr. Eisenach

1. Proponents of net neutrality claim that if we want broadband Internet access to operate in a manner that preserves the Internet's open character, then the best approach is to establish that expectation in advance through regulation.

   a. Do you agree with this approach? Will regulation-before-the-fact preserve and promote the Internet's openness better than, let's say, targeting an actual market failure or anti-competitive behavior that has occurred?

Answer: I do not agree that regulation is needed to protect the open nature of the Internet. Indeed, broadband networks have operated without the sort of regulation now being considered from the very beginning – for nearly two decades – and the number of alleged (not necessarily actual) Net Neutrality violations advanced by Net Neutrality advocates can still be counted on one hand.

   b. In a dynamic, ever-changing environment such as the Internet, is there a greater justification for ex ante regulation as compared to ex post enforcement?

Answer: No. Ex ante regulation is especially costly in dynamic markets, where it inhibits the innovation and technological progress which are responsible for improving consumer welfare creating economic growth. Regulations take years – in the case of Net Neutrality, a decade and counting – to put in place, while markets may be transformed in a matter of months. Ex post enforcement of competition principles, on the other hand, has the capacity to adjust as markets change.

2. I asked this question at the hearing, but would like you to give a more detailed response in writing. It has been argued that antitrust analysis is purely a numbers game that doesn't take into account important non-economic values.

   a. Do you agree? Does an antitrust analysis only consider financial and economic values, or can it, in fact, constitute a broader consumer welfare-based analysis that looks at other consumer values?

Answer: Antitrust answer is focused on protecting the competition and, by so doing, enhancing consumer welfare. The underlying values behind antitrust are grounded in the

The opinions expressed in these responses are my own and do not necessarily represent the views of the American Enterprise Institute or any other organization with which I am affiliated.

principles of individual liberty and empowerment: By precluding anticompetitive actions that may create or preserve monopoly power, they ensure that all Americans have an opportunity to enter markets and compete on an equal footing. At the same time, they promote and protect the ability of all citizens to create and market products and services that are valued by their fellow citizens and consumers – without political interference or excessive government control. In the realm of speech, antitrust prevents large and powerful entities from using unfair practices to prevent others from speaking out, while at the same time protecting the rights of all parties (the powerful as well as the weak) to engage in speech-related commerce so long as they do so without engaging in exclusionary or other harmful conduct. To be sure, the antitrust laws are not social policy, and they do not provide a basis for "industrial policy" or legitimize policies that consciously seek to favor one group or business over another. But whatever maybe said in favor of such policies, they cannot in general be promoted as favoring "consumer welfare."

3. It has been claimed that we have had a *de facto* net neutrality policy regime for the past 20 years. Do you agree with this observation? Why or why not?

Answer: The answer to this question depends someone on how one defines "net neutrality policy." It is simply not accurate to suggest that the FCC has had in place regulations that resemble in any meaningful way the regulations now being considered. It is, however, true that the "un-regulatory" policies put in place beginning under the Clinton Administration in the late 1990s have resulted in the most open and empowering communications technology in history, and in that sense have advanced the causes espoused by many Net Neutrality advocates.

4. It has been claimed that the Internet needs "basic rules of the road to ensure that it remains open." Do you agree with this sentiment? Would adopting clear rules provide marketplace certainty and promote investment? If so, what rules specifically should we adopt?

Answer: The basic rules of the road required for the Internet to continue to prosper are contained in the extensive laws and regulations already in place, including the antitrust laws, Section 5 of the Federal Trade Commission Act, and a wide variety of privacy and consumer protection laws and regulations in place at both the Federal and state levels. The "basic rules" being proposed by the FCC, on the other hand, would create the impetus for further regulation, litigation and lobbying activity that lead to tremendous regulatory uncertainty and thereby impede investment and innovation.

The opinions expressed in these responses are my own and do not necessarily represent the views of the American Enterprise Institute or any other organization with which I am affiliated.

5. Some net neutrality proponents argue that without government regulation, certain content providers may be prohibited from getting their content online. Do you agree or disagree with this statement and why?

Answer: There is no basis for concluding that ISPs would discriminate against content providers. Rather, the net neutrality rules would themselves prove to be discriminatory, as the FCC set out to decide which classes of Internet users should be given favorable treatment and which should be discriminated against. The current proposals, for example, prohibit ISPs from charging content providers to use their networks, but place no restrictions on their ability to charge consumers, who as a result would bear the full costs of supporting the network.

6. You testified that free market principles should guide the interactions of a dynamic internet ecosystem. However, another witness testified that there should be an internet market "open to all." Are these two principles compatible under economic theory?

Answer: The "open to all" thesis is a canard. The question is who will pay for what. As described in my response to question 5, under the net neutrality rules as proposed, consumers pay for 100 percent of the network while content and other edge providers are given free access. So, "open to all" means "open to all corporations but only open to consumers for a fee." In a market-driven system, costs are allocated based on the value created and the benefits received by all parties.

7. It has been said that there is a "strong argument that Internet access is a 'telecommunications service'" within the definitions of the Communications Act.
    a. Do you agree with this assertion? Why or why not?

Answer: I am an economist and not an attorney, but it is my opinion that the FCC's decisions finding that the "information service" aspect of Internet access is inseparable from the telecommunications aspect, and therefore that Internet access is not appropriately classified as a telecommunications service, are sound from an economic perspective.

    b. How would classifying Internet access as a Title II "telecommunications service" result in the regulation of the larger Internet ecosystem? Are you concerned that it could possibly ensnare other things like content, applications or edge providers? How could that impact the Internet?

Answer: Yes. Classifying Internet access as a Title II service would risk setting off a free-for-all in which all firms in and around the Internet ecosystem would seek favorable treatment under the resulting rules. Because computing and communications are inextricably interwoven in the modern Internet architecture, and becoming more so, there are no clear boundaries by which to distinguish between "exempt" and "non-exempt" services. The result would be the politicization of decisions regarding relationships between players in the Internet ecosystem which heretofore have been made through pragmatic, flexible, market-based processes.

8. I've heard concerns that vertical contracts between ISPs and content providers – such as "paid prioritization" agreements and differentiated pricing structures – will only harm consumers and the Internet marketplace overall. It has been claimed that the proposed FCC regulations are necessary to "preserve" the freedom and openness that has until now been a central characteristic of the Internet.

    a. Are these concerns warranted?

Answer: To the extent vertical contracts and pricing structures evolve from market-based negotiations, subject to oversight under the antitrust and consumer protection statutes, they are highly likely to increase consumer choice and improve consumer welfare. Concerns to the contrary are not warranted.

    b. Are there any benefits or efficiencies that consumers will gain from such arrangements?

Answer: Yes. "Zero-rating" or "sponsored data" plans are a specific example. Under such plans, content providers subsidize the ability of "marginal" consumers (those who cannot afford to pay the full costs of mobile data plans) to access online content, such as Facebook or Twitter. Under such plans, content providers pay more and consumers pay less, thus benefiting consumers. From a broader economic perspective, such "competitive price discrimination" increases overall economic efficiency by allowing content providers and ISPs to recoup the fixed costs of providing their services while still offering the most price-sensitive consumers the ability to participate, and offering all consumers the positive "network effects" generated by extending the Internet ecosystem.

Questions for the Record

Sept. 17, 2014 Judiciary Committee Hearing

Senator Lee

For Dr. Eisenach:

1. At the Committee's hearing, you expressed concern that FCC net neutrality regulations might encourage rent-seeking behavior. In particular, you mentioned that the FCC has had a regrettable history of encouraging rent seeking by special interests.

   a. Please elaborate on the FCC's past experience with rent-seeking behavior by regulated parties.

   Answer: As Nobel Prize winner Ronald Coates discussed in his 1959 article on "The Federal Communications Commission" (Attachment A), the FCC's ability to allocate broadcast licenses, set prices and determine other economic rights is in effect the power to allocate wealth among private parties. The affected parties react by employing lobbyists, attorneys and others in an effort to turn the Commission's decision in their favor. I describe the history of rent seeking at the FCC in a paper jointly authored with Hal Singer, "Avoiding Rent-Seeking in Secondary Market Spectrum Transactions." (Attachment B.)

   b. Do you believe the proposed net-neutrality regulations could lead to similar problems?

   Answer: Yes. By establishing itself as the arbiter of what services can be provided by ISPs to other firms in the Internet ecosystem, and at what prices, the FCC would create powerful incentives for all such firms to engage in rent seeking, that is to seek to expand or contract the Commission's authorities (depending on their self-interests) and to assure that pricing and other regulatory decisions are set in such a way as to contribute to their profitability. Firms which feel they would benefit from the FCC's "non-discrimination" rules will have strong incentives to have them enforced as expansively as possible, including, for example, challenging in court any efforts by the Commission to forbear from or exercise discretion in its use of such authority.

2. Apart from the net-neutrality regulations discussed at the hearing, I would like to ask you about a related subject concerning the future of the Internet: the transition of oversight of the domain name system from the U.S. National Telecommunications and Information Administration to the independent Internet Corporation for Assigned Names and Numbers (ICANN).

   a. A number of groups and individuals have expressed concerns with the Administration's vague announcement that it would not renew its contract with ICANN—and that ICANN must implement a new mechanism, built on a multi-stakeholder model, that maintains the openness of the Internet. Some of these groups have proposed a minimum set of protections that should be in place before the United States agrees to relinquish its oversight. What protections do you believe ICANN should implement before the United States relinquishes its oversight, and why are such protections necessary?

Answer: The IANA function which is immediately at issue in the transition announced by the Department of Commerce is inherently technical in nature, but the technical outcomes that result from that process have potentially far reaching implications. Heretofore, technical decisions have been made on technical grounds through a transparent process, with the U.S. government serving as a backstop against politicization. Before any changes are made, it is essential for the U.S. government to be assured that whatever new process is put in place is both transparent and insulated from politicization.

    b. If the transition is not completed in a thoughtful way, is there any potential for other governments or intergovernmental organizations to hijack the Internet and threaten its openness?

Answer: Yes.

    c. In your opinion, assuming adequate protections are in place, will the proposed transition create a more open and freedom-enhancing Internet?

Answer: In my opinion, the effect of the transition depends both on how it is structured and on the going-forward effectiveness of U.S. diplomacy in the Internet space. The fact that the U.S. is in the position of being pressured to divest the IANA function is a signal that we have not been as effective as we would like in persuading the international community of the value of having a strong U.S. role in these issues.

RESPONSES OF NUALA O'CONNOR TO QUESTIONS SUBMITTED
BY SENATORS LEAHY AND LEE

KEEPING THE INTERNET
OPEN • INNOVATIVE • FREE

www.cdt.org

1634 Eye Street, NW
Suite 1100
Washington, DC 20006

Nuala O'Connor's Responses to Questions for the Record
Sept. 17, 2014 Senate Judiciary Committee Hearing

October 9, 2014

United States Senate Subcommittee on the Judiciary
Washington, DC 20510-6275

Dear Chairman Leahy,

Thank you for the opportunity to testify at the hearing of the Senate Committee
on the Judiciary entitled "Why Net Neutrality Matters: Protecting Consumers and
Competition Through Meaningful Open Internet Rules" on September 17, 2014.
Following are my responses to written questions from the Committee for the
formal Committee record.

Question from Senator Leahy

1. Some have said that if the FCC adopts strong rules to promote net
    neutrality, it could undermine our Nation's message to oppressive
    regimes that restrict free expression online and otherwise control the
    Internet. Isn't there a fundamental difference between rules to ensure
    that the Internet remains free, open and competitive, and regulating the
    Internet to oppress?

    *Answer: Yes. CDT has long advocated for strong and narrowly tailored
    rules that preserve the fundamental openness of the Internet so that it
    can remain a vibrant platform for ideas, expression, and innovation of all
    kinds. The Internet's power to transform communications and promote
    free expression flows from certain technical characteristics that have
    defined the Internet since its inception. These characteristics are not
    immutable, however, and are increasingly subject to pressure. To
    maximize the Internet's potential to advance human rights, the Internet
    must remain free from centralized controls, open to the fullest range of
    content and services, and truly global. Establishing rules to preserve
    Internet neutrality is one way to prevent the imposition of content
    gatekeeping and other burdens on expression and competition by those
    in a position to control individuals' ability to access the global network.*

Questions from Senator Lee

1. Apart from the net-neutrality regulations discussed at the hearing, I would
    like to ask you about a related subject concerning the future of the
    Internet: the transition of oversight of the domain name system from the
    U.S. National Telecommunications and Information Administration to the

P +1-202-637-9800   F -1-202-637-0968   E info@cdt.org

independent Internet Corporation for Assigned Names and Numbers (ICANN).

a. A number of groups and individuals have expressed concerns with the Administration's vague announcement that it would not renew its contract with ICANN—and that ICANN must implement a new mechanism, built on a multi-stakeholder model, that maintains the openness of the Internet. Some of these groups have proposed a minimum set of protections that should be in place before the United States agrees to relinquish its oversight. What protections do you believe ICANN should implement before the United States relinquishes its oversight, and why are such protections necessary?

Answer: CDT, along with many other stakeholders and interested parties, have cautioned against ICANN assuming the IANA functions oversight before a reformed accountability structure for ICANN is in place. This accountability structure should ensure that the IANA functions are not vulnerable to capture or manipulation by any stakeholder group – particularly governments – and that the continuity and stability of the Internet is assured. This structure should be based upon key principles including maintaining the primacy of the ICANN multistakeholder model, securing the support and engagement of the global Internet community, protecting both the IANA functions and ICANN generally from government capture, and ensuring a commitment to transparency and openness in all of ICANN's work.

b. If the transition is not completed in a thoughtful way, is there any potential for other governments or intergovernmental organizations to hijack the Internet and threaten its openness?

Answer: CDT is fully supportive of the transition of the oversight of the IANA functions. The Internet community has begun the process of developing a transition proposal; we believe this proposal will be well thought-out, will be multistakeholder in its nature and will ensure the continuity and stability of the Internet and will be resistant to hijack and capture. We join many other stakeholders engaged in this process in rejecting the idea that the US government's role in the DNS should replaced by another government or group of governments or an intergovernmental organization. The need to avoid the potential for government capture of the IANA functions oversight, or of ICANN more generally, will continue to be a touchstone in the process to develop the transition proposal.

c. In your opinion, assuming adequate protections are in place, will the proposed transition create a more open and freedom-enhancing Internet?

Answer: Yes; we believe that the successful transition of the oversight of the IANA functions will lead to a greater confidence in the multistakeholder model and in the distributed management and

*governance of the Internet, both in the US and abroad. This will result
in a more stable, resilient, and open Internet.*

Sincerely,

Nuala O'Connor

NATIONAL ASSOCIATION of REALTORS®

Steve Brown, AB, CIPS, CRS, GREEN
2014 President

Dale A. Stinton
Chief Executive Officer

GOVERNMENT AFFAIRS
DIVISION
Jerry Giovaniello, Senior Vice President
Gary Weaver, Vice President
Joe Ventrone, Vice President
Scott Reiter, Vice President
Jamie Gregory, Deputy Chief Lobbyist

September 16, 2014

The Honorable Patrick J. Leahy
Chairman
Senate Judiciary Committee
437 Russell Senate Office Building
Washington, DC 20510

The Honorable Chuck Grassley
Ranking Member
Senate Judiciary Committee
135 Hart Senate Office Building
Washington, DC 20510

Dear Chairman Leahy and Ranking Member Grassley:

On behalf of the more than one million members of the NATIONAL ASSOCIATION OF REALTORS® (NAR), I write in advance of your hearing entitled: "Why Net Neutrality Matters: Protecting Consumers and Competition Through Meaningful Open Internet Rules" to express NAR's belief that open internet rules are necessary to protect our members, who are primarily independent contractors and small businesses, as well as their clients.

As you know, the Federal Communications Commission (FCC) has recently proposed and has sought comment on new Open Internet rules that would permit Internet service providers to discriminate technically against and impose new tolls on American businesses that operate on the Internet. Permitting these actions would be disruptive to our members' businesses that have come to rely on an open Internet. Moreover, these actions would be especially harmful for small businesses and start-ups competing against larger companies that can afford such tolls. In order to continue the economic boom enabled by Internet innovation, NAR supports and has urged the FCC instead to adopt open Internet rules that will protect against blocking, discrimination, access charges, and paid prioritization.

The Internet has been a driving force for innovation for decades, and our members, their Customers, and local communities are benefiting from this innovation every day. The economic growth and job creation fueled by the open Internet is unprecedented in American economic history. This growth has been fostered by the Federal Communications Commission (FCC) under both Republican and Democrat administrations for over a decade.

Our members, who identify themselves as REALTORS®, represent a wide variety of real estate industry professionals. REALTORS® have been early adopters of technology, and are industry innovators who understand that consumers today are seeking real estate information and services that are fast, convenient and comprehensive. Increasingly, technology innovations are driving the delivery of real estate services and the future of REALTORS®' businesses.

Streaming video, Voice over Internet Protocol, and mobile applications are commonly used in our businesses today. In the future, new technologies, like virtual reality and telepresence among others, will be available that will no doubt require open internet access unencumbered by technical or financial discrimination.

NAR supports preserving an open Internet that in turn, promotes small business, job creation and personal liberty. We wish to see the FCC implement strong and enforceable rules of the road to protect the free and open Internet that includes no-blocking and non-discrimination. If left as proposed, the current FCC rule would harm Main Street businesses, such as REALTORS®, and their ability to be competitive in the high-speed, 21st century world.

REALTOR® is a registered collective membership mark which may be used only by real estate professionals who are members of the NATIONAL ASSOCIATION OF REALTORS® and subscribe to its strict Code of Ethics.

The benefits of broadband Internet for innovation and economic development are unparalleled. But we'll lose those tremendous benefits if the Internet does not remain an open platform, where Americans can innovate without permission and with low barriers to launching small businesses and creating jobs. Given this reality, it is important that this Committee work with the FCC to enact and preserve open Internet policies that promote competition between Internet application and service providers. NAR is ready to work with you on this important issue.

Sincerely,

Steve Brown
2014 President, National Association of REALTORS®

cc: Members of the Senate Judiciary Committee

 ELECTRONIC FRONTIER FOUNDATION

**WRITTEN TESTIMONY OF CORYNNE MCSHERRY
INTELLECTUAL PROPERTY DIRECTOR, ELECTRONIC FRONTIER FOUNDATION
HEARING ON NETWORK NEUTRALITY
BEFORE THE SENATE JUDICARY COMMITTEE**

September 17, 2014

I. Overview

An open, neutral, and fast Internet has sparked an explosion of free expression, innovation, and political change and has become an essential tool for basic communication. Internet-based services help us learn, find jobs, organize politically and socially, file tax returns, manage our healthcare, connect to family and friends, and contribute to our common culture.

The principles of openness and neutral handling of data were crucial to the development of the Internet and were once reinforced by competition that allowed dissatisfied users to vote with their wallets. Now, though, companies with quasi-monopoly power over Internet access have grown and begun to abuse that power.

Most Americans have only one or two realistic choices for broadband, making normal market forces inadequate to protect the openness that has characterized the Internet. ISPs have economic incentives to leverage their ownership of the transmission infrastructure at the expense of Internet users, and switching costs and consumer lock-in further undermine the ability of marketplace forces to prevent discriminatory practices.

Regulators can play an important role in curbing such abuse. The Federal Communication Commission ("FCC") is currently considering this issue.[1] While its goals are laudable, it has sabotaged itself by basing the effort on its authority to promote broadband adoption under Section 706 of the Telecommunications Act.[2] The D.C. Circuit Court of Appeals explained in *Verizon v. FCC*[3] that the FCC cannot impose meaningful non-discrimination obligations on Internet access providers under Section 706. We have therefore urged the FCC to reclassify broadband as a "telecommunications service" governed by Title II of the Communications Act.[4] Reclassification will give the FCC the authority it needs to do its part to support the open Internet.

Because of the danger of over-regulation, we have recommended that the FCC regulate narrowly and deliberately. Net neutrality rules should promote user choice, permissionless innovation, and an application-blind network. Clear and simple prescriptive rules would minimize the practical costs of regulation, particularly for small businesses and new entrants.

We have also recommended that the FCC revisit the open access rule that was once so effective in promoting competition in Internet access services. A rule enabling new entrants to use existing infrastructure could create competition and enable consumers to leave services that undermine the open and neutral Internet.

Finally, broadband should be covered by meaningful transparency rules to help enforce nondiscrimination requirements and give the public the information it needs to create a competitive market. We offer detailed suggestions below to assist in that effort.

---

[1] In the Matter of Protecting and Promoting the Open Internet, Notice of Proposed Rulemaking (hereinafter "NPRM"), GN Docket No. 14-28 (May 15, 2014).
[2] 47 U.S.C. § 1302(a), (b).
[3] 740 F.3d 623 (D.C. Cir. 2014).
[4] 47 U.S.C. § 151 et seq.

ELECTRONIC FRONTIER FOUNDATION

II. About EFF

EFF is a member-supported nonprofit organization devoted to protecting civil liberties and free expression in technology, law, policy, and standards. With over 27,000 dues-paying members, EFF is a leading voice in the global and national effort to ensure that fundamental liberties are respected in the digital environment.

EFF has campaigned both in the United States and abroad against ill-considered efforts to block, filter, or degrade access to the public Internet. EFF is actively developing and promoting technological tools that help consumers and public interest groups investigate whether ISPs are interfering with the traffic to and from users' computers. EFF was among the first to independently discover the precise nature of Comcast's 2007 interference with BitTorrent and other peer-to-peer applications.

III. The FCC Should Regulate Broadband Under Title II, not Section 706

A. The FCC's Goals Are Laudable, But Its Proposed Rules Do Not Serve Those Goals

The FCC and the D.C. Circuit Court of Appeals identified several serious issues facing the open Internet, including:

- "[B]roadband providers' potential disruption of edge-provider traffic [is] itself the sort of 'barrier' that has 'the potential to stifle overall investment in Internet infrastructure'";[5]

- Broadband Internet access providers "have incentives to interfere with the operation of third-party Internet-based services that compete with the providers' revenue generating telephone and/or pay-telephone services";[6]

- "[B]roadband providers' position in the market gives them the economic power to restrict edge-provider traffic and charge for the services they furnish edge providers . . . the provider functions as a 'terminating monopolist' . . . [and has] this ability to act as a 'gatekeeper'";[7]

- "[E]nd users are unlikely to [switch to a competing broadband provider]" as "end users may not know" that their broadband provider is behaving in non-neutral ways and "even if they do have this information [consumers] may find it costly to switch."[8]

- In light of recent history, "the threat that broadband providers would utilize their gatekeeper ability to restrict edge-provider traffic is not . . . 'merely theoretical.'"[9]

Given these threats, regulators can and should take steps to protect the open Internet.

The FCC, however, has offered proposals that run directly contrary to its purported intent by *permitting* discriminatory treatment of edge providers. It proposes a rule against the blocking of "lawful content,

---

[5] *Id.* at 642-43, citing *In the Matter of Preserving the Open Internet,* FCC Rcd. 17905, 17969 (2010) at ¶ 120. (hereinafter *Open Internet Order*).
[6] *Id.* at 645-46 citing *Open Internet Order* at ¶¶ 22-24.
[7] *Id.* at 646, citing *Open Internet Order* at ¶ 24.
[8] *Id.* at 646-647, citing *Open Internet Order* at ¶ 27.
[9] *Id.* at 648, citing *Open Internet Order* at ¶ 35.

ELECTRONIC FRONTIER FOUNDATION

applications, services or non-harmful devices, subject to reasonable network management."[10] The FCC also proposes a rule against "commercially unreasonable practices" with another explicit carve-out for "reasonable network management."[11] These rules would forbid broadband providers from engaging in several kinds of discrimination, but simultaneously allow them to negotiate special arrangements with some edge providers, so long as such arrangements are "commercially reasonable."

There are several problems with these proposals. First, the proposed rules implicitly bless the blocking of "unlawful" content. This puts ISPs in the position of a court, effectively enjoining content and applications that might or might not be lawful.[12] Such blocking could require snooping on the data habits of its users, even if a court order were required. And ISP practices purportedly aimed at curtailing unlawful activities often interfere with lawful content and activities, posing the same dangers to competition, innovation, and openness as other non-neutral practices. For example, if ISPs deploy blocking mechanisms in the name of copyright enforcement, innovators who want to offer new products and services may have to negotiate with ISPs, hat in hand, to ensure that their products will not be thwarted by these mechanisms.[13]

Second, and more broadly, the proposed rules offer a murky set of guidelines that are more likely to line the pockets of telecommunications lawyers than protect the open Internet. Many practices may be dressed up as "commercially reasonable" or necessary for "reasonable network management," but still undermine an open and neutral Internet and the free expression and commerce that depend on it. A "commercially reasonable" standard, paired with a "reasonable network management" exception is too vague to be meaningful, and likely difficult to enforce. This is a recipe for litigation and confusion. ISPs have every incentive to quietly discriminate and make deals with established incumbents and then litigate the "reasonableness" of those decisions before the FCC on a case-by-case basis if they are caught. They can afford that risk and expense; innovators and users cannot.

Ironically, the "commercially unreasonable practices" rule and the "reasonable network management" exception are also a recipe for regulatory overreach. While the NPRM lays out a variety of possibilities for what the "commercially unreasonable" rule could accomplish,[14] it remains unclear what is and is not "reasonable," which will potentially give the FCC veto power over innovation.[15] Broadband providers should not have that power, and neither should the FCC.

Taken together, the proposed rules would inevitably be abused to discourage the emergence of new Internet-based services. Commenter Etsy, Inc., noted that its business would likely have failed if it had to pay for priority access to consumers.[16] Other small businesses and their investors have echoed such concerns.[17]

---

[10] NPRM at App. A §§ 8.5, 8.7.

[11] *Id.* at App. A. § 8.7.

[12] *See generally* Electronic Frontier Foundation Comments, GN Docket No. 09-191, (Jan. 14, 2010), avail. at https://www.eff.org/files/filenode/nn/EFFNNcomments.pdf.

[13] *Id.* at 17.

[14] NPRM ¶¶ 116-138.

[15] At least one mobile service provider has found "commercial reasonableness" to be a difficult, uncertain, and anti-competitive standard. *See* Petition for Expedited Declaratory Ruling of T-Mobile USA, Inc., *Reexamination of Roaming Obligations of Commercial Mobile Radio Service Providers and Other Providers of Mobile Data Services,* WT Docket No. 05-265, at 13 and Exhibit 1, Declaration of Dirk Mosa ¶ 10 (May 27, 2014).

[16] Etsy, Inc. Comments, GN Docket No. 14-28 at 5 (July 8, 2014).

[17] *See, e.g.* https://www.techdirt.com/articles/20140710/17450827845/kickstarter-etsy-dwolla-all-speak-out-net-neutrality-why-fccs-plan-is-dangerous-to-innovation.shtml; http://openmic.org/files/Open%20MIC%20et%20al_GN%20Docket%20No.%2014-28_Comment.pdf; http://engine.is/wp-content/uploads/Company-Sign-On-Letter.pdf.

ELECTRONIC FRONTIER FOUNDATION

Of course this problem is not confined to a realm of pure commerce. Thanks in large part to the innovative technologies that have been able to flourish on the open Internet, the Internet has become our public square, our newspaper, and our megaphone. The Supreme Court rightly called the Internet "the most participatory form of mass speech yet developed."[18] In a 2009 speech, then Secretary of State Hillary Clinton credited Internet platforms with giving a voice to "ordinary citizens . . . to organize political movements, or simply exchange ideas and information."[19] The 2010 election cycle, for example, featured citizen videos dealing with a variety of campaign issues, including illegal immigration, health care reform, education and teachers' unions, the federal budget deficit, bank bailouts, and taxes.[20] A 2012 study found that 39% of all American adults have used social media to engage in civic or political activities.[21]

Paid prioritization, blocking, access charges and other discriminatory practices could transform this extraordinary engine for civic discourse into something more like the old broadcast model, where a few powerful companies had inordinate power over the public sphere. Internet censorship already occurs via a variety of means, and will become all the more dangerous without network neutrality.[22]

The risks go further still. Across the country, people depend on high-speed Internet to access a variety of public and nonprofit services. Hospitals, libraries, firefighters, churches, schools, and social service organizations need a fast and open Internet, but such entities are unlikely to negotiate with quasi-monopolies for acces to the "fast lane."[23] Instead they, and those that rely upon them, are more likely to be relegated to the "minimum access" slow lane, with little recourse.

According to a recent Pew Center survey, many Internet experts fear that "commercial pressures affecting everything from Internet architecture to the flow of information will endanger the open structure of online life."[24] Unfortunately, the FCC's proposed rules are at best ineffective against such a threat.

B. The FCC Cannot Protect the Open Internet Under Section 706

Many of the flaws in the proposed rules stem from the FCC's continued reliance on Section 706. The D.C. Circuit's decision in *Verizon v. FCC*[25] gives the FCC broad statutory authority under Section 706, *except* when it comes to addressing the very practices that "erode Internet openness," i.e. net neutrality.[26]

In the *Verizon* decision, the D.C. Circuit held that the FCC has authority under Section 706 to promote the deployment of high-speed Internet service, and that the FCC had a good basis for concluding that access providers' "disruption of edge-provider traffic" through discriminatory practices threatened that deployment by reducing incentives to invest at the edges of the network.[27] But the court went on to hold that any regulations promulgated under Section 706 authority cannot be the sort of regulations that would create common carrier

---

[18] *Reno v. ACLU*, 521 U.S. 844, 863 (1997) (citing *ACLU v. Reno*, 929 F. Supp. 824, 883 (E.D. Pa. 1996)).
[19] Hillary Clinton, U.S. Sec'y of State, Remarks to U.S. Global Leadership Coalition (Dec. 7, 2009), available at http://www.state.gov/statecraft/index.htm.
[20] CitizenTube Blog, The 2010 Election on YouTube by the Numbers, Nov. 1, 2010, http://www.citizentube.com/2010/11/2010-election-on-youtube-by-numbers.html.
[21] *See* http://www.pewinternet.org/2012/03/12/main-findings-10/.
[22] *See generally*, https://www.eff.org/free-speech-weak-link; https://www.eff.org/issues/bloggers-under-fire.
[23] *See, e.g.,* http://www.washingtonpost.com/blogs/the-switch/wp/2014/05/16/why-the-death-of-net-neutrality-would-be-a-disaster-for-libraries/.
[24] Net Threats, Pew Research Internet Project, July 3, 2014, http://www.pewinternet.org/2014/07/03/net-threats/.
[25] 740 F.3d 623 (D.C. Cir. 2014).
[26] NPRM ¶ 26.
[27] 740 F.3d at 523, 640-45.

ELECTRONIC FRONTIER FOUNDATION

status.[28] It is clear from the court's decision that the FCC cannot impose an effective "anti-discrimination obligation [on] broadband providers."[29]

The very characteristics that will make the open Internet rules effective at achieving their goal are the characteristics that the D.C. Circuit identified as hallmarks of common carriage, and thus impermissible without reclassification. The worrisome ISP practices that the FCC identified in its NPRM, from Comcast's blocking of peer-to-peer communications to Verizon's ban on tethering apps to pay-for-priority proposals,[30] have at their core an ISP's decision to favor or disfavor certain Internet traffic — in other words, to discriminate. But a firm rule prohibiting "unreasonable discrimination" is precisely what the D.C. Circuit said the FCC cannot impose under Section 706.[31]

The opinion also suggested that without reclassification, the FCC *must* permit ISPs to engage in discriminatory paid prioritization — that is, levels of service made available to some edge providers and denied to others. In discussing the no-blocking rule, the D.C. Circuit held that such a rule must, for example, allow Verizon to "charge an edge provider like Netflix for high-speed, priority access while limiting all other edge providers to a more standard service."[32] This is the essence of a practice that threatens the open Internet and the "virtuous cycle" of investment.

The D.C. Circuit suggested that *some* rules aimed at preserving the open Internet will be legally permissible under the FCC's Section 706 authority,[33] but the *Verizon* decision makes clear that such rules must be limited in scope, effect, or definiteness to pass muster. A "commercially reasonable" standard, said the court, cannot be applied in a "restrictive manner" that prevents broadband providers from making "individualized decisions."[34] Also, any particular application of such a rule that is seen as overly "restrictive" will be subject to an "as applied" legal challenge.[35]

C.   A Better Way Forward: Reclassification, Bright-Line Rules

1.   *Reclassify*

The FCC can enact some species of "Open Internet" rules using its Section 706 authority, but the more effective those rules are in both wording and application, the more their lawfulness can be questioned. If it reclassifies broadband service provision as a telecommunications service, however, it can solve this problem.

Reclassification is pure common sense. First, broadband Internet access *is* a telecommunications service. The Telecommunications Act of 1996 defined telecommunications as "the transmission, between or among points specified by the user, of information of the user's choosing, without change in the form or content of the information as sent and received."[36] This plainly includes broadband Internet access.

Second, reclassification brings the goals and law of net neutrality into alignment. "Net neutrality" is very close to the much older legal concept of common carriage that applies to most telecommunications

---

[28] *Id.* at 650.
[29] *Id.* at 655.
[30] NPRM ¶¶ 18, 41.
[31] *Verizon* 740 F.3d 623, 655-58.
[32] *Id.* at 658.
[33] 740 F.3d 623, 652 (quoting *Cellco Partnership v. FCC*, 700 F.3d 534, 547 (D.C. Cir. 2012); NPRM ¶¶ 114-116.
[34] 740 F.3d at 657.
[35] 740 F.3d at 652.
[36] 47 U.S.C. § 153(43) (emphasis added).

services. The FCC applied common carrier non-discrimination rules to telephone service for most of the last century, and that same regulatory scheme helped foster the Internet as we know it today. Broadband Internet access providers perform much the same function once performed by phone lines: they provide the last mile connection to the consumer. The author of the phrase "net neutrality" has called it "the twenty-first century's version of common carriage."[37]

Third, there is little question that the FCC has the legal power to reclassify. In *Brand X* the Supreme Court accepted the FCC's prior classification under *Chevron* deference.[38] It did not rule on the merits of the classification, though four justices suggested that the FCC's classification was "implausible" or beyond the agency's authority.[39] The majority noted that a change in circumstances or even administration could justify a change in the classification of broadband Internet access service.[40] The D.C. Circuit has also signaled that reclassification is an appropriate path forward.[41]

Finally, reclassification could help clarify not only the basis for the FCC's authority, but also its limits. The FCC should not be focused on regulating "the Internet," (the content carried on the wires) but the wires themselves, i.e., the underlying transmission network. Net neutrality rules should seek to ensure that broadband carriers' "telecommunications" services occur in a non-discriminatory way. Title II authority will help orient the FCC in precisely that direction.

2. Light, limited, bright-line regulation

Net neutrality regulation should promote user choice, permissionless innovation, and an application-blind network.[42] In keeping with these goals, such rules should include prohibitions on blocking, application-specific discrimination, and paid prioritization.[43] Internet access providers should not be permitted to charge special fees for the right to reach that provider's Internet service customers. This is not to say that all tiering of service must be banned; companies could still impose application neutral bandwidth charges. But Internet access providers should never be able to take advantage of their position to effectively direct subscribers toward or away from particular applications, services, or content.

In addition, we have suggested that the FCC forbear from any common carrier regulation that is not clearly essential to meet the above goals and to clarify that its proposed regulations would not reach noncommercial providers of broadband Internet access service, whether they are individuals who operate open Wi-Fi networks at home or public-minded entities that provide free Internet access in their local communities. Federal regulation of these noncommercial, public-spirited initiatives is not necessary to vindicate the openness, competition, innovation, and free expression of the open Internet.

[37] TIM WU, THE MASTER SWITCH 236 (2010).
[38] *NCTA v. Brand X Internet Services*, 545 U.S. 967, 980 (2005).
[39] *Id.* at 1003 (Breyer, S. concurrence, "within the agency's discretion, but barely") and 1006 (dissenting opinion of Justice Scalia, joined in part by Justices Souter and Ginsburg); *see also id.* at 1005 ("implausible reading of the statute").
[40] *Id.* at 981.
[41] *Verizon*, 740 F.3d 623, 650.
[42] *See generally* Barbara van Schewick, *Network Neutrality and Quality of Service: What a Non-Discrimination Rule Should Look Like*, CENTER FOR INTERNET AND SOCIETY, (June 2012), http://cyberlaw.stanford.edu/files/publication/files/20120611-NetworkNeutrality_0.pdf.; *see also* http://media.law.stanford.edu/publications/archive/pdf/schewick-statement-20100428.pdf.
[43] *Id.*

ELECTRONIC FRONTIER FOUNDATION

IV.   **Open Access to Last-Mile Connections Could Mitigate the Power to Discriminate Through Market Competition, Reducing the Need for More Intrusive Regulation**

The market cannot correct abuses of power by ISPs when consumers lack a real choice among providers. One potential regulatory response is the creation of access obligations, such as line sharing, to allow for competition over shared infrastructure.

Following the enactment of the Telecommunications Act of 1996, the FCC imposed a range of competitive last-mile access remedies called for in the Act. Soon thereafter, however, the FCC began to deregulate broadband Internet access.[44] As a result, in 2014 neither cable nor telephone company broadband Internet access is subject to meaningful last-mile access obligations. The *Verizon* court recognized that approximately 14-24 million Americans had no access to broadband,[45] and end users with inadequate service "may have no option to switch, or at least face very limited options," noting that "as of December, 2009, nearly 70 percent of households lived in census tracts where only one or two wireline or fixed wireless firms provided broadband service."[46]

Unfortunately, it is currently unclear whether merely imposing last-mile obligations on the U.S. marketplace today will have the desired effects. The situation in 2014 is significantly different than it was in 2002; regulators now at least need to study open access in the fiber, cable, and wireless contexts as well as copper.

We have encouraged the FCC to investigate open access requirements, looking into the effects of past access regulation on competition in the DSL markets; the effects of access regulation on competition in markets outside the United States, such as in the European Union; the economic and technical feasibility of line sharing in the U.S. cable broadband access market and in the emerging U.S. FTTH market; and the likely effects of line sharing and similar access remedies on innovation, competition, consumer welfare, and privacy and First Amendment freedoms on the Internet.

V.   **Mobile Broadband Users Also Need a Neutral Internet**

The marketplace for mobile technologies that depend on high-speed Internet access has blossomed since the FCC's Open Internet Order in 2010.[47] As the FCC noted, minority communities are more likely than other groups to access the Internet on a mobile device instead of a home wire-line connection.[48] The mobile-related cloud broadband and supporting services industry is worth tens of billions of dollars, and grows each year.[49]

Given widespread dependence on mobile Internet access, the Internet should be no less neutral on mobile platforms. Yet examples of discriminatory practices by mobile providers abound. For example, AT&T blocked Apple's FaceTime application over AT&T's mobile data network in 2012.[50] In the same year, Verizon

---

[44] *Cable Modem Declaratory Ruling and Notice of Proposed Rulemaking*, 14 March 2002; *see generally Verizon*, 740 F.3d 623, 631 (describing history of FCC's exempting broadband providers from Title II obligations beginning in 2002).

[45] *Id.* at 641 (citation omitted) (applying "broadband" benchmark of "four megabytes per second (mbps) for end users to download content from the Internet—twenty times as fast as the prior threshold—and one mbps for end users to upload content.").

[46] *Id.* at 647 (citation omitted).

[47] *See* Duggan and Smith, *supra*, note 54.

[48] *See Mobile Technology Fact Sheet*, PEW RESEARCH INTERNET PROJECT (January 2014), http://www.pewinternet.org/fact-sheets/mobile-technology-fact-sheet/.

[49] *See generally* Roger Entner, *The Wireless Industry: The Essential Engine of US Economic Growth*, RECON ANALYTICS, (May 2012), http://reconanalytics.com/wp-content/uploads/2012/04/Wireless-The-Ubiquitous-Engine-by-Recon-Analytics-1.pdf.

[50] *See* David Kravets, AT&T Holding FaceTime Hostage is No Net-Neutrality Breach, WIRED.COM (Aug. 22, 2012) http://www.wired.com/2012/08/facetime-net-neutrality-flap/.

ELECTRONIC FRONTIER FOUNDATION

reached a $1.25 million settlement with the FCC for refusing to allow tethering on smartphones. [51] AT&T and T-Mobile both forbid users from using peer-to-peer file sharing applications. [52]

The 2010 Open Internet order prohibited the blocking of "lawful websites" and "applications that compete with the provider's voice or video telephony services." [53] Given the expanded diversity of applications that provide voice and video on the Internet, the wording of this rule is now too vague to accomplish its goals.

In particular, mobile broadband service providers should not be allowed to prohibit tethering. Restrictions on tethering are discriminatory and anti-innovative. The FCC has successfully protected tethering via the C Block open access rules. Such protections should extend to all mobile Internet access services.

Zero-rating is also worrisome. Zero-rating refers to the practice of not counting data to and from certain websites or services toward users' monthly data limits. T-Mobile's recent announcement of its Music Freedom plan is one example of zero-rating: users can stream all the music they want from certain services without worrying about their data limit. [54] This arrangement, however, discourages users from trying other music streaming sites not in T-Mobile's list (which might host alternative artists) since those sites will count towards users' data caps. Zero-rating is a type of data discrimination: it allows a mobile broadband provider to influence what services, websites, and applications people are more likely to use. In this way zero-rating allows mobile broadband providers to pick winners instead of leaving that determination to the market.

VI. Meaningful Transparency

Transparency is critically important. Without adequate information, a customer experiencing a problem with broadband service may punish the wrong party, blaming the application vendor, device maker, or herself for the problem. As a result, customers will not be able to express their preferences by switching ISPs. This interferes with the market's ability to protect consumers and correct improper ISP practices. Application innovators also need enough information about ISP practices to enable them to develop new applications and protocols that work reliably without asking permission from ISPs.

Transparency is also vital to enforcement. As we have seen, ISPs are willing to secretly engage in discriminatory practices on their networks and then lie about those practices to the public. [55] Strong transparency requirements will help regulators stop ISPs from saying one thing about their network management practices while doing another.

[51] See In re Complaint of Free Press Against Cellco Partnership d/b/a Verizon Wirless for Violating Conditions Imposed on C Block of Upper 700 Mhz Spectrum (June 6, 2011), available at http://www.freepress.net/sites/default/files/fp-legacy/FreePress_CBlock_Complaint.pdf and Federal Communications Commission, News Release: Verizon Wireless to Pay $1.25 Million to Settle Investigation into Blocking of Consumers' Access to Certain Mobile Broadband Applications (July 31, 2012) http://transition.fcc.gov/Daily_Releases/Daily_Business/2012/db0731/DOC-315501A1.pdf.
[52] See AT&T Wireless Customer Agreement § 6.2, available at https://www.att.com/shop/en/legalterms.html?toskey=wirelessCustomerAgreement#whatAreTheIntendedPurposesOfDataServ and T-Mobile Terms and Conditions §18, available at http://www.tmobile.com/Templates/Popup.aspx?PAsset=Ftr_Ftr_TermsAndConditions&print=true.
[53] NPRM ¶ 21.
[54] See Lily Hay Newman, T-Mobile Is Making Certain Types of Data Use Free. Which Is Suspicious., SLATE.COM (June 27, 2014) http://www.slate.com/blogs/future_tense/2014/06/27/t_mobile_isn't_counting_speedtests_or_certain_music_streaming_toward_users.html.
[55] See Seth Schoen, "Comcast and BitTorrent," (Sep. 13, 2007) https://www.eff.org/deeplinks/2007/09/comcast-and-bittorrent; Fred Von Lohmann, "FCC Rules Against Comcast for BitTorrent Blocking" (Aug. 3, 2008), https://www.eff.org/deeplinks/2008/08/fcc-rules-against-comcast-bit-torrent-blocking.; See Peter Eckersley, Comcast Needs to Come Clean, ELECTRONIC FRONTIER FOUNDATION (October 25, 2007) https://www.eff.org/deeplinks/2007/10/comcast-needs-come-clean.

ELECTRONIC FRONTIER FOUNDATION

A.   Advantages and Disadvantages of the Existing Transparency Rule

The existing transparency rule is vague.[56] Most ISPs have complied by including a short passage on their websites describing generally how they deal with congestion, with statistics about how advertised speeds compare to the true speeds users experience. In order to generate these statistics, many of the largest ISPs have taken part in the FCC's Measuring Broadband America study, which uses volunteers across the country to measure broadband speeds.[57] The study averages data about latency, download, and upload speed over one month. This program has helped ensure that the throughput speeds ISPs advertise to customers match the throughput speeds they actually deliver.

While this is a good start, the current disclosure requirements regarding network management practices are too vague and the reported statistics cannot reveal performance issues due to peering, co-location, or content delivery network (CDN) agreements, such as the recent problems Comcast and Verizon subscribers had with slow Netflix download speeds.[58] The Measuring Broadband America program only takes measurements with respect to servers designed explicitly for testing, the connections to which are almost always uncongested. In the latest Measuring Broadband America study, the authors even went out of their way to *exclude* data that showed congestion due to peering issues.[59]

B.   A Stronger Transparency Rule

Effective transparency requires two kinds of disclosure. The first is a simple disclosure at the point of sale that includes the 95% percentile minimum and maximum speeds the user will experience to a realistic population of well-connected servers, as well as clear warnings about any fast lanes, premium services, blocking or filtering that the user will not have a simple and practical way to avoid.

The second should be a more detailed technical disclosure posted on the ISP's website, which would include CDFs of the sorts of statistics already reported, as well as statistics concerning jitter (the variability in the latency of packets), uptime, and packet loss. These metrics are essential for predicting and debugging the performance of many types of network applications including voice and video over IP; online gaming; and common tools for software development and website administration.

Additionally, these measurements need to capture the customer's experience when talking to end points do not have special peering arrangements with the ISP. Without such measurements the resulting statistics are unlikely to match a customer's true Internet experience.

Finally, any meaningful transparency rule must require ISPs to provide more frequent disclosures as well as detailed disclosures about their network management practices as soon as these network management practices are put into place, if not before. We support the portion of the FCC's proposed transparency rule that requires ISPs to disclose such information "in a timely manner."[60] Any content-specific discrimination, including blocking, throttling, or traffic-shaping, should be explicitly listed in whatever disclosure the ISP

---

[56] *In the Matter of Preserving the Open Internet*, FCC Rcd. 17905, 17937 (2010).

[57] Federal Communications Commission, *Measuring Broadband America*, https://www.fcc.gov/measuring-broadband-america.

[58] See Associated Press, *Cogent CEO: Comcast purposefully slowed down Netflix streaming*, SAN JOSE MERCURY NEWS (May 8, 2014) http://www.mercurynews.com/business/ci_25723988/cogent-ceo-comcast-purposefully-slowed-down-netflix-streaming; Jon Brodkin, *Netflix tells customer, "The Verizon Network is Crowded Right Now"*, ARS TECHNICA (June 4, 2014) http://arstechnica.com/information- technology/2014/06/netflix-tells-customer-the-verizon-network-is-crowded-right-now/.

[59] FCC's Office of Engineering and Technology and Consumer and Governmental Affairs Bureau, *Measuring Broadband America 2014: A Report on Consumer Wireline Broadband Performance within the U.S.*, at 27.

[60] NPRM appendix A, rule 8.3c.

makes to satisfy the rule —not buried deep within the legalese of a Terms of Service document.

C.   Minimizing the Costs of Transparency

Many ISPs would not face a large burden in collecting high-quality transparency data, as the types of measurements we have described are already commonly used in order to diagnose network problems and enhance network performance. The Measuring Broadband America program could also be used to obtain high-quality data without imposing high costs and burdens on ISPs that do not already have extensive performance data about their networks, or the internal capacity to start efficiently collecting and reporting that data.

D.   Privacy Must Be Preserved

The FCC is considering whether ISPs should disclose information about users' data, application, and device usage.[61] In most cases, ISPs should not have sufficient access to provide application- or device-specific reports. ISPs' monitoring what devices had connected to a user's router, what devices are tethered to a user's phone or tablet, or what applications were running on those devices would constitute a deep violation of the subscriber's privacy. A better approach that is consistent with user privacy would put users, rather than carriers, in charge of acquiring such information through applications or software that they can control on their own devices and networks. ISPs should not invade users' privacy in order to provide details on application or device-specific usage.

E.   Transparency Must Extend to Edge Providers

The emerging environment of discriminatory peering and co-location practices is a dire threat to innovation on the Internet. The parties most threatened by these developments are those who are trying to make novel and unanticipated uses of the network, including startup companies, open source projects, and developers of new network protocols. The next startup that attempts to offer innovative video streaming products will not have the deep pockets and negotiating strength of Netflix and YouTube.

To counteract the danger of these practices, transparency should include the terms of any peering, co-location, or CDN hosting arrangements ISPs make with other parties. By requiring ISPs to publish the contractual details of these arrangements (as well as any necessary technical data), other parties will be able to request the same reasonable and nondiscriminatory terms without significant negotiation and transaction costs.

VII.   Conclusion

Net neutrality is best accomplished with light regulation setting forth clear rules forbidding discriminatory and anti-competitive practices that threaten the openness of the Internet. The FCC can accomplish this without congressional action, but only if it both reclassifies broadband as a telecommunications service and forbears from imposing any regulations that are not strictly necessary to protect the open Internet.

---

[61] NPRM ¶ 73.

**Written Testimony of
Casey Rae
VP for Policy and Education
Future of Music Coalition**

**In the
"Why Net Neutrality Matters: Protecting
Consumers and Competition Through Meaningful
Open Internet Rules"
Hearing**

Senate Judiciary Committee

September 17, 2014

Future of Music Coalition (FMC) is pleased to submit the following written testimony for

the record in this important hearing on preserving an open Internet. FMC is a nonprofit organization founded in 2000 by musicians, composers, independent label owners, technologists and artist advocates. Our goal is a diverse musical culture where artists flourish, are compensated fairly for their work, and where fans can find the music they want.

For the past fourteen years, FMC and our artist allies have made a consistent case for accessible communications networks that allow for creative expression, innovation and entrepreneurship. In fact, we have been involved in conversations about net neutrality since before the term was coined. Preserving an open Internet is vitally important to our organization and to the musicians and composers with whom we work. Musicians intuitively understand the dangers of pay-to-play environments, because they have experienced the negative impacts of corporate consolidation in radio and the structural payola it helped engender. This is why thousands of musicians and independent labels are already on record in various FCC proceedings to make the case for clear rules of the road to prohibit Internet Service Providers from picking winners and losers online based on their business—or even political—preferences.

Musicians across genres have consistently gone to bat for net neutrality at concerts, before Congressional committees and in letters and filings. Those in favor of preserving an open Internet include R.E.M., Erin McKeown, OK Go, Kronos Quartet, Pearl Jam, tUnE-yArDs, Nicole Atkins, Preservation hall Jazz Band, Boots Riley of The Coup, and thousands more across the country. All of these creators support a legitimate digital marketplace where a great song, idea or innovation has a chance to find an audience.

By now, it should be obvious that musicians and other creators use the Internet in practically every aspect of their lives and careers—from connecting with fans to booking tours, to selling music and merchandise to collaborating with other artists. Musicians who were around before broadband remember how difficult it was to accomplish simple things like letting people know where and when you were performing, to say nothing of the limitations of physical distribution. By contrast, an artist today can publish their music globally with a tap of a screen or a click of a mouse. Creators of every conceivable background and discipline are able to engage with audiences on their own terms without having to ask permission. This is a powerful thing.

While it is clear that the Internet has created challenges for musicians and other creators, there is no denying that digital technology has made many things easier for countless artists who otherwise would have faced tremendous barriers to entering the marketplace.

Much has been made about the current economic conditions for musicians and composers online. It is certainly the case that artists continue to grapple with many of the changes brought on by technological evolution, but it is also true that any possible solutions to these difficulties are more likely to come from an open, accessible Internet rather than a closed system that serves a privileged few. Artists simply want the opportunity for their creative expression to compete its own merits, and not have their success be pre-determined by a handful of powerful ISPs.

Currently, the music community is experiencing yet another shift, from downloads to streaming. Musicians and composers are not a monolithic group, and there are differences of opinion about which models are appropriate. This is as it should be: the music industry was never one single way of doing business, but rather a diverse array of approaches based on the individual goals of participants. This diversity is to be celebrated, particularly when it comes to emerging technologies. For example, it's not uncommon these days to hear from a musician that thinks Spotify is not a sustainable model for artists. Perhaps this musician prefers Bandcamp, which allows pricing flexibility and greater opportunities to directly engage with listeners. What happens if an ISP decides that Spotify can pay more and blocks or otherwise interferes with traffic from the smaller platform? What if an ISP charges overages for data on a certain application, but exempts traffic from its preferred partners? Musicians have been down this road before with commercial radio ownership consolidation and institutional payola. A pay-to-play Internet would be devastating to small-to-medium sized enterprises in both the music and technology sectors. And it would be bad for fans that deserve the opportunity to patronize the lawful platforms of their choosing—particularly those that provide better economic returns to creators and allow for new ways for artists to take charge of their lives and careers.

Telecommunications and cable companies have an important role to play in a functional 21st century media ecosystem. There is nothing inherently wrong with their desire to operate profitable businesses, but they must not be allowed to do so at the expense of those who depend on open networks to express themselves creatively and pursue their own entrepreneurial goals. It is important to remember that creative expression—including a diverse array of lawful, licensed music—is a chief reason people go online. Musicians and other artists are entirely aware that part of what has driven the expansion of broadband is their creativity and the innovations that enable them to reach fans.

The work of artists must be valued in a way that is commensurate with demand; there is still a great deal to be done to ensure that creators are treated fairly in the digital age. But policymakers would do upcoming generations of artists a disservice should they allow ISPs to dictate economic terms for creators for sole the purpose of expanding their own bottom lines. Without meaningful rules to prevent discrimination and anticompetitive behavior, this is exactly what will occur.

For several iterations of this debate, Future of Music Coalition and our friends in the broader cultural sector have been content with making the case for basic rules of the road to preserve access and innovation online. Having closely examined the FCC's currently proposed rules, however, we feel strongly that the best course of action is for the Commission to reclassify broadband Internet service as a common carrier under Title II of the Telecommunications Act. In addition to the thousands of artists and independent labels in the official record, more than two-dozen prominent arts and cultural organizations in all 50 states have also urged the FCC to adopt the strongest rules possible. They join more than 3 million Americans from all walks of life calling overwhelmingly for reclassification. At this point, it is hard to ignore the evidence: the FCC has received the most public comments in any docket in history—99 percent of which demand the placement of broadband Internet service under Title II.

Nothing in the ISP arguments in any way convinces us that broadband Internet service should not exist under a common carrier framework. The giant telecommunications and cable companies would probably like to think that musicians and other creators aren't sophisticated enough to understand what they're trying to do, which is no less than establish a pay-to-play Internet where only the biggest companies can thrive. But artists and the vast majority of Americans know that you can't have a free market without the ability to compete. The FCC must take the necessary steps to ensure that creativity and entrepreneurship can continue to flourish online. And this means reclassification.

The main barrier appears to be political will. This is where Congress can help. Access and innovation are not bipartisan concerns; we have seen members of this very committee tweeting during the State of the Union address. Where do you think Twitter came from? The answer is an open Internet where one can build and promote the next amazing innovation without having to ask permission or pay a toll to an ISP. Whether it's outreach to constituents or delivering an amazing song, the ability to utilize the most important communications platform in history without the interference of gatekeepers should be of utmost importance to each of you. Common carrier is not some left-field concept. It is a bedrock principle that has informed communications policy for nearly a hundred years—a particularly lucrative century for incumbent companies such as AT&T that built durable empires under its consumer-friendly provisions.

Some would raise the specter of lawsuits to discourage the FCC from doing what it should to protect the interests of entrepreneurs and the public. It is important to understand that there is but one test that the FCC must pass, and that is justifying its decision to reclassify. Given that the Supreme Court has already validated a previous decision to do so, the government will likely persevere in its argument that a move to Title II is not "arbitrary and capricious." Actually, a return to the prior designation is sober and informed, as the past decade has proven that users subscribe to broadband service in order to access the Internet, not to purchase a suite of bundled "information services" from an ISP. Upon reclassification, we hope that the ISPs will recognize that litigation is ill-considered and destined to fail.

The FCC has the legal authority to prevent discrimination and paid prioritization online; it only needs to exercise this authority. We are unconvinced, however, that its current proposal under Section 706 is the way in which to do so.

Meaningful rules must be enforceable. We take Chairman Wheeler at his word that he will be aggressive in the application of a "commercial reasonableness" standard under 706. But can the same be said for future leadership? What guarantee do we have that an after-the-fact approach to enforcement will prevent the ISPs from taking advantage anywhere they can and then deploying their armies of lawyers and lobbyists to justify their mischief? Clear net neutrality rules under Title II will let the ISPs know up front what is and isn't permissible. This is the regulatory structure that the FCC must put forward in its rulemaking, one that is already endorsed by more than three million

Americans who have filed comments with the Commission.

Congress must be willing to show support to the FCC as it establishes clear rules of the

road to preserve access and innovation for generations to come. When you do, rest

assured that Future of Music Coalition and our peers and allies across the creative sector

will have your back. Thank you for the opportunity to share our perspectives as you

consider these important matters.

Casey Rae
Future of Music Coalition
1615 L ST NW, Suite 520
www.futureofmusic.org

**Statement of the Computer & Communications Industry
Association (CCIA)**

Why Net Neutrality Matters: Protecting Consumers and Competition
Through Meaningful Open Internet Rules

**Committee on the Judiciary
U.S. Senate**

September 17, 2014

CCIA hereby submits its statement for the record of the above-referenced hearing. CCIA is an international organization that represents companies of all sizes in the high technology sector, including computer software, electronic commerce, telecommunications, and Internet products and services.

Ever since our involvement in the antitrust case that resulted in the break-up of AT&T in the early 1980s, CCIA has been a strong and consistent advocate for open networks and full and fair competition. When the World Wide Web was launched in the early 1990s and for more than a decade following, dial-up connections to the Internet were common carrier telecommunications services subject to Title II of the Communications Act. AOL, Compuserv, Yahoo!, Amazon, Google, and eBay, on the other hand, were unregulated information services with nondiscriminatory access to the networks. After the FCC also classified both cable and telco provided broadband Internet access connections as unregulated "information services" in 2002-2005, CCIA worked vigorously for enforceable rules to keep the underlying transmission networks open for end users and so-called "edge providers" of online content and services. CCIA was a founding member of the Open Internet Coalition which at first championed enforceability of the FCC's 2005 Internet Policy Statement, that aimed to give consumers rights regarding online access to the services and content of their choice free of blocking. Comcast, in a case involving throttling of BitTorrent, challenged the enforceability of the FCC Internet policy in court and won. The Open Internet Coalition then began to focus on a modified, light touch common carrier framework for broadband Internet access.

In 2010 the FCC adopted Open Internet rules, which were then invalidated early this year in *Verizon v. FCC*, largely because Internet access was still classified as an information service, rather than as an essential two-way telecommunications service.

Post *Verizon*, American residential, business and nonprofit Internet consumers are all without any legal protections for the open Internet access they have come to expect and rely on in their daily life and work. Given our broadband Internet access network operators' newly confirmed freedom from legal obligations to end-users, open Internet access is at risk.

Despite the IAPs' claims that Title II reclassification will hamper incentives to investment in the network, no clear causal link has been articulated to support this contention. In fact, as Free Press has documented, Cable and Telecommunications companies invested *more* money in their networks when they were regulated as a Title II service. Furthermore, the IAPs have requested to be classified under Title II in the past in order to get the tax breaks and universal service subsidies that accompany it. Not surprisingly, IAPs did not complain then that such a classification would diminish their incentives to invest.

What is clear from the open Internet comments submitted to the FCC, however, is that without open access safeguards, investment and innovation in over-the-top Internet applications and services – which would need either the implicit or explicit permission of the IAPs – would be in real jeopardy. For the Internet marketplace to thrive, investors in start-ups need confidence that their products and services will be easily accessible to all online over the Internet.

Where network facilities competition is limited to duopoly or oligopoly conditions, the IAPs have basic economic incentives to profit from scarcity and congestion on their existing networks rather than invest in comprehensive upgrades.[1] Google Fiber and community broadband networks are only just getting started in a handful of cities and towns.

---

[1] See James J. Heaney, *Why Free Marketeers Want to Regulate the Internet*, DE CIVITATE (Sep. 15, 2014), *available at* http://www.jamesjheaney.com/2014/09/15/why-free-marketeers-want-to-regulate-the-internet/ for economic analysis of need for regulatory safeguards for Internet access.

So the FCC must continue to promote greater network competition, which will spur greater investment by the IAPs. Meanwhile, the FCC must use its clear legal authority over telecommunications to prevent degradation of our Internet access. The IAPs' empty threat that open Internet rules will cause them not to invest in their networks is the same one they use traditionally to oppose any FCC action they do not like. Only companies with dominant positions facing insufficient competition can even get an audience for such threats. In a truly competitive market the need to beat the competition incentivizes investment and innovation.

Antitrust law is designed to protect trade and commerce from unfair business practices and remedy anticompetitive market conduct by dominant firms and monopolies that reduces or eliminates competition. However, antitrust cases typically consume massive financial resources from both the private sector and the government and usually take years, and sometimes more than a decade, to prosecute. Furthermore, legal precedent around a firm's "duty to deal" with its competitors is murky and often contradictory, but it is generally recognized that even monopolists do not have to supply their competitors. Therefore, taking an antitrust approach to open Internet will not give the market the certainty necessary to ensure innovation and investment in all layers of the Internet.

Antitrust enforcement generally works best in markets where competition is the norm and not the exception. Under such conditions, individual cases can be used to restore a competitive market when a company acquires market power and uses it anti-competitively. Where markets are chronically less than competitive for structural reasons, expert agencies are generally tasked with ensuring that market power is not continually abused. Using antitrust enforcement to supervise a chronically non-competitive market is less desirable than the supervision of an expert agency tasked with promoting consumer welfare, as replacing an expert agency with a patchwork quilt of generalist court rulings is more expensive, creates more uncertainty, and does little to protect startups and smaller competitors who are often forced from the market before the court proceedings are finalized.

However, promoting competition is recognized as only part of the FCC's continuing obligation to protect "the public interest, convenience and necessity" regarding the universal availability of communications by wire and radio spectrum. The agency has the authority to make rules governing public access to everything from radio and TV stations to voice telephony, from satellite services to emergency services. Vibrant competition among communications companies certainly has public benefits that the FCC encourages and well recognizes, but the expert agency has specific responsibility for public communications services that goes beyond just disciplining behavior among commercial competitors.

The Internet is a network of interconnected networks that exchange data traffic at dozens of exchange points (IXPs) in the U.S. alone and many more around the globe. Online information service platforms pay for their own long-haul transit and larger ones often build or buy capacity from more localized content delivery networks (CDNs). Up to this point, markets are competitive. However, even when a U.S. business or household has a couple of choices for Internet access, once signed up with a particular company, that IAP has a monopoly on local delivery of Internet traffic to that subscriber. That is, the business or household not only must use that IAP for uploads, but nothing can be downloaded except through that chosen IAP. This terminating access monopoly provides an IAP the leverage to charge online content providers such as Netflix unlimited access tolls just to "open the door" and let the subscriber's requested video streaming through. That's true despite the fact that the subscriber has already paid monthly for that service. No party is getting or asking for anything "for free" here. The terminating monopoly also allows an IAP to impose discriminatory data caps that exempt its own affiliated content, such as premium sports or TV shows, but render other video choices that use equivalent bandwidth relatively more expensive. IAPs have a similar incentive and ability to charge competing providers of cloud and data storage services for local network access while their own cloud service would be free of such tolls, and therefore less expensive. Since end users cannot easily switch to a competing IAP that would not disadvantage their over-the-top choices, strong open Internet rules are urgently needed.

Even if IAPs do not have any intentions of discriminating against small businesses or nonprofits, selling priority speeds or quality of service to the largest online content companies will have the inevitable result of degrading throughput to other edge providers given the finite capacity of their networks. And once the harm is done, it will not only be too late for an aggrieved start-up to bring an antitrust case it cannot afford, it will be too late for the FCC to crack down and unwind all the contracts for paid prioritization that have proliferated. That's why the FCC must not waste time in adopting enforceable open Internet rules.

The impact of the FCC's decision on open Internet rules will be felt far into the future, not just in the U.S., but also around the world where the governments of many diverse nations take cues from ours. People everywhere need Internet access free from restrictions so they can access products and services, including personally empowering information online. While the term "net neutrality" has grown controversial in the U.S. and is susceptible to many conflicting definitions, the consensus goal of maintaining open Internet access is a strong bipartisan one that in fact the U.S. government works toward regularly at international multi-stakeholder meetings regarding Internet management. While the U.S. opposes any international regulation of the Internet, and cautions against national government restrictions like censorship and data localization mandates, we would certainly not take issue with any other nation's efforts to enshrine their own citizens' right to open Internet access into law, which is exactly what the FCC is aiming for in its current proceeding. And that task is of paramount importance for the growth and long-term health of the US economy.

National Cable & Telecommunications Association
25 Massachusetts Avenue, NW, Suite 100
Washington, DC 20001-1431
(202) 222-2300

Rick Chessen
Senior Vice President
Law and Regulatory Policy

(202) 222-2445
(202) 222-2448 Fax
rchessen@ncta.com

May 14, 2014

Marlene H. Dortch
Secretary
Federal Communications Commission
445 12th Street, S.W.
Washington, D.C. 20554

Re: Protecting and Promoting the Open Internet, GN Docket No. 14-28

Dear Ms. Dortch:

On behalf of the National Cable & Telecommunications Association ("NCTA"), I write to underscore our deep concerns regarding recent proposals to reclassify broadband Internet access services (or some component thereof) as telecommunications services subject to Title II of the Communications Act. As explained in NCTA's prior comments in this docket,[1] the existing transparency rules provide a strong foundation for promoting Open Internet principles, and, to the extent the Commission determines that additional safeguards are necessary, the *Verizon* decision provides ample leeway to adopt such measures pursuant to Section 706 of the Telecommunications Act.[2] In light of that recently confirmed authority, it is wholly unnecessary to pursue a Title II reclassification theory. It also would be immensely destabilizing. Indeed, any effort to subject broadband Internet access services to common carrier regulation would do far more harm than good, as such a heavy-handed framework would discourage network investment necessary to fuel the "virtuous cycle" of deployment, innovation, and adoption that the Commission has long sought to promote under Section 706.

As the Commission and numerous stakeholders have recognized, cable operators and telecommunications companies have made massive private investments in broadband networks, unleashing innovation and dramatically increased consumer welfare.[3] The Commission's 2002 determination and subsequent reaffirmations that broadband Internet access is an integrated information service without any severable telecommunications service component were a critical factor in creating the stable regulatory climate that attracted investment and enabled the Internet

---

[1]   Comments of the National Cable & Telecommunications Association, GN Docket No. 14-28 (filed Mar. 26, 2014).

[2]   *Verizon v. FCC*, 740 F.3d 623 (D.C. Cir. 2014).

[3]   Federal Communications Commission, *Connecting America: The National Broadband Plan*, at XI (2010).

to become a key driver of our economy and a central aspect of our lives.[4] In fact, the Commission and the Department of Justice ("DOJ") sought Supreme Court review in the *Brand X* case to prevent the imposition of common carrier regulation on broadband services based in large part on the concern that such regulation would entail significant burdens that could prevent or delay the deployment of "new broadband infrastructure, particularly in rural or other underserved areas."[5] The Court upheld the Commission's information-service classification based on the "factual particulars of how Internet technology works and how it is provided."[6]

As a threshold matter, it is far from clear that the Commission could simply abandon the fact-based classification it adopted and repeatedly confirmed over the past 12 years. The classification of broadband Internet access "turns on the nature of the functions that the end user is offered,"[7] and those functions have not materially changed since the Commission analyzed them in its previous orders. Notably, cable operators have *never* provided broadband transmission as common carriers. Moreover, where, as here, such a classification has engendered "serious reliance interests," and any effort to reclassify broadband Internet access would contradict "factual findings ... which underlay [the FCC's] prior policy," the Commission would need to "provide a more detailed justification than what would suffice for a new policy created on a blank slate."[8] At a minimum, pursuing Title II reclassification would plunge the broadband industry into a lengthy period of uncertainty while a new round of appellate proceedings ran its course—a process that can be easily avoided by relying on the roadmap provided by the *Verizon* court.

But even assuming the Commission could lawfully reclassify broadband services, it would be profoundly counterproductive to do so. The burdens and uncertainty associated with Title II regulation (or even the threat of such regulation) would deter broadband providers from making the substantial additional investments required to deploy new and upgraded broadband infrastructure. As noted, the Commission and DOJ emphasized that very risk in their petition in

---

[4]   *Inquiry Concerning High-Speed Access to the Internet Over Cable and Other Facilities*, Declaratory Ruling and Notice of Proposed Rulemaking, 17 FCC Rcd 4798 (2002) ("*Cable Modem Declaratory Ruling*"); *see also, e.g., Appropriate Framework for Broadband Access to the Internet over Wireline Facilities*, Report and Order and Notice of Proposed Rulemaking, 20 FCC Rcd 14853 (2005) (classifying wireline broadband services as information services); *Appropriate Regulatory Treatment for Broadband Access to the Internet Over Wireless Networks*, Declaratory Ruling, 22 FCC Rcd 5901 (2007) (classifying wireless broadband services as information services).

[5]   Petition for Writ of Certiorari, U.S. Dept. of Justice and FCC, *FCC v. Brand X Internet Servs.*, No. 04-277, at 25-26 (Aug. 27, 2004) ("*Brand X* Cert Petition").

[6]   *Nat'l Cable & Telecomms. Ass'n v. Brand X Internet Servs.*, 545 U.S. 967, 991 (2005).

[7]   *Cable Modem Declaratory Ruling* ¶ 38.

[8]   *FCC v. Fox Television Stations, Inc.*, 556 U.S. 502, 515 (2009).

the *Brand X* case,[9] and it remains just as serious today. The Commission has estimated that reaching the broadband deployment goals set forth in the *National Broadband Plan* could require as much as $350 billion in private investment,[10] but the specter of Title II regulation would significantly diminish network providers' ability to attract that level of investment. A wide array of financial analysts and industry observers have reached the same conclusion, arguing emphatically that the threat of Title II reclassification would damage broadband providers, discourage infrastructure investment, stifle job growth, and harm consumers.[11]

Indeed, in other contexts where the government has imposed public utility-style regulation, such an approach has led to chronic *under*-investment in basic infrastructure. One need only examine our nation's ailing public infrastructure to appreciate the potential dangers to the continued expansion and growth of broadband networks.[12] The contrast is striking when one compares the crisis in public utility infrastructure with the dynamism and stable investment in broadband Internet services.[13]

---

[9] *Brand X* Cert Petition at 25-26.

[10] *See* FCC Staff Presentation, *September 2009 Commission Meeting*, at 45 (Sep. 29, 2009), http://hraunfoss.fcc.gov/edocs_public/attachmatch/DOC-293742A1.pdf.

[11] *See, e.g.*, Anna-Maria Kovacs, *The Internet Is Not a Rotary Phone*, Re/code, May 12, 2014, *available at* http://recode.net/2014/05/12/the-internet-is-not-a-rotary-phone/ (comparing robust investment in broadband in the U.S. to diminished investment in Europe, which "has continued to regulate its telecommunications industry along the lines of Title II"); Bret Swanson, *Title II Communications Is the 'Slow Lane'*, Tech Policy Daily, May 13, 2014, *available at* http://www.techpolicydaily.com/communications/title-ii-communications-slow-lane/ (explaining that "[a]s the mostly unregulated Internet piles success upon success, boosting bandwidth and transforming each industry it touches, with no end in sight, the old, heavily regulated, Title II network is barely an afterthought and is rapidly approaching full retirement"); *see also* Letter of Robert W. Quinn, Senior Vice President, AT&T, to Marlene H. Dortch, Secretary, FCC, GN Docket No. 14-28, at 2-4 (May 9, 2014) ("AT&T May 9 Letter") (summarizing other analysts' commentary on the risks of Title II reclassification theories).

[12] A recent study found that most of America's drinking water infrastructure is nearing the end of its useful life and will need $1 trillion in investment in the coming decades, and that America's electric grid will require a $736 billion shot in the arm by 2020 to keep it from failing. *See* American Society of Civil Engineers, *2013 Report Card for America's Infrastructure*, *available at* http://www.infrastructurereportcard.org. The same study found that one in three major U.S. roads is in poor or mediocre condition and that repairing and maintaining these roads will require an estimated $170 billion in annual investment, and that one in four bridges is either functionally obsolete or structurally deficient. *Id.*

[13] Broadband speeds have increased 1500 percent in the last decade. Michael Powell, *Keynote Remarks: 2014 Cable Show* (Apr. 29, 2014), at 3, *available at* https://www.ncta.com/sites/prod/files/NCTA-MichaelPowellKeynoteRemarks_0.pdf.

And the risks associated with Title II regulation would extend far beyond the chilling of investment and innovation by broadband Internet access providers. If the transmission component(s) of broadband Internet access were to be treated as distinct telecommunications services, there is no sound principle that would justify limiting such a classification to last-mile providers; to the contrary, other entities that provide transmission (such as backbone providers and content delivery networks) could become subject to Title II.[14]

Nor could the Commission overcome such obstacles by forbearing from unwanted and overbroad aspects of Title II. Any such undertaking would be massively complex and contentious, given the myriad provisions that are included in Title II and relevant Commission precedent. As a result, the forbearance process *itself* would engender enormous uncertainty, as the Commission has previously recognized.[15] And any grant of forbearance would be subject to judicial challenge and/or potential revocation by a later Commission.

Moreover, subjecting broadband access providers to regulation under Title II would not even accomplish the goal that reclassification proponents apparently seek. Reclassification would not support a categorical prohibition on Internet "fast lanes" any more than Section 706 would. Section 202 of the Act does not impose a duty of "nondiscrimination," but rather proscribes only "unjust" or "unreasonable" discrimination.[16] The relevant precedent makes clear that carriers subject to this standard have considerable flexibility to differentiate among customers for various legitimate business reasons.[17] Accordingly, whatever the Commission's ultimate judgment about the potential benefits and harms associated with paid prioritization and

---

Moreover, as the Commission is aware, America's Internet providers have invested well over $1 trillion dollars since 1996 to make America's Internet world-class. *See Inquiry Concerning the Deployment of Advanced Telecommunications Capability to All Americans in a Reasonable and Timely Fashion, and Possible Steps to Accelerate Such Deployment Pursuant to Section 706 of the Telecommunications Act of 1996, as Amended by the Broadband Data Improvement Act*, Eighth Broadband Progress Report, 27 FCC Rcd 10342 (2012).

[14] As AT&T has pointed out, reclassification of last-mile transmission under Title II also could import the broken intercarrier compensation scheme to the exchange of Internet traffic, among various other unintended and disruptive consequences. *See* AT&T May 9 Letter at 5.

[15] *See Brand X* Cert Petition at 28 (explaining that "forbearance authority is not in this context an effective means of remov[ing] regulatory uncertainty that in itself may discourage investment and innovation").

[16] 47 U.S.C. § 202(a).

[17] *See, e.g., Orloff v. FCC*, 352 F.3d 415 (D.C. Cir. 2003) (upholding carriers' ability to offer differential discounts to retail customers); *Southwestern Bell Tel. Co. v. FCC*, 19 F.3d 1475, 1481 (D.C. Cir. 1994) (upholding carriers' ability to enter into individualized contracts); *Ameritech Operating Cos. Revisions to Tariff FCC No. 2*, Order, DA 94-1121 (CCB 1994) (upholding reasonableness of rate differentials based on cost considerations).

Ms. Marlene Dortch
May 14, 2014
Page 5

similar arrangements, any such practices will have to be reviewed on a case-by-case basis pursuant to general standards promulgated by the Commission, regardless of whether the Commission seeks to rely on Section 706 or Title II.

As reflected in our recent comments, NCTA seeks to be a constructive partner in any new dialogue about new Open Internet rules. While the substance of proposed rules can be fairly debated, there is no sound reason to pursue reclassification under Title II.

Sincerely,

/s/ Rick Chessen

Rick Chessen

July 30, 2014

The Honorable Penny Pritzker
Secretary
U.S. Department of Commerce
1401 Constitution Avenue NW
Washington, D.C. 20230

Dear Secretary Pritzker:

The public discussion surrounding net neutrality has heated up, with all sides of the debate – large Internet service providers (ISPs), online content providers, the media and individual Americans – publicly voicing their opinions on how best to protect the Open Internet. Now it is time for our voice to be heard. We, the undersigned smaller, regional and medium-sized broadband ISPs, are at the leading edge of technology for broadband Internet, video and voice services that bridge the digital divide. We have heavily invested in rural areas and small towns and cities to bring much needed high speed connectivity to residents, as well as to local businesses, governments, schools, libraries, and health care facilities. We recognize that quality broadband services – and the adoption of those services by consumers – are crucial to economic development and the creation of jobs in the markets we serve.

Congress and the FCC have laid the groundwork for this constant stream of investment and the jobs that it produces through a consistent, bipartisan federal policy of light-touch regulation. The FCC, however, is now considering proposals in its *Open Internet* rulemaking that could put the brakes on broadband investment in the very markets that are most in need. The undersigned broadband providers are fully committed to openness, but we have serious concerns about the FCC's move toward a heavy-handed regulatory approach that would apply the outdated common carrier regulatory regime of Title II of the Communications Act to broadband Internet access service providers.

First and foremost, there is no problem identified that would justify putting more costs and burdens on our resources and our networks. We have strong incentives to meet the needs of our residential and commercial customers and a lengthy track record of doing just that. Does the federal government really need to heap costly, complex new regulations on our companies? We have no incentive to interfere with our customers' ability to access the Internet content of their choice. Nor is there any evidence that we have done so. Simply put, there is no net neutrality problem to be solved, and certainly no problem that would warrant the imposition of onerous regulation.

If the government nevertheless wants to impose new rules, Title II is a poor choice for that authority. None of the companies below is today subject to common carrier regulations with respect to retail broadband Internet access service. Consumers should not be burdened with the costs required for us to retain lawyers to interpret Title II and to administer the reporting and other rules that will no doubt go along with it. The time, regulatory uncertainty and costs associated with a Title II regime would deter investment in new broadband services and discourage our banks from providing capital for deployment of new infrastructure and improvements. These problems would be compounded if our broadband subscriber base must absorb price increases resulting from the potential for new fees attributable to the Universal Service Fund, Telecommunications Relay Service, and other programs. Given the widely acknowledged challenges this country faces in persuading all Americans to adopt broadband, any policy that results in higher costs for providers and new fees for consumers should be a non-starter.

Our goal has been to invest in new and advanced broadband services for our customers and to connect our institutions, not to invest in new lawyers, regulatory staff, and paperwork or to raise customer's costs with new government taxes and fees. We are striving each and every day to keep our existing customers satisfied and to attract new customers – and we thought that was the goal of Congress and the FCC as well. With millions of Americans still lacking any broadband options, the FCC should be focused on identifying strategies to encourage private investment in broadband deployment, not taking steps that make it more difficult and more expensive for such investment to take place.

We want to maintain an Open Internet. We believe that new, heavy-handed regulation is not necessary to achieve that result, and are committed to having an open dialogue with the FCC about how best to create a regulatory framework that maintains openness without sacrificing investment, innovation, and opportunity for all Americans. For all the reasons discussed above, the regulatory obligations and legal uncertainties associated with Title II should not be part of the process.

Sincerely,

Aeronet Wireless Broadband Corp.	Alamo Broadband Inc.
Alaska Communications	AllureTech/CoffeyNet www.atwy.net
Alsat Wireless	Amarillo Wireless
BackWoods Wireless	BendBroadband
A Better Wireless, NISP, LLC	Blaze Broadband
BridgeNet Wireless	Bright House Networks
Broadband VI	California Broadband Services
Central Coast Internet	Central Virginia Technology Group, LLC dba CVALINK Broadband
Cherry capital connection, llc	CKS Wireless
Columbia Energy, LLC	Consolidated Communications

Country Connections, LLC

CresComm WiFi, LLC

Crossroads Wifi

Cyber Broadband Inc.

Cybernet1, Inc.

Digital Passage, Inc.

DSLbyAir, LLC

Eagle Communications

Eastern Indiana Wifi,Inc.

Eastern Oregon Telecom, LLC

eCom Direct, Inc.

ECSIS.NET, LLC

Epic Touch Company

Ethoplex

Evans Telecommunications Company

e-vergent.com LLC

Excel.Net, Inc.

FairPoint Communications

First Step Internet, LLC

Fourway Computer Products, Inc.

FTX Networks, LLC

General Communication, Inc.

Grand County Internet Services, Inc.

GVTC

Hawaiian Telcom

Highspeedlink.net

Hudson Valley Communications | Hudson Valley Wireless

Imagine Networks

Intelligent Computing Solutions

InvisiMax

Jefferson Telecom

JMF Solutions, Inc.

KWISP Internet

Mediacom Communications Corporations

Midcontinent Communications

Monroe Telephone Company

Myakka Communications, Inc.

Net-Change.Com

New Signals Wireless LLC

New Wave Net Corp.

NewWays Networking, LLC

North State Communications

Northern Neck Wireless Internet Services, LLC

On-Ramp Indiana, Inc.

Outback Internet LLC

Pioneer Telephone Cooperative

Plains Internet

Razzo Link, Inc.

REACH4 Communications

Sandhills Wireless / Echelon Internet Services

Shelby Broadband

SightLine Wireless

Sjoberg's, Inc.

SkyWerx Industries, LLC

Smart City

Southern Ohio Communication Services Inc.

Suddenlink Communications

Triad Wireless

Velocity Online, Inc.

Vom.Com

Winters Broadband LLC

Zirkel Wireless

Phoenix Broadband, LLC

Pixius Communications, LLC

Portative Technologies

Rainier Connect

Red Shift Internet Services

SCS Broadband

Shenandoah Telecommunications Company

Silver Star Communications

Sky Valley Network, LLC

Slopeside Internet

Smithville Communications

Southwest Texas Telephone Company

Tnet Broadband Internet, LLC

Valnet Holdings, LLC

Vista Beam

Vyve Broadband

XL Broadband, Inc.

September 9, 2014

The Honorable Penny Pritzker
United States Secretary of Commerce
U.S. Department of Commerce
1401 Constitution Ave., NW
Washington, D.C. 20230

Dear Madam Secretary,

As manufacturers and suppliers of the high-tech equipment used by broadband providers, content providers and users, the undersigned have a unique perspective on the impact that Internet regulation has had and could have on the past and future innovation and opportunities in the broadband marketplace. Computer and electronics manufacturers are a critical part of a positive cycle of investment, innovation, and consumer demand that has made the Internet the world's biggest driver of economic development. The Administration must act to protect against calls for utility-like common carrier regulation that would threaten demand for Internet infrastructure, reduce incentives for investment, hinder innovation and jeopardize this success.

Broadband Internet deployment and adoption grew and flourished in a light-touch regulatory environment that encouraged heavy investment in the infrastructure needed to support the innovative new services that have become the trademark of the Internet economy. When broadband Internet service providers sought to invest billions of dollars over the past decade to develop and deploy advanced broadband services, they turned to the manufacturing industry, which creates and builds all the myriad physical components of broadband infrastructure from routers and servers to amplifiers and fiber nodes.

The high-tech manufacturing industry has created more than 600,000 jobs in the past four years, [1] contributing nearly $450 billion to the U.S. economy in 2012 alone. [2] In his 2014 State of the Union address, President Obama emphasized the important role that high-tech manufacturing has had, and will continue to have, in the nation's economic recovery by announcing a $140 million initiative to promote job growth in the high-tech manufacturing sector. [3] Overall, infrastructure equipment spending is expected to grow from $38.6 billion in 2013 to $42.9 billion in 2017. [4] Between the physical assets that serve as the foundation of the Internet and the devices used by consumers to connect to the Internet, high-tech manufacturing has led the way to ensure that "the United States is better-positioned for the 21st century than any other nation on Earth."[5]

Continued investment in the build-out and improvement of existing infrastructure will lead to even better broadband services and innovations, resulting in greater consumer demand and greater economic growth. It is expected that IP traffic in North America will grow from 16,607 petabytes of data in 2014 to 40,545 petabytes in 2018. [6] This rapid increase in demand will require significant private investment. But continued investment is by no means guaranteed.

Proposals to reclassify broadband Internet access as a "Title II" service – today reserved largely for landline telephone service – threaten to remove incentives to invest in broadband growth and improvement. Because Title II allows for so little flexibility and innovation, it would undercut substantially the broadband providers' incentives to make the investments necessary to fund network deployments and upgrades. Indeed, the Federal Communications Commission's determination to leave Internet access services largely unregulated incentivized both investment and innovation and the Internet's potential as a mechanism for economic growth was realized.

Reclassifying broadband Internet access service as a Title II service would be harmful to the economy and would create unnecessary obstacles to achieving the Administration's goal of promoting broadband deployment and adoption. A sudden shift from the existing light-touch approach – which has been an unqualified success and the basis for billions of dollars in investments – to the prescriptive regime of Title II would be extremely disruptive to the broadband marketplace. Resources that would normally be spent on building and improving infrastructure would instead be spent complying with burdensome regulatory obligations, and uncertainty regarding future profitability would deter additional private investments. If investment in broadband services declines, it will set off a domino effect of decreased investment and innovation throughout the manufacturing sector and into the economy as a whole. Title II reclassification would likely delay the full potential for additional broadband investment during the uncertainly resulting from further court scrutiny. If the Commission nonetheless determines that it must fashion ISP regulations, we urge it to exercise authority under Section 706 rather than Title II. [7]

---

[1] Katie Lobosco, *Why Obama is pushing high-tech manufacturing.* CNN Money, http://money.cnn.com/2014/03/03/smallbusiness/high-tech-manufacturing-obama/ (March 3, 2014)

[2] U.S. Department of Labor, Bureau of Labor Statistics, Employment and Output by Industry, *available at* http://www.bls.gov/emp/ep_table_207.htm.

[3] President Barack Obama, State of the Union Address (Jan. 28, 2014) ("*2014 State of the Union*")

[4] Telecommunications Industry Association, TIA's 2014-2017 ICT Market Review & Forecast 3-9 (2014).

[5] 2014 State of the Union.

[6] Cisco, Cisco Visual Networking Index: Forecast and Methodology, 2013–2018 1 (2014), *available at* http://www.cisco.com/c/en/us/solutions/collateral/service-provider/ visual-networking-indexvni/VNI_Hyperconnectivity_WP.html.

[7] 47 U.S.C. § 1302(b); see also *Verizon v. FCC*, 740 F.3d 623, 635-42 (D.C. Cir. 2014).

The Federal Communications Commission has previously declined past invitations to regulate broadband Internet service as a Title II service, wisely recognizing the essential role that flexibility and innovation would play in the success of the Internet economy. We urge the administration to support our efforts to ensure that the Internet economy can continue to thrive.

Sincerely,

ACS Solutions
ADTRAN
ActiveVideo Networks
Alcatel-Lucent
Alticast
ARRIS
BlackArrow
Blonder Tongue
Broadcom
Cisco
Commscope
Concurrent Computer
Drake
dLink
Ericsson
Gainspeed, Inc.
Harmonic
IBM
ILS Technologies
Intel
NetCracker Technology
NSN
Pace
Panasonic Corporation of North America
Penthera Partners
RGB
Rovi
Sandvine
Sumitomo Electric Lightwave
Synacor
This Technology
Universal Remote Control
Walker & Associates

May 13, 2014

Federal Communications Commission
445 12th Street, SW
Washington D.C. 20554

Dear Chairman Wheeler and Commissioners Clyburn, Rosenworcel, Pai, and O'Rielly:

For more than a decade, America's broadband companies (including companies that depend on the broadband ecosystem) have worked to ensure that their customers can enjoy access to world-class broadband services consistent with the Commission's clearly articulated core Internet freedoms. An open Internet is central to how America's broadband providers operate their networks, and the undersigned broadband providers remain fully committed to openness going forward. We are equally committed to working with the Commission to find a sustainable path to a lawful regulatory framework for protecting the open Internet during the course of the rulemaking you are launching this week. That framework must promote investment and opportunity across the Internet economy, from network providers to app developers, for the benefit of American consumers.

In recent days, we have witnessed a concerted publicity campaign by some advocacy groups seeking sweeping government regulation that conflates the need for an open Internet with the purported need to reclassify broadband Internet access services as Title II telecommunications services subject to common carrier regulation. As demonstrated repeatedly, the future of the open Internet has *nothing* to do with Title II regulation, and Title II has *nothing* to do with the open Internet. As it did in 2010, the Commission should categorically reject efforts to equate the two once and for all.

The high stakes of this debate have already been demonstrated. Today's regulatory framework helps support nearly 11 million jobs annually in the U.S. and has unleashed over $1.2 trillion dollars of investment in advanced wired and wireless broadband networks, as well as an entirely new apps economy. We see an average of over $60 billion poured into cable, fiber, fixed and mobile wireless, phone, and satellite broadband networks each and every year. And broadband gets better every year: the average broadband speeds jumped 25 percent in 2013 alone, highlighting there are no "slow lanes" in today's Internet.

Yet even the potential threat of Title II had an investment-chilling effect by erasing approximately ten percent of some ISPs' market cap in the days immediately surrounding the Title II announcement in 2009/10. Today, Title II backers fail to explain where the next hundreds of billions of dollars of risk capital will come from to improve and expand today's networks under a Title II regime. They too soon forget that a decade ago we saw billions newly invested in the latest broadband networks and advancements once the Commission affirmed that Title II does not apply to broadband networks.

Reclassification of broadband Internet access offerings as Title II "telecommunications services" would impose great costs, allowing unprecedented government micromanagement of all aspects of the Internet economy. It is a vision under which the FCC has plenary authority to regulate rates, terms and conditions, mandate wholesale access to broadband networks and intrude into the business of content delivery networks, transit providers, and connected devices. Indeed, groups pushing the Title II approach fail to acknowledge that their path forward is in fact a slippery slope that would provide the Commission sweeping authority to regulate all Internet-based companies and offerings. In defending their approach, Title II proponents now argue that reclassification is necessary to prohibit "paid prioritization," even though Title II does not discourage—let alone outlaw— paid prioritization models. Dominant carriers operating under Title II have for generations been permitted to offer different pricing and different service quality to customers.

Not only is it questionable that the Commission could defensibly reclassify broadband service under Title II, such an action would greatly distort the future development of, and investment in, tomorrow's broadband networks and services. America's economic future, as envisioned by President Obama and congressional leaders on both sides of the aisle, critically depends on continued investment and innovation in our broadband infrastructure and app economy to drive improvements in health care, education and energy. Under Title II, new service offerings, options, and features would be delayed or altogether foregone. Consumers would face less choice, and a less adaptive and responsive Internet. An era of differentiation, innovation, and experimentation would be replaced with a series of "Government may I?" requests from American entrepreneurs. That cannot be, and must not become, the U.S. Internet of tomorrow.

We should seek out a path forward together. All affected stakeholders need and want certainty and an end to a decade of legal and political wrangling. All parts of the Internet community should be focused on working together to develop next-generation networks, applications, and services that will be critical to our global competitiveness and enhance opportunities for all Americans. Yet, those demanding the Title II common carrier approach are effectively compelling years—if not decades—of endless litigation and debate. The issues at stake would include not simply regulating the Internet under Title II, but also which specific provisions of the monopoly-era statute apply to modern broadband networks. Collectively, we would face years more of uncertainty and, as a result, an economy deprived of the stable regulatory framework needed to promote future investment, innovation and consumer choice.

As it begins its rulemaking process, the Commission should reaffirm its commitment to the light-touch approach that has ensured America's leadership throughout the Internet ecosystem, from networks to services, from applications to devices. The U.S. experience was not a foregone conclusion. It was the result of courageous and bipartisan leadership that rejected old regulatory mandates in favor of a new, nimble paradigm of government oversight. We urge you to continue down that path at this critical juncture.

Sincerely,

Thomas R. Stanton
Chairman & CEO
ADTRAN

Amy Tykeson
CEO
BendBroadband

Glen Post
President & CEO
CenturyLink

Robert Currey
Chairman & CEO
Consolidated Communications

Gary Shorman
President & CEO
Eagle Communication

Anand Vadapalli
President & CEO
Alaska Communications

Steve Miron
Chairman & CEO
Bright House Networks

Tom Rutledge
President & CEO
Charter Communications

Patrick J. Esser
President
Cox Communications

Paul H. Sunu
CEO
FairPoint

Randall L. Stephenson
Chairman & CEO
AT&T

Brian Sweeney
President
Cablevision

Brian L. Roberts
Chairman & CEO
Comcast

Steve Largent
President & CEO
CTIA – The Wireless Association

Maggie Wilderotter
Chairman & CEO
Frontier

Ronald Duncan
President & CEO
GCI

Eric Yeaman
President & CEO
Hawaiian Telcom

Rocco Commisso
Chairman & CEO
Mediacom Communications

Patrick McAdaragh
President & CEO
Midcontinent Communications

John Evans
Chairman & CEO
Nelson County Cable and
Evans Telecommunications
Co.

Michael Powell
President & CEO
National Cable &
Telecommunications
Association

Chris French
President & CEO
ShenTel Communications

Richard J. Sjoberg
President & CEO
Sjoberg's Cable

Jerald L. Kent
Chairman & CEO
Suddenlink

Grant Seiffert
President
Telecommunications Industry
Association

Robert D. Marcus
Chairman & CEO
Time Warner Cable

Walter B. McCormick, Jr.
President & CEO
USTelecom

Lowell C. McAdam
Chairman & CEO
Verizon

United States Senate
WASHINGTON, DC 20510

May 13, 2014

The Honorable Thomas Wheeler
Chairman
Federal Communications Commission
445 12th Street, S.W.
Washington, D.C. 20554

Dear Chairman Wheeler:

We write to reiterate our strong concerns with any proposal that would have the Federal Communications Commission (FCC) apply monopoly-era Title II regulations to our nation's competitive and dynamic broadband economy.

The growth of the Internet and the rapid adoption of mobile technology have been great American success stories, made possible by a light regulatory touch for the entire online ecosystem. This approach has freed Internet innovators and users at the edge, the core, and the last mile to offer services, to build networks, and to buy and sell products based on market demand; no government permission has been necessary.

Imposing common carrier-style regulation upon any part of the Internet would be a dangerous rejection of this successful policy course, potentially impeding the development and adoption of new Internet technologies and services, and threatening future investment in next-generation broadband infrastructure.

The courts have twice struck down ill-advised and unauthorized attempts by the FCC to regulate the Internet. Unfortunately, you have chosen to have the FCC again undertake a politically corrosive rulemaking, relying upon new and untested court-defined powers rather than upon clear Congressional intent and statutory authority.

Of even greater concern would be using Title II of the Communications Act to regulate broadband, which some voices have called for in recent days. So-called "net neutrality" restrictions are unnecessary, but using Title II reclassification to impose them would create tremendous legal and marketplace uncertainty and would undermine your ability to effectively lead the FCC.

Rather than attempting further legal contortions to encumber modern communications networks with last century's rules, the Commission should work with the Congress to develop clear statutory authority and direction for the agency so that it can be a productive regulator for the 21st century marketplace. If the Commission will not do that, we urge it to reject new "net neutrality" regulations, particularly any which rely upon Title II.

Sincerely,

MITCH McCONNELL
Senate Republican Leader

JOHN CORNYN
Senate Republican Whip

JOHN THUNE
Senate Republican Conference Chairman

JOHN BARRASSO, M.D.
Senate Republican Policy Committee
Chairman

ROY BLUNT
Senate Republican Conference Vice-Chairman

JERRY MORAN
National Republican Senatorial
Committee Chairman

September 15, 2014

Tom Wheeler, Chairman
Federal Communications Commission
445 12th Street, SW
Washington, DC 20554

Dear Chairman Wheeler:

We urge you not to base new net neutrality regulations on Title II. Attempting to retrofit the onerous set of regulations developed for the monopoly telephony network onto the Internet would be a disaster for Internet users everywhere. That's why it has been rejected by four FCC Chairmen (of both parties), leading Democratic Senators as early as 1998, 74 House Democrats as late as 2010,[1] *all* Congressional Republicans, and the entire broadband industry.

Government *should* be able to police any deals between broadband companies and content providers to make sure they don't harm consumers or competition. But the FCC doesn't need Title II to do that. The FCC has already claimed vast authority under Section 706, including the power to issue new net neutrality rules.

Title II won't actually do what those pushing it claim: **Title II would *not* ban "paid prioritization."**[2] It's not even yet clear what that vague term means, but it would certainly include some deals that would actually *help* users.

If anything, Title II would probably make paid prioritization *more* likely:[3] Title II's costs and price controls could force broadband providers to turn to paid prioritization as a new revenue source. Globally, **imposing Title II would validate efforts by European carriers to impose sender-pays rules**, the default assumption of the Title II-style regimes in Europe. That means American web companies would have to pay European carriers to deliver traffic to European users — the very opposite of net neutrality.

Title II would undermine 15 years of American insistence around the world that the Internet shouldn't be regulated under traditional telecom rules. That would only play into the hands of the bizarre alliance of European carriers and repressive governments who have fought hard to transfer Internet governance from the bottom-up, multistakeholder model of ICANN to the United Nations' International Telecommunication Union and its "International Telecommunication Regulations."[4] That, in turn, would make censorship and surveillance easier around the world, while slowing broadband deployment to the world's poor and underserved.

---

[1] *See* Berin Szoka, *Democrats Tell FCC Not to Regulate Broadband as a Utility — Back in 1998*, TECHFREEDOM (June 20, 2014), http://bit.ly/1nQlzM3.

[2] Under Section 202, the FCC can only require that differences in rates for prioritization are "just and reasonable." Thus, Title II would actually enshrine prioritization into law.

[3] *See, e.g.*, George S. Ford & Lawrence J. Spiwak, *Tariffing Internet Termination: Pricing Implications of Classifying Broadband as a Title II Telecommunications Service*, PHOENIX CENTER POL'Y BULL. NO. 36 (Sept. 2014), *available at* http://www.phoenix-center.org/PolicyBulletin/PCPB36Final.pdf (arguing that the FCC may be legally required to set prices for carrying traffic).

[4] Larry Downes, *Why is the UN Trying to Take over the Internet?*, FORBES (Aug. 9, 2012), http://www.forbes.com/sites/larrydownes/2012/08/09/why-the-un-is-trying-to-take-over-the-internet/.

Validating the imposition of Title II-style telecom rules would jeopardize the "zero-rating" plans that Facebook, Google, Twitter, Wikipedia and others have launched to get the world's poor online — just as overzealous interpretation of the FCC's 2010 Open Internet Order forced MetroPCS to abandon plans to offer free YouTube as part of a mobile service plan geared towards low-income consumers in American inner cities.[5]

In the U.S., innovative **web companies would not be safe from Title II**. Contrary to *recent* assertions, there is no such thing as "reclassification." The FCC can only *re-open* the complex mess of definitions left murky by Congress in the 1996 Act. Re-interpreting these to make broadband a Title II service would likely sweep in other services, too. If this FCC can identify a "transmission" component in broadband, what will stop a future FCC from reaching the same conclusion about VoIP, video services, content delivery networks, hosting, or many other services at the core of the Internet?[6]

VoIP pioneer Jeff Pulver, founder of Vonage, knows better. Having fought hard to get the FCC to keep VoIP out of Title II, he recently warned that the "**madness of applying Title II means declaring everything telecom**. It requires an entirely new standard and ends 60 years of precedent underlying the telecom versus information services distinction. … I have no idea how to judge the difference between IP transmission and IP services for the purposes of my next startup. I will not be able to explain it to investors, because the **line exists entirely in the mind of whoever happens to be Chairman of the FCC.** Applying Title II to IP networks creates a new Federal Computer Commission with authority to weigh in on everything connected to an IP network, in other words — everything."[7] This very slippery slope may explain why Google and Facebook have been silent on the push for Title II.

Title II includes a slew of burdensome regulations, from price controls to tariffs and listings of prices, which economists have long known facilitate collusion among regulated companies and make markets *less* competitive. Title II is appropriate only for true, "natural" monopolies, where competition is impossible. Otherwise, it is a self-fulfilling prophecy, tending to discourage new competition.

Every previous FCC Chairman, regardless of party affiliation, has attempted to protect Internet services from common carriage regulation. Bill Kennard, President Clinton's second FCC Chairman, was perhaps most instrumental in drawing a **clear, bright line between the Internet and Title II.** Kennard knew that imposing the "morass" of traditional telephone regulations on broadband would discourage cable companies and telcos from building out competing infrastructure. His **"vigilant restraint" under Title I unleashed over a trillion dollars in investment in the U.S. That meant much greater deployment and faster speeds than European countries that stuck to a Title II model.**[8] That approach has benefitted underserved Americans most, which is why the NAACP,[9] Minority Media and

---

[5] *See* Protecting & Promoting the Open Internet, *ICLE & TechFreedom Policy Comments*, GN Docket No. 14-28, 24-32 (July 17, 2014), *available at* http://bit.ly/1m0go1J; *see also* Matthew Lasar, *MetroPCS: The Open Internet on a Budget?*, ARSTECHNICA (Feb. 16, 2011), http://bit.ly/1xTSGcB.

[6] *See* Protecting & Promoting the Open Internet, *TechFreedom & ICLE Legal Comments*, GN Docket No. 14-28, 24-32 (July 17, 2014), *available at* http://bit.ly/1pcZHLu.

[7] Jeff Pulver, *Fear & Loathing as Telecom Policy*, HUFFINGTON POST (Aug. 6, 2014), http://www.huffingtonpost.com/jeff-pulver/fear-and-loathing-as-tele_b_5654881.html.

[8] *See* Christopher S. Yoo, *U.S. vs. European Broadband Deployment: What do the Data Say?*, 13-21 (June 2014), *available at* https://www.law.upenn.edu/live/files/3352-us-vs-european-broadband-deployment.

[9] *See* Protecting & Promoting the Open Internet, *Comments of the Communications Workers of America & the National Association for the Advancement of Colored People*, GN Docket No. 14-28, 24-32 (July 15, 2014), *available at* http://bit.ly/1r54LEz.

Telecommunications Council and 42 other minority organizations have opposed Title II.[10]

Kennard's policies have continued for sixteen years and drawn broad bipartisan support. Re-opening Title II would shatter this consensus. Proponents acknowledge the problems with Title II, but say the FCC can waive them away through "forbearance." **Forbearance is an illusion.** An increasingly activist FCC has made forbearance almost impossible to justify. Legally, it's not clear the FCC can lower that bar[11] or forbear at all if broadband providers have the "terminating monopoly" the FCC claims.[12] But even if the FCC could forbear, it's not likely to do so— lest a future Republican FCC use forbearance to gut the Telecom Act. And of course those talking about "Title II Lite" today would fight forbearance in practice. Even if possible, forbearance would become a political football and a tool for the FCC to pressure companies to do things the FCC could not legally require. The FCC has a long history of abusing such leverage. In short, **Title II is a Trojan Horse for far more than net neutrality.**

We urge you to maintain the bipartisan consensus against Title II.

The Communications Act clearly directs the FCC to recommend new legislation to Congress.[13] You should use that power to propose legislation that once and for all resolves questions regarding the FCC's authority over broadband with clear, specific language focused on core net neutrality concerns.

We recommend that **such legislation should forever bar application of Title II to the Internet, narrowly focus Section 706, and remove barriers to deployment at all levels of government.** Government should make it as easy as possible for the private sector to build broadband networks, both to upgrade existing networks and to build new networks. Far from encouraging competition, Title II would choke it.

Mister Chairman, **please don't break the Net** by imposing Title II. Before acting on Title II, please consider the petition hosted at DontBreakThe.Net, which concludes, "Competition, not endless litigation and political bickering over Title II, should be your legacy."

Respectfully,

---

[10] *See* Protecting & Promoting the Open Internet, *Comments of the National Minority Organizations*, GN Docket No. 14-28, 24-32 (July 15, 2014), *available at* http://bit.ly/1nu7ClY.

[11] *See* Protecting & Promoting the Open Internet, *TechFreedom & ICLE Legal Comments*, GN Docket No. 14-28, 32-48 (July 17, 2014), *available at* http://bit.ly/1pcZHLu.

[12] *See* Ford & Spiwak, *supra* note 3, at 16.

[13] Communications Act of 1934, Pub. L. No. 73-416, § 4, 48 Stat. 1064, 1066 (1934) (codified at 47 U.S.C. 154(k)(4)).

INDIVIDUALS *(Organizations listed here are for identification only)*

Berin Szoka, President, TechFreedom

Geoffrey A. Manne, Executive Director, International Center for Law & Economics

Scott Banister, Co-founder, IronPort & Zivity

Richard Bennett, High Tech Forum

Babette Boliek, Associate Professor of Law, Pepperdine University

Donald J. Boudreaux, Professor of Economics, George Mason University

Henry N. Butler, Foundation Professor of Law, George Mason University

Bartlett Cleland, Managing Director, Madery Bridge

Robert W. Crandall, Nonresident Senior Fellow, Economic Studies Program, Brookings Institution

Larry Downes, Project Director, Georgetown Center for Business and Public Policy, McDonough School of Business, Georgetown University

Richard A. Epstein, Laurence A. Tisch Professor of Law, New York University

Hance Haney, Program Director, Technology and Democracy Project

Gene Hoffman, Co-founder, eMusic & Vindicia

Justin (Gus) Hurwitz, Assistant Professor of Law, University of Nebraska

Thomas A. Lambert, Wall Chair in Corporate Law and Governance, University of Missouri

Roslyn Layton, Strand Consult

Stan Liebowitz, Ashbel Smith Professor of Economics, University of Texas, Dallas

Jason Llorenz, Attorney, Researcher, Rutgers University

Daniel Lyons, Associate Professor of Law, Boston College

Fred McChesney, de la Cruz-Mentschikoff Endowed Chair in Law and Economics, University of Miami

David S. Olson, Associate Professor of Law, Boston College

Jeff Pulver, Founder, Vonage, FreeWorldDialup & Pulver.com

Glen O. Robinson, Former FCC Commissioner (1974-76) and David and Mary Harrison Distinguished Professor of Law Emeritus, University of Virginia

Paul H. Rubin, Dobbs Professor of Economics, Emory University

Hal Singer, Senior Fellow, Progressive Policy Institute

Michael E. Sykuta, Associate Professor of Economics, University of Missouri

ORGANIZATIONS

TechFreedom

International Center for Law & Economics

American Commitment

Center for the Analysis of Property Rights & Innovation

Center for Boundless Innovation in Technology

Center for Financial Privacy and Human Rights

Center for Individual Freedom

Citizens Against Government Waste

Competitive Enterprise Institute

Information Technology & Innovation Foundation

Institute for Liberty

Institute for Policy Innovation

Less Government

Lincoln Labs

MediaFreedom

NetCompetition

National Taxpayers Union

RedState

THE WALL STREET JOURNAL.
WSJ.com

OCTOBER 29, 2009, 7:45 P.M. ET

. . . Or Barrier to Broadband Investment?

Who's going to build the information superhighway?

By ORRIN HATCH AND JIM DEMINT

Last week, Chairman Julius Genachowski and his Democratic colleagues on the Federal Communications Commission (FCC) began rewriting federal regulations governing the Internet and broadband communications. According to Mr. Genachowski, the Internet today is a failed market in which neither entrepreneurs nor consumers are treated fairly.

If this is news to you (especially if you're reading this on a Web site while simultaneously uploading photos to your family blog and streaming music from an online radio station), you're not alone.

The Internet is one of the only aspects of our economy and national life free from government regulation. Mr. Genachowski and his colleagues see this as a bad thing. We disagree.

If there is a perfect encapsulation of the success of Washington's current hands-off approach to the Internet, it's the popular "There's an app for that" advertising campaign. Since the latest introduction of smart phones like Apple's iPhone and Blackberry's Curve, independent software developers have created tens of thousands of applications for mobile devices. There are apps for gamers, bloggers, couch potatoes, foodies, health-care providers and every other niche market you can imagine. These applications have improved people's lives and satisfied consumer demand.

And it has all happened without a Washington politician or bureaucrat moving a muscle.

This isn't a coincidence. If the Internet were invented by a politician or worse, managed by bureaucrats, cell phones would still look like bricks and the information superhighway would still be a dirt road. If there is any sector of our economy where competition is so fierce and where the pace of innovation is so rapid that government interference would only get in the way, it is the Internet and telecommunications market.

The Internet has grown because of a virtuous and mutually beneficial circle: network operators provide ever-increasing speed and bandwidth; content providers one-up each other with game-changing innovations; and consumers adapt and adopt at lightning speed.

Ten years ago, we effectively had no broadband marketplace. Dial-up Internet was common, but not ubiquitous. Consumers had a choice of service providers, but they were typically confined to walled gardens of preselected or preferred content. The broadband revolution led us out of that desert. Instead of dog-paddling, we could surf the net, choosing between broadband service offered by traditional phone and cable companies and, now, wireless companies as well.

Compare that to the last decade of success at government dominated companies like Fannie Mae, Freddie Mac, GM or Chrysler.

Yet despite an overwhelming record of innovation, and customer satisfaction, Washington wants to replace the judgment of consumers with that of politicians and bureaucrats.

Net neutrality may sound like fairness but it is actually the opposite. Bandwidth is finite—like the finite number of lanes on a highway—and network providers must innovate in order to accommodate the burgeoning traffic. As they invest billions of private dollars in new and improved networks, they should rightly expect to set prices and manage those networks as they see fit.

If the FCC takes control of the Internet, we'll have the inevitable result of all poorly designed regulations: business decisions prejudiced by politicians and political decisions prejudiced by corporations. Keep in mind, we're talking about the most competitive, efficient and consumer-driven industry in the global economy.

Is it reasonable to believe committees of suits in Washington—with hearings and markup meetings and regulatory comment periods—can keep up with the competitive pressures of the Internet economy?

To ask the question is to answer it. There is a time and place for federal economic regulation, but the middle of a recession is not the time, and the Internet is certainly not the place.

Mr. Hatch is a Republican senator from Utah. Mr. DeMint is a Republican senator from South Carolina.

ADDITIONAL SUBMISSIONS FOR THE RECORD

A list of material and links can be found below for Submissions for the Record not printed due to voluminous nature, previously printed by an agency of the Federal Government, or other criteria determined by the Committee:

Journal of Law and Economics, The, R.H. Coase, October 1959, article:
http://www.jstor.org/stable/724927.

Federal Communications Law Journal, Jeffrey A. Eisenach and Hal J. Singer, June 2013, article:
http://www.fclj.org/wp-content/uploads/2013/09/65-3-Singer.pdf.

Social Science Research Network (SSRN), Jerry Brito et al., April 12, 2010, article:
http://papers.ssrn.com/sol3/papers.cfm?abstract ▮ id=1587058&download=yes.

American Enterprise Institute, Jeffrey A. Eisenach, Ph.D., economic study:
http://www.aei.org/files/2012/10/17/-broadband-competition-in-the-internet-ecosystem ▮ 164734199280.pdf.

Eisenach, Jeffrey A., and Ilene Knable Gotts, "In Search of a Competition Doctrine for Information Technology Markets: Recent Antitrust Developments in the Online Sector," paper:
http://www.techpolicydaily.com/wp-content/uploads/2014/06/In-Search-of-a-Competition-Doctrine-for-Information-Technology-Markets-Eisenach-Gotts.pdf.

Federal Communications Commission (FCC), Electronic Comment Filing System, September 4, 2014, online posting:
http://apps.fcc.gov/ecfs/comment/view?id=6018327622.

www.ingramcontent.com/pod-product-compliance
Lightning Source LLC
Chambersburg PA
CBHW081107170526
45165CB00008B/2361